MODERN CRITICAL THEORY
AND CLASSICAL LITERATURE

MNEMOSYNE

BIBLIOTHECA CLASSICA BATAVA

COLLEGERUNT

J.M. BREMER · L.F. JANSSEN · H. PINKSTER

H.W. PLEKET · C.J. RUIJGH · P.H. SCHRIJVERS

BIBLIOTHECAE FASCICULOS EDENDOS CURAVIT

C.J. RUIJGH, KLASSIEK SEMINARIUM, OUDE TURFMARKT 129, AMSTERDAM

SUPPLEMENTUM CENTESIMUM TRICESIMUM

IRENE J.F. DE JONG AND J.P. SULLIVAN (EDITORS)

MODERN CRITICAL THEORY
AND CLASSICAL LITERATURE

MODERN CRITICAL THEORY
AND
CLASSICAL LITERATURE

EDITED BY

IRENE J.F. DE JONG

AND

J.P. SULLIVAN

E.J. BRILL
LEIDEN · NEW YORK · KÖLN
1994

The paper in this book meets the guidelines for permanence and durability of the Committee on Production Guidelines for Book Longevity of the Council on Library Resources.

Library of Congress Cataloging-in-Publication Data

Modern critical theory and classical literature / edited by Irene J.F. de Jong and J.P. Sullivan.
 p.   cm. — (Mnemosyne, bibliotheca classica Batava, Supplementum, ISSN 0169-8958 ; 130)
  Includes bibliographical references (p.) and index.
  ISBN 9004095713 (alk. paper)
  1. Classical literature—History and criticism—Theory, etc.
I. Jong, Irene J. F. de. II. Sullivan, J. P. (John Patrick)
III. Series.
PA35.M63   1993
880'.09—dc20   93-4053
                                                                         CIP

Die Deutsche Bibliothek – CIP-Einheitsaufnahme

Modern critical theory and classical literature / ed. by Irene J. F. De Jong and J. P. Sullivan. – Leiden ; New York ; Köln : Brill, 1993
  (Mnemosyne : Supplementum ; 130)
  ISBN 90–04–09571–3
NE: Jong, Irene J. F. de [Hrsg.]; Mnemosyne / Supplementum

ISSN   0169-8958
ISBN   90 04 09571 3

© *Copyright 1994 by E.J. Brill, Leiden, The Netherlands*

PRINTED IN THE NETHERLANDS

CONTENTS

PREFACE

In 1990 the editors of this volume were approached by the Classics editor of E.J. Brill with the request to compile a volume which would attempt to show the applicability of the methodologies of various modern theories of literary criticism to the study of Greek and Roman literature. In selecting authors, the editors have aimed at a representative coverage, in terms of themes, gender, Latin-Greek, and even nationality, although the requirement that papers be produced in (or translated into) English did place constraints on the selection of authors from the non-English-speaking world. Most of the papers printed here are new, some are revised versions of papers presented elsewhere. The editors would like to express their thanks to Emilie van Opstall for her help in compiling the general bibliography.

Irene J.F. de Jong
J.P. Sullivan

During the final stages of the preparation of this book for the press, the sad news was received of the death of J.P. Sullivan. This volume is dedicated to his memory.

Irene J.F. de Jong

INTRODUCTION
CRITICAL CONTINUITY AND CONTEMPORARY INNOVATION

BY

J.P. SULLIVAN

In recent decades the study and teaching of literature in Europe and the Americas have been radically influenced by modern critical theory in its various forms. Although the influence and the leading exponents of these various theories and approaches have been most noticeable in the study of modern literatures and culture, there has also been a perceptible impact of these theories in the study of Greco-Roman literature and, more broadly, in the examination of the mythologies, culture and *mentalité*, as far as that can be reconstructed, of Greece and Rome.

The rubrics attached to this group of theories are not always precise, and individual practitioners will often deny the applicability of such rubrics to their own work. These theories moreover often represent specific focuses of interest in literary phenomena, methods of approach to literary works, or even ideological perspectives on culture in general (including literature) rather than mutually exclusive conceptual systems. Nor is their prime concern always with literature, or even art in the broad sense. The situation therefore bears little resemblance to the conflict in evolutionary theory between Darwinism and Creationism or, in astrophysics, between the theory of the "Big Bang" and the Continuous Creation of Matter. Such terms as "New Criticism," (sometimes prefaced by the dismissive adjectives "old" or "aging"), Structuralism and its continuation (or reactive response), Deconstructionism,[1] are not to be put in the same logical category as Reader-Response Theory in its various forms such as *Rezeptionsästhetik*, although there may be theoretical connections between them. Semiotics is not an alternative to Poetics or Narratology, since it subsumes them. Hermeneutics,

---

[1] It is not always remembered that the term "deconstruction" came into being in the context of Structuralism. It was taken from a sentence of Derrida's discussing the achievements of Structuralism in which he was merely questioning the epistemological basis of that general theory and the principles it used and calling for a re-examination of some of its polarities, premisses, and conclusions. This not altogether happy term seemed to catch on as applied to a certain group of critics at Yale: Derrida himself, Paul de Man, Geoffrey Hartman, and J. Hillis Miller; Harold Bloom would probably reject the description: see Davis and Schleifer (1985) viii, Lehman (1991) 24. Since then it seems to have attached itself to other "French" theorists or critics such as Tzvetan Todorov and Michel Riffaterre, and even (to his dismay) to the late Michel Foucault.

to take another example, is a venerable, indeed ancient, way of dealing with literary texts, from Aristotle through Schleiermacher and Boekh;[2] as reformulated by Hans-Georg Gadamer and others, it may invoke Marxist, feminist, neo-historical, and psychoanalytical perspectives just as easily as it once deployed allegory and symbolism, or the more conventional triad of philology, history and philosophy.

How valid or, more importantly, how valuable or illuminating, these different theories, perspectives, and methods are for the study of classical literature or culture is still, not surprisingly in view of the conceptual confusions, a matter of some dispute (benevolent or hostile) among classical scholars themselves.

The discipline of Classics, as academically defined, comprehends the total study of the ancient Mediterranean cultures of Greece and Rome, not least their transmitted texts and their influence on later vernacular literatures; it may also be extended to their interactions, historical and literary, with contiguous areas, the provinces of other disciplines, such as Biblical Studies and Egyptology. The investigation of these cultures, and the study, often with important pedagogical, not to say ideological, implications, of their literary heritage, has in the past made profitable use of other disciplines. Indeed it is sometimes claimed that it is at the points of intersection with other disciplines that classics has recently made most progress, or at least has generated the liveliest debate. The utility of, say, archaeology for our general knowledge of the ancient world was accepted in the eighteenth and nineteenth centuries, although not without some opposition. Similarly, although classical Luddites may still be encountered, few would dispute the contributions made, even to purely philological studies, by the great computerized *Thesaurus Linguae Graecae* (and its Latin *parerga*). This in turn was a small part of the computer revolution in the second half of the twentieth century, which has been compared variously to the introduction of the alphabet, the substitution of the codex for the papyrus roll, and the invention of printing.

Yet it is to the more controversial comparative investigation of other cultures, to anthropology, in short, and its effects on classical studies in the nineteenth and early twentieth centuries that we should look for a more suitable analogy to the present situation in the study of the classical literatures. It is not unreasonable to see in the work of the so-called Cambridge school of Sir James Frazer, J.E. Harrison, A.B. Cook, and F.M.

---

[2] For eighteenth- and nineteenth-century Hermeneutics and its connection with Biblical exegesis as well as the interpretation of key classical texts, see Laks and Neschke (1990); an introduction to later developments is offered by Mueller-Volmer (1989). For the rejection of the method by pure "philologists" such as Hermann, and the consequences for classical studies, see Selden (1990) 158. For the application of modern hermeneutics to classical texts, see e.g. Kresic (1981), Benjamin (1988) and Galinsky (1992).

Cornford, with its emphasis on the underlying ritual basis of myth,[3] a foreshadowing of later work on classical culture that we accept with greater readiness. The Cambridge school at least ensured a more understanding audience for the widely differing insights of E.R. Dodds, J.-P. Vernant, M. Detienne, and W. Burkert.[4] Anthropological fieldwork on oral cultures even added further dimensions to the long-debated Homeric Question, initiated by F.A. Wolf's *Prolegomena ad Homerum* (1795). The work of the Parrys, *père et fils*, after much initial scepticism and with some remaining reservations, has been embraced by Homeric scholars for the new light they shed on the composition of the *Iliad* and *Odyssey*.[5]

Indeed it was the discipline of anthropology again, at least in its Gallic manifestation in the work of Claude Lévi-Strauss (b.1908), together with the new approach to structural linguistics and semiotics pioneered by Ferdinand de Saussure (1857-1913), that introduced into classical studies the seminal ideas of Structuralism.[6] Propp, notably in his *Morphology of the Folk Tale* (Russian original, 1928), while the work of other Russian formalists moved in the same direction. The structuralist approach was particularly well adapted to the study of myth and mythological narratives, but its influence would soon be felt in other areas of classical studies.

Fashions in critical theory and practice must seem to the classical philologist to be changing with bewildering rapidity in the second half of the twentieth century. The New Criticism of English and American poetry and prose was initially associated with I.A. Richards, and then with such scholar-poets as Cleanth Brooks, John Crowe Ransom, Allen Tate, R.P. Blackmur, Robert Penn Warren, and William K. Wimsatt, and with such journals as *Hound and Horn* and *The Kenyon Review*. It came to include (despite differences) Kenneth Burke in the U.S. and, in Britain, William Empson and

---

[3] For recent re-evaluations of the work of this school, see Peacock (1988), Ackerman (1991) and Calder (1991).

[4] See most recently Bremmer (1989). For some representative work by the authors mentioned, see the bibliography s.v. Strauss (1985) 67 has remarked: "more than a few studies of Greco-Roman antiquity have made a provocative and stimulating use of anthropological scholarship...and not only studies of ancient literature or religion, but of ancient history as well." For some suggestive insights into the relationship between anthropology and the classics, see Redfield (1991) 11, who points to the progression from Mommsen to Weber in Germany; Fustel de Coulanges to Durkheim in France; and to the English traditions centering on Frazer and Robertson Smith; for a discussion of the interrelation and the benefits, see Humphreys (1978) and Winkler (1990) 8. There is a relationship between Cambridge "myth criticism" and the archetypal criticism of literature to be found in Bodkin (1934), Wheelwright (1954; 1962) and Frye (1957); cf. n. 7 below.

[5] Wolf's *Prolegomena* was recently republished; details are in the bibliography. For the Parrys' contribution to the study of Homer, see especially Parry (1971).

[6] See, e.g. Pucci (1971) 103 for the influence of Structuralism in the Classics. The basic documents for Lévi-Strauss' methodology are still *Structural Anthropology* (1967) and *The Savage Mind* (1966). On Saussure, see most conveniently Culler (1986); for some criticisms of Saussurian theory, Lyons (1969) 56.

the *Scrutiny* circle of F.R. Leavis. It even produced pronounced ripples in the study of classical literature in the sixties.[7] New Criticism, like Poststructuralism and Deconstruction, is a vague term, and perhaps better characterized as an approach to reading texts rather than a theoretical system of literary analysis. Its discernible principles had some roots at least in the critical work and modernist poetic practice of Ezra Pound and T.S. Eliot. (Theories of the literary *persona* or the Image, for instance, which had served a number of critics well, despite their difficulties, can be traced back to Pound.[8]) In so far as the theory of the New Critics could be articulated, it stressed the autonomy of the work of art ("the well-wrought urn") with a rejection of biographical and historical explanations of its creation and value.[9] It looked instead at imagery, paradox, ambiguity, irony, and poetic tension as the informing characteristics of the best poetry.

The literary values espoused by New Critics tended to elevate, or canonize, certain literary forms, the lyric, satire, and the novel, as opposed to epic or didactic poetry, and also certain authors such as the Metaphysical poets (as well as certain modernist poets like them) as opposed to the Romantics and Victorians. Despite the stress on formal aspects of poetry and narrative, the relationship of art to "life", a subtler form of the ancient insistence on the intimate link between art and morality, was smuggled back in the Southern agrarian values of some of the earlier New Critics, the conservative, almost religious, respect for tradition of those who followed T.S. Eliot, the insistent Puritan morality of Yvor Winters (notably in *Maule's Curse*), and the demands of the more secular *Scrutiny* group for an Arnoldian, "life-enhancing" dimension found embodied in the novels of Jane Austen, Joseph Conrad, Henry James, and, latterly, D.H. Lawrence.

The New Criticism, however, as the dominant mode of literary analysis, was eventually challenged by Structuralist Poetics, which promised a science of literary interpretation through the investigation of the structures of

---

[7] Most obviously seen in some of the contributions to the classical journal *Arion*, which began publication in 1961. For a retrospective survey of the New Criticism, see Willingham (1989) 24. For F.R. Leavis and his colleagues, see Mulhern (1979). As an approach to literature, New Criticism did not go unchallenged even in its own time. Opposition came from Chicago neo-Aristotelianism, which adopted an aggressive formalism based on older theories, stressing plot structure, motive, character and genre, as in e.g. Booth (1961), and from myth criticism, best exemplified by Frye (1957), which took in literature as just one aspect of its search for cultural archetypes.

[8] See Elliott (1982) for a discussion of the history and difficulties of the concept of *persona*.

[9] See, for example, the rejection of the Intentional and Affective Fallacies by W.K. Wimsatt in *The Verbal Icon* (1954) and of any non-textual concepts of "sincerity" or the intimate relationship of biographical information to the work of art. The best exposition of New Critical principles and objectives is Ransom (1941). For the empiricist underpinning of their implicit theory, see Berman (1988) 26.

literature.[10] Not much later Structuralist critical theory in all its many forms seemed in turn to yield before the onslaught of a more sceptical "poststructuralist" approach to language and literature, an approach based on different "epistemological" deductions from Saussurian semiotics. This sceptical perspective was given the *omnium gatherum* title, Poststructuralist Theory, and referred to by its commonest shibboleth, Deconstruction.[11] There would be even newer debates about Modernism and Postmodernism. Interestingly enough for the classicist, Deconstructionists too professed to base their insights — or their *aporiai* — on the close reading favoured by the New Critics, and (for different purposes) by philologists.

Not that the break between these different approaches seems all that abrupt for classicists attracted to them. The insightful examination of poetic closure by Barbara Herrnstein Smith (1968), based on the methods of New Criticism, were easily assimilated by the Gallic *nouvelle vague*, specifically by Hamon (1975). It was later recommended as a useful approach to classical texts in *Materiali e discussioni per l'analisi dei testi classici*, the flagship of intertextuality (and narratology).[12] At very least, the insistence of the New Critics on the autonomy of the literary work and the rejection of such biographical or psychological notions as "sincerity" surely prepared the way for the emphasis on the text as opposed to the artist. As often happened in imperial Rome, the relegation of the writer was but a prelude to the death of the author.

The apparently sweeping success of Deconstruction in English and Modern Language departments,[13] where it became almost *the* paradigm of contemporary critical theory, would have its reverberations in certain classical circles, most noticeably and (some would say) appropriately in Cambridge, the home of the anthropological approach to Classics.[14]

To summarize the methods (rather than the results) of the various writers who march under the banner, not always of their own chosing, of Deconstruction is no easy matter, although few would deny the challenge they presented to reigning assumptions and unexamined certaities, particularly about the independent existence of the text. The Deconstructionists however are now being challenged in their turn on personal, academic, philosophical, and political grounds by more ideological critics, who object to this overly sceptical, if not nihilistic, approach to literary interpretation, and the

---

[10] Notably in the work of Barthes, Todorov, and Genette. For an early discussion, see Culler (1975). Some representative writings of these authors are listed in the bibliography s.v.

[11] The most useful guides here are Lentriccia (1980), Culler (1982) and Goodheart (1984). For further objections, but also acknowledgement of its benefits, see Eagleton (1983) 127, Abrams (1989) 333; 397.

[12] See Fowler (1989), who cites Hammon (1975) 495.

[13] For an incisive survey of the history, see Bergonzi (1990).

[14] See the bibliography s.v. Goldhill, Henderson and Wyke.

intellectual (and political) passivity which is arguably its consequence.[15] Again, the objection is to the focus on the *intrinsic* features of language and literature; the implicit denial of the *extrinsic* connections of literature with the world, history, society, and political action — *il n'y a pas de hors-texte* — and that includes, in a way, the reader, who must surrender himself or herself to the text's own deconstruction. The most prominent of these ideological opponents would be neo-Marxist and feminist theorists, as well as some more traditional critics, such as René Wellek and M.H. Abrams, whose affinities or sympathies with New Criticism are obvious enough. The subordination of the text's content, affect, and even structure to a concentration on the deceptive play of language seemed an abnegation of the critic's task, however broadly conceived, rather than an advance.

CONTEMPORARY THEORIES AND CURRENT ANXIETIES

It is naturally not to the purpose here to examine the various philosophical theories, Hegelian idealism, dialectical materialism, Husserlian phenomenology, Heideggerian or Sartrean existentialism, Gadamerian hermeneutics, Wittgensteinianism, logical analysis, and ordinary language philosophy, or even the semiotic theories of Saussure and Pierce that supposedly inspire or validate many of the metacritical theories presently in vogue.[16] Nor is there space to consider the wider pedagogical implications of contemporary critical theory (or just "theory") as it now prevails in some North American universities, where it bids fair to usurp the functions of the Philosophy (and other) departments, particularly for those who find the intellectual nourishment of Anglo-Saxon empiricism and ordinary language analysis jejune and unsatisfying by comparison with the intellectual feasts provided by continental philosophy and the new theoretical discourse in general. (Naturally classicists too are welcome to pursue the epistemological and sociological ramifications of critical theory, but then they write *qua* theorists or philosophers or sociologists rather than *qua* classical scholars. They might however remember John Miller's comment: "numerous critics of literature who enter the burgeoning field of literary theory become somewhat like most professors who shift into administrative posts: Rarely do they return."[17]) A discussion of the ambiguities of "modernism" versus "postmodernism" may also be deferred, despite the striking presence of the classics in the writing of such archpriests of "modernism" (in one sense of

---

[15] The most accessible critique of the philosophical foundations of Derrida's theories, for instance, is Searle (1983). On the political implications, see Eagleton (1983) 127, who is careful to exclude Derrida himself from his strictures.

[16] A sensible guide to the underlying philosophies of the different approaches is provided by Berman (1988).

[17] *Vergilius* 33 (1987) 118.

the term) as James Joyce, Ezra Pound, and T.S. Eliot. The last two indeed still inspire the more informal investigations into literary tradition and reception that preceded the more "scientific" methods known as *Textrezeptionstheorie*, which is discussed below. The almost closed world of classical culture and classical texts is also spared the intellectual agonizing about what is, or should be counted as, "literature" or how far literature can be separated from culture in general. For all practical purposes, our *données* exclude such options, which is not to deny the relevance of analogous questions posed by modern critical theorists about canonicity.

Instead of looking at the underlying philosophical, linguistic or sociological bases of these critical theories and methods, it may be more helpful for our present purposes initially to examine their manifest, if sometimes overlapping, areas of interest, since it is generally accepted that literary critics and literary theorists tend to have at least four discernible, although not always clearly delimited, focuses: the author, the work, the reality or universe to which it relates (including of course its economic and historical dimensions), and the audience or readership.[18]

Focus on the first concentrates on the genesis of the literary work, the nature of inspiration, the poet's voice, the relation of the individual talent to the literary tradition or collective archetypes, to the singer's or writer's racial and historical context, and even the role in artistic creation of unconscious wishes and fantasies. The second invites considerations of meaning, structure, language, and style, of the interrelation of theme and content, of genre and other modes of analysis. Then the theorist may turn to the relation of the work to the real world, past and present, or even to some spiritual, moral or aesthetic universe. Finally, in the examination of the moral, aesthetic and psychological affects of literature, theoretical questions arise about the nature of audience response; the constitution of meaning and evaluation; the establishment of critical canons; and the justification of literature in terms of pleasure, morality, utility, and education. These often entail broader issues of social control and hierarchical power, literary prescription, pornography, and moral or political censorship.

In contemporary critical theory, the first focus has become almost limited to psychoanalytical and phenomenological criticism, since biographical enquiries had been sternly excluded by the New Critics and rendered meaningless by structuralist and post-structuralist theory. The Romantic view that poetry was the language of feeling and that the temperament and morality of the poet was to be discovered, indirectly expressed, in the work was easily transmuted into a Freudian view that the important elements in a work of fiction are the elements of the author's personality or his unconscious wishes or conflicts. Alternatively, for the phenomenological

---

[18] Abrams (1989) 3 uses the terms "expressive," "objective," "mimetic," and "pragmatic" for his discussion of these four areas.

critics such as Georges Poulet (1964) a literary work would embody the
author's unique mode of consciousness, which the reader would then ideally
reconstitute in his reading of the text. The phenomena of consciousness,
properly, that is transcendentally, defined, were the constituents not only of
the world but also of the literary work.[19]

The Death of the Author was loudly proclaimed in Roland Barthes'
famous *pronunciamento* in the late sixties,[20] and the demise was echoed by
Pierre Macherey, Michel Foucault and others. The author was but the
epiphenomenal node of ideological or cultural influences, an epistemological
or semiotic construct of the *Zeitgeist* or the unconscious, a processor of
preformed materials through historical templates, or even the mere channel
of language itself. In any case the author had been sadly misused in debates
about literature and culture. Nietzsche, who also divorced the author from
the work, put it more vividly in his *Genealogy of Morals* (3.4): the author
is only a condition of the work, the soil from which it grows, perhaps only
the manure on that soil. D.H. Lawrence's slogan: *Never trust the artist: trust
the tale* offered the same advice, and even E.M. Forster had written in 1925
that "all literature tends towards the condition of anonymity...it wants not to
be signed". (This should bother classical scholars the less, accustomed as
they are to dealing with anonymous texts and such troublesome authors as
Homer and the Greek tragedians or the writer(s) of the *Historia Augusta*,
where the biographical information is scanty, untrustworthy, or non-
existent.[21] For Nietzsche even Homer, the poet of the *Iliad* and the
Odyssey, was "an aesthetic judgement".)

The emphasis then of New Criticism, and of Structuralist and Deconstructionist criticism alike, was centered largely on the text, which was strictly
separated from the author. The difference between the competing theories
lay in the problems perceived and the techniques of analysis and interpretation favoured. (Close reading however remained a methodological practice.)

One difference between the earlier and later forms of this emphasis might
be detected. This was to be seen in the degrees of strictness observed in
separating the text from the "real world," from "Life." The New Critics
stressed the autonomy of the text, despite its firm anchoring in an established literary tradition; they insisted that the world created within the work
of art was self-subsistent and was only to be judged by internal criteria.
Nevertheless, to make the point once again, they were prone to introduce,

[19] For bravura examples of psychoanalytical criticism, see Wilson (1941); for a discussion
of phenomenological criticism, Magliola (1989) 101.

[20] Barthes (1968) 14. Literary biographies of a popular and scholarly sort are as popular as
ever, although there is a prudent tendency to avoid straight deductions from the work to the
artist and vice versa. The person that suffers is now generally distinguished from the artist that
creates, although exceptions are made in the case of such authors as D.H. Lawrence.

[21] See, e.g. Lefkowitz (1982) on the sad state of literary biography in classical times.

almost surreptitiously, concepts of external significance, such as moral coherence and aesthetic vision. The allied followers of Leavis and Winters certainly looked for a relationship to life, even specific "life-enhancing" qualities immanent in their favoured texts, even though this was not be confused with the more traditional search for a moral message.[22]

Even more extreme was the Deconstructionist slogan: "Nothing outside the text!" For the Deconstructionist, the text was no more (and no less) than the interplay of signs, whose stability and reference, as far as extrinsic meaning went, was shifting and dubious, because of the nature of language in general and literary language in particular. A text might yield a plurality of meanings, and the establishment of the validity of any *one* meaning was, to use an over-used term, highly "problematic." *Jouissance*, as advocated by Roland Barthes, the Philodemus of modern critics, rather than mundane reference or truth, would be the recommended guide for the reader in this inevitable polysemy.

This sceptical, indeed negative, view must be contrasted with the critical innovations fostered by Structuralism proper in the formal analysis of the text, particularly in such areas as poetics, genre, and narrative. These were found to be of considerable value for the understanding and criticism of classical literature. Obvious examples are Narratology and Intertextuality as developed by G.B. Conte.[23] It has not been to their disadvantage that connections with ancient critical theory and the terminology of classical rhetoric, and even with Humanist scholarship, were easily made.

Intertextuality, for instance, offered itself as a more dynamic form of *Quellenforschung*, the traditional search by philological commentators for models, parallels, allusions, echoes, borrowings, and even plagiarism in ancient authors.[24] At the same time it connects with such ancient concepts as *imitatio* and *aemulatio*.[25] Allusions and references are not a display of *doctrina* or, worse, gratuitous padding or evidence of a lack of inspiration or originality, but a positive trope, constituting a rhetoric of its own and the assertion of the new work's place in literary history.

It has to be admitted that Intertextuality, a word coined by Julia Kristeva, can be broadened until it becomes, as described by Worton and Still (1990:xi) "a promiscuous inter-discipline, or even a trans-discipline." By

---

[22] Some representative texts are reprinted in Selden (1988) 494.

[23] Some of these studies have developed an extensive theoretical vocabulary of their own; see e.g. de Jong (1987), Winkler (1985), and Prince (1987) for Narratology (Todorov's term). As Conte remarks in discussing Intertextuality and the concept of "functional opposition," *il linguaggio imita gli strumenti del metodo*.

[24] In the broader modern sense of the word. As it is first used (by Martial, for instance), it simply means claiming the authorship of another's work with or without one's own additions.

[25] Bloom (1973) postulates an almost Oedipal "anxiety of influence" in authors which induces them to overthrow or deface their important models. For the anticipation of Intertextuality in ancient Imitation theory, see Hooley (1990).

contrast with other sorts of formalism, Intertextuality has presupposed that
the text cannot exist as an hermetic or self-sufficient or closed system, since
it permeated with references, quotations, allusions and other influences, and
has set up a dialogue with them. (The writer is first a reader.) So, although
Intertextuality was in essence a text-oriented critique, once external factors,
social, political, religious, are seen to affect a text, which now included any
signifying structure including the Book of Nature and even social codes, a
much wider horizon is opened up. When it is further argued that the reader's
experience of some practice or theory unknown to the author may lead to
fresh interpretations, we move into the contiguous area of Text and
Response.

The severance of the author from the text had meant that its meaning was
no longer to be located in the unknowable intentions or unconscious drives
of some writer. But is meaning so easily locatable in the possibly
polysemous text itself? As if in response to such a dilemma, a strong
connection was now discerned by various critics between the text and the
reader. Indeed it was in this relationship or interaction that significant
communication, indeed the very existence of the artistic work, the literary
phenomenon, was to be somehow located.

Holland (1968), for example, had proposed that the appreciation of a
literary work was an experience structured by the reader's unconscious as
well as by the text itself. Riffaterre (1982) argued more generally that the
literary phenomenon lies in the relation between the unchanging text and the
reader, and not between text and author, or text and reality. "Formal analysis
bears on the text...; on the internal relationships among words; on forms
rather than contents..."[26]

The rigid formalism of this latter position pointed to a need to re-examine
both the external relations of the text and its readership. This emphasis on
the audience, that is to say on reader-response, was most carefully
articulated by Wolfgang Iser (1978), following in the steps of H.-G.
Gadamer. For Iser the text consists in "an effect to be experienced" rather
than "an object to be explored". This incidentally led to a rethinking of the
literary history and critical evaluation of classical texts along the lines of the
new *Textrezeptionsgeschichte* and -*ästhetik* outlined by H.R. Jauss (1982;
1990). Unfortunately, the whole notion of "readership" or "audience"
continues to present problems. Are we to think of the reader as the passive
receptor of the work or the active creator of meaning and value, or even as
the mediator between the text and external reality, including political action.

---

[26] Riffaterre (1982) 24-25; 90. Later he says of a poem: "it is based entirely on words
arranged in advance, prefabricated groups, whose meaning has not to do with things, but rather
with their role in a system of signifiers... Any interpretation tending to immobilize this
mechanism by reducing the text to reality and to the static atomism of the dictionary fails to
recognize the function of poetry as an experience of alienation." (41-2)

Is that readership the first (for the classicist, the ancient) audience, the implied reader, the competent or ideal reader, a postulated super-reader, or a circle of like-minded readers? Attempts by classicists to reconstruct the audiences of an Augustan literary event or an ancient novel or the Neronian court circle merely scratch the surface of the problem.[27]

Although the *Nachleben* of classical writings has long been of interest to philologists, from this more modern perspective the notion of a objective, immutable, and recoverable text, along with the historical consciousness implicit in it, has to be abandoned in favour of the assumption of "an horizon of expectation" entertained by the original audience and constituted by expectations of genre, models and tradition, as well as the social and historical ambience. Any new work that transcends this horizon then sets up a new horizon in turn, as the work's reception and influence demands a more thoughtful reading. The aesthetic distance created between this and the expectations of the original audience will disappear for a later audience with its now revised horizon of expectation. Our own understanding — and evaluation — of a literary work will derive from the constantly changing aesthetic resonances of the work among later audiences until it is brought into contemporary existence, creating once again its own receptive audience. There is a continuing dialogical and incremental relationship: all interpretations contribute to the unfolding of the immanent significance of the work. Reception is the starting point of evaluation, as well as of the assessment of canon formation.

This approach involves many difficulties. It has however analogies, as was mentioned earlier, in the views held by Ezra Pound and T.S. Eliot about the interrelation of tradition and the individual talent and the importance of the classics in translation. Eliot had claimed that each new work of art altered the arrangement of all previous works of art in the *musée imaginaire* of European literature. Pound's interest in "creative" translation, such as Elizabethan adaptations of Seneca, Pope's *Iliad*, and indeed his own *Homage to Sextus Propertius*, would lead to his tendentious claim: "The Classics only exist in translation!" Both were arguing against the objective self-subsistency of the particular work: the classics are only valuable, indeed viable, in so far as they are transmissible as living works to later generations and continue to influence later literature and other forms of artistic expression (drama, opera, ballet, and now cinema). These indeed may be regarded as the most significant forms of *Textrezeptionsgeschichte*, and they are much more easily documented than the putative reactions of the general or special reading public in any given era, since these may in any case be skewed by contemporary censorship and various religious, educational and

---

[27] Iser (1978) worked with the concept of "an implied reader"; Fish (1980) postulated "the competent reader" and "the cultured audience". For investigations of into the relationship between classical authors and their audience, see now Woodman and Powell (1993).

social pressures. Such an approach, evaluating the documentable influences
of classical works on later writings rather than the postulated effects on their
readership, has never lacked its defenders and practitioners. It therefore
continues to provide a less systematic form of *Rezeptionstheorie*.[28]

Finally there is the unavoidable, if often disguised, problem that bulks
large in any discussion of critical theories of literature (ancient as well as
modern). This is the specifically extrinsic dimension of literature, the
"World", in all its contemporary, historical, ethical, aesthetic, or even
metaphysical dimensions. This Other sits at the table, as it were, along with
the other players: the author, the text, and the reader. However this Other is
constituted, as the objectively real (physical or metaphysical — everything
that is the case) or the sometimes subjective, sometimes objective, ethical
and aesthetic universe, its claims are pressing, although they can be (and
are) resisted. (In ancient critical theory both of these objective and subjective
aspects were subsumed in the theories of "*mimesis*"; artistic "imitation"
reflected both the external physical world and the ethical world of human
life and conduct.)

The relationship of literature to the world of facts, introspection or action
has been the disputed province of numerous theorists: from Plato and
Aristotle to Nietzsche, Marx, and Freud, and latterly Foucault, Althusser,
and Lacan. These larger theories, which are as much "sociological" as
metaphysical, like those based on religion and "morality" (sacred or
profane), tend to scrutinize civilization and culture as a whole, not just
literature and art. Their broader purview, however, does not *ipso facto*
negate their potential contributions to the understanding and evaluation of
classical literature, even if, for example, Marxist and neo-Marxist theory has
been (illogically) discredited by the collapse of the Soviet Union and most
of its satellites.[29]

To take one example, contemporary feminist theory may alienate some
philologists because, like Marxism, it has a decidedly activist side to it.[30]
One of its prime aims, in examining Greco-Roman civilization as a whole,
or classical literature in particular, is to reclaim women's past from its

---

[28] The basic texts are Pound's "Notes on Elizabethan Classicists", "Translators of Greek:
Early Translators of Homer", conveniently reprinted in Pound (1954) 227, 249; Eliot's
"Tradition and the Individual Talent in Eliot" and "Seneca in Elizabethan Translation" in Eliot
(1951) 13, 65.

[29] For Marxist theory and the Classics, see e.g. *Arethusa* (1985). For a useful introduction
to the whole subject, see Eagleton (1976) and Williams (1977). For a sample of the literary
comments of Marx and Engels, see Baxandall and Morawski (1973). For a recent analysis of
aspects of Greek literature along Marxist lines, see Rose (1992).

[30] See e.g. Richlin (1991) on the potential of feminist theory to empower women in the
present, not least in academe and in classical studies in particular. Good introductions to
feminist theory are Showalter (1986) 3-17 and Tong (1990); for its application to classical
studies, see Keuls (1985), Cantarella (1987) and Richlin (1992).

suppression in the traditional patriarchal, or phallocratic, social systems. Feminist theory has therefore concerned itself as much with the significant silences that exclude women in male-authored texts as with the misogynistic representations or stereotyping of women in ancient male authors. Part of its goal will be to recover what few female voices, such as Sappho's, have managed to survive from the classical past, even though they have been misrepresented by the predominantly male values of the ancient and modern world. There are implications in this for canon formation, which according to feminist theory is to be seen not as the objective establishment of the best and the worst, but rather as a literary hierarchy determined by cultural, political and ideological considerations — and not least by the unconscious desire to mimimize the role and importance of the female in society and in literature. An appreciation of this leads to the concept of a "feminist" reader who sceptically probes the underlying male assumptions and omissions in a given text, and the alternative readings possible — the perspective of "gynocritics" (*la gynocritique*). Feminist theory however is not unified beyond its espousal of the most general goals, and it has, naturally enough, affinities to other sociological perspectives such as Marxism and psychoanalysis, including the Lacanian variety. Like them, it can focus on the genesis of the literary work and on its impact on the audience. Indeed some feminists have argued strongly for a pluralism of theory and practice, by contrast with the separatist strand of Lesbian theory. This last can invoke such classical sources as the works of Sappho and the recurrent motif of the Amazon in ancient and modern sources. Its implications are thought-provoking. It is provocative in that it calls into question the literary representation of sexual differences and gender — and here it may be linked with similar investigations, notably those of Foucault, into the conceptualization of homoerotic love, with all the implications that has for the interpretation of certain classical texts.[31]

These radical investigations in classical studies contrast strongly with the attempt by the New Right in the United States to appropriate most of the classical canon to its own political agenda. There have been similar attempts at such appropriation from the early Christian period through the Renaissance into the nineteenth century, when classical literature became the didactic instrument of "higher" spiritual, educational or counter-revolutionary purposes. Indeed even the supposedly value-neutral critical theories that concentrate on the intrinsic characteristics of literature are not immune to ideological analysis — and political application. Religious, political, and even philosophical insistence that literature be part of a greater spiritual culture, and even at its service, is a call common to Platonic utopias, the requirements of the Inquisition and the *Index librorum prohibitorum*, as well

---

[31] See Winkler (1990) 2 and Halperin (1990) 41. Both take as their starting point the work of Foucault.

as the unreformed Writers' Union of the USSR. (Islamic *fatwas* against blasphemous literature cannot escape the notice of any reader of newspapers.)

This brief and necessarily crude sketch of various critical systems should not overlook the contributions they have provided to the eclectic critic concerned with the interpretation of classical literature. Such concepts as systematic ambiguity, imagery and figuration, *persona*, textual subversion, polyphony and dialogic, focalization, the carnavalesque, closure — the list could be multiplied — are now taken for granted in our investigations[32] and should be able to co-exist comfortably enough with older technical terms such as paradosis and stemmatics.

THE CONTINUITY OF ANCIENT AND MODERN CRITICISM AND THEORY

The disjunction between the principles and practice of earlier critics in this last half-century, even in the late eighteenth century (if we take Hermann as the first advocate of the limiting view of classical philology), and the most up-to-date of critical theorists may not seem to the historian of criticism or classical scholarship as abrupt, or as radical, as might be supposed.[33] The more intriguing question that presents itself is whether there is a greater discontinuity between the preoccupations, assumptions, and conclusions of *ancient* literary critics and those of their more modern avatars.

It is evident enough that *some* modern critical debates are no more than continuations of perennial enquiries. The concept of genre was adumbrated, and even regulated, by Aristotle; it remained a systematic concern of the Alexandrian scholar-poets; it was adapted for their own purposes by Quintilian and other educators; it was later exhaustively codified by J.C. Scaliger in the Renaissance; and it still prompts lively and sometimes liberating dialogue.[34] Canon formation, a particularly Alexandrian interest, embraced also by Quintilian for his propaedeutic purposes, has taken on a new and dynamic dimension as its underlying presuppositions are challenged by feminists and multiculturalists.[35] Allegorical interpretation goes back to

---

[32] How far "difference," "trace," and "supplement" will prove useful is still a matter of debate.

[33] For a forceful presentation of this point, see Selden (1990) 174, although I do not agree with the pessimism of his conclusions. Some guidance to the friendly reception of critical theory by classicists will be found in Rosenmeyer (1988), the volumes of *Arethusa* cited in the bibliography below and in the general bibliography.

[34] For ancient classification theories, see Russell (1981) 148, where the contributions are discussed of Plato, Aristotle, Proclus, Cicero, Horace, Quintilian, Menander Rhetor, pseudo-Dionysius; see Pfeiffer (1968) 182 for the Alexandrian contributions to the debate. Most of the relevant texts are in Russell and Winterbottom (1972). Grube (1965) is still the best survey.

[35] On genre and canon formation see the discussions by Fowler (1982) 37; 213. The same author (1989) has some interesting speculations on the future of genre theory.

the sixth and fifth centuries B.C., to Pherecydes of Syros, Anaxagoras, and Metrodorus of Lampsacus. Refined as a method of interpretation by Stoics such as Annaeus Cornutus and neo-Platonists such as Porphyry and Proclus its attractions are as compelling to Northrop Frye and Paul de Man as they were to Dante. Literary history too, in forms that seem perhaps somewhat unsophisticated now, goes back to Aristotle and the industrious cataloguers and classifiers of Alexandria and Pergamum. Various formalist analyses of narrative, drama, and style in general still tend to return, for comparisons and contrasts, to their classical roots. Ancient examples of *explication de texte* and hermeneutical or "critical" readings may be found in Plato's *Protagoras*, the treatise *On the Sublime*, and Dionysius of Halicarnassus' *On the Classical Orators* and *On the Arrangement of Words*.

In a less explicit way various classical writings concern themselves with the theoretical bases of modern critical practice: notably semiotics, hermeneutics, deconstruction, psychoanalysis and reader-response criticism.[36] The discussion of matters semiotic in Plato's *Cratylus*, and then in Aristotle and the Stoical and Sceptical philosophers (noticeably in the interpretation of omens, oracles, and dreams as well as literature) is easily connected with current semiological interests. Such prolegomena are scattered through the Platonic corpus and Aristotle's *Poetics* and *Rhetoric*. Similarly both Plato and Aristotle concerned themselves with the impressionable psychology of the reader. Plato's fear that immoral fictions would adversely affect the character of the reader (*Rep.* 377-397) was countered by Aristotle's theory of *catharsis* (*Pol.*1342a; *Poet.*1449b27).

One noticeable resemblance between ancient literary criticism and contemporary critical theory is that there is little agreement about the limitations of the literary critic's field; attempts to fence it off from aesthetics in general, linguistic theory and epistemology, history, moral philosophy, psychology, and rhetoric are generally unsuccessful.[37]

Because our foundational classical texts have dealt with literature as part of a larger philosophical perspective, they have served as inspiration for a number of modern conceptual systems. Karl Marx wrote his dissertation on Epicurus' atomism; Nietzsche was a professor of classical philology at Basel; Freud drew extensively on classical myth and drama for his terminology; Bakhtin derived inspiration from Menippean satire for his investigation of Rabelais and the novel; and even Foucault has to invoke ancient authors from Plato to Artemidorus in his *History of Sexuality*. The

---

[36] Noted by Kennedy (1989) xi. The relevance of modern semiotic theory to classical studies is pressed by Rubin (1978-9) 17 in an examination of Eco (1976).

[37] Noted by Russell (1981) 1.

study of classical influences on the thinking of the modern moulders of cultural and literary studies is still in its infancy.[38]

On a less portentous level, it is worth noticing how the word "rhetoric" has replaced the word "logic" in the analysis of literary modes (e.g. "the rhetoric of fiction," "the rhetoric of motives," or "the rhetoric of criticism"), when not replaced by more *au courant* metaphors such as "code" and "decoding" (from Prague and elsewhere). Similar borrowings from classical theory and terminology are to be found in Derrida's use of the Plato's *pharmakon* for his own specific purposes.[39] *Ekphrasis* has been found a useful critical tool for the explication of modern as well as ancient literary phenomena.[40] Again, examples could be multiplied.

The epistemological nihilism of Gorgias and Antiphon, the relativism of Protagoras, and the scepticism of the Pyrrhonists, as reported by Sextus Empiricus, seem to surface again in the dubieties of the unstable sign as expounded by Derrida, who even resuscitates the belief shared by Gorgias, Cratylus, Lucretius, and Varro in the heuristic value of the pun. Gorgias, in particular, merits attention in that he impatiently stated that nothing exists; if it does, it is not knowable; and even if it could be known, it could not be communicated to anyone else.[41] By rejecting the search for valid epistemological foundations for discourse as a chimera, he could then refine language as a pragmatic tool, which could be pressed into service in the defence of Helen of Troy and whatever other causes the sophist might decide to take up. Such pragmatism was bitterly opposed by Plato, who did believe in attainable knowledge and despised sophistic orators, since, like some modern critics, they obviously felt that they had only to be interesting rather than informative or truthful. This sophistic stance, typified by the anthropocentric relativism of Protagoras, is arguably a less anxiety-laden attitude that of some Deconstructionists, who openly despair of the epistemological validity or stability of any literary interpretation, but continue to wander in the wilderness, offering subtle analyses of selected literary texts, while elevating the critic to the status of the creative artist, who has no inhibiting theories to prevent him practising his craft.

Some of these resemblances or apparent borrowings may be regarded as fortuitous. Fortuitous too may be the resemblances between the positive discussions of Nothingness and Absence in Heidegger, Gadamer and some deconstructionist critics and the more sceptical examinations of the concept in Plato's *Parmenides* (160b ff.) and *Sophist* (237a ff.), although philosophi-

---

[38] See the perceptive survey of Selden (1990) 166: he traces the lineages of Marx-Benjamin-Althusser-Jameson; Nietzsche-Derrida-Bakhtin-Foucault; Freud-Norman O. Brown-Jacques Lacan-Harold Bloom, but, as he admits, this is only to cite the most familiar names. For the growing importance of Bakhtin in literary studies, see the bibliography s.v.

[39] See Derrida (1981); for other examples, Kennedy (1989) xii.

[40] For references see Fowler (1991) and Bartsch (1989).

[41] See Guthrie (1969) 193.

cal grammar is involved in both. In any case the similarities may help restore some of the dynamic power to Greek literary theory which has been weighted down by centuries of formalistic investigations of the classics and their co-option by conservative political and educational systems.

A case in point is how modern treatments of ancient rhetoric emphasise the purely analytical aspects of its study in the later Greco-Roman world. Yet its origins in fifth-century Greece indicate that rhetoric was originally conceived as a mechanism of power in the emergent democracies. The significance of the "science" of oratory was not lost on Thucydides, Plato, or Isocrates: the Word was intended to master, not just map, the world. The term "Persuasion" only masks what we nowadays might describe as the imposition of "hegemony" (à la Gramsci) or "privileging" or (in different times) "hypnosis" or "brain-washing" — it is au fond the exercise of power through any language but the language of physical violence. Gorgias had frankly described it as "force" and compared it to magic or the administration of drugs in his exculpation of Helen. The dilution of the prime purpose of oratory and rhetoric in the later etiolated analyses of rhetorical handbooks and the unreal exercises of the schools is analogous to the change in the purpose of Science from mastering (Bacon would say "torturing") the physical world to the supposedly disinterested enquiries of "pure" research.

The excessive concern of ancient critics after Plato and Aristotle with the *stylistic* analysis of poetry and prose, especially oratory, substituted the study of the means for the study of the end. This was sometimes protested, but even those protests, as Tacitus's *Dialogus* makes clear, had to recognise the underlying realities of power, hierarchy, and even censorship inherent in the new political vocabularies. Aristotle's intensive analysis of the art of rhetoric was prompted by the belief that the *techne* of oratory is at the service of political ends, not least the class struggle between rich and poor endemic in every civic polity, as he frequently points out in his *Politics* (e.g. 1226a). The power of words could be the impulse to political change, as is evident enough in Thucydides' analysis of the corruption of language in the interests of revolution and reaction. The historian remarks in his description of the prototypical Corcyrean revolution: "to fit in with the change of events, words, too, had to change their usual meanings" (3.5).[42]

If knowledge is power, then mastery of the definition of knowledge would confer even greater power. Who controls the language controls the forms of thinking about politics (and everything else) in privileging certain terms over others. Political discourse has action as its ultimate end, and the inhibiting of free speech is effectively a deterrent to political action, whether as promulgated in Plato's ideal Republic or as lamented by Tacitus in his discussion of the decay of political theory under autocracy.

---

[42] For a discussion of Thucydides' (and Gorgias') belief that language was to be used for mastering the world of events, see Parry (1970) 15.

No wonder then that the stress on form, even on the pleasures of literature, was constantly combatted by different authors and for different reasons. Strabo takes issue with Eratosthenes' denial of knowledge to Homer, and therefore with the latter's opposition to the didactic function of literature. His espousal of pleasure as Homer's chief justification fore-shadows the better argued theoretical position of Philodemus.[43]

If we go back to the four divisions used to categorize the chief concerns of different literary critics and theorists (Author, Text, World, and Audi-ence), some further suggestive analogies can be drawn between ancient and modern criticism.

The author is curiously absent from the narration of events in epic, although the text may be that of the omniscient narrator. The tenuous status of "the author" is clear from the fact that he invokes a higher source for his narrative, not social formations or pressures, or even the bardic epic tradition (*la langue*, in Saussurian terminology), but the Muse(s) or some other divine source of inspiration (Hermes, Apollo or Dionysus). Little attention was paid to the personality of the author or poet, perhaps because of the very communal nature of artistic production in archaic Greece. The romantic view of literature as a form of self-expression was alien to Greek thinking, but the idea of some divine or daemonic inspiration that took over the poet dominated early Greek discussions of poetry: the speaker is not so much Homer as the Muse who speaks through him. Consequently early Greek criticism has little interest in authorial intent and looks to the text itself for critical illumination. Only later will some interest in the author's genius and individuality manifest itself, in Alexandrian chronological research, in the Peripatetic biographers, and in such later works as pseudo-Longinus' *On the Sublime*. And this interest was hardly salutary, since the biographers would use the literary works to draw crude inferences about the author's life and attitudes (hence the reputation of Euripides for misogyny and the strange views of Augustine about Apuleius.[44]) The more famous critics show little interest in the personality or motivations of the writer. The text therefore became the main object of concern in later literary criticism and theory, hence the unremitting analysis of formal features of oratory, prose and poetry: grammar, metrics, the study of tropes, metaphor, literary kinds, and so on.

As for the extrinsic referentiality of literature, the main concept around which the debate revolved in ancient literary theory was that of *Mimesis*. Like the modern "Picture Theory of Language" this concept of Art as an

---

[43] On Philodemus, see Innes (1989) 215.

[44] See Nagy (1989) and Slings (1990). The "I" in ancient literature is, as the Deconstruction-ist critic would say, highly problematic. The Pindaric "I" is not identifiable with the lyric poet who picks up his fee for a job well done for Hieron of Syracuse. For Latin literature, see Veyne (1964).

"imitation" or some kind of representation of the World, was a seductive concept which dominated ancient criticism. If we leave aside such meanings of *Mimesis* as the re-enactment of a composer's work by a performer (itself a very problematic concept) or the re-enactment in ritual of a myth,[45] then two important issues involved in ancient discussions of *Mimesis* may be distinguished. First, there is the *Mimesis* that is concerned with the representation of reality, however philosophically defined, by artistic means (*ut pictura poesis*), and then there is the imitation (in various ways) of earlier authors by later writers, what we now term Intertextuality.[46]

The first kind of *Mimesis* entailed Plato's rejection of poetry as real *mimesis*, since it is rather the *mimesis* of *doxa*, human opinion, an unreliable reflection of the transcendent world of Forms. Aristotle counters with the view that poetry reflects *universalia in re*, rather than the specific events of human life and history. Poetry is therefore more philosophical, in his view, than history. Plato's attempt to elevate philosophy over poetry is not unlike modern attempts to elevate literary theory to the level of creative writing, its very subject of investigation. This problem of how literature relates to the real world continued to plague ancient theorists. They offered a number of answers, one of the more important being "Allegory", which aimed to solve the problem of the non-correspondence of literary statements with external facts through various modes of interpretation. The texts had to be read properly, or, as we might now say, "decoded," in order to understand the true meanings of the text. The method in altered form is still acceptable in modern critical theory,[47] but its roots, as was observed earlier, go back to the fifth and sixth centuries. Aristotle also managed to break away from the "mimetic" picture of artistic discourse by his insistence that rhetoric at least was not "mimetic" but was pragmatic, and aimed to change the world, not reflect it, as did poetry and prose forms allied to it.

Another prime concern for ancient critics and theorists of literature was the nature of audience response. On the more scientific level no one was more assiduous than Aristotle in his investigations of the machinery of audience affect in his examination of "Plausibility" in the *Rhetoric*. Aristotle was interested in the mastery of the audience by the orator and the rhetorician. Just as the mastery of nature by means of scientific analysis was the aim of his biological works, so the search for the ideal system of government is the object of his political works — not least in the anatomies of the Athenian and other systems of government. The significance of the power of rhetoric, i.e. the definition of ruling concepts, of rhetoric as the manipulation of language for a particular purpose, was no more lost on

---

[45] On these meanings, see Nagy (1989) 47.

[46] See Russell (1981) 112.

[47] See e.g. de Man (1981) and his discussion of "allegories" of reading in Greenblatt (1981). On Hellenistic allegorization, see now Dawson (1992).

Aristotle than it would be on Foucault. Aristotle was willing to substitute the hegemonic language of persuasion (democratic terms) for the crude terminology of force in the eternal struggle between rich and poor in the city state. (The language of force even in democratic societies is well expressed in Thucydides' Melian dialogue.) His political analysis underlies and justifies his scientific analysis of rhetoric, and by natural extension, his analysis of poetics and even his sociological justification of the effects of tragedy.

Aristotle saw that the nature of the audience's response determines the techniques of rhetoric, and indeed of literature in general. Analysis of the forms of persuasion was the first step to the scientific mastery of rhetoric, and thus the main avenue at that time to political power. This should be the aim of rhetoric as a science, as a teachable subject. This aim is frequently lost sight of in the oversubtle analyses of the Hellenistic and Roman theoreticians of rhetoric such as Cicero and Quintilian. Teleologically, however, the aim of all this mastery of the spoken (and written) word was political and ideological power, however unrealistic this aim became in changed political conditions, when military intervention was so obviously more direct and effective. The power of rhetoric was however soon transferred to the saving of men's souls, to the religious rather than the secular sphere. It would later emerge as a powerful religious force in secular affairs once again, as political and social conditions changed.

Mimesis as the imitation, adaptation, and emulation of other authors becomes an important subject of discussion in the Hellenistic period. It would greatly concern Horace, and later such Renaissance worthies as Ben Jonson. It is naturally tied to the important question of reader or audience reception. The old paradigm is the later author, who looks to earlier originals for inspiration, guidance, and material to be borrowed, adapted, or even perverted; to precursors who are to be admired and praised; improved on or surpassed; or even challenged or confuted. The obvious case in point here would be Vergil and the ramifications of his relations with Homer, Hesiod, Apollonius Rhodius, Theocritus, Ennius, and Lucretius, which inspired much critical comment later about *aemulatio, imitatio*, and even plagiarism. As even Velleius Paterculus noticed (1.17): talent is fed by emulation; jealousy and admiration both fire the wish to imitate.

But the classical investigation of reader-response was of course not limited to this. It is no great exaggeration to claim that the most ancient discussions of literature are audience-oriented. Poetry was seen as a means of producing effects, not expressing the author's *psyche*. Self-expression, Art for Art's sake, are more modern, if out-dated, concepts. For the ancient critic the audience is seen as the responsive and reactive reader. Theophrastus (fr. 65 Wimmer) specifies the effect of literature on the audience: pleasure, curiosity, conviction, emotional stimulus to action: he therefore puts poetry and oratory in the same category, and he distinguishes them from the work of the philosopher, who is primarily concerned with facts and truth.

Plato above all was concerned with the impact for good or ill on the citizen audience of the faulty representations of reality and truth purveyed by poet and sophist. His answer, since according to his way of thinking the audience would imitate the lessons of dramatic art, was a rigid censorship, and the elimination of poets from his ideal state. Aristotle's different philosophical viewpoint allowed him to defend the utilitarian value of poetry as both philosophically educational and also emotionally valuable in his theory of *Catharsis*. This utilitarian value ascribed to poetry leads at once to the potent set of concepts in ancient literary criticism that revolves around the distinction of *utile* and *dulce* in the production of art. These concepts above all concern reader-response. The didactic function, indeed the didactic *nature* of poetry had long been a given in the implicit rationale for poetry's place in society — not for nothing has Homer been described as the Bible of the Greeks. Plato and some predecessors had come to question this concept not because they offered a different view of poetry, but because the teachings of poetry as they knew it, were in fact wrong or at best unreliable or unprovable or just unphilosophical. It was left to Philodemus to argue the case best for the pleasure element *per se* in poetry. The idea that poetry should serve a social purpose, that is should be didactic (indeed provocative) is still part and parcel of neo-Marxist and feminist theory, while modern literary education assumes automatically that the close critical study of relevant texts (including selected classical texts) is a potent part of a humanistic education, a more humanistically useful element of that education than, say, the philological study of Sanskrit or Tibetan texts, or entomology and vulcanology. This may be seen as just another version of the common (but not universal) ancient belief that literature should have utility — enlightenment and moral improvement, if not political action — as well as pleasure or aesthetic appreciation as its goal.

To see analogies and resemblances between ancient and contemporary literary and cultural theory is, it would seem, easy enough. How profound these connections are will continue to be a matter of debate.

The present volume can do no more than present a sample of the possibilities for the possibly fruitful engagement between modern critical theory and the study of Greek and Roman classical literature. The intention was to dispel some of the incomprehension that surrounds this interaction. Not all of those who were invited to contribute could do so and the editors are therefore all the more grateful to those who were willing to contribute their time and patience to this enterprise. A brief guide to the contents of the volume may prove helpful.

Of the less controversial methodologies, Narratology is applied by I. de Jong to Homer. Using the modern concept of "embedded focalization", the presentation of a character's perceptions, thoughts, and emotions by the narrator in a narrator-text, she challenges the *idée reçu* that Homeric characters have no secret or hidden thoughts. Intertextuality in its strict meaning, the *conscious* and purposive allusion by an author to other texts, is exemplified by M. van Erp's analysis of Theocritus' Thirteenth Idyll, which demonstrates, through its repeated invocations of Homer, the clash between the heroic world of Heracles and the unheroic world in which Hylas disappears. G. W. Most scrutinizes Plato's ingenious *explication de texte* in *Protagoras* and shows how "contextuality" provides a more reliable critical anchor than other approaches.

In the broader and more debated areas of critical theory, S. Goldhill explores the ramifications for the study of classical texts of work of Derrida and others, taking the theme of Helen's depiction in different Greek authors as a particularly striking "exemplarity". R.S. Caldwell applies Freudian and Lacanian psychoanalytical theory to uncover the deeper significances of the Danaid trilogy as represented by Aeschylus' *Supplices*. Speech-Act theory, as pioneered by J.L. Austin (1962) and further explored by Searle (1969), is applied by R. Cohen as a new methodological tool for the investigation of certain plays of Plautus. D.P. Fowler demonstrates how the modern concept of "poetic closure" can provide valuable insights in the exploration of certain classical Latin texts. C. Segal brings the principles of modern hermeneutics to help unravel the Tereus' episode in Ovid's *Metamorphoses*. The important branch of Reader-Response theory, Jauss' aesthetics of reception, is critically analyzed by R. Nauta, who uses Horace's famous Soracte Ode as a touchstone of the theory. M. McDonald pursues the alternative route of examining the effects of the apprehension and transmutation of a classic text, Sophocles' *Electra*, by later artists (here Strauss' opera on the subject) and the insights, some feminist, into the original that are thereby generated.

BIBLIOGRAPHY

Abrams M.H. (1989) *Doing Things with Texts. Essays in Criticism and Critical Theory*, ed. M. Fisher (New York-London: 1989).
Ackermann R. (1991) *The Myth and Ritual School: J.G. Frazer and the Cambridge Ritualists* (New Haven: 1991).
Arethusa 6 (1973), *Women in Antiquity*.
Arethusa 7 (1974), *Psychoanalysis and the Classics*.
Arethusa 8 (1975), *Marxism and the Classics*.
Arethusa 10 (1977), *Classical Literature and Contemporary Literary Theory*.
Arethusa 16 (1983), *Semiotics and Classical Studies*.
Arethusa 19 (1986), *Audience-Oriented Criticism and the Classics*.
Atkins C.D. and Morrow L. (1989) *Contemporary Literary Theory* (Boston: 1989).
Austin J.L. (1962) *How to do Things with Words*, ed. J.O. Urmson and M. Sbisa (Oxford: 1962).

Bakhtin M. with P.N. Medvedev (1978) *The Formal Method in Literary Scholarship: a Critical Introduction to Sociological Poetics*, trans. K.J. Wehrle (Russian original, 1928) (Baltimore: 1978).

Bakhtin M. (1981) *The Dialogic Imagination*, ed. M. Holquist, trans. C. Emerson and M. Holquist (Austin, Texas: 1981).

Barthes R. (1968) "The Death of the Author", in *Image, Music, Text*, ed. and trans. S. Heath (London: 1968).

—— (1975) *The Pleasure of the Text*, trans. R. Miller (New York: 1975).

Bartsch S. (1989) *Decoding the Ancient Novel* (Princeton: 1989).

Baxandall S. and Morawski S. (eds.) (1973) *Marx and Engels on Literature and Art* (St. Louis: 1973).

Benjamin A. (ed.) (1988) *Post-Structuralist Classics* (London-New York: 1988).

Bergonzi B. (1990) *Exploding English: Criticism, Theory and Culture* (Oxford: 1990).

Berman A. (1988) *From the New Criticism to Deconstruction: The Reception of Structuralism and Poststructuralism* (Urbana-Chicago: 1988).

Bloom H. (1973) *The Anxiety of Influence. A Theory of Poetry* (Oxford: 1973).

Bodkin M. (1934) *Archetypal Patterns in Poetry* (London: 1934).

Booth W.C. (1961) *The Rhetoric of Fiction* (Chicago: 1961).

Bremmer J. (ed.) (1989) *Interpretations of Greek Mythology* (London: 1989).

Burkert W. (1979) *Structure and History in Greek Mythology and Ritual*, trans. P. Bing (Berkeley: 1979).

—— (1983) *Homo Necans: the Anthropology of Ancient Greek Sacrificial Ritual and Myth*, trans. P. Bing (Berkeley: 1983).

Calder W.M. (ed.) (1991) *The Cambridge Ritualists Reconsidered, Illinois Classical Studies Supplement* 2 (Atlanta: 1991).

Cantarella E. (1987) *Pandora's Daughters. The Role and Status of Women in Greek and Roman Antiquity*, trans. M.B. Fant (Baltimore: 1987).

Cohen R. (ed.) (1989) *The Future of Literary Theory* (London: 1989).

Collier P. and Geyer-Ryan H. (1990) *Literary Theory Today* (Cambridge: 1990).

Conte G.B. (1986) *The Rhetoric of Imitation. Genre and Poetic Memory in Virgil and Other Latin Poets* (Ithaca, N.Y.: 1986).

Culler J. (1975) *Structuralist Poetics: Structuralism, Linguistics, and the Study of Literature* (London: 1975).

—— (1981) *The Pursuit of Signs — Semiotics, Literature, Deconstruction* (Ithaca, N.Y.: 1981).

—— (1982) *On Deconstruction: Theory and Criticism after Structuralism* (Ithaca, N.Y.: 1981).

—— (1986) *Ferdinand de Saussure* (Ithaca, N.Y.: 1986).

Davis R.C. and Schleifer R. (eds.) (1989) *Contemporary Literary Criticism: Literary and Cultural Studies* (New York-London: 1985).

Dawson D. (1992) *Allegorical Readers and Cultural Revision in Ancient Alexandria* (Berkeley: 1992).

de Man P. (1981) "Pascal's Allegory of Persuasion", in Greenblatt (1963).

Derrida J. (1981) "Plato's Pharmacy", in *Dissemination*, trans. B. Johnson (Chicago: 1981).

Detienne M. and Vernant J.-P. (1978) *Cunning Intelligence in Greek Culture and Society*, trans. J. Lloyd (Brighton: 1978).

Dodds E.R. (1951) *The Greeks and the Irrational* (Berkeley: 1951).

Eagleton T. (1976) *Marxism and Literary Criticism* (Berkeley: 1976).

—— (1983) *Literary Theory: An Introduction* (Oxford: 1983).

Eco U. (1976) *A Theory of Semiotics* (Bloomington: 1976).

Eliot T.S. (1951) *Selected Essays* (London: 1951).

Elliott R.C. (1982) *The Literary Persona* (Chicago: 1982).

Fish S. (1980) *Is there a Text in this Class? The Authority of Interpretive Communities* (Cambridge, Mass.-London: 1980).

Foucault M. (1970) *The Order of Things*, trans. (London: 1970).

—— (1980) *Power and Knowledge*, trans. (London: 1980).

—— (1978-1986) *The History of Sexuality*, trans. R. Hurley (New York: 1978-1986).

Fowler A. (19820 *Kinds of Literature: An Introduction to the Theory of Genres and Modes* (Oxford: 1982).

—— (1989) "The Future of Genre Theory: Functions and Constructional Types", in Cohen (1989).

Fowler D.P. (1989) "First Thoughts on Closure: Problems and Prospects", *Materialii e discussioni per l'analisi dei testi classici* 22 (1989) 75-122.

—— (1991) "Narrate and Describe: The Problem of Ekphrasis", *Journal of Roman Studies* 81 (1991) 25-35.

Frye N. (1957) *The Anatomy of Criticism. Four Essays* (Princeton: 1957).

Gadamer H.-G. (1961) *Wahrheit und Methode* (Tübingen: 1961).

—— (1976) *Philosophical Hermeneutics*, trans. D.E. Linge (Berkeley: 1976).

Galinsky K. (ed.) (1992) *Hermeneutics and Empiricism* (Frankfurt am Main-New York: 1992).

Genette G. (1980) *Narrative Discourse*, trans. J. Lewin (New York: 1980).

Gentili B. (1990) *Poetry and its Public in Ancient Greece*, trans. A.T. Cole (Baltimore: 1990).

Goldhill S. (1984) *Language, Sexuality, Narrative: the Oresteia* (Cambridge: 1984).

—— (1991) *The Poet's Voice: Essays on Poetics and Greek Literature* (Cambridge: 1991).

Goodheart E. (1984) *The Skeptic Disposition in Contemporary Criticism* (Princeton: 1984).

Greenblatt S. (ed.) (1981) *Allegory and Representation* (Baltimore: 1981).

Grube G.M.A. (1965) *The Greek and Roman Critics* (London: 1965).

Guthrie W.K.C. (1969) *A History of Greek Philosophy* vol. III: *The Fifth-Century Enlightenment* (Cambridge: 1969).

Hamon P. (1975) "Clausules", *Poétique* 6 (1975) 495-526.

Halperin D. (1990) *One Hundred Years of Homosexuality* (New York-London: 1990).

Hardin R.F. (1989) "Archetypal Criticism", in Atkins (1989).

Harriott R. (1969) *Poetry and Criticism before Plato* (London: 1969).

Henderson J. (1989) "Satire writes 'woman': Gendersong.", *Proceedings of the Cambridge Philological Society* 35 (1989) 50-80.

Holland N.N. (1968) *The Dynamics of Literary Response* (New York: 1968).

Hooley D.M. (1990-1) "On Relations between Classical and Contemporary Imitation Theory: Some Hellenistic Suggestions.", *Classical and Modern Languages* 11 (1990-1) 77-92.

Hoy D.C. (1978) *The Critical Circle: Literature and History in Contemporary Hermeneutics* (Berkeley: 1978).

Humphreys S.C. (1978) *Anthropology and the Greeks* (London: 1978).

Innes D.C. (1989) "Philodemus", in Kennedy (1989).

Iser W. (1978) *The Act of Reading: A Theory of Aesthetic Response*, trans. (London: 1978).

Jauss H.R. (1982) *Towards an Aesthetic of Reception*, trans. T. Bahti (Minneapolis: 1982).

—— (1982) *Aesthetic Experience and Literary Hermeneutics*, trans. M. Shaw (Minneapolis: 1982).

—— (1990) "The Theory of Reception: A Retrospective of its Unrecognized Prehistory", in Collier (1990).

de Jong I.J.F. (1987) *Narrators and Focalizers. The Presentation of the Story in the Iliad* (Amsterdam: 1987).

Kennedy G.A. (ed.) (1989) *The Cambridge History of Literary Criticism* vol. 1: *Classical Criticism* (Cambridge: 1989).

Keuls E.C. (1985) *The Reign of the Phallus: Sexual Politics in Ancient Athens* (New York: 1985).

Kresic S. (ed.) (1981) *Contemporary Literary Hermeneutics and the Interpretation of Classical Texts* (Ottawa: 1981).

Laks A. and Neschke A. (1990) *La naissance du paradigme herméneutique: Schleiermacher, Humboldt, Boekh, Droysen* (Lille: 1990).

Lefkowitz M. (1982) *The Lives of the Greek Poets* (London: 1982).

Lehman D. (1991) *Signs of the Times: Deconstruction and the Fall of Paul de Man* (New York: 1991).
Lentriccia F. (1980) *After the New Criticism* (London: 1980).
Lévi-Strauss C. (1966) *The Savage Mind*, trans. (London-Chicago: 1966).
—— (1967) *Structural Anthropology*, trans. C. Jacobson and B.G. Schoepf (New York: 1967).
Lyons J. (1969) *Introduction to Theoretical Linguistics* (Cambridge: 1969).
Magliola R. (1989) "Like the Glaze on a Katydid-Wing: Phenomenological Criticism", in Atkins (1989).
Mueller-Vollmer K. (ed.) (1989) *The Hermeneutics Reader* (New York: 1989).
Mulhern F. (1979) *The Moment of 'Scrutiny'* (London: 1979).
Nagy G. (1989) "Early Greek Views of Poets and Poetry", in Kennedy (1989).
Parry A. (1970) "Thucydides' Use of Abstract Language", *Yale French Studies* 45 (1970) 3-20.
Parry M. (1971) (ed. A. Parry) *The Making of Homeric Verse: The Collected Papers of M. Parry* (Oxford: 1971).
Peacock S.J. (1988) *Jane Ellen Harrison: the Mask and the Self* (New Haven: 1988).
Pfeiffer R. (1968) *History of Classical Scholarship from the Beginnings to the End of the Hellenistic Age* (Oxford: 1968).
Poulet G. (1964) *The Interior Distance*, trans. E. Coleman (Ann Arbor: 1964).
Pound E. (1954) (ed. T.S. Eliot) *Literary Essays of Ezra Pound* (London: 1954).
Prince G. (1987) *A Dictionary of Narratology* (Lincoln, Nebraska-Aldershot: 1987).
Propp V. (1968) *Morphology of the Folktale*, trans. (Austin, Texas: ^{2}1968).
Pucci P. (1971) "Lévi-Strauss and Classical Culture", *Arethusa* 4 (1971) 103-17.
Ransom J.C. (1941) *The New Criticism* (New York: 1941).
Redfield J. (1991) "Classics and Anthropology", *Arion* 1.2 (1991) 5ff.
Richards I.A. (1936) *The Philosophy of Rhetoric* (Cambridge, Mass.: 1936).
Richlin A. (1991) "Zeus and Metis: Foucault, Feminism, Classics", *Helios* 18.2 (1991) 160ff.
—— (ed.) (1992) *Pornography and Representation in Greece and Rome* (New York-Oxford: 1992).
Riffaterre M. (1982) *The Semiotics of Poetry* (New York: 1982).
Rose P.W. (1992) *Sons of the Gods, Children of Earth: Ideology and Literary Form in Ancient Greece* (Ithaca, N.Y.: 1992)
Rosenmeyer T.G. (1988) *DEINA TA POLLA: A Classicist's Checklist of Twenty Literary-Critical Positions*, Arethusa Monographs 12 (Buffalo: 1988).
Rubin N. Felson (1978-79) "Eco's Semiotics: a Classicist's Perspective", *Helios* 6.2 (1978-79) 17-32.
Russell D.A. and Winterbottom M. (eds.) (1972) *Ancient Literary Criticism: The Principal Texts in New Translations* (Oxford: 1972).
Russell D.A. (1981) *Criticism in Antiquity* (Berkeley: 1981).
Scaliger J.C. (1561) *Poetikes Libri VII* (Lyons: 1561).
Searle J.R. (1969) *Speech Acts: an Essay in the Philosophy of Language* (Cambridge: 1969.
—— (1983) "The World Turned Upside Down", *New York Review of Books* (October 27, 1983) 74-79.
Segal C. (1968) "Ancient Texts and Modern Literary Criticism", *Arethusa* 1:1 (1968) 1-25.
Selden D.L. (1990) "Classics and Contemporary Criticism", *Arion* n.s. 1.1 (1990) 155-178.
Selden R. (1988) *The Theory of Criticism from Plato to the Present. A Reader* (New York: 1988).
Showalter E. (ed.) (1986) *The New Feminist Criticism: Essays on Women, Literature, Theory* (London: 1986).
Slings S.R. (1990) "The I in Personal Archaic Lyric: an Introduction", in S.R. Slings (ed.) *The Poet's I in Archaic Greek Lyric* (Amsterdam: 1990).
Smith B.H. (1968) *Poetic Closure, How Poems End* (London: 1968).
Steiner G. (1984) *Antigones* (Oxford: 1984).

Strauss B.S. (1985) "Ritual, Social Drama and Politics in Classical Athens", *American Journal of Ancient History* 10 (1985) 67.

Sutton W. (1963) *Modern American Criticism* (Englewood Cliffs, N.Y.: 1963).

Thompkins J.P. (1990) *Reader-Response Criticism* (Baltimore: 1990).

Todorov T. (1988) *Literature and its Theorists: a Personal View of Twentieth-Century Criticism* (London: 1988).

—— (1992) *Genres of Discourse* (Cambridge: 1992).

Tong R. (1990) *Feminist Thought: A Comprehensive Introduction* (London: 1990).

Vernant J.-P. (1980) *Myth and Society in Ancient Greece*, trans. J. Lloyd (London: 1980).

Veyne P. (1964) "Le 'je' dans le *Satiricon*", *Revue des Études Latines* 42 (1964) 301-24.

Wheelwright P. (1954) *The Burning Fountain: a Study in the Language of Symbolism* (Bloomington, Ind.: 1954).

—— (1962) *Metaphor and Reality* (Bloomington, Ind.: 1962).

Williams R. (1977) *Marxism and Literature* (Oxford: 1977).

Willingham J.R. (1989) "The New Criticism: Then and Now", in Atkins (1989).

Wilson E. (1941) *The Wound and the Bow* (Boston: 1941).

Wimsatt W.K. (1954) *The Verbal Icon: Studies in the Meaning of Poetry* (Nashville, Kentucky: 1954).

Winkler J.J. (1985) *Auctor & Actor: A Narratological Reading of Apuleius' "Golden Ass"* (Berkeley: 1985).

—— (1990) *The Constraints of Desire: the Anthropology of Sex and Gender in Ancient Greece* (New York-London: 1990).

Winters Y. (1938) *Maule's Curse*, in *In Defence of Reason* (London: 1960).

Wolf F.A. (1989) *Prolegomena ad Homerum*, translation and introduction by A. Grafton and G.W. Most (Princeton: 1989).

Woodman T. and Powell J. (eds.) (1993) *Author and Audience in Latin Literature* (New York-London: 1993).

Worton M. and Still J. (eds.) (1990) *Intertextuality: Theory and Practices* (Manchester: 1990).

Wyke M. (1984) *The Elegiac Woman and her Male Creators: Propertius and the Written Cynthia* (diss. Cambridge: 1984).

BETWEEN WORD AND DEED:
HIDDEN THOUGHTS IN THE *ODYSSEY*

BY

IRENE J.F. DE JONG

INTRODUCTION

One of the main characteristics of narrative fiction, one which sets it apart both from other literary genres and from real life, is its capacity to portray the unspoken thoughts, feelings, and perceptions of a person other than the speaker. This capacity has been effectively exploited by writers in various ways, one of which is to acquaint the reader with a character's secret inner life, which differs considerably from his outward behaviour, his words and gestures. A novel which immediately springs to mind here is Dostoyevski's *Crime and Punishment*, in which the reader shares with Raskolnikov his terrible secret. Other noteworthy examples are the novels of Virginia Woolf and James Joyce, in which the technique of unspoken thought even acquires thematic centrality. In this paper I will argue that yet another famous narrative text should be added to this list: the *Odyssey*. As far as I know, this work has not yet figured in discussions of the technique by literary theorists; rather, it is suggested that we are dealing here with a relatively recent, novelistic device.[1] This is less surprising, when we realize that even Homerists seem to be largely unaware of the existence of unspoken thought in Homer, as may be gathered from statements like the following:

> So wird der Mensch mit seinem Tun identisch, und er läßt sich von seinem Tun her vollständig und vollgültig erfassen; er hat keine verborgenen Tiefen... In dem sachlichen Bericht den das alte Epos vom Tun und Reden der Menschen erstattet, wird alles ausgesagt was die Menschen sind, weil sie eben nur das sind was sie tun und reden und leiden.
>
> (Fränkel 1951: 112-3)

---

* I would like to thank Mrs. A.M. van Erp Taalman Kip and S.R. van der Mije for their comments and suggestions, and Mrs. B. Fasting for her correction of my English. The research for this article was made possible by a fellowship from the Royal Netherlands Academy of Arts and Sciences.

[1] Scholes and Kellogg (1966) 175-81 only mention the Homeric monologue, which, however, is not unspoken; according to Kahler (1973) 15, epic is concerned primarily with deeds and physical incidents; Cohn (1978) discusses only novels from the period 1850-1950.

Handlungsverläufe vollziehen sich im steten Wechsel von Wort und Tat. Diese
sind die einzigen Ausdrucksmittel des Epos.

(Barck 1976: 32)

Homeric man, being objective, has no innerness. He expresses himself completely
in words and acts, and is thus completely known to his fellows. He has no hidden
depths or secret motives; he says and does what he is.

(Redfield 1975: 21)

A recurrent element in these quotations is the combination "word and deed".
These scholars, recalling Peleus' words in *Iliad* 9.443 that a hero should be
a 'speaker of words and a doer of deeds' (μύθων τε ῥητῆρ' ... πρηκτῆρά τε
ἔργων), imply that Homeric heroes only act and speak, and, accordingly, that
the Homeric text consists only of actions and speeches.[2] The most radical
of the three scholars just quoted is Redfield, who claims that the Homeric
hero "is completely known *to his fellows*" (my italics). To counter this claim
one needs only think of Odysseus' many lying tales in the *Odyssey*. There
are also expressions like ἐξαύδα, μὴ κεῦθε νόῳ; μυθήσομαι οὐδ'
ἐπικεύσω; ἄπτερος ἔπλετο μῦθος,[3] etc. which all suggest that Homeric
speakers were able either to speak out or to conceal their thoughts. Fränkel's
statement is ambiguous. Does the sentence "er hat keine verborgene Tiefen"
betray the same naive credulity in the sincerity of Homeric characters as
Redfield's, or does he mean that the interior of Homeric characters remains
no secret *for the reader*? This is at any rate the position of Auerbach in his
famous *Mimesis*:[4]

... Homer's personages vent their inmost heart in speech; what they do not say to
others, they speak in their own minds, so that the reader is informed of it.

However, this contention has not gone unchallenged either. In the first place,
there is Beßlich's fine study on Odyssean silences, both those mentioned
explicitly by the narrator, and those which the reader himself is left to infer.
In the second place, there is Griffin's chapter on Homeric characterization
in his *Homer on Life and Death* (1980), in the course of which he deals
with places where the narrator himself "explicitly tells us of the psychology
underlying the words and acts of characters" and others where the reader is

---

[2] Cf. also Mattes (1958) 21, Whitman (1958) 118, Russo and Simon (1968) 47-8, and De
Romilly (1984) 13, 26, 31, 45.

[3] This expression has, I think, been convincingly analysed by Latacz (1968): the thoughts of
a character do not become ἔπεα πτερόεντα, i.e. remain unexpressed.

[4] Auerbach (1953) 6; cf. Schwinge (1990) 5: "Wenn der Erzähler aber nun ... innere
Vorgänge seiner Personen direkt benennt, so um *dem Hörer* auch in dieser Hinsicht das
Geschehen in jedem einzelnen Fall transparant werden zu lassen; ihn keinen Augenblick einer
möglichen Ungewißheit auszuliefern" (my italics).

left to infer that psychology.[5] Together, Beßlich and Griffin have shown that not everything is externalized in the Homeric epics, either by the characters or by the narrator. Both scholars occasionally mention examples of unspoken thought, but the pervasiveness and thematic significance of this device in the *Odyssey* have not yet been explored fully. Let us begin by taking a closer look at the phenomenon itself.

UNSPOKEN THOUGHT AS A FORM OF EMBEDDED FOCALIZATION

Thought, like speech, can be presented directly, in the form of a monologue, or indirectly. Since monologues in Homer are always spoken aloud, the only form of unspoken thought found is the indirect one. In terms of the narratological theories of Genette and Bal, we are dealing with a form of *embedded focalization*. Embedded focalization is the narrative situation in which a primary narrator-focalizer represents in the narrator-text the perceptions, thoughts, emotions, or words (indirect speech) of characters, e.g.:

(1) Bond Street fascinated her; Bond Street early in the season; its flags flying, its shops, no splash; no glitter; one roll of tweed in the shop where her father had bought his suits for fifty years; a few pearls; salmon on an iceblock.

(Virginia Woolf, *Mrs. Dalloway*)

or

(2)   τὸν δὲ νόησεν
ἑλκόμενον πρόσθεν πόλιος· ταχέες δέ μιν ἵπποι
ἕλκον ἀκηδέστως κοίλας ἐπὶ νῆας Ἀχαιῶν.

and she saw him
being dragged in front of the city, and the running horses
dragged him ruthlessly toward the hollow ships of the Achaians.

(*Il.* 22.463-5)[6]

In the first passage we look at Bond Street through Clarissa Dalloway's fascinated eyes, while in the second we share Andromache's horrified perception of Hector being dragged towards the Greek ships. In both passages there are specific indications that we are dealing with the consciousness or focalization of the characters, rather than that of the primary narrator-focalizer (henceforth the narrator): in passage (1) the

---

[5] Such reading between the lines is categorically forbidden by Kakridis (1970), advocated by Winkler (1990) 143: "It would also be methodologically constricted to assume that Homer is an utterly transparent narrator, always telling us all that can be known."

[6] All quotations are from the Oxford Classical Text (Monro and Allen, Monro). The translations are R. Lattimore's (*The Odyssey of Homer*, New York: 1965) with occasional changes.

personal note of "[the shop] where her father had bought his suits for fifty years", in passage (2) the emotional word ἀκηδέστως, 'ruthlessly'. Only here the wordgroup ἀκηδέστως, ἀκήδεστος, and ἀκηδής is found in narrator-text as against 10 occurrences in direct speech.

In both passages it is the narrator who verbalizes Mrs. Dalloway's and Andromache's perceptions; the characters themselves do not speak. The implication is that only the reader is informed about these perceptions and feelings, and not the characters in the story. This implication is not always relevant; thus in passage (1) there are no other characters present, while in passage (2) Andromache's feelings are no secret. In most of the instances of embedded focalization in the *Iliad* secrecy plays no role.[7] The implication can, however, be exploited with great effect, when thoughts are *deliberately* left unspoken by a character and there is a discrepancy between the knowledge of the reader, who is aware of what is going on in the mind of the character, and that of the other characters in the story, who are not.[8] This happens frequently in the *Odyssey*.

That the Homeric narrator was aware of the 'unspokenness' of embedded focalization can be illustrated quite simply from his use of the monologue form to present a character's thoughts, as opposed to the embedded focalization form: the monologue form is used when a character is alone, cannot be overheard by others and hence can safely utter what he thinks. The embedded focalization form is used when other characters are present.[9] Thus, at the beginning of book 6 of the *Odyssey* we find first a monologue by Odysseus, in which he asks himself where he has landed this time (110-26); then, when he stands opposite Nausicaa, his deliberation as to how to approach the girl takes the form of embedded focalization (141-8), since she is clearly not meant to overhear his thoughts.

Let us now look at the ways in which the device of unspoken thought is used in the *Odyssey*.[10] I will concentrate on the second half of the poem, the story of Odysseus' homecoming, which contains most of the instances. The champion of unspoken thought is, of course, Odysseus himself.

ODYSSEUS' UNSPOKEN THOUGHTS

The point of departure for Odysseus' secrecy is the following instruction which Athena gives him as soon as he lands on the shore of Ithaca:

---

[7] See De Jong (1987) 102-123.

[8] See Bal (1985) 110.

[9] Hentze (1905) 23 and Scully (1984) 13 mention other criteria for choosing between the two forms: the monologue form allows the poet to characterize a person and to explain more fully his motives.

[10] The importance of thoughts in the *Odyssey* (as opposed to actions and words) is noted but not worked out systematically by Austin (1975) 180 and Rutherford (1985) 144.

(3) "εἴπω θ' ὅσσα τοι αἶσα δόμοις ἔνι ποιητοῖσι
κήδε' ἀνασχέσθαι· σὺ δὲ τετλάμεναι καὶ ἀνάγκῃ,
μηδέ τῳ ἐκφάσθαι μήτ' ἀνδρῶν μήτε γυναικῶν,
πάντων, οὕνεκ' ἄρ' ἦλθες ἀλώμενος, ἀλλὰ σιωπῇ
πάσχειν ἄλγεα πολλά, βίας ὑποδέγμενος ἀνδρῶν."

"[I am here] to tell you all the troubles you are destined to suffer
in your well-built house; but you must, of necessity, endure
and you must not tell any man or woman that you have
come home from your wanderings, but you must suffer
much grief in silence, standing and facing men in their violence."

(*Od.* 13.306-10)

In order to make it easier for Odysseus to remain incognito, the goddess
changes his outward appearance. It is up to Odysseus, however, to adapt his
behaviour and never drop his mask.

The first test follows in the next book. Eumaeus tells "the stranger"/
Odysseus about the insolent behaviour of the suitors. The latter reacts as
follows:

(4) ὁ δ' ἐνδυκέως κρέα τ' ἤσθιε πῖνέ τε οἶνον,
ἁρπαλέως ἀκέων, κακὰ δὲ μνηστῆρσι φύτευεν.

and he ate his meat and drank his wine, quietly,
greedily and without speaking, and devised evils for the suitors.

(*Od.* 14.109-10)

Reacting with angry or excited words to Eumaeus' information would betray
Odysseus' real identity. Hence he remains silent, but the embedded
focalization (κακὰ ... φύτευεν) reveals to the reader — although not to
Eumaeus — what is at the same time going on in his mind. Unspoken
thoughts take the place of words.[11]

The confrontation with the friendly Eumaeus requires only a modicum of
self-restraint on Odysseus' part. The situation changes, however, when he
meets with physical and verbal abuse, as Athena predicted he would in
passage (3). The first time it is the goatherd Melantheus who reviles
(17.215-32) and then kicks (233-4) him. Physically, our hero manages to
keep his footing (ἔμεν' ἀσφαλέως), and this is his mental reaction:

(5) ὁ δὲ μερμήριξεν Ὀδυσσεὺς,
ἠὲ μεταΐξας ῥοπάλῳ ἐκ θυμὸν ἕλοιτο,
ἦ πρὸς γῆν ἐλάσειε κάρη ἀμφουδὶς ἀείρας.
ἀλλ' ἐπετόλμησε, φρεσὶ δ' ἔσχετο.

---

[11] For the simultaneity of Odysseus' outward and inward reaction, see Beßlich (1966) 80-1.
Less well Stanford (1958) *ad loc.*: "O. 'wolfs' his food because he wants to give his immediate
attention to the planning of revenge on the suitors".

and he pondered within him
whether to go for him with his cudgel, and take the life from him,
or pick him up like a jug and break his head on the ground. Yet
still he stood it, and kept it all inside him.

(*Od.* 17.235-8)

The interesting point here is that Odysseus weighs two aggressive alternatives, but in fact chooses a third course of action: to do nothing at all.
Although he is very much provoked (cf. earlier ὄρινε δὲ κῆρ 'Οδυσῆος:
216) he follows Athena's instructions. Unspoken thoughts take the place of
action. At the same time, the embedded focalization (μερμήριξεν...ἀείρας)
makes clear — to the reader — what he would very much have liked to
do.[12] If we recall the rough treatment of Thersites by the Iliadic Odysseus
in *Iliad* 2, we can imagine how he would have reacted in normal circumstances. The insight we are given into Odysseus' mind makes his actual
restraint all the more clear ... and admirable. Eumaeus, who is present at the
confrontation between Odysseus and Melantheus, does *not* restrain himself:
he reacts not with the kind of deeds Odysseus had in mind, but with words
(238-46).

The confrontation with Melantheus forms the prelude to an even tenser
situation, when the suitor Antinous throws a footstool at Odysseus. This is
what happens:

(6)   ὁ δ' ἐστάθη ἠΰτε πέτρη
ἔμπεδον, οὐδ' ἄρα μιν σφῆλεν βέλος 'Αντινόοιο,
ἀλλ' ἀκέων κίνησε κάρη, κακὰ βυσσοδομεύων.

but he stood up to it, steady
as a rock, nor did the missile thrown by Antinous shake him,
but he shook his head in silence, in the depths of his heart devising evils.

(*Od.* 17.463-5)

Once more, Odysseus keeps his footing, both literally (he does not fall) and
figuratively (he does not retaliate). But inwardly his anger against the suitors
is mounting. The verb used here, βυσσοδομεύειν, explicitly means 'to plan
inwardly, in the interior (βυσσός≈βένθος) of one's mind'. Thus there is a
suspenseful contrast, to be savoured only by the reader, between Odysseus'
outward immobility, highlighted by the comparison with a rock,[13] and the
turmoil of his inward feelings. Some verses later Odysseus does react with
words (468-76), coolly maintaining the adopted identity of a beggar: ἀλλ'
εἴ που πτωχῶν γε θεοὶ καὶ ἐρινύες εἰσίν, 'Αντίνοον πρὸ γάμοιο τέλος
θανάτοιο κιχείη ('therefore, if there are any gods or any furies for beggars,

---

[12] Voigt (1934) 80.
[13] For rock or stone as a symbol of steadfastness, cf. 19.494: ἔξω δ' ὡς ὅτε τις στερεὴ λίθος
ἠὲ σίδηρος.

Antinous may meet his death before he is married': 475-6). Thus the embedded focalization κακὰ βυσσοδομεύων replaces action and is itself replaced by carefully chosen words.

The next point at which Odysseus has to curb himself occurs at the beginning of book 18. Spurred on by the suitors, the beggar Irus and the "beggar" Odysseus engage in a wrestling contest. As the fight begins, Odysseus deliberates on the course of action to follow:

(7) ἢ ἐλάσει' ὥς μιν ψυχὴ λίποι αὖθι πεσόντα,
ἦέ μιν ἦκ' ἐλάσειε τανύσσειέν τ' ἐπὶ γαίῃ.
ὧδε δέ οἱ φρονέοντι δοάσσατο κέρδιον εἶναι,
ἦκ' ἐλάσαι, ἵνα μή μιν ἐπιφρασσαίατ' Ἀχαιοί.

whether to hit him so that the life would go out of him, as he
went down, or only to stretch him out by hitting him lightly.
And in the division of his heart this seemed best to him,
to hit him lightly, so the Achaeans would not be suspicious.

(*Od.* 18.90-4)

The first alternative (to kill Irus outright), which recalls Odysseus' — suppressed — impulse in passage (5), is what he would normally have done. The second alternative (to lay Irus down gently) is dictated by reason. It is this alternative which he chooses. In this passage we find explicitly expressed what in the previous passages had remained implicit, viz. the motive for Odysseus' restraint: to avoid attracting the attention of the suitors (and thus giving away his true identity).

By far the most elaborate restraint scene is found at the beginning of book 20. It is triggered by the laughter of female servants on their way to their lovers, the suitors. This is almost more than Odysseus can bear, as he lies awake, troubled by worries about the suitors:

(8) πολλὰ δὲ μερμήριζε κατὰ φρένα καὶ κατὰ θυμόν,
ἠὲ μεταΐξας θάνατον τεύξειεν ἑκάστῃ,
ἦ ἔτ' ἐῷ μνηστῆρσιν ὑπερφιάλοισι μιγῆναι
ὕστατα καὶ πύματα· κραδίη δέ οἱ ἔνδον ὑλάκτει.
ὡς δὲ κύων ἀμαλῇσι περὶ σκυλάκεσσι βεβῶσα
ἄνδρ' ἀγνοιήσασ' ὑλάει μέμονέν τε μάχεσθαι,
ὥς ῥα τοῦ ἔνδον ὑλάκτει ἀγαιομένου κακὰ ἔργα.

and much he pondered in the division of mind and spirit,
whether to spring on them and kill each one, or rather
to let them lie this one more time with the insolent suitors,
for the last and latest time; but his heart was barking within him.
And as a bitch, facing an unknown man, stands over
her callow puppies, and barks and longs to fight, so Odysseus'
heart was barking inside him as he looked on these wicked actions.

(*Od.* 20.10-6)

Once more Odysseus feels a strong urge to go into action. The intensity of his agitation (cf. 9: ὠρίνετο θυμός) is indicated by πολλά (10, only here in combination with μερμήριζε), the metaphor ὑλάκτει (13, 16), and the simile triggered by that metaphor: ὡς δὲ κύων ... (14-6). Barking inwardly is almost a paradox, since barking normally involves quite a bit of noise. The verb symbolizes Odysseus' aggression, his eagerness to act (cf. in the simile: ὑλάει μέμονέν τε μάχεσθαι). The bitch of the simile, which barks because it wants to protect its tender puppies, also reveals the reason for Odysseus' aggression: he feels he must protect his house against the threat posed by the suitors and the disloyal maids.[14] The intensity of Odysseus' feelings requires a mighty act of self-restraint. Since he is alone he can talk aloud in a monologue (18-21), even reprimand himself (ἠνίπαπε: 17, καθαπτόμενος: 22). He urges himself to endure (note the thrice repeated τέτλαθι, ἔτλης, ἐτόλμας) by calling to mind his successful defeat of the Cyclops. His words have the desired effect: τῷ δὲ μάλ᾽ ἐν πείσῃ κραδίη μένε τετληυῖα νωλεμέως (23-4, note the unique combination κραδίη ... τετληυῖα). Thus once again the rational alternative, to let the maids go to their lovers, prevails over the irrational one, to kill them. The reader, however, will hardly fail to notice the menacing tone of 'for the last and latest time' (ὕστατα καὶ πύματα: 13) in Odysseus' unspoken thoughts;[15] soon the unfaithful maids will be killed by their master.

After this powerful act of self-restraint there follows a repetition of incidents: once more Odysseus is reviled by the goatherd Melanthius (cf. passage 5) and he reacts with silence and inward brooding (20.183-4, cf. passage 6); once more a suitor, Ctesippus, throws an object at him (cf. passage 6),[16] but this time we observe a change in Odysseus' reaction:

(9)   ὁ δ᾽ ἀλεύατ᾽ Ὀδυσσεὺς
ἦκα παρακλίνας κεφαλήν, μείδησε δὲ θυμῷ
σαρδάνιον μάλα τοῖον

                              Odysseus avoided
this by an easy shift of his head. And he inwardly smiled
a very sardonic smile.

(Od. 20.300-2)

Whereas the first time Odysseus was actually hit, this time he easily avoids the projectile, a cow-foot, by ducking. The acts of the suitors, even their insolence, become more and more ineffective.[17] Odysseus' inward reaction

---

[14] See Rose (1979) 26-30.
[15] The expression recurs only once, in what seems to be a mixture of a wish and a curse by Penelope (4.684-5).
[16] This is actually the *third* time an object is thrown at him, but the second time (18.394-8) contains no passage of unspoken thought.
[17] See Fenik (1974) 186-7.

is different too: knowing that the moment of revenge is near, he no longer 'plans evil for the suitors', but smiles 'very[18] sardonically' at their powerless insolence.[19]

Thus the reader sees how a menacing and superior tone slowly creeps into Odysseus' unspoken thoughts, while until the very end the suitors remain unaware of the danger threatening them. 'For', as the narrator remarks, 'who would think that one man, alone in a company of many men at their feasting, though he were a strong one, would ever inflict death upon him and dark doom?' (22.12-4). Some lines later the moment of revelation comes. Finally Odysseus can say and do what he had wanted to say and do all the time: he can call the suitors dogs, denounce their behaviour in the palace, openly announce their death (35-41) ... and kill them.

But the suitors are not the only ones from whom Odysseus hides his emotions and plans. There is Penelope too, who must remain unaware of his identity even longer. The test comes in book 19, in the course of the intimate conversation between the queen and the "beggar". The latter has just told a lying tale, in which Odysseus played an important role (165-202). Penelope reacts to the story with a flood of tears and starts lamenting 'her husband sitting next to her' (209), as the narrator says, explicitly noting the irony of the situation.[20] This emotional reaction, which reveals Penelope's loyalty and love for him, does not leave Odysseus unaffected:

(10)   αὐτὰρ Ὀδυσσεὺς
θυμῷ μὲν γοόωσαν ἐὴν ἐλέαιρε γυναῖκα,
ὀφθαλμοὶ δ᾽ ὡς εἰ κέρα ἕστασαν ἠὲ σίδηρος
ἀτρέμας ἐν βλεφάροισι· δόλῳ δ᾽ ὅ γε δάκρυα κεῦθεν.

> But Odysseus
> in his heart had pity for his wife as she mourned him,
> but his eyes stayed, as if they were made of horn or iron,
> steady under his lids. Thus he craftily hid his tears.

(Od. 19.209-12)

Odysseus inwardly pities Penelope — note the affective reference to her as ἐὴν... γυναῖκα, which parallels ἐὸν ἄνδρα in 209 — but outwardly he

---

[18] The intensifier μάλα τοῖον is otherwise found only in direct speech (*Od.* 11.135 and 23.282). I differ with Stanford (1958) *ad loc.*, who does not consider the smile to be a secret (he takes θυμῷ as 'in his anger' instead of 'in his heart') and takes μάλα τοῖον as implying a gesture. Cf. also the *Lexikon des frühgriechischen Epos* s.v. θυμός, B 13aβ ("still für sich").

[19] For Odysseus' smiles in the later books of the *Odyssey*, see Levine (1984). In my view, Odysseus' sardonic smile is scornful (Ameis-Hentze and Levine) rather than bitter (Stanford 1958) *ad loc.*

[20] Dekker (1965) 232, Emlyn-Jones (1984) 5.

remains composed. As in passage (6), the narrator points up Odysseus'
outward composure by means of a double comparison: 'like horn or iron'.[21]

It will take until 23.232 before Odysseus no longer needs 'to craftily hide
his tears', and can embrace his wife and openly weep. It is interesting to
note, however, that the actual recognition of Odysseus by Penelope comes
about precisely because Odysseus for once loses his self-control: he reacts
angrily to Penelope's proposition to move the marital bed (23.181-204).[22]
It is this anger, and the intimate knowledge revealed on this occasion, which
finally convince her that he is indeed Odysseus. So the one instance when
Odysseus loses his composure has positive rather than negative results.

There is one person in the *Odyssey* who remains unaware of Odysseus'
return even longer than the suitors and Penelope: his father Laertes. When
in book 24 Odysseus goes out to visit him in the country, he finds him
clothed in rags and working in his garden (226-31). The sight of his father
elicits tears from Odysseus, and everything seems to point to a quick
reunion. Instead, Odysseus once more decides against expressing his
feelings:

(11) μερμήριξε δ' ἔπειτα κατὰ φρένα καὶ κατὰ θυμὸν
κύσσαι καὶ περιφῦναι ἑὸν πατέρ' ἠδὲ ἕκαστα
εἰπεῖν, ὡς ἔλθοι καὶ ἵκοιτ' ἐς πατρίδα γαῖαν,
ἦ πρῶτ' ἐξερέοιτο ἕκαστά τε πειρήσαιτο.
ὧδε δέ οἱ φρονέοντι δοάσσατο κέρδιον εἶναι,
πρῶτον κερτομίοις ἐπέεσσιν διαπειρηθῆναι.

and [he] deliberated then in his heart and spirit
whether to embrace his father and kiss him and tell him
everything, how he was come again to his own dear country,
or question him first about everything, and make trial of him.
In the division of his heart this way seemed best to him,
first to make trial of him and speak with provoking words.

                                                        (*Od.* 24.235-40)

Scholars have condemned the poet for trying Laertes for so long and without
a clear reason.[23] Now it is true that Odysseus' revenge scheme against the
suitors has been carried out, and there is no longer any need for secrecy. But
he has not yet completed his 'homecoming' scheme. He still has to put
Laertes' attachment to him to the test (cf. his announcement to do so in 216-
8), just as he had done with the other members of his *oikos*. He wishes to
be recognized as son, just as before he has been recognized as master,

[21] For iron as a symbol of steadfastness, see 19.494 (quoted in note 13) and especially 5.190-
1: οὐδέ μοι αὐτῇ θυμὸς ἐνὶ στήθεσσι σιδήρεος, ἀλλ' ἐλεήμων.
[22] Cf. Stanford (1963) 57: "revealing his deeper feelings spontaneously for the first time since
his return home", Rutherford (1986) 160: "Here Odysseus' celebrated caution and control
vanish".
[23] See Fenik (1974) 47-50.

father, king, and husband.[24] But if there is one thing which this instance of unspoken thought (and the ensuing lying tale) makes clear, it is that secrecy, dissimulation, and restraint are innate, not to say incorrigible, traits of Odysseus' character. I will come back to this point in my conclusion.

And finally, in the case of Odysseus and Telemachus the period of secrecy is much shorter. In 16.11 Odysseus sees his son for the first time, and in 16.167ff. Athena allows him to make himself known. Having done so Odysseus freely lets his tears flow: κὰδ δὲ παρειῶνǀ δάκρυον ἧκε χαμᾶζε· πάρος δ' ἔχε νωλεμὲς αἰεί (190-1). Only now does the narrator tell us that previously Odysseus has had to restrain his feelings. Nowhere, however, did the text record such a moment — as when Odysseus faces the suitors, Penelope, and his father. There is one passage, however, which contains perhaps a hint of Odysseus' unexpressed feelings. I am referring to the passage at the beginning of book 16, in which Eumaeus greets Telemachus after his safe return from his trip to Pylos and Sparta:

(12)   θαλερὸν δέ οἱ ἔκπεσε δάκρυ.
ὡς δὲ πατὴρ ὃν παῖδα φίλα φρονέων ἀγαπάζῃ
ἐλθόντ' ἐξ ἀπίης γαίης δεκάτῳ ἐνιαυτῷ,
μοῦνον τηλύγετον, τῷ ἔπ' ἄλγεα πολλὰ μογήσῃ,
ὣς τότε Τηλέμαχον θεοειδέα δῖος ὑφορβὸς
πάντα κύσεν περιφύς, ὡς ἐκ θανάτοιο φυγόντα.

                    and the swelling tear fell from him.
And as a father, with heart full of love, welcomes his only
and grown son, for whose sake he has undergone many hardships
when he comes back in the tenth year from a distant country,
so now the noble swineherd, clinging fast to godlike
Telemachus, kissed him even as he had escaped dying.

(*Od.* 16.16-21)

Scholars have noted that the simile in this passage contains several role-reversals: Eumaeus plays the role of a father; and the son, Telemachus, has made a journey similar to that of Odysseus.[25] One of the effects of these reversals is that Eumaeus' emotional and affective reaction at the sight of Telemachus can be read as the reflection of Odysseus' inward feelings at seeing his son for the first time after twenty years.[26]

Odysseus' early self-identification in the case of Telemachus makes the latter an accomplice to his revenge scheme against the suitors. Now

---

[24] For defenses of the passage, see Clarke (1967) 25, Wender (1978) 56-62, and Falkner (1989) 41-8.

[25] See Podlecki (1971) 89, Moulton (1977) 132-3, and Foley (1978) 7.

[26] Rutherford (1986) 157 has also connected 16.16-21 and 190-1, but analyses the first passage somewhat differently: "the spontaneous joy and openness of the swineherd's greeting to his young master ... provide a perfect foil to the silent presence of the disguised Odysseus in the background."

Telemachus, too, must suppress his feelings towards them for a long time. We will see whether he is as successful in this respect as his father.

TELEMACHUS' UNSPOKEN THOUGHTS

Telemachus receives from Odysseus more or less the same instructions as the latter had received from Athena in book 13 (passage 3):

(13) "εἰ δέ μ' ἀτιμήσουσι δόμον κάτα, σὸν δὲ φίλον κῆρ
τετλάτω ἐν στήθεσσι κακῶς πάσχοντος ἐμεῖο,
ἤν περ καὶ διὰ δῶμα ποδῶν ἕλκωσι θύραζε
ἢ βέλεσιν βάλλωσι· σὺ δ' εἰσορόων ἀνέχεσθαι."

"But if they maltreat me in the house, then let the dear heart
in you even endure it, though I suffer outrage, even
if they drag me by the feet through the palace to throw me out of it,
or pelt me with missiles; you must still look on and endure it."

(Od. 16.274-7)

Again we find the key words 'endure' and 'put up with' (τετλάτω, ἀνέχεσθαι, cf. 13.307). In comparison with Athena, Odysseus gives a more detailed foreshadowing of the mischief which will befall him: 'if they pelt me with missiles'. He also allows Telemachus to react with gentle words, which might make the suitors change their mind (278-9).

As we have seen, when Antinous throws a footstool at Odysseus in book 17, Odysseus manages to control himself, even though he has been hit (passage 6). This is Telemachus' reaction:

(14) Τηλέμαχος δ' ἐν μὲν κραδίῃ μέγα πένθος ἄεξε
βλημένου, οὐδ' ἄρα δάκρυ χαμαὶ βάλεν ἐκ βλεφάροιϊν,
ἀλλ' ἀκέων κίνησε κάρη, κακὰ βυσσοδομεύων.

But Telemachus sustained in his heart a great sorrow over
the blow, but he did not let fall from his eyes any groundward
tear, but shook his head in silence, in the depths of his heart devising evils.

(Od. 17.489-91)

To some extent Telemachus is copying the behaviour of his father (491= 465), but the reader also gets to know his inward feelings of grief for Odysseus; the negated clause οὐδ' ... βάλεν suggests that normally — but for Odysseus' instructions — he would have burst into tears.

The second time that an object is thrown at his father, Telemachus reacts with gentle words (18.406-9), as his father had advised him in 16.278-9.

The last time the suitors harass Odysseus, the father is able to smile about it (passage 9), but the son reacts with angry words (20.304-19): he says that he would rather die than continue watching (ὁράασθαι) the insolent behaviour of the suitors, as he has done until now (τέτλαμεν εἰσορόωντες).

In other words, Telemachus in his anger neglects Odysseus' command to εἰσορόων ἀνέχεσθαι (16.277). The difference between the reactions of Odysseus and Telemachus points up the latter's youthful and inexperienced temperament.[27]

Telemachus' temporary loss of control does not endanger the revenge scheme and he soon regains his calm (338ff.). Thus, when he is again provoked, and this time is himself the direct butt of the suitors' attacks (Τηλέμαχον ἐρέθιζον: 374), he is outwardly very composed:

(15)   ὁ δ᾽ οὐκ ἐμπάζετο μύθων,
      ἀλλ᾽ ἀκέων πατέρα προσεδέρκετο, δέγμενος αἰεί,
      ὁππότε δὴ μνηστῆρσιν ἀναιδέσι χεῖρας ἐφήσει.

                                        but he paid no attention,
      but looked across at his father silently, always waiting
      for the moment when he would lay his hands on the shameless suitors
                                                    (Od. 20.384-6)

Telemachus is no longer paying attention to the suitors' words, but the insight which the narrator gives us into his mind (δέγμενος ... ἐφήσει) speaks volumes: in his youthfulness he is impatient (note αἰεί, ὁππότε δή) to begin the punishment of the 'shameless' suitors. Whereas at the beginning of this book Odysseus (29, 39) was still pondering the question of *how* to kill the suitors (ὅππως δὴ μνηστῆρσιν ἀναιδέσι χεῖρας ἐφήσει), for Telemachus it is now only a matter of *time* (ὅππότε δή). His certainty that the moment of revenge is near is reflected in the use of the future indicative (ἐφήσει) instead of the optative, which is elsewhere found after δέγμενος.[28] In 21.431, finally, a movement of Odysseus' eyebrows puts an end to Telemachus' long waiting, and their revenge can begin.

We see that in general Telemachus matches his father in restraint, only once losing his temper, with no untoward consequences. His unspoken thoughts reveal — to the reader — his real feelings (grief, impatience, and, of course, revenge), which characterize him as a young man. But father and son are not the only members of the family who are capable of hiding their thoughts and feelings. There is also Penelope.

PENELOPE'S UNSPOKEN THOUGHTS

In 16.303 Odysseus announces to Telemachus that Penelope is to be excluded from their revenge scheme, and indeed she is not reunited with

---

[27] Note that all three casts elicit a critical comment from the other suitors as well: 17.483-7, 18.401-4, and 20.322-37.

[28] Cf. Il. 2.794; 7.415; 9.191; 18.524; Od. 23.91, and see Monro (1891) 283.

Odysseus until 23.205ff.[29] This situation, in which Odysseus is present in the palace without Penelope knowing it, yields numerous ironies, dramatic scenes, and moments of suspense, as well as two fascinating passages of unspoken thought.

The first occurs in that famous and much disputed scene of 'Penelope before the suitors' (18.158-303). It all begins with a passage of unspoken thought ... by Athena:

(16) Τῇ δ' ἄρ' ἐπὶ φρεσὶ θῆκε θεὰ γλαυκῶπις Ἀθήνη,
κούρῃ Ἰκαρίοιο, περίφρονι Πηνελοπείῃ,
μνηστήρεσσι φανῆναι, ὅπως πετάσειε μάλιστα
θυμὸν μνηστήρων ἰδὲ τιμήεσσα γένοιτο
μᾶλλον πρὸς πόσιός τε καὶ υἱέος ἢ πάρος ἦεν.

But now the goddess, gray-eyed Athene, put it in the mind
of the daughter of Icarius, circumspect Penelope,
to show herself to the suitors, so that she might all the more
open their hearts, and so that she might become more precious
to her husband and son, more than she had been before this.

(Od. 18.158-62)

It is very important to distinguish here between the idea which Athena puts into Penelope's mind and the goddess's intentions in doing so, which are disclosed only to the reader, and not to Penelope.[30] Thus Penelope mentions to her servant Eurynome the idea of appearing before the suitors (165) but, rationalizing this strange and sudden impulse, provides her own motive: she wants to talk to Telemachus (166-8). This she does in 215-25, but she does more. She announces to the suitors that the moment — carefully defined by Odysseus when leaving for Troy — has come to remarry (257-73). She adds that it grieves her that the suitors fail to woo her in the usual fashion, viz. by offering many presents (274-80). The reader, usually so well informed, is unprepared for Penelope's sudden announcement to remarry, and eagerly awaits a comment by the narrator explaining how her words are to be taken. What is she up to? Instead of the narrator, however, it is Odysseus who evaluates Penelope's speech for us:

(17) Ὣς φάτο, γήθησεν δὲ πολύτλας δῖος Ὀδυσσεύς,
οὕνεκα τῶν μὲν δῶρα παρέλκετο, θέλγε δὲ θυμὸν
μειλιχίοις ἐπέεσσι, νόος δέ οἱ ἄλλα μενοίνα.

<hr>

[29] The moment of recognition is very much disputed: see Harsh (1950), Amory (1963) 100-21, Vester (1968), Emlyn-Jones (1984), and Murnaghan (1987) 118-47. Analysts like R. Merkelbach and D. Page have, of course, their own radical solutions to this question.

[30] This distinction is made by Beßlich (1966) 139, Müller (1966) 118-9, Vester (1968) 430, Emlyn-Jones (1984) 10, and Hölscher (1988) 248; but not by Whitman (1958) 303, Merkelbach (1969) 12, and Austin (1975) 208.

She spoke, and much-enduring great Odysseus was pleased
because she beguiled gifts out of them, and enchanted their spirits
with sweet words, while her mind felt differently.

(Od. 18.281-3)

We are dealing here with a highly complex passage: Penelope's unspoken
thoughts (she said X, but thought Y) are presented as part of Odysseus'
unspoken thoughts (he was pleased because she said X, but thought Y). Not
surprisingly, the passage has produced a wealth of interpretations.[31] One
of the more popular is that Odysseus is pleased because he knows that
Penelope is not seriously considering remarriage and only solicits gifts under
false pretenses. Odysseus knows Penelope's secret thoughts, either (1)
because in the original version of the poem the recognition of husband and
wife took place much earlier, and the revenge scheme, the first stage of
which is the announcement, was planned by them together, or (2) because
we are to suppose — and Odysseus would know — that Odysseus' parting
speech, which she quotes in 259-70, was invented by her, or (3) because the
narrator simply provides him with this, strictly speaking, illogical knowledge. My own interpretation of this passage is as follows. To start with, I
think that Penelope is seriously proposing remarriage, as witness her words
in 19.571-81 and 21.68-79.[32] It is true that in the two other places where
the expression νόος δέ οἱ ἄλλα μενοίνα occurs (2.91-2 and 13.380-1) the
implication is clearly that Penelope is promising to remarry, but does in fact
have other plans, i.e., is *not* considering remarriage. There, however, the
νόος δέ-clause contrasts with a 'promise of marriage' μέν-clause, but in
passage (17) it contrasts with an 'eliciting gifts and charming through sweet
words' μέν-clause. What are these sweet words? They cannot refer to
Penelope's announcement to remarry, since the words she uses are far from
sweet: she speaks of 'hateful marriage' (στυγερὸς γάμος: 272) and refers to
herself as 'accursed me' (οὐλομένης ἐμέθεν: 273). No, the sweet words
must be the last part of her speech, in which she subtly suggests that the
suitors should bring her gifts (274-80). Nowhere does she directly address
or criticize them, but she speaks in general about suitors from the past and
uses third person verb forms. Of course, her final words ἀλλότριον βίοτον
νήποινον ἔδουσιν cannot but refer to the (reprehensible) behaviour of her
own suitors; if, however, we compare this speech with her earlier, angry one
(16.417-33), it may be seen as (relatively) sweet.[33] Odysseus is highly
appreciative of Penelope's businesslike attitude; even though she loathes her

---

[31] See, amongst others, Page (1955) 124-6, Müller (1966) 121-2, Vester (1968) 432, Fenik
(1974) 120, Levine (1983) 177, Emlyn-Jones (1984) 11, Murnaghan (1987) 131-2, Hölscher
(1988) 246-7, and Byre (1988) 172-3.

[32] Page, Vester, and Byre (see previous note) also take her words as serious.

[33] Hölscher (1988) has missed the point when he refers to lines 18.274-80 as a "Schelte"
(245) and "das heftige Mißfallen" (250).

enemies and abhors the idea of marrying one of them, she still manages to elicit gifts from them. She uses sweet words though her feelings towards them are anything but sweet. This, in my view, is the meaning of νόος δέ οἱ ἄλλα μενοίνα here. Only Odysseus, not the love-struck suitors (cf. 212-3), notices the insincerity of Penelope's sweet tone; the latter hasten to shower presents on her (284-301). Of course Odysseus also smiles, because he knows Penelope's remarriage will never take place. We see that Athena's goals of 160-2 have been reached: the suitors are even more smitten with desire for Penelope, while she has enhanced her value to her husband, exploiting the desire of the suitors to replenish his treasury.

The second instance of Penelope's silent thoughts is found at the beginning of book 23. She has just been told by Eurycleia that Odysseus has returned and killed the suitors. In the ensuing dialogue we see Penelope displaying scepticism (11-24), joy (32-3), and again disbelief (59-68). In the end she decides to go down to the hall and take a look herself: ὄφρα ἴδωμαι ἄνδρας μνηστῆρας τεθνηότας, ἠδ' ὃς ἔπεφνεν (83-4). It is clear from her last words ('the man who killed them') that Penelope is still not convinced that the avenger is really Odysseus. The oscillation of her mind, wavering between hope and fear, belief and disbelief continues in the magnificent passage of unspoken thought which now follows:

(18)   πολλὰ δέ οἱ κῆρ
ὅρμαιν', ἢ ἀπάνευθε φίλον πόσιν ἐξερεείνοι,
ἢ παρστᾶσα κύσειε κάρη καὶ χεῖρε λαβοῦσα.
ἡ δ' ἐπεὶ εἰσῆλθεν καὶ ὑπέρβη λάϊνον οὐδόν,
ἕζετ' ἔπειτ' Ὀδυσῆος ἐναντίη, ἐν πυρὸς αὐγῇ,
τοίχου τοῦ ἑτέρου· ὁ δ' ἄρα πρὸς κίονα μακρὴν
ἧστο κάτω ὁρόων, ποτιδέγμενος εἴ τί μιν εἴποι
ἰφθίμη παράκοιτις, ἐπεὶ ἴδεν ὀφθαλμοῖσιν.
ἡ δ' ἄνεω δὴν ἧστο, τάφος δέ οἱ ἦτορ ἵκανεν·
ὄψει δ' ἄλλοτε μέν μιν ἐνωπαδίως ἐσίδεσκεν,
ἄλλοτε δ' ἀγνώσασκε κακὰ χροΐ εἵματ' ἔχοντα.

She spoke, and came down from her chamber, her heart pondering
much, whether to keep away and question her dear husband,
or to go up to him and kiss his head, taking his hands.
But then, when she came in and stepped over the stone threshold,
she sat across from him in the firelight, facing Odysseus,
by the opposite wall, while he was seated by the tall pillar,
looking downward, and waiting to find out if his majestic
wife would have anything to say to him, now that she saw him.
She sat a long time in silence, and her heart was stupefied.
At one time she would look at him full in the face,
at another she would fail to recognize him because of his poor clothes.

                                                          (*Od.* 23.85-95)

I submit that this passage, in which nothing is said but all the more is thought, would not be out of place in any modern novel; it invites comparison with the following quotation from Virginia Woolf's *Mrs. Dalloway*:

'And how are you?' said Peter Walsh, positively trembling; taking both her hands; kissing both her hands. She's grown older, he thought, sitting down. I shan't tell her anything about it, he thought, for she's grown older. She's looking at me, he thought, a sudden embarrassment coming over him, though he had kissed her hands ... Exactly the same, thought Clarissa; the same queer look; the same check suit; a little out of the straight his face is, a little thinner, dryer, perhaps, but he looks awfully well, and just the same. 'How heavenly it is to see you again!' she exclaimed.

Let us take a closer look at the Homeric passage. It opens with an internal deliberation by Penelope, as she descends from her room, in the form of embedded focalization: should she remain at a distance and question 'her husband', or should she go up to him and kiss him? The words φίλον πόσιν are intriguing: is this Penelope's focalization, or is the narrator intruding upon her focalization and substituting his — and the reader's — knowledge that the man is Odysseus?[34] I would prefer to connect the words with Penelope, without, however, taking this to mean that she *recognizes* Odysseus at this very moment. The two alternative actions which she considers (questioning him or kissing him) both require her to at least *accept the possibility* that the stranger is her husband. The second alternative (kissing) shows her as passionate and emotional as she was in her conversation with Eurycleia (cf. especially 32-3). When she enters the hall, however, she adopts neither alternative but, without saying or doing anything, seats herself opposite Odysseus (the name derives of course from the narrator). The focus now switches to Odysseus and we get to know *his* unspoken thoughts: he waits for his wife to speak first. Odysseus' feelings at this point are wavering too: the verb ποτιδέχεσθαι indicates that he expects Penelope to speak; the dependent εἰ+optative clause, however, suggests that he is not sure whether she will indeed do so.[35] And Penelope, to whom we now move back again, does not speak. For the benefit of the reader the narrator explains why: stupefaction has taken hold of her; one minute she looks the stranger in the face (and is inclined to believe that he might be Odysseus), and the next she looks at his poor clothing and cannot believe that this is her husband.

This wordless exchange between man and wife, fascinating and complex in itself, becomes even more so by the interpretations which the characters

---

[34] For such intrusions, see De Jong (1987) 108-9. Stanford (1958) chooses the second interpretation, Ameis-Hentze and Russo and Fernandez-Galiano and Heubeck (1992) the first.

[35] For the analysis of this type of εἰ-clause, see Wakker (1986) 164.

involved add to it. The first to react is Telemachus, who, unaware of Penelope's inner turmoil, and in general not very understanding towards his mother, angrily demands an explanation for her silence (97-103). His assessment σοὶ δ' αἰεὶ κραδίη στερεωτέρη ἐστὶ λίθοιο is wide of the mark, as the reader knows from her silent thoughts in 87. Provoked by Telemachus, Penelope finally speaks, but to him, not to Odysseus, repeating what the narrator had already told us in 93: she is too stupefied to speak (105-7). Why is she stupefied? The text is not explicit on this point — nor have many commentators asked themselves this question. Taking as the only possible clue ἀγνώσασκε κακὰ χροΐ εἵματ' ἔχοντα (95) — the fact that Odysseus is still wearing his rags was stressed in 22.487-91 — I would suggest that Penelope is stupefied by the fact that the man she is looking at, the 'beggar' with whom she had talked an entire evening without recognizing him, now turns out to be — or at any rate is said to be — Odysseus. In other words, she cannot reconcile what she is seeing to what she has heard; she is still sceptical. Her scepticism is reflected in her use of the conditional clause εἰ δ' ἐτεὸν δὴ ἐστι 'Οδυσσεύς ('if he really is Odysseus': 107-8).[36] For this woman, who is herself wily, neither outward appearances nor words are to be trusted. Odysseus, who is as wily and suspicious as his wife, is better able to appreciate her behaviour than Telemachus: he smiles (111). Once more, he shows that he can even read her mind (cf. passage 17), when he rightly guesses her unexpressed thought of 95: νῦν δ' ὅττι ῥυπόω, κακὰ δὲ χροΐ εἵματα εἶμαι, τοὕνεκ' ἀτιμάζει με καὶ οὔ πώ φησι τὸν εἶναι (115-6). Later, after the recognition, Penelope will give a fuller explanation of her hesitation: she was afraid that if she took it on faith that the beggar was Odysseus — since she did not recognize him she could do no more than that — she might be disappointed again should he turn out *not* to be Odysseus, or, worse, turn out to have committed adultery like Helen (214-24).

The two passages of unspoken thought provide us with fascinating insights into the workings of Penelope's mind; we get to know intimately her cleverness and cautiousness. For once, the reader is not the only one to appreciate these insights; they are shared by Odysseus, who, being so much like Penelope, can read her mind.

We are left with the suitors. So far, we have only met them in the role of the objects or even the victims of the secret thoughts of Odysseus, Telemachus and Penelope. But they, too, can entertain silent thoughts.

---

[36] For the sceptical nuance of εἰ+ indicative (especially when there is an attitudinal modifier present, here ἐτεόν), see Rijksbaron (1984) 69. Marquardt (1985) 40-2 and Roisman (1987) 63 suggest that it is at this point that Penelope recognizes Odysseus. This leads Marquardt to the following assessment of Penelope's stupefied silence: "It is not surprising that her initial reaction upon facing that idealized and long-awaited husband .... is a blend of elation, relief, disillusionment, resentment, possibly even shame..."

THE SUITORS' UNSPOKEN THOUGHTS

The suitors usually behave like braggarts and loudmouths. But even they are occasionally subtle enough to keep their inner feelings secret. This occurs for the first time in book 16. Penelope has heard about the suitors' ambush of Telemachus, and she decides to go down to the hall and question them about this (418-330). One of the suitors, Eurymachus, reassures her that none of them would ever consider harming Telemachus (435-46). His speech is capped with:

(19) ῍Ως φάτο θαρσύνων, τῷ δ' ἤρτυεν αὐτὸς ὄλεθρον.

> So he spoke, encouraging her, but himself was planning
> the murder.

> (*Od.* 16.448)

Juxtaposing the suitor's real intentions and his speech, the narrator makes clear the insincerity of Eurymachus' 'reassuring' words. Penelope accepts his statement and retreats, but later — and this is typical for her tongue-in-cheek character — she makes clear that she is aware of the suitors' insincerity: εὖ μὲν βάζουσι, κακῶς δ' ὄπιθεν φρονέουσι (18.168).

The suitors are insincere not only towards Penelope but also towards Telemachus. Thus when the latter has returned safely from his trip to Pylos and Sparta (notwithstanding the ambush by the suitors) they react as follows:

(20) ἀμφὶ δέ μιν μνηστῆρες ἀγήνορες ἠγερέθεντο
ἐσθλ' ἀγορεύοντες, κακὰ δὲ φρεσὶ βυσσοδόμευον.

> Around him the haughty suitors clustered. They all were speaking
> him fair, but in the deep of their hearts were devising evils.

> (*Od.* 17.65-6)

The second half of line 66 occurs several times in connection with Odysseus' and Telemachus' unspoken thoughts (see passages 6 and 14), but its juxtaposition with ἐσθλ' ἀγορεύοντες underlines the depravity of the suitors.

The last instance of unspoken thoughts shows a different aspect of the suitors' negative characterization, their misplaced self-confidence. It occurs in the scene of the bow contest. Before the actual trial begins, Antinous announces that he does not think that any of the suitors will be able to string the bow, since only a man like Odysseus can do this. His speech is capped as follows:

(21) ῍Ως φάτο, τῷ δ' ἄρα θυμὸς ἐνὶ στήθεσσιν ἐώλπει
νευρὴν ἐντανύειν διοϊστεύσειν τε σιδήρου.

So he spoke, but the spirit inside his heart was hopeful
that he would be able to string the bow and shoot throught the iron.

(Od. 21.96-7)

For the reader, Antinous' words are ironical in two senses: (1) when he says
that there is no man present like Odysseus, he cannot know that in fact
Odysseus himself is present;[37] and (2) when he says that nobody will be
able to string the bow, words which his secret thoughts prove to be
insincere, he is unwittingly speaking the truth. But his unspoken thoughts
tell us something else about Antinous: this leader of the suitors, in both
word and deed, in his heart turns out to actually equate himself with
Odysseus; he fully expects[38] that he will be able to do what only Odysseus
can do. His role as leader and his pretensions will make him the prime
target of Odysseus' revenge, as the narrator announces (to the reader) in the
lines immediately following upon his secret embedded focalization (98-9).

CONCLUSION

The preceding pages have amply demonstrated the presence of the
purportedly modern novelistic device of unspoken thought in the oldest
narrative text of West European literature, the Homeric epics. They have
also shown that these texts, apparently filled with only words and events,
also allow room for thought, which may take the place of deeds or words,
or be juxtaposed to them. Whereas embedded focalization — the form which
unspoken thought takes in Homer — occurs both in the *Iliad* and in the
Odyssey,[39] the potential secrecy inherent in this narrative mode is fully
exploited only in the second poem, in particular in its second half,
Odysseus' homecoming. Almost all the characters involved have their
reasons for harbouring secret thoughts, and the phenomenon of unspoken
thought acquires a thematic relevance on the level of the characterization of
individual personae, as well as on that of the poem as a whole.

The device unmasks the suitors as depraved and vain, thus contributing
to their portrayal as 'bad guys', who deserve to be butchered by Odysseus.

In the case of Telemachus, the device makes clear two things. Throughout
the *Odyssey* we see Telemachus aspiring to emulate his father: like him he
makes a modest 'odyssey' of his own, shows himself to be wily,[40] and
fights like an accomplished Iliadic warrior. We are now able to add that as
regards self-restraint, another of Odysseus' characteristic traits, Telemachus

---

[37] See Dekker (1965) 262, who notes this irony, not the second one.
[38] The verb ἔλπω usually has an optimistic tone in Homer, see J.N. O'Sullivan in the *Lexikon des frühgriechischen Epos*, s.v.
[39] In both epics it occupies about 5% of the total text.
[40] See for this aspect of his character, Austin (1969).

on all but one occasion manages to match the composure of his father during the confrontations with the suitors. At the same time, his unspoken thoughts reveal his youthful temperament: he wants to cry when Odysseus is hit by Antinous' footstool, and eagerly awaits the moment of revenge.

Where Penelope is concerned, the device of unspoken thought helps us to get a clearer idea of her proverbial prudence and cleverness (cf. her stock epithet περίφρων), which she displays not only towards the enemy, the suitors, but also towards Odysseus.

And finally, there is Odysseus himself. Not once does he lose his self-control when provoked by the suitors or disloyal servants, nor when faced with his wife, who is crying over him, and his father, who is debasing himself as a sign of mourning for him. His capacity to endure is proverbial (cf. his stock epithet πολύτλας), but whereas in the first half of the *Odyssey* his endurance was put to the test mainly in physical circumstances, in the second half it is mental strength which is required of him.[41]

In addition to characterizing Odysseus and Penelope individually, the analysis of their unspoken thought has also brought to the fore their 'like-mindedness' (ὁμοφροσύνη).[42] In the first place, Odysseus is the only one who understands what is going on inside Penelope's head even without her disclosing her thoughts. In the second place, their exceptional, almost superhuman self-restraint is described (by other characters) in very identical terms:

(22) (Athena about Odysseus)
"ἀσπασίως γάρ κ' ἄλλος ἀνὴρ ἀλαλήμενος ἐλθὼν
ἵετ' ἐνὶ μεγάροις ἰδέειν παῖδάς τ' ἄλοχόν τε·
σοὶ δ' οὔ πω φίλον ἐστὶ δαήμεναι οὐδὲ πυθέσθαι,
πρίν γ' ἔτι σῆς ἀλόχου πειρήσεαι..."

"Anyone else come home from wandering would have run happily
off to see his children and wife in his halls; but it is not
your pleasure to investigate and ask questions, not till
you have made trial of your wife..."

(*Od.* 13.333-6)

and

(23) (Telemachus about Penelope)
"οὐ μέν κ' ἄλλη γ' ὧδε γυνὴ τετληότι θυμῷ
ἀνδρὸς ἀφεσταίη, ὅς οἱ κακὰ πολλὰ μογήσας
ἔλθοι ἐεικοστῷ ἔτεϊ ἐς πατρίδα γαῖαν·
σοὶ δ' αἰεὶ κραδίη στερεωτέρη ἐστὶ λίθοιο."

---

[41] See Rutherford (1986).
[42] Cf. on this subject: Austin (1975) 181-238, Foley (1978), and Marquardt (1985) 48.

"No other woman, with spirit as stubborn as yours, would keep back
as you are doing from her husband who, after much suffering,
came at last in the twentieth year back to his own country.
But always you have a heart that is harder than stone within you."

(*Od.* 23.100-3)

In the third place, Odysseus and Penelope share the epithet ἐχέφρων, which
rather than 'having a good mind' appears to mean 'restraining one's mind',
said of a person "who does not allow his impulses and thoughts to lead to
wrong words or actions".[43] Their capacity to control their emotions, to
remain silent, or to say something other than what they feel, marks Penelope
and especially Odysseus as the typical heroes of the *Odyssey*, poem of
disguise and dissimulation. They do exactly what the central hero of the
Iliad, Achilles, detests: ἐχθρὸς γάρ μοι κεῖνος ὁμῶς Ἀΐδαο πύλησιν ǀ ὅς χ᾽
ἕτερον μὲν κεύθῃ ἐνὶ φρεσίν, ἄλλο δὲ εἴπῃ ("for as I detest the doorways
of death, I detest that man, who hides one thing in the depths of his heart,
and speaks forth another": *Il.* 9.312-3). In contrast to this Iliadic ideal, the
message — or rather one of the messages — of the *Odyssey* seems to be
that secret thinking is at times to be preferred to speaking or acting. Or as
Redfield aptly puts it: "Achilleus beherrscht seine Mitwelt im Tun und
stirbt... Odysseus herrscht nur in Gedanken und überlebt."[44]

BIBLIOGRAPHY

Ameis K.F. and Hentze C. (1894-1909) *Homers Odyssee* (Leipzig: 1894-1909).
Amory A. (1963) "The Reunion of Odysseus and Penelope", in *Essays on the Odyssey*, ed. C.H.
    Taylor (Bloomington: 1963) 100-21.
Auerbach E. (1953) *Mimesis. The Representation of Reality in Western Literature* (transl. by
    W.R. Trask, Princeton: 1953).
Austin N. (1969) "Telemachos Polymechanos", *California Studies in Classical Antiquity* 2
    (1969) 45-63.
—— (1975) *Archery at the Dark of the Moon. Poetic Problems in Homer's Odyssey* (Berkeley-
    Los Angeles: 1975).
Bal M. (1985) *Narratology. Introduction to the Theory of Narrative* (Toronto: 1985).
Barck C. (1976) *Wort und Tat bei Homer* (Hildesheim: 1976).

---

[43] Stanford (1963) 33; cf. H.W. Nordheider in the *Lexikon des frühgriechischen Epos*, s.v.:
"klug, vorsichtig, (mit Selbstkontrolle)", and Winkler (1990) 136-7. This interpretation of
ἐχέφρων accords well with the original meaning of ἔχω, which is 'hold' or 'retain' rather than
'have' (I thank C.J. Ruijgh for this observation).

[44] (1968-9) 75. The same idea has been voiced by Stanford (1963) 33, but, in my opinion,
far too strongly (and with little understanding for the *Iliad*): "In so far as Homer has any moral
message in the *Iliad* and the *Odyssey* it comes to this: only by Ulyssean self-control and
moderation can men achieve victory in life. In contrast the wrathful, vainglorious Achilles, the
arrogant, grasping Agamemnon, the headstrong Ajax, the self-centered, unscrupulous Autolycus,
paid their penalties."

Beßlich S. (1966) *Schweigen, Verschweigen, Übergehen. Die Darstellung des Unausgesprochenen in der Odyssee* (Heidelberg: 1966).

Byre C.S. (1988) "Penelope and the Suitors before Odysseus: *Odyssey* 18.158-303", *American Journal of Philology* 109 (1988) 159-173.

Clarke H.W. (1967) *The Art of the Odyssey* (Englewood Cliffs, N.J. 1967, reprint Bristol 1989).

Cohn D. (1978) *Transparant Minds: Narrative Modes for Presenting Consciousness in Fiction* (Princeton: 1978).

Dekker A.F. (1965) *Ironie in de Odyssee* (Leiden: 1965).

Emlyn-Jones C. (1984) "The Reunion of Penelope and Odysseus", *Greece and Rome* 31 (1984) 1-18.

Falkner T.M. (1989) "'Επὶ γήραος οὐδῷ: Homeric Heroism, Old Age and the End of the *Odyssey*", in T.M. Falkner and J. de Luce (ed.) *Old Age in Greek and Latin Literature* (Albany N.Y.: 1989) 21-67.

Fenik B. (1974) *Studies in the Odyssey* (Wiesbaden: 1974).

Foley H.P. (1978) "Reverse Similes and Sex Roles in the *Odyssey*", *Arethusa* 11 (1978) 7-26.

Fränkel H. (1951) *Dichtung und Philosophie des frühen Griechentums* (München: 1951).

Genette G. (1972) "Discours du récit", in *Figures III* (Paris: 1972). English translation by J.E. Lewin, *Narrative Discourse* (Ithaca N.Y.: 1980).

Griffin J. (1980) *Homer on Life and Death* (Oxford: 1980).

Harsh P.W. (1950) "Penelope and Odysseus in *Odyssey* XIX", *American Journal of Philology* 71 (1950) 1-21.

Hentze C. (1905) "Die Chorreden in den homerischen Epen", *Philologus* 64 (1905) 254-68.

Hölscher U. (1988) *Die Odyssee. Epos zwischen Märchen und Roman* (München: 1988).

de Jong I.J.F. (1987) *Narrators and Focalizers. The Presentation of the Story in the Iliad* (Amsterdam: 1987).

Kahler E. (1973) *The Inward Turn of Narrative*, transl. R. and C. Winston (Princeton: 1973).

Kakridis J.Th. (1970) "Dichterische Gestalten und wirkliche Menschen bei Homer", in *Das Altertum und jedes neue Gute. Festschrift für W. Schadewaldt zum 15.3.1970*, ed. K. Gaiser (Stuttgart: 1970) 51-64.

Latacz J. (1968) "ἄπτερος μῦθος-ἄπτερος φάτις: 'ungeflügelte Worte'", *Glotta* 46 (1968) 27-47.

Levine D.B. (1983) "Penelope's Laugh. *Odyssey* 18.163", *American Journal of Philology* 104 (1983) 172-8.

—— (1984) "Odysseus Smiles. *Odyssey* 20.301, 22.371, 23.111", *Transactions and Proceedings of the American Philological Association* 114 (1984) 1-9.

Marquardt P. (1985) "Penelope πολύτροπος", *American Journal of Philology* 106 (1985) 32-48.

Mattes W. (1958) *Odysseus bei den Phäaken* (Würzburg: 1958).

Merkelbach R. (1969) *Untersuchungen zur Odyssee* (München: ²1969).

Monro D.B. (1891) *A Grammar of the Homeric Dialect* (Oxford: ²1891).

Moulton C. (1977) *Similes in the Homeric Poems* (Göttingen: 1977).

Müller M. (1966) *Athene als göttliche Helferin in der Odyssee. Untersuchungen zur Form der epischen Aristie* (Frankfurt-Heidelberg: 1966).

Murnaghan S. (1987) *Disguise and Recognition in the Odyssey* (Princeton: 1987).

Page D. (1955) *The Homeric Odyssey* (Oxford: 1955).

Podlecki A.J. (1971) "Some Odyssean Similes", *Greece and Rome* 18 (1971) 81-90.

Redfield J.M. (1968-69) "Über die *Odyssee*", *Antaios* 10 (1968-69) 55-75.

—— (1975) *Nature and Culture in the Iliad. The Tragedy of Hector* (Chicago: 1975).

Rijksbaron A. (1984) *The Syntax and Semantics of the Verb in Classical Greek* (Amsterdam: 1984).

Roisman H.M. (1987) "Penelope's Indignation", *Transactions and Proceedings of the American Philological Association* 117 (1987) 59-68.

de Romilly J. (1984) *"Patience mon coeur". L'essor de la psychologie dans la littérature grecque classique* (Paris: 1984).

Rose G.P. (1979) "Odysseus' Barking Heart", *Transactions and Proceedings of the American Philological Association* 109 (1979) 215-30.

Russo J. and Simon B. (1968) "Homeric Psychology and the Oral Epic Tradition", *Journal for the History of Ideas* 29 (1968) 483-98.

Russo J. and Fernández-Galiano M. and Heubeck A. (1992) *A Commentary on Homer's Odyssey III* (Oxford: 1992).

Rutherford R.B. (1985) "At Home and Abroad. Aspects of the Structure of the *Odyssey*", *Proceedings of the Cambridge Philological Society* 31 (1985) 133-50.

—— (1986) "The Philosophy of the *Odyssey*", *Journal of Hellenic Studies* 106 (1986) 145-162.

Scholes R. and Kellogg R. (1966) *The Nature of Narrative* (Oxford: 1966).

Schwinge E.-R. (1990) "Aristoteles und die Gattungsdifferenz von Epos und Drama", *Poetica* 22 (1990) 1-20.

Scully S. (1984) "The Language of Achilles. The ὀχθήσας Formulas", *Transactions and Proceedings of the American Philological Association* 114 (1984) 11-27.

Stanford W.B. (1958) *The Odyssey of Homer*. I-II (Frome-London: ²1958).

—— (1963) *The Ulysses Theme. A Study in the Adaptability of a Traditional Hero* (Oxford: ²1963).

Thornton A. (1970) *People and Themes in Homer's Odyssey* (London: 1970).

Vester H. (1968) "Das 19. Buch der *Odyssee*", *Gymnasium* 75 (1968) 417-34.

Voigt C. (1934) *Überlegung und Entscheidung. Studien zur Selbstauffassung des Menschen bei Homer* (Berlin 1934, cited from the reprint Meisenheim am Glan: 1972).

Wakker G.C. (1986) "Conditionele bijzinnen met finale nuance in het Grieks", *Lampas* 19 (1986) 159-74.

Wender D. (1978) *The Last Scenes of the Odyssey* (Leiden: 1978).

Whitman C.H. (1958) *Homer and the Heroic Tradition* (Cambridge Mass.: 1958).

Winkler J.J. (1990) *The Constraints of Desire. The Anthropology of Sex and Gender in Ancient Greece* (New York-London: 1990).

THE FAILURE OF EXEMPLARITY

BY

SIMON GOLDHILL

> 'Us *Canoniz'd*' — John Donne
> "'I am an invalid, Dr. Middleton", he said,
> "I am unable to cope with analogies."' —
> George Meredith

What relation between theory and practice is being promoted by the format that I have been asked to follow in this volume — an exposition of a critical theory followed by an exemplary reading of a classical text? What place is being projected for methodological enquiry by the definition of various schools of criticism in opposition to classics and classical texts? There's classics and *then* there's...theory? There are some important questions that are in danger of being occluded in this mandate, and I want to begin by outlining four areas of worry.

The first risk in this organizational strategy is of implying that methodology is a supplement to reading rather than what makes reading possible. The greatest of all critical fictions is the claim of 'no methodology' — a claim which may be naive but is never innocent. As Eagleton famously wrote 'An opposition to theory usually means an opposition to other people's theories and an ignorance of one's own'.[1] Classics always has been a constantly developing, historically contingent, ideologically laden study. What 'modern critical theory' has placed on the agenda is the question of how explicit, how sophisticated and how self-aware a discussion of each and every critic's inevitable commitment to a methodology is to be.

The second risk of the Smorgasbord approach to theories is of implying that there is a range of discrete theories, each waiting to be intellectually evaluated and then adopted or rejected, wholly or piecemeal. While it is difficult to imagine an engagement with theory that did not privilege intellectual evaluation — the unexamined life is not worth living for a critic above all — it must not be forgotten that the degree to which a critical theory's questions or strategies are mobilized or absorbed into classics as a discipline also involves an institutional sociology. Each classicist is also involved in a network of power relations that police the academy: a

---

[1] Eagleton (1983) viii.

philologist's choice to avoid a discussion of the underpinnings of philology in a theory of language is a strategy to be comprehended within a continuing history of the profession. Adopting a feminist perspective on classics as a subject and as an institution will also always depend on — or at least affect — your (self-)positioning within the academy.

The third area of worry is also concerned with the discreteness of the theories allowed a voice here, and involves a more complex set of issues. On the one hand, such an approach may make it harder to see the necessary connections between fields: an adequate 20th-century feminist theory, for example, could hardly hope to avoid an engagement with psychoanalysis.[2] On the other hand — and to my mind more importantly — such a strategy may also silence certain questions that link the various turns to theory, questions that concern authority, meaning and the nature of exemplification. For the exploration of the past from the present requires a scrupulous attention to the aims and procedures of producing meaning. Is a critic committed to uncovering an author's meaning? Or an ancient reader's meaning? Or what is tacit or unrecognized to an ancient reader/writer but can be seen by the outsider's gaze of the historical anthropologist? Or a meaning for the present — to confirm or contest, inspire or threaten the modern? Can — should — these different approaches to meaning be kept separate? The very name, Classics, invokes the *exemplary* (and problematic) status of the past in an especially marked way. When a classicist claims to offer a Feminist (Psychoanalytic, Marxist, Traditional... whatever) reading of an ancient text, what gestures of appropriation, what commitments to what epistemological stances are being made or excluded? Marxism with Marx, Psychoanalysis with Freud (and Lacan), make clear appeals to an authority that is modern, to ground an engagement with the past. What is the status of such an appeal? Is it of a different kind from other (modern) readings or merely a more clearly articulated version of a process of appropriation necessarily enacted in reading the past from the present? When a classicist claims to offer a Feminist (etc.) reading, is he or she committed to a particular set of questions, either in the form of certain strategies or tools of analysis, or in the sense of excluding some forms of enquiry as invalid? Is he or she committed to a type of — or even a particular — answer to such questions — as, for example, a mechanistic application of a theoretical model is sometimes used in a circular fashion to 'prove' or 'support' via literature the claims of the theory? The very format of individual papers analyzing discrete theories with exemplary readings may help conceal both that there are such prior, difficult and often unbroached questions linking the different theoretical enterprises, and also that the

---

[2] See e.g. Butler (1990); Brennan (1989); Gallop (1982); Mitchell (1974).

exemplary itself is an integral element of the theoretical difficulties facing classics in particular.

This leads to my fourth worry. Since Kant (in particular) the relation between a theory — or a general principle — and its exempla — or instances — has been increasingly viewed as less than straightforward. Of course, within the scope of a paper of this length, a description of any important body of theoretical work will tend to be partial, and any example, equally, will tend to be limited and, to a degree, misrepresentative. But there is a more general argument about a necessary gap, a necessary interplay of difference, between examples and general cases. For Kant, who was instrumental in setting this question on the agenda, it is both a historical problem of teaching from the past, since the 'historical structure of the example as such causes a perpetual deferral within the pedagogical scene, given that the ideal which the example represents is always beyond attainment';[3] and a metaphysical problem since philosophy's dependence on examples — without examples, philosophy 'gropes, uncertain and trembling, among meaningless concepts'[4] — is partly what distinguishes philosophy from (the ideal of) pure science.[5] The distinction between the example as the (unobtainable) ideal model and the example as the specific case (which may become exemplary) continues to provoke aesthetic and political debate. As Marx wrote of the glorious Greek example, 'the difficulty we are confronted with is not, however, that of understanding how Greek art and epic poetry are associated with certain forms of social development. The difficulty is that they still give us aesthetic pleasure and are in certain respects regarded as a standard and unobtainable ideal'.[6] How and why Greek literature may be exemplary is part of a lengthy discussion on the nature of exemplification.

This set of problems is particularly pertinent to the work of Jacques Derrida and to what has been called 'deconstruction' or 'post-structuralism' — my theoretical remit for this volume. For Derrida has repeatedly interrogated the boundaries between the language of criticism and the language of the objects criticised, between philosophy and literature, between theory and illustration, as he pursues his analysis (and performance) of writing as a practice. As he puts it, most notoriously and apophthegmati-cally, 'il n'y a pas d'hors-texte'. Or as de Man writes with equal brusque-ness, 'the difference between' literature and criticism is 'delusive'.[7] One

---

[3] Lloyd (1989) 15, a fine study. For further on Kant see Gadamer (1975) 37, 253-8; for further on the historical nature of the example see Stierle (1972); Quint (1982); Hampton (1990).

[4] Kant's remark, from the preface to *The Metaphysical Foundation of Natural Sciences*, is discussed by Caruth (1988) 26.

[5] See the excellent study of Caruth (1988).

[6] Marx (1970) 217.

[7] De Man (1979) 19.

aim of this paper will be to show that since the modern works I am meant
to be discussing challenge the very possibility of maintaining the discreteness of theoretical exposition and literary reading, it would only be by
ignoring the claims of the theory I am discussing, that I can fulfil — or
avoid sending back — my remit. This conclusion — opaque, perhaps, at
present — will be approached gradually by a discussion of some aspects of
exemplification. And since I will need to approach exemplary material in
modern and ancient texts, the self-reflexivity of this discussion is evident,
inevitable and difficult. Indeed, since I have begun with some theoretical
questions and will end with some comments on Homer and tragedy, I might
seem finally to have reproduced something at least of the editors' requirements, even as I claim to be refusing them. (Such worrying about the self-
reflexive lures of writing is often taken as an exemplary sign of post-
structuralist criticism — the endless suspicion of another question?) It is
worth stating from the outset, however, that my questions about exemplification are not broached because I think criticism can do without the exemplary, but because this necessary aspect of criticism is all too rarely
considered.

Moreover, the difficulty of giving a theoretical exposition of Derrida's
work (followed or supported by exemplary demonstrations) is in itself a
topos of writing about Derrida and post-structuralism. Rudolph Gasché
writes of literary criticism's adoption of Derridean strategies that the
'reduction [of Derrida's debate with philosophy] to a few sturdy devices for
the critic's use represents nothing less than an extraordinary blurring and
toning-down of the critical implication of this philosopher's work'.[8] Or
books like Christopher Norris' *Deconstruction: theory and practice* offer sly
or self-defensive or despairing gestures of apology: 'What follows is...a
deferred involvement with the writings of Derrida, and not to be taken on
trust as a handy or "objective" survey of deconstructionist method. If there
is one applied lesson to be taken away, it is the powerlessness of ready-
made concepts to explain or delimit the activity of writing'.[9] Or, from
Derek Attridge, 'the raîson d'être of the present volume...is unmistakably at
odds with Derrida's own thinking'.[10] I too...by quoting such (exemplary)
remarks manipulate in turn the protocols of *recusatio* — as I hesitate before
my editors' request to list 'the sturdy devices' for 'the interested neophyte'.[11]

---

[8] Gasché (1979) 180; see also Gasché (1986).

[9] Norris (1982) xiii.

[10] Attridge (1992) 7. A good discussion of the problem is also to be found in Ulmer (1985).

[11] While listing these useful introductions: Harrari (1979); Young (1981); Norris (1982);
Culler (1983); Ulmer (1985); Spivak's introduction to Derrida (1976), and Derrida's own
attempt, Derrida (1981). 'The interested neophyte' is the editors' intended audience.

In the following pages, I shall be looking at three different aspects of exemplification: the process of framing and contextualization of examples (particularly with regard to the example of linguistics and philology); the functioning of counter-examples and polarities (particularly with regard to Homeric models of female behaviour); the interplay of exemplification and narrativization (particularly with regard to tragic narrative). Each of these concerns broaches a major area of discussion among the writers collected under the aegis of post-structuralism, and I will trace — exemplify — some ways in which my work has been informed by this heterogeneous body of texts. (I follow here the exemplary sleight of hand of Kant who negotiates the difficulty of admitting influence and resisting mere copying as follows: 'Following *[Nachfolge]* which has reference to a precedent and not imitation *[Nachahmung]* is the proper expression for all influence which the products of an exemplary *[exemplarischen]* author may exert upon an other'.[12]) Before this, however, I wish very briefly to sketch some of the background as to why exemplification must be seen as a fundamental topic.

The discovery of classics in the Renaissance is a discovery of exemplarity.[13] The ancient world provided a model and pinnacle of literature, of (heroic) behaviour, of philosophical reasoning: 'probably no descriptive term for literature and history was more universal in the Renaissance than "examples" or had a longer history'.[14] Part of this long history is to be found in Greek and Roman rhetorical theories, which have their roots in Aristotle's treatment of *paradeigmata* as a standard tool of argumentation (*Rhet.* 2. 20ff). Part is also to be found in Greek and Roman culture's use of myth as paradigmatic stories: τὸν σὸν παράδειγμ' ἔχων, τὸν σὸν δαίμονα...ὦ Οἰδιπόδα, as Sophocles' chorus sings, 'taking your's as an example, your fate, Oedipus...'.[15] Part is to be found in a tradition which includes Homer's treatment of Telemachus and Orestes but which finds its acme in Plutarch — the exemplary life as model and philosophical paradigm. The use of exemplars is indeed an integral part of the Greek and Roman education system and is already being debated by Plato, not only in the *Laws* and the *Republic* but also in the *Protagoras*, where Protagoras is made to say that teachers offer 'panegyrics of the good men of old, so that the child may be inspired to imitate them and long to be like them' (326a). In the modern era, Marx famously said of the participants of the French Revolution that they 'performed the task of their time in Roman costume

---

[12] Kant (1982) 138-9. On Kant's punning between *Nachahmung*, 'following', and *Nachmachung*, 'imitation' in *The Critique of Judgement* see Derrida (1981b) 10-11.

[13] See Hampton (1990) for extensive bibliography and discussion.

[14] Wallace (1974) 280. See also the works cited in n. 3.

[15] S. *O.T.* 1193-5; the exemplarity of Oedipus is discussed by Vernant (1981) 63-86; Segal (1981) 207-48; Goldhill (1986) 199-221.

and with Roman phrases'.[16] And Freud echoes Sophocles in the discovery of an exemplary Oedipus 'within us all'. One could multiply such examples, not least with Derrida's readings of Plato as a founding text of Western metaphysics...[17] This question of the exemplary nature of the ancient world and its effects has not yet finished being debated.

WHAT A TO-DO IN THE LANGUAGE LAB: EXAMPLES AND FRAMING

> 'Winged words are also clubs; language is a lure; paradise is also the inferno of discourse' — Monique Wittig
> '"Most things should be tacit," said Walter, "I often wish everything was."' — Ivy Compton-Burnett

It is, however, first with modern linguistics and philology that I wish to explore the example. The example is an integral part of linguistic analysis: almost any page of linguistics or any philological analysis will include normative, paradigmatic cases to demonstrate grammatical, semantic and other assertions. One particular branch of linguistics, however, namely, speech act theory, makes particular claims for the way in which examples should be formulated and analysed. (Both the fact that speech act theory — in the work of one of its main theoreticians, John Searle — has entered into a very public and strongly felt debate with the deconstruction of Derrida, and the fact that, with the growth of speech act theory in classics, my own work on Aeschylus has been criticized from a similar perspective, help motivate the following analysis.[18]) Now speech act theory, like deconstruction, is the work of a range of scholars who do not necessarily agree, and in particular several critics have pointed out how the widely read work of John Searle attempts to delimit the elegant equivocations of J.L. Austin, whose ideas he claims to expound and expand.[19] On the one hand, Austin, who first developed the opposition between constative and illocutionary utterances — that is, between the descriptive sentence or statement and the performative expression such as 'I promise' or 'I apologize' — repeatedly shows in *How To Do Things With Words* how this opposition collapses so that the constative appears as a subset of the illocutionary. On the other hand, not only Searle but also structural linguists such as Benveniste, and

---

[16] Marx (1977) 11.

[17] See Derrida (1981c) 61-172; (1987); and for an explicit discussion of the role of Greek influence, Derrida (1992).

[18] Derrida (1988); Searle (1977); (1983). Goldhill (1984) is discussed by Clark and Csapo (1991), Judet de la Combe (1989-90).

[19] See for discussion and bibliography Petrey (1990).

students of transformational grammar such as Katz, have attempted to maintain, police and strengthen the opposition in the face of Austin's tricky argumentation.[20] (Katz writes a chapter entitled 'How to save Austin from Austin'...) I shall be concerned, however, with a general and largely shared principle of speech act theory — and, incidentally, of its development into pragmatics and relevance theory[21] — and how this principle is discussed by Austin himself. For the clarion call that unites speech act theorists is 'the total speech-act in the total speech situation'[22]. That is, to understand a linguistic utterance, it must be viewed within a context and as a performance: meaning is constituted through 'the total situation in which an utterance is issued'[23] (and thus not merely inherent in language). The disembodied, decontextualized linguistic example of the laboratory cannot do justice to the functioning of language.

Now with regard to literary criticism and the theory of 'performative language', Derrida, Fish, Felman and others have analyzed at length both the paragraphs where Austin excludes from consideration performative utterances spoken on stage or in a poem because they are 'in a peculiar way hollow'; and also the paragraphs where Austin declares his allegiance to the difficult and ideologically charged concept of 'ordinary language in ordinary circumstances'.[24] Furthermore, a series of scholars have ignored Austin's exclusions and made excellent applications of speech act theory to literary texts.[25] What I intend to do here — with this much introduction — is to look at a section of Austin's analysis where he considers what might be implied by the idea of the 'total speech situation'. This largely ignored passage offers an instructive (and witty) comment on the problem of linguistic exemplarity. It is entitled 'the circumstances of the utterance', and begins (77):

> An exceedingly important aid is the circumstances of the utterance. Thus we may say 'coming from *him*, I took it as an order, not as a request'; similarly the context of the words 'I shall die someday', 'I shall leave you my watch', in particular the health of the speaker, make a difference how we shall understand them.

---

[20] Benveniste (1971); Katz (1977).

[21] See for a good introduction to pragmatics and relevance theory Sperber and Wilson (1986); Grice (1975) and the other contributors to Cole and Morgan (1975); Levinson (1983) with good bibliography; Searle (1969) is influential in this work.

[22] Austin (1962) 52.

[23] Austin (1962) 52.

[24] Felman (1980); Derrida (1988); Fish (1980).

[25] See e.g. Felman (1980); Ohman (1973); Pratt (1977); Elam (1984); Rivers (1983). For a fuller discussion of speech act theory and literature see Petrey (1990), and for speech act theory and things Greek, see Martin (1989); Herzfeld (1985). I have not seen Rip Cohen's contribution to this volume.

This is an apparently straightforward point that would seem basic to any theory of pragmatics or rhetoric. 'Who says what to whom' is a defining aspect of an utterance; and that such contextualization will 'make a difference' to meaning and understanding is not hard to affirm. Austin adds the following paragraph, however (ib.):

> But in a way these resources are over-rich: they lend themselves to equivocation and inadequate discrimination; and moreover, we use them for other purposes, e.g. insinuation. The explicit performative rules out equivocation and keeps the performance fixed, relatively.

This paragraph systematically undoes the apparently straightforward point of the first paragraph. 'But in a way' introduces both a qualification and, in 'in a way', an equivocation. 'These resources are over-rich: they lend themselves to equivocation and lack of discrimination': the circumstances of an utterance are too much, 'over-rich'; they produce an *excess*, over and above language resources, an excess that threatens control and the 'success' of a communication by introducing 'equivocation and lack of discrimination'. The 'total speech situation' is worryingly excessive as much as it is 'an exceedingly important aid'. So, too, such circumstantial factors may add different performative forces to an utterance: they are used for other purposes, such as 'insinuation', which confuse the simplicity or explicitness of the performative. 'The explicit performative', however, like 'I promise' or 'I apologize', rules out equivocation — except under certain ... circumstances. Such explicitness can keep the performative fixed, that is, without equivocation or lack of discrimination. Or rather it may keep the performative fixed, 'relatively'. The final adverb with fine wit precisely adds a note of equivocation, even a lack of discrimination. Austin — typically — as he worries about equivocation, equivocates, finally.

What this paragraph highlights is the problem of what counts as the circumstances of an utterance, and how such over-rich possibilities may or may not affect understanding. For Austin, the requirement of 'the total speech-act in the total speech situation' brings a hesitant recognition and *exclusion* of 'circumstances' as the excess that threatens the fixedness of performance. A linguistic example must be framed by the context in which it is uttered: but the framing circumstances destabilize with excess that very determination of meaning. Thus Austin tries to use the nature of the performative — its explicitness — to rule out the dangers of the equivocal context. The frame is framed thus by its content...

This problem of contextualization and framing is integral to the written text. If words gain sense from their context — their circumstances of utterance — where is the limit to reading a word 'in context'? As sentence expands to paragraph to scene to act to play...the threat is of 'an uncontrollable echoing: a mad round of verbal associations'[26] as reading becomes 'absorbed in a kind of metonymic skid, each synonym adding to its neighbour some new trait, some new departure'.[27] One particular aspect of post-structuralist reading that has challenged both classical philology and traditional literary criticism is the desire to take at full value what is often treated merely as a piety — the need to determine meaning *in context*. For context is an ever expanding frame, or series of frame(s) on frame(s)... When we turn to drama — and speech *act* theory with its *performatives* borrows much vocabulary at least from drama — the (social) frame of performance — the stage, the audience(s), collectively and individually, the theatre, democracy, Athens... — is equally kaleidoscopic. When Derrida writes '*Il n'y a pas d'hors-texte*', he is in part stressing that each context, each frame, becomes the content, the text, of another frame: context offers, as Austin shows, not the comfort of the secure control or determination of meaning, so much as equivocations and worries about relative fixedness. Context spreads and stains the integrity of meaning.

Post-structuralist critics have focused on this *dissemination* of meaning, the openness that is produced by reading the network of signifiers that make up (con)text(s). Not a drift towards, nor (even) a celebration of 'meaninglessness', but an awareness of the excess of meaning produced by reading; not 'anything goes' — that constant fantasy (or nightmare) of bourgeois social control — but a question of how far to go, of where to bring the end to the 'uncontrollable echoing'; not (just) 'playfulness', but a scrupulous attention to the '*vols de langage*', the 'flights/thefts of language'. Such an awareness of the indeterminacy and excess of language is peculiarly difficult for the authoritative voice of the critic and his/her writing. Much of the difficulty of style that is associated with post-structuralist writing is a result of or response to — in part at least — the necessary attempt to negotiate the self-reflexive tension between the authoritative pronouncement of the critic and the claims of the indeterminacy or excess of language.

My first example of writing about examples, then, has emphasized the difficulty that stems from the process of framing, crucial to exemplification. Derrida refers to the problematic interplay between frame and content, generalization and example, as the 'logic of the parergon' and argues that 'the structure of framing effects is such that no totalization of the border is even possible. The frames are always framed: thus, by some of their content'[28] — as we saw with my framed example of Austin's discussion of circumstance. Rather than introduce a rigid delimitation of inside and outside, argument and example, framing functions as a source and site of difference that undermines the rigid delimitation of the boundaries of sense

---

[26] Hartman (1981) 111.

[27] Barthes (1975) 92.

[28] Derrida (1975) 99.

and the sense of boundaries. So Barbara Johnson writes in her remarkable study 'The Frame of Reference', 'the frame thus becomes not the borderline between the inside and the outside, but precisely what subverts the applicability of the inside/outside polarity to the act of interpretation'.[29] Hence, my initial hesitation to accede directly to a model of theoretical exposition and classical example (a necessary and impossible divide).

MAKING AN EXAMPLE OF WOMAN

> 'The generic woman seems to have a remarkable faculty for swallowing the individual' — George Meredith

For the Greek world, Homer even when nodding, is the exemplary text: the paradigm not merely of the genre of epic but of the very possibilities of literature to inform, to teach, to illustrate. How the heroes Odysseus and Achilles are exemplary, however, is itself a question posed in and by the *Iliad* and the *Odyssey*.[30] The characters of the *Iliad* themselves debate, especially with Achilles, the nature of his behaviour, and finally even the gods censure the best of the Achaeans for his excess. The *Odyssey*'s focus on ἄνδρα, 'a/the man', as I have discussed elsewhere,[31] repeatedly raises a doubt about how exemplary, how generalisable a figure Odysseus is as 'man'. What I wish briefly to gloss here, however, is a moment when a figure is said to be instructive for women in general.

The arrival of the suitors in the Underworld is the triumph and glory of Odysseus and Penelope attested to by Agamemnon. He juxtaposes Penelope to his own wife, Clytemnestra (24.197-202):

τεύξουσι δ' ἐπιχθονίοισιν ἀοιδὴν
ἀθάνατοι χαρίεσσαν ἐχέφρονι Πηνελοπείῃ,
οὐχ ὡς Τυνδαρέου κούρη κακὰ μήσατο ἔργα,
κουρίδιον κτείνασα πόσιν, στυγερὴ δ' ἀοιδὴ
ἔσσετ' ἐπ' ἀνθρώπους, χαλεπὴν δέ τε φῆμιν ὀπάσσοι
θηλυτέρῃσι γυναιξί, καὶ ἥ κ' εὐεργὸς ἔῃσιν.

---

[29] Johnson (1980) 128. I have discussed this with regard to Theocritus' pervasive framing devices in Goldhill (1990) 223-61.

[30] A much discussed topic. See e.g. Redfield (1975); Schein (1984), and, specifically on paradeigmata, Willcock (1964), and the recent stimulating work of Slatkin (1991); for my go at it, see Goldhill (1990) 1-108 with further bibliography to which can be added Taplin (1992). All quotations from Homer in this chapter are taken from the Oxford Classical Text of T.W. Allen.

[31] Goldhill (1990) 1-5.

> The immortals will furnish a pleasing song
> For humans in honour of constant Penelope.
> What a contrast with the daughter of Tyndareus, who devised
> Evil and killed her wedded husband! A hateful song
> Will there be among men for her. She provides a harsh sentence
> On the whole race of women, even one who works nobly.

Penelope, who has helped preserve her husband's status by her constancy and proper attitudes (ἀγαθαὶ φρένες 194), is praised, and promised a glorifying immortality of song. Clytemnestra, who has destroyed her husband, the speaker of these lines, will have an equally immortal song of hate addressed to her. A polarity is drawn up which rehearses both a standard aesthetic discourse (the opposition of praise/blame, celebration/hate) and a standard moral discourse (the good woman preserves her home/husband/attitudes, a bad woman corrupts and destroys her home/husband/attitudes). Yet if Penelope is exemplary, it is Clytemnestra who provides the model for women in general (θηλυτέρῃσι γυναιξί); indeed, even a woman who is εὐεργός, good and noble at the work by which a woman's place is defined, still is (to be) stained by the φῆμις — the words, report, sentence, judgement, reputation — that has been established by Clytemnestra. This rhetoric of misogyny has been read by critics as an 'understandable',[32] 'natural'[33] move for the shamefully betrayed husband, 'generalizing from his personal experience',[34] and as the beginnings of a Greek tradition of misogynistic writing: 'Agamemnon here looks ahead to the formation of a tradition of misogyny that, as he acknowledges it, is based on paying attention to some examples and not to others'.[35] Exemplary Penelope is viewed thus as 'a counter-example at the center of the story'[36] of man's necessary distrust of women.

Indeed, the effects of this spread of the *phêmis* of Clytemnestra can be seen in the preceding speech of Amphimedon, one of the slaughtered suitors, which prompts Agamemnon's exclamation of praise and blame. For Amphimedon highlights the deceptiveness of Penelope — the quality which has distinguished the dangerous Clytemnestra — even wrongly attributing to her a role in the bow competition at which the suitors died.[37] The deceptive woman at the centre of the house is a threat differently instantiated in Penelope and Clytemnestra — but both instantiations contribute to a discourse of gender evaluation. So, indeed, in the first Nekuia, Agamemnon frames his praise of Penelope with a repeated

[32] Wender (1978) 38.

[33] Eisenberger (1973) 181-2.

[34] Stanford (1978) *ad* 11.441-2.

[35] Murnaghan (1987) 125.

[36] Murnaghan (1987) 124.

[37] For discussion and bibliography on Amphimedon's speech see Goldhill (1988).

injunction to beware all women (11.440-456): 'Never be gentle with a woman/wife [γυναικί]', says Agamemnon, 'nor tell her the whole story...Not that for *you*, Odysseus, death will come from a woman/wife at any rate [ἔκ γε γυναικός]. For Penelope is so firm and knows well in her heart what is to be counselled...But anchor your ship in your fatherland secretly and not openly. For there is no trustworthiness [πιστά] in women/wives [γυναιξί]'. Again, the rhetorical generalization of Clytemnestra frames Penelope as a counter-example to womankind's tendencies to untrustworthiness, and sets up a narrative of concern about Penelope's trickiness that can never be quite controlled by Odysseus' wariness.[38]

These comments of Agamemnon on Clytemnestra and Penelope are offered in response to Odysseus' own generalization (11.436-9) that Zeus has hated the race of Atreus in an extraordinary way γυναικείας διὰ βουλάς, 'through the plans of women/wives'. He specifies both Clytemnestra, who manufactured a deception against her husband, and Helen, through whom so many died. The example of Helen here is particularly interesting, since in the Telemachy the visit to Helen and Menelaus provides a climax to the education of Telemachus, Odysseus' son. In Sparta, Helen, as hostess, drugged the drinks with a potion to remove grief, and she and her husband swap tales of Odysseus and Helen at Troy, after which Telemachus with an expression of grief goes to bed.[39] In the *Iliad*, as she excoriates herself to Hector, Helen declares that her marriage to Paris will make them 'the subject of song for future generations' (6.358). In Sparta, in the presence of Telemachus, we see the production of such a literary representation (in the voices of Helen and Menelaus themselves). Helen, however, as the juxtaposition of Odysseus making an example of her and Telemachus being entertained by her suggests, offers a difficult example for the discourse of exemplary praise and blame that we have been tracing. Like Clytemnestra, she is the source of destruction and a figure of violent deception and sexual transgression. Yet she is depicted in the centre of the household celebrating a wedding as Telemachus arrives; and as he leaves, she gives the boy a gown (πέπλος) for his bride on his own wedding day as a memorial of herself (15.126-7):

μνῆμ' Ἑλένης χειρῶν πολυηράτου ἐς γάμου ὥρην
σῇ ἀλόχῳ φερέειν
A memorial of Helen's hands for the time of your much-desired wedding
For your bride to wear.

This moment's potential for irony and prediction is hard to evaluate: what is Telemachus to recall of Helen on his wedding day? Eustathius marks the difficulty when he points out the ambiguity of πολυηράτου, 'much desired'.

---

[38] See the fine study of Katz (1991).
[39] This scene is discussed with bibliography in Goldhill (1988).

I have translated it with γάμου, 'marriage', but it can equally well go with 'Helen', for whom being much desired (πολυηράτου) has led to her being 'much husbanded' (πολυάνορος...γυναικός Aeschylus *Agamemnon* 62) and so great a threat to the institutions of marriage.[40] Apollonius of Rhodes — always an instructive reader of Homer — twice has Jason use a gown that he has been given by Hypsipyle, the queen of Lemnos whom he slept with and deserted on his journey towards the Golden Fleece and Medea. On the first occasion, Jason is following Medea's advice on how to complete her father's demands by engaging in magic rituals to protect his body. He puts on a robe, a gift of Hypsipyle, described as (3.1206) ἀδινῆς μνημήιον εὐνῆς, 'a memorial of their intense sex'. As Hunter comments, 'Jason dresses himself in an advertisement of his tendency to leave women behind'.[41] The second occasion is when Jason and Medea are luring her brother Apsyrtus to his death. They give him another robe that Hypsipyle had given Jason. This robe (πέπλος) had been used by Dionysus when he had 'clasped the beautiful breasts of Ariadne, whom Theseus had deserted' (4.432-4). This cloak still has the 'divine smell' (ἀμβροσίη ὀδμή 4.430) of that encounter with another deserted and 'much loved' female. For Apollonius, gifts of robes are memorials of past desertions, transgressions and encounters...

Penelope herself uses Helen in an example that has not failed to provoke readers of the *Odyssey*. As she asks Odysseus for forgiveness for not recognizing him immediately, she explains that her coldness comes from fear of deception. She adds (23.218-24):

οὐδέ κεν Ἀργείη Ἑλένη, Διὸς ἐκγεγαυῖα
ἀνδρὶ παρ' ἀλλοδαπῷ ἐμίγη φιλότητι καὶ εὐνῇ,
εἰ ᾔδη ὅ μιν αὖτις ἀρήιοι υἷες Ἀχαιῶν
ἀξέμεναι οἶκόνδε φίλην ἐς πατρίδ' ἔμελλον.
τὴν δ' ἦ τοι ῥέξαι θεὸς ὤρορεν ἔργον ἀεικές·
τὴν δ' ἄτην οὐ πρόσθεν ἑῷ ἐγκάτθετο θυμῷ
λυγρήν, ἐξ ἧς πρῶτα καὶ ἡμέας ἵκετο πένθος.

For nor would Argive Helen, daughter of Zeus,
Have made love with a foreign man,
If she had known that the war-like sons of the Achaeans
Were destined to bring her back home again to her dear fatherland.
But god made her do the outrageous deed.
Before that, she did not cherish that bitter madness in her heart,
That madness from which grief has come to us also from the first.

The logic of this exemplum is hard to appreciate and the passage, since the Hellenistic commentators, has often been condemned — predictably — as

---

[40] The Oxford text punctuates with a comma after χειρῶν to try to remove this ambiguity.
[41] Hunter (1989) ad 1203-6. See also Rose (1985).

'inauthentic'.[42] The most recent edition of the *Odyssey*, however, explains it as follows: 'Penelope uses this apparent digression...to explain and justify her own conduct...Penelope's analysis of the actions of Helen is calculated to draw the listener's (Odysseus') attention to a comparison with her own behaviour...She seeks to justify [her steadfastness].' The editors add, however, 'Equally, she attempts to win sympathy for Helen by showing that her actions were the result of divine influence: she could not recognize her infatuation for what it was until the consequences of her action were visible'.[43] Helen on this reading is being set up first as a counter-example to Penelope, but second as a sympathetic figure, led to err by the gods. The *Odyssey* opens with Zeus declaring that humans are wrong to blame the gods for their own tendency to transgress and thus to be punished (1.32-43). The sexual and social transgression of Aegisthus is Zeus' example. Aegisthus is a model for the suitors, whose transgressions and punishment structure the moral discourse of the epic. Here, however, Penelope allows a different sense of causation for that exemplary narrative of sexual and social transgression, Helen.

The figure of Helen, then, does not simply 'mediate' between the poles of the bad Clytemnestra and the good Penelope (as a structuralist account might put it). Rather we have detailed here a more complex rhetoric of exemplarity. On the one hand, the exemplary wife, Penelope, is not only invested with an uncertainty and trickiness to match her husband's wariness and to ground Agamemnon's warnings, but also is subordinated to Clytemnestra, as the exemplary is construed as exceptional. On the other hand, the parallel between Helen and Clytemnestra that Odysseus develops, is manipulated in quite different ways in the text, as Telemachus is entertained by Helen, and carries home a memorial of her for his own wedding, and as Penelope 'sympathetically' explores their difference. The polarized discourse of transgression and fulfilment of a female role *slips*, as exemplary becomes exceptional, framed by the suspicion of the transgressive; and as the transgressive becomes the site of a pedagogical and sympathetic encounter. With Helen hosting at home in Sparta, what image of the patriarchal *oikos* can stand unmined by suspicion, untested by wariness? Stanford highlights the problem neatly if un-self-consciously. As I quoted him earlier, he says that Agamemnon's misogyny is a case of 'generalizing from his personal experience'. The full gloss is 'generalizing from his personal experience of one woman (or two, if we include Helen)'. The conditional with which the figure of Helen is invested destabilizes the polarized evaluative discourse. (The 'if' in 'wife'?) Helen is (to be) included, for sure; Helen counts — but for what? As Helen's tale is recounted in the *Odyssey*, it becomes harder and harder to account for her

---

[42] Good discussion and bibliography in Katz (1990) 183-7.

[43] Fernandez-Galiano and Heubeck (1991) *ad loc.*

figuration within the polarities of female evaluation. Or is this instability itself just the exemplary trope of misogyny — οὐκέτι πιστὰ γυναιξί — a trope that reminds us that punishment is not the only normative/narrative response to transgression?

My second exemplary text has demonstrated, then, a difficulty in patrolling the polarity of example/counter-example (as the question of what counts is opened). The hierarchical opposition of 'good woman'/'bad woman' (and attendant oppositions e.g. 'pleasing song'/'hateful song') inverts and 'discomposes'[44] around the figure of Helen (and her songs...). This is how Derrida describes a strategic move in what he calls, with characteristic hesitation, '"deconstruction"': 'In a traditional philosophical opposition we do not have a peaceful co-existence of facing terms but a violent hierarchy. One of the terms dominates the other (axiologically, logically etc), occupies the commanding position. To deconstruct the opposition is above all, at a particular moment, to reverse the hierarchy'.[45] There is a further necessary step, however: one must put into 'practice an *overturning* of the classical opposition *and* a general *displacement* of the system. It is only on this condition that deconstruction will provide itself the means of intervening in the field of oppositions it criticizes and which is also a field of non-discursive forces'.[46] Elsewhere Derrida talks of the need 'to work through the structured genealogy of [a philosophical discourse's] concepts in the most scrupulous and immanent fashion, but at the same time to determine, from a certain external perspective that it [the philosophical discourse] cannot name or describe, what this history may have concealed or excluded, constituting itself as history through this repression in which it has a stake'.[47] Derrida's treatment in *De la grammatologie* of speech and writing in Rousseau is the best known working through of such a set of ideas, where the privileging of speech (as presence, as direct communication) over writing (as secondary, flawed, dangerous) is shown to depend on the repression of a shared structuring of difference and deferral inherent in the signifying processes of both speech and writing: the delays, absences and gaps that are used to characterize writing in the privileging of speech are shown to be integral to speech also. This argument is also aimed at Saussure and structural linguistics: the term 'post-structuralist' is coined specifically for Derrida's work because of its challenge to the binarism of the structuralists Saussure and Lévi-Strauss (as much as their commitment to the privileging of 'voice' over 'writing' — 'phonocentrism'). This challenge is

---

[44] 'Discompose', although awkward, seems a better translation than 'decompose', the term that Richard Howard adopts. The term is taken from Barthes (1975b) 'décomposer', (1977) 63: as Barthes says (1977) 69: 'what matters is not the discovery, in a reading of the world and of the self, of certain oppositions but of encroachments, overflows, leaks, skids, shifts, slips...'.

[45] Derrida (1972) 392, translated by Culler (1983) 85-6.

[46] Derrida (1982) 329.

[47] Derrida (1981) 15-16.

particularly provocative at the level of the sign itself, where for Saussure the hierarchical polarity of signifier and signified is fundamental. The celebrated punning and fragmentation of words in Derrida is a part of the inversion and displacement of that polarity — as Derrida traces (and sets free) 'les vols des signifiants', 'the flights/thefts of the signifier', rather than attempting to pass untrammeled through the signifier towards the signified.

What I have offered by way of a reading of Homer — partial as it inevitably is — is not, despite the evident concern for the inversions and displacements of a polarised, normative discourse, an application of a 'sturdy device' extracted from this Derridean project. Rather, it is a reading that draws on a wide range of intellectual sources and provocations, not least from the study of representation undertaken by a network of feminist theorists.[48] Indeed, it is not a reading that aims to prove or disprove any claim of Derrida's; nor a reading that is made possible solely by Derrida. At best, it is a reading that has been stimulated in part by an engagement with Derrida's writing, and that aims to allow more extensive implications of the discussion to emerge by a juxtaposition of my reading of Derrida with my reading of Homer.

Except, of course, I chose to focus on this aspect of Homer's epic precisely so that I could discuss example/counter-example with regard to Derrida's exposition...

NARRATIVE AND PARADIGMS: EXEMPLIFICTION

> 'Dreadful to think of! She was one of the creatures who are written about.' — George Meredith

The exemplarity of Helen and Clytemnestra continues throughout Greek tragedy. My third example is from Euripides — and Euripides is an exemplary reader of Homer — who in his play *Electra* has Electra argue with Clytemnestra herself precisely about her and Helen's exemplarity. Electra begins with a self-reflexive remark on beginnings, and an explicit paralleling of Helen and Clytemnestra (1060-66):

λέγοιμ' ἄν· ἀρχὴ δ' ἥδε μοι προοιμίου·
εἴθ' εἶχες, ὦ τέκουσα, βελτίους φρένας.
τὸ μὲν γὰρ εἶδος αἶνον ἄξιον φέρειν
Ἑλένης τε καὶ σοῦ, δύο δ' ἔφυτε συγγόνω,
ἄμφω ματαίω Κάστορός τ' οὐκ ἀξίω.
ἣ μὲν γὰρ ἁρπασθεῖσ' ἑκοῦσ' ἀπώλετο,
σὺ δ' ἄνδρ' ἄριστον Ἑλλάδος διώλεσας...

---

[48] E.g. the writers collected in the following collections: Miller (1986); Flyn and Schweikart (1986); Abel (1982); Showalter (1985).

I will speak. This will be the beginning of my introduction:
Would that you had, mother, better sense.
For your appearance is worthy of winning praise,
Both your's and Helen's; but you are two of a kind in nature,
Both useless and both not worthy of Castor.
For she was snatched and corrupted willingly,
You destroyed the best man in Greece...

As Penelope is praised in the *Odyssey* for ἀγαθαὶ φρένες, 'good sense', so Electra here wishes her mother had 'better sense', βελτίους φρένας. Homer (*Od.* 3.265-72) allows Clytemnestra an initial good sense, φρεσὶ ἀγαθῆσι, as Penelope allowed Helen a similar dispensation ('not before...' τὸ πρὶν μέν 3.265/οὐ πρόσθεν 23.223); Electra dispenses with a narrative of gradual corruption. Clytemnestra's appearance (εἶδος — that which distinguishes Homer's heroic women and goddesses) is worthy of praise (αἶνος) as is Helen's. As Agamemnon in Homer promised praise and blame for Penelope and Clytemnestra, here Electra allows Clytemnestra a measure of praise as a foil to the reproach to come. For the 'praise-worthy form' is to be contrasted with the 'unworthy nature' (ἔφυτε...οὐκ ἀξίω) — a fifth-century interest in *phusis*, which also shifts *eidos* towards a polarization of 'real nature'/'mere *appearance*'. The duals (rendered by 'both'/'you two') emphasize the pairing of the sisters as equally vain — Helen because she was destroyed/corrupted (ἀπώλετο) willingly (and here Electra speaks against not only Penelope's exoneration of Helen as the dupe of the gods but also the writing of contemporary figures such as Gorgias); Clytemnestra because she destroyed (διώλεσας) the best man (Achilles' Iliadic title here used of Agamemnon) of Greece. The punning that enforces the parallel narrative of corrupt destruction recalls the exclamation of the Homeric Odysseus on how the family of Atreus is god-hated, because through Helen 'many of us were destroyed', πολλοὶ ἀπωλόμεθ'.

Electra's fifth-century redeployment and development of the Homeric Odysseus' expression leads into an attack on any woman who uses make-up in her husband's absence (1069-79), before she returns to the comparison with Helen (1080-5):

κaίτοι καλῶς γε σωφρονεῖν παρεῖχέ σοι·
ἄνδρ' εἶχες οὐ κακίον' Αἰγίσθου πόσιν,
ὃν Ἑλλὰς αὐτῆς εἵλετο στρατηλάτην·
Ἑλένης δ' ἀδελφῆς τοιάδ' ἐξειργασμένης
ἐξῆν κλέος σοι μέγα λαβεῖν· τὰ γὰρ κακὰ
παράδειγμα τοῖς ἐσθλοῖσιν εἴσοψίν τ' ἔχει.

Yet it was possible for you to show virtue in a really fine way.
You had a man for a husband no worse than Aegisthus,
A man Greece had chosen as her own general.
Since Helen, your sister, had perpetrated such deeds,
You could have gained great fame. For evil is
An example for good, and attracts men's gaze.

Electra stresses Clytemnestra's inability to show virtue (σωφρονεῖν), an archetypal female quality (as she had wished her mother had better sense). For since Helen had so transgressed, Clytemnestra could have won great glory by maintaining the rules of virtue. 'For evil is an example — παράδειγμα — for good'. The mutual dependence of the categories 'good' and 'bad', and indeed the paradigmatic status of the bad, its ability to compel attention in the sight of men (εἴσοψιν — a *hapax*), goes to the heart of tragedy in the theatre (the place for looking), where the exempla of transgressions have such contested paradigmatic value for the good citizen. Where Plato requires a city to allow only literature that extols the virtues of the good as exemplary and didactic models, Euripides' Electra stresses the necessary display and paradigmatic value of evil by which the glory (κλέος) of the noble is won. Helen should have been a paradigm for Clytemnestra not to follow but to mark her difference.

Electra here recalls Clytemnestra's own argumentation in fragments. Clytemnestra states the possible reasons for killing Iphigeneia, but concludes (1027-29):

νῦν δ᾽ οὕνεχ᾽ Ἑλένη μάργος ἦν ὅ τ᾽ αὖ λαβὼν
ἄλοχον κολάζειν προδότιν οὐκ ἠπίστατο,
τούτων ἕκατι παῖδ᾽ ἐμὴν διώλεσεν.

But as things are, it was because Helen was lustful, and because her man
Did not know how to get and punish his treacherous wife,
That he destroyed my child.

The destruction (διώλεσεν) that Clytemnestra stresses is the sacrifice of Iphigeneia; the cause is first Helen's lewdness, her lustfulness, and second Menelaus' failure to control her. ('The contempt strong women feel for weak men' — Denniston. Generalizing from...?) Clytemnestra separates herself (and Aegisthus) from Helen (and Menelaus) — and from Agamemnon (and Cassandra). It is in response to this diacritical account that Electra constructs her rhetorical parallelization of her mother and aunt.

Clytemnestra has been reminded earlier by the chorus of her inability to recall suitable models. They respond to the story of the sun's shocked response to Thyestes' consumption of his own children as follows (737-46):

λέγεται <τάδε>, τὰν δὲ πί-
    στιν σμικρὰν παρ᾽ ἔμοιγ᾽ ἔχει,
στρέψαι θερμὰν ἀέλιον
χρυσωπὸν ἕδραν ἀλλάξαν-
    τα δυστυχίᾳ βροτείῳ
θνατᾶς ἕνεκεν δίκας.
φοβεροὶ δὲ βροτοῖσι μῦθοι
κέρδος πρὸς θεῶν θεραπείαν.
ὧν οὐ μνασθεῖσα πόσιν
κτείνεις, κλεινῶν συγγενέτειρ᾽ ἀδελφῶν.

Thus the story goes. It produces
Scant belief in me,
That the gold-faced sun
Changed its warm station
For mortal misfortune
For the sake of human justice.
But fearful myths for humans
Are useful for worship of the gods.
You forgot this when you killed
Your husband, sister of famous brothers.

I have discussed elsewhere both the extraordinary rhetoric whereby a chorus offers an exemplary tale only to distance itself from its own story, and the self-reflexive pronouncement of the usefulness of *muthoi* for religion (as this chorus performs in precisely such a frightening *muthos*).[49] Here, I want to focus first on the difficulty of the chorus' description of the exemplary narrative that they have just offered, and second on the connecting relative ὧν, translated as 'you forgot *this*', literally 'which things/figures'. To what does it refer? How much of the exemplary narrative and its choral commentary is it to be assumed that Clytemnestra failed to remember? θνατᾶς δίκας indeed is notably ambiguous, since it can mean not only 'human justice' in the sense of 'punishment meted out to humans' by the gods, but also 'human vengeance', that is, the punishment Atreus meted out on Thyestes, as well as a more general sense of 'justice' or 'right', that is, 'for the sake of proper order among humans'. Nor is δυστυχίᾳ βροτείῳ any easier: 'for a mortal's i.e. Thyestes' misfortune' is how Denniston construes it; Wilamowitz, followed by Stinton, takes it generally 'for mankind's detriment'; Wecklein, differently, construes it as 'because of human blindness'. The narrative which is to be exemplary is glossed by the chorus in a way which leaves it open to plays of interpretation which construct quite different versions of the relations between man, god, transgression and punishment. What, then, of ὧν? Denniston relates it closely to μῦθοι: 'you

---

[49] Goldhill (1986) 244-59.

do not remember these tales of warning'[50]. Stinton[51] takes it closely with θεῶν — 'you did not remember the gods' — because, he argues, it would be extraordinary — 'perverse'[52] — to criticize Clytemnestra for forgetting a story which is probably untrue. Cropp suggests that the chorus is 'recommending attention to "fearful piety-inducing tales" *in general*'[53]. The lack of precision in ὧν opens the possibility of a range of reference to the preceding exemplum and discussion of exemplarity. As Stinton shows, it is hard to delimit the reference without prejudging the use of the example.

What I hope to have highlighted by this brief discussion of figures in a play much concerned with exemplary models and paradigms of behaviour[54] is three points about narrative and exemplification. First, examples themselves are narrativized — told as narrative — and as such are open to the plays and openness of the narrative form. (This problem has been brilliantly analyzed in Kant by Caruth.[55]) The example's narrative form always threatens to produce an excess of signification beyond the controlling lines of the case it is designed to illustrate. Second, the positioning of examples *within* a narrative not only produces the interplay of the narrativized example in tension with the framing narrative, but also requires a recognition of the constant recontextualization and realignment of the example — as Electra's attack on Clytemnestra's exemplary destructiveness must be viewed in relation not only to Clytemnestra's own argument but also to the unfolding tragic narrative of violence.[56] This leads to my third point: this constant recontextualization also involves an intertextual dynamic, as the exemplary narrative is construed within a tradition of exemplification. In the case of Euripides, it is especially Homer that I have emphasized here; Aeschylus and other fifth-century writers would need to be included also. The force of exemplification also depends on a history of exemplification. As Classics teaches us...

*

In this paper, I have tried to offer some reasons why an exposition of critical theory, followed by an exemplary reading, raises a network of difficult

---

[50] Denniston (1939) *ad loc.*

[51] Stinton (1978) 79-82.

[52] Cropp (1988) ad 745.

[53] Cropp (1988) ad 745.

[54] For a discussion of the play along these lines see Goldhill (1986) 248-64.

[55] Caruth (1988). For a brilliant post-structuralist discussion of the plays and the openness of narrative, see Felman (1977). Barthes (1975) remains exemplary.

[56] These two first problems lead to certain well-known cruces about exemplarity, such as the fourth stasimon of the *Antigone*, where exemplarity is again explicitly marked, and critically problematic: see Sourvinou-Inwood (1988); (1989); Winnington-Ingram (1980) 102-9; but the general problem is less commonly discussed, even in tragedy.

questions about exemplification, which open into post-structuralist writings and into classical literature — its reading and its construction as classical. Exemplification cannot be dispensed with — as this essay has repeatedly... exemplified: it is a necessary ground of criticism. That criticism's necessary grounds are also open to question and fraught with difficulty is at least one very general point that can be extracted from this engagement with Derrida and Classics...

BIBLIOGRAPHY

This bibliography contains only the works referred to in my chapter. Since it is designed for English speakers I have always, where available and suitable, given a reference to the translations of works in languages other than English. The works marked with an asterisk are especially useful for those wishing to learn about Derrida and post-structuralism.

Abel E. (ed.) (1982) *Writing and Sexual Difference* (Brighton: 1982).
*Attridge D. (ed.) (1992) *Jacques Derrida: Acts of Literature* (London-New York: 1992).
Austin J. (1962) *How To Do Things With Words* (Oxford: 1962).
*Barthes R. (1975) *S/Z* (London: 1975), trans. A. Miller.
—— (1975b) *Roland Barthes par Roland Barthes* (Paris: 1975).
—— (1977) *Roland Barthes by Roland Barthes* (New York: 1977), trans. R. Howard.
Benveniste E. (1971) "Analytical Philosophy and Language", in *Problems of General Linguistics* (Miami: 1971), trans. M. Meeks.
Brennan T. (ed.) (1989) *Between Feminism and Psychoanalysis* (London-New York: 1989).
Butler J. (1990) *Gender Trouble: Feminism and the Subversion of Identity* (New York-London: 1990).
Caruth K. (1988) "The Force of Example: Kant's Symbols", *Yale French Studies* 74 (1988) 17-37.
Clark M. and Csapo E. (1991) "Deconstruction, Ideology and Goldhill's Aeschylus", *Phoenix* 45 (1991) 95-125.
Cole P. and Morgan J. (1975) *Syntax and Semantics 3: Speech Acts* (New York: 1975).
Cropp M. (1988) *Euripides: Electra* (Warminster: 1988).
*Culler J. (1983) *On Deconstruction: Theory and Criticism after Structuralism* (London: 1983).
*de Man P. (1979) *Allegories of Reading: Figural Language in Rousseau, Nietzsche, Rilke and Proust* (New Haven-London: 1979).
Denniston J. (1939) *Euripides: Electra* (Oxford: 1939).
Derrida J. (1972) *Marges de la Philosophie* (Paris: 1972). [See Derrida 1982]
—— (1975) "The purveyor of truth", *Yale French Studies* 52 (1975) 31-113.
*—— (1976) *On Grammatology* (Baltimore: 1976), trans. G. Spivak.
*—— (1981) *Positions* (Chicago: 1981), trans. A. Blass.
—— (1981b) "Economimesis", *Diacritics* 11.2 (1981) 3-25, trans. R. Klein.
*—— (1981c) *Dissemination* (Chicago: 1981), trans. B. Johnson.
*—— (1982) *Margins — of Philosophy* (New York: 1982), trans. A. Bass.
—— (1987) *The Post Card: from Socrates to Freud and Beyond* (Chicago: 1987), trans. A. Bass.
*—— (1988) *Limited Inc*, ed. G. Graff (Evanston: 1988).
—— (1992) "'Nous autres Grecs'", in *Nos Grecs et leurs modernes*, ed. B. Cassin (Paris: 1992).
*Eagleton T. (1983) *Literary Theory: an Introduction* (Oxford: 1983).
Eisenberger H. (1973) *Studien zur Odyssee* (Wiesbaden: 1973).

Elam K. (1984) *Shakespeare's World of Discourse* (Cambridge: 1984).

*Felman S. (1977) "Turning the Screw of Interpretation", *Yale French Studies* 55-56 (1977) 94-207.

—— (1980) *Le scandale du corps parlant* (Paris: 1980).

Fernandez-Galiano M. and Heubech A. (1991) *A Commentary on Homer's Odyssey: III* (Oxford: 1991).

Fish S. (1980) "How to do Things with Austin and Searle", in *Is There a Text in This Class?* (Cambridge, Mass.: 1980).

Flyn E. and Schweickart P. (edd.) (1986) *Gender and Reading: Essays on Readers, Texts and Contexts* (Baltimore: 1986).

Gadamer H.-G. (1975) *Truth and Method* (New York: 1975).

*Gallop J. (1982) *The Daughter's Seduction: Feminism and Psychoanalysis* (Ithaca-London: 1982).

*Gasché R. (1979) "Deconstruction as Criticism", *Glyph 6: Textual Studies* (Baltimore: 1979).

—— (1986) *The Tain of the Mirror: Derrida and the Philosophy of Reflection* (Cambridge Mass.: 1986).

Goldhill S. (1984) *Language, Sexuality, Narrative: the Oresteia* (Cambridge: 1984).

—— (1986) *Reading Greek Tragedy* (Cambridge: 1986).

—— (1988) "Reading Differences: the *Odyssey* and Juxtaposition", *Ramus* 17 (1988) 1-31.

—— (1990) *The Poet's Voice: Essays on Poetics and Greek Literature* (Cambridge: 1990).

Grice P. (1975) "Logic and Conversation", in Cole and Morgan (1975).

Hampton T. (1990) *Writing from History: the Rhetoric of Exemplarity in Renaissance Literature* (Ithaca-London: 1990).

*Harari J. (ed.) (1979) *Textual Strategies: Perspectives in Post-Structuralist Criticism* (Ithaca: 1979).

*Hartman G. (1981) *Saving The Text: Literature/Derrida/Philosophy* (Baltimore: 1981).

Herzfeld M. (1985) *The Poetics of Manhood: Contest and Identity in a Cretan Mountain Village* (Princeton: 1985).

Hunter R. (1989) *Apollonius of Rhodes: Argonautica Book III* (Cambridge: 1989).

*Johnson B. (1980) *The Critical Difference* (Baltimore: 1980).

Judet de la Combe P. (1989-90) "La force argumentative du dérisoire: *Agamemnon* 931-43", *Sacris Erudiri* 31 (1989-90) 210-37.

Kant I. (1982) *Critique of Judgement* (Oxford: 1982), trans. J.C. Meredith.

Katz J. (1977) *Propositional Structure and Illocutionary Force* (Hassocks: 1977).

Levinson S. (1983) *Pragmatics* (Cambridge: 1983).

Lloyd D. (1989) "Kant's Examples", *Representations* 28 (1989) 34-55.

Martin R. (1990) *The Language of Heroes: Speech and Performance in the Iliad* (Ithaca: 1990).

Marx K. (1970) *A Contribution to the Critique of Political Economy* (Moscow: 1970).

—— (1977) *The Eighteenth Brumaire of Louis Bonaparte* (Moscow: 1977).

Miller N. (ed.) (1986) *The Poetics of Gender* (New York: 1986).

Mitchell J. (1974) *Psychoanalysis and Feminism: Freud, Reich, Lang and Women* (New York: 1974).

Murnaghan S. (1987) *Disguise and Recognition in the Odyssey* (Princeton: 1987).

Norris C. (1982) *Deconstruction: Theory and Practice* (London: 1982).

Ohmann R. (1973) "Literature as Act", in *Approaches to Poetics* ed. S. Chatman (New York: 1973).

Petrey S. (1990) *Speech Acts and Literary Theory* (New York-London: 1990).

Pratt M.L. (1977) *Towards a Speech-Act Theory of Literary Discourse* (Bloomington: 1977).

Quint D. (1982) "'Alexander the pig': Shakespeare on History and Poetry", *Boundary 2* 10.3 (1982) 49-67.

Redfield J. (1975) *Nature and Culture in the Iliad: the Tragedy of Hector* (Chicago: 1975).

Rivers E. (ed.) (1986) *Things Done With Words: Speech Acts in Hispanic Drama* (Newark: 1986).

Rose A. (1985) "Clothing Imagery in Apollonius' *Argonautika*", *Quaderni Urbinati di Cultura Classica* 21 (1985) 29-44.

Schein S. (1984) *The Mortal Hero: an Introduction to the Iliad* (Berkeley: 1984).

Searle J. (1969) *Speech Acts* (Cambridge: 1969).

—— (1977) "Reiterating the Differences", *Glyph* 1 (1977) 198-208.

—— (1983) Review of J. Culler *On Deconstruction* in *New York Review of Books* October 27th (1983) 74-9.

Segal C. (1981) *Tragedy and Civilization: an Interpretation of Sophocles* (Cambridge Mass: 1981).

Showalter E. (ed.) (1985) *The New Feminist Criticism* (New York: 1985).

Slatkin L. (1991) *The Power of Thetis: Allusion and Interpretation in the Iliad* (Berkeley: 1991).

Sourvinou-Inwood C. (1988) "Le mythe dans la tragédie, la tragédie à travers le mythe: Sophocles *Antigone* 944-987", in *Métamorphoses du mythe en Grèce antique* (Geneva: 1988), ed. C. Calame.

—— (1989) "The Fourth Stasimon of Sophocles' *Antigone*", *Bulletin of the Institute of Classical Studies* 36 (1989) 141-165.

Sperber D. and Wilson D. (1986) *Relevance: Communication and Cognition* (Cambridge: 1986).

Stanford W. (1978) *The Odyssey of Homer* (London: ^{2}1978).

Stierle K. (1972) "L'Histoire comme example, l'example comme histoire", *Poétique* 10 (1972) 176-198.

Stinton T. (1978) "'Si credere dignum est': Some Expressions of Disbelief in Euripides and Others", *Proceedings of the Cambridge Philological Society* 22 (1978) 60-89.

Taplin O. (1992) *Homeric Soundings* (Oxford: 1992).

Ulmer G. (1985) *Applied Grammatology: Post(e)-Pedagogy from Jacques Derrida to Joseph Beuys* (Baltimore-London: 1985).

Vernant J.-P. (1981) "Oedipus without his Complex", in Vernant J.-P. and Vidal-Naquet P. *Myth and Tragedy in Ancient Greece* (Brighton: 1981).

Wallace J. (1974) "'Examples are the Best Precepts': Readers and Meanings in seventeenth-century poetry", *Critical Inquiry* 11 (1974) 273-80.

Wender D. (1978) *The Last Scenes of the Odyssey* (Leiden: 1978).

Willcock M. (1964) "Mythological Paradeigmata in the *Iliad*", *Classical Quarterly* 14 (1964) 141-54.

Winnington-Ingram R. (1980) *Sophocles: an Interpretation* (Cambridge: 1980).

*Young R. (ed.) (1981) *Untying the Text: a Post-Structuralist Reader* (Boston: 1981).

AESCHYLUS' *SUPPLIANTS*: A PSYCHOANALYTIC STUDY

RICHARD S. CALDWELL

> "If you want to know more about feminin-
> ity, enquire from your own experiences of
> life, or turn to the poets..."
>
> (Freud 1933: 135)

THE NEW DATE OF THE *SUPPLIANTS*

For several reasons, not least the role of the chorus as protagonist, the *Suppliants* was long regarded as the earliest extant Greek tragedy. Basing their theories on the twin assumptions that an artist's style must evolve in a progressive organic continuum and that the art form itself evolves by a similar logic, critics regarded the play as closest to the supposed choral predecessors of genuine tragedy.[1] But the publication in 1952 of a papyrus fragment (*Oxy. Pap.* 2256.3, Lesky 1954), showing that the play must have been produced after 467, probably in 463, placed the *Suppliants* in the same period as the *Oresteia* and the *Prometheus* and implied that Aeschylus used the chorus as the protagonist not because he had to, but because he wanted to.

Now that the dating of the play seems to have been settled, it might be thought that other questions, previously decided by reference to the supposedly primitive nature of the *Suppliants* would be open to different approaches and fresh answers. For it is clear that the new dating, while it demonstrated the inadequacy not only of former interpretations but also of former methods of interpretation, did not in itself provide any new solutions. Nevertheless, forty years after the papyrus publication many important questions still remain, both specific (e.g., the role of the chorus as protagonist, the characterization of Danaos, the significance of Io, the meaning of Zeus) and general (how are we to understand this strange drama, so full of love and death, of politics and fantasy?).

---

[1] "The *Supplices* or *Suppliant Women* of Aeschylus is generally regarded as the earliest of extant Greek plays. It is certainly the most primitive, and perhaps, in the common opinion of scholars, the most stiff, helpless, and unintelligible." Murray (1930) 7.

THE DANAID TRILOGY

Only a few fragments remain of the other plays in the trilogy (the *Egyptians* and the *Danaids*), but with the help of other references to the myth it is possible to make a rough reconstruction. It is probable that in the second play the Danaids married their cousins, perhaps as the result of a battle in which the Egyptians were victorious. On the wedding night, which would take place presumably in the interval between the second and third play, the Danaids, at the urging of their father, kill their husbands; the sole exception to this mariticide is Hypermestra, who spares Lynkeus. In the final play Hypermestra is exonerated by Aphrodite and her sisters are in some way reconciled to marriage.[2]

PSYCHOLOGICAL INTERPRETATIONS

Despite the intimations of Méautis two generations ago,[3] it was not until recently that studies appeared emphasizing the perspicuity and accuracy of Aeschylus' powers of psychological observation (e.g., Devereux 1976). Psychoanalytic investigation of Aeschylean drama, however, has tended to be confined to the *Oresteia* and, less often, to the *Prometheus*; any interest in the psychological meaning of the other plays, including the *Suppliants* has been usually peripheral and unsystematic. Attempts by the psychoanalyst D. Kouretas (1957) and by the classicist R. Murray (1958) to apply contemporary psychology to the *Suppliants* have been, for different reasons, less than completely successful. Although Murray's analysis of the imagery of the Io motif in the *Suppliants* is one of the finest works of Aeschylean scholarship, his references to such psychic phenomena as the "death wish," "atavistic obsession," "deep but unconscious feeling," and "subconscious" identification are handicapped by the lack of a psychological framework in which to locate these phenomena. Thus, while the fact of neurotic obsession is recognized (referred to as "half sight," "curiously warped understanding," or "confused, blinded mental processes"), investigation of the nature and cause of the obsession in the Danaids' relationship with their father is omitted entirely. Similarly, the Danaids' identification with their ancestress Io is regarded as an involved allegory rather than as a psychological determinant of the Danaids' behavior (Murray 1958: 72,69,53,26,69,70,83). Kouretas' treatment of the *Suppliants*, on the other hand, is so summary as to be nearly superficial, leaves major elements of the drama unexplained or inexplicable, and, as we shall see, contains some questionable psychology.

---

[2] For a reasonable reconstruction of the trilogy, see Winnington-Ingram (1961).

[3] Méautis (1936) 58 refers to Aeschylus as "ce fin psychologue ... cet observateur profond de l'âme humaine."

Of central importance is the hostility of the Danaids toward marriage with their cousins, an aversion which forces certain questions upon the critic of the play. Are the Danaids opposed to their cousins alone or to men in general? What is the cause of their aversion?[4] The reasoning of those who hold that the Danaids are opposed specifically to marriage with their cousins is usually based upon the force and violence which characterize the pursuit of the Danaids by the Aigyptids. But it must be kept in mind that our knowledge of the Aigyptids is based almost entirely on what the Danaids say they feel about them. This is an often overlooked aspect of any dramatic situation — what one character says about another is not necessarily to be accepted as fact (or better, as anything but subjective fact).[5] The view which seems to have widest acceptance may be represented by Winnington-Ingram's statement (1961: 144) that "the violent approach of the sons of Aigyptos has warped the feminine instincts of the Danaids and turned them against marriage as such." But this is neither more plausible nor more logical than to hold that the warped feminine instincts of the Danaids cause any sexual encounters to be regarded as acts of violence. Nor would this be a characteristic peculiar to the Danaids alone; one of the major themes of both mythology and psychology is the virginal perception of sexual encounter as rape, a dread of "the fight of the sexes as a deadly issue of violence, abuse, and defeat" (Thass-Thienemann 1967: 365). To say that the Danaids are opposed to marriage with the Aigyptids because of the violence of the latter may be true, but is not necessarily an exhaustive statement of causality; to say that the Danaids are opposed to *all* marriage because of the violence of the Aigyptids is *petitio principii* and true only if the absence of other determinants can be shown.

The cause of the "warped feminine instincts" of the Danaids has been studied by Kouretas, who finds in the Danaids "la personalité des femmes qui ont peur de la maternité avec négation de leur rôle de partenaire sexuel (frigidité) et attitude agressive envers le sexe masculin" (1957: 597). This view, virtually a word for word restatement in psychoanalytic terms of that of Méautis,[6] is unfortunately not developed by Kouretas beyond the statement of the Danaids' oedipal attachment to their father, his "counter-oedipal complex" in regard to them, and a few remarks on the "masculinity

---

[4] See Garvie (1969) 215-224 for the range of scholarly answers to these questions.

[5] The Aigyptids themselves do not make an appearance in the first play of the trilogy, and we can say nothing at all about the nature of their subsequent appearances. They are, to be sure, represented by a Herald who is the epitome of violence, but, given the usual character of heralds in Greek tragedy, it is not necessary that his attributes mirror those of his masters. Furthermore, if the Danaids are indeed hostile to all men and any marriage, then even if it were to be proven that the Aigyptids were absolute villains we would still be entitled to believe that there must be factors *within* the Danaids which cause them to fear all men and not merely some men.

[6] Compare Kouretas (1957) 598 with Méautis (1936) 49.

complex" in women. The Danaids are seen as arrested in an unresolved oedipal fixation upon their father Danaos, a situation which inhibits their femininity, leads to aggressive and masculine behavior, and prevents the extension of their sexual feelings to men other than their father.

The view of Kouretas, which emphasizes the "masculinity complex" of the Danaids, recalls Freud's description of three alternate developmental processes which are caused by the female castration complex:

> The discovery that she is castrated is a turning-point in a girl's growth. Three possible lines of development start from it: one leads to sexual inhibition or neurosis, the second to a change of character in the sense of a masculinity complex, the third, finally, to normal sexuality (1933: 126).

For Kouretas, the Danaids would fall into the second category, since they demonstrate

> la prédominance de tendances actives et agressives qui aboutissent à des conflits avec l'entourage et surtout avec ce que la femme possède en elle de feminin. ... La peur de la féminité mobilise les tendances masculines, qui à leur tour augmentent le trouble ... l'envie ou la jalousie de la masculinité qui hante les femmes ainsi névrosées, dont la rivalité avec l'homme et l'agressivité se dissimulent sous une forme plus ou moins tolérable (1957: 597-598,602).

This position, however, does not correspond with the text of the *Suppliants* nor is it psychoanalytically self-evident. The Danaids are clearly depicted by Aeschylus as the very antithesis of masculinity. As Murray points out, "The Danaids emphasize throughout the play their femininity and contrast it to the predatory masculinity of the generic male" (1958: 27-28). In his study of Aeschylus' characterization of women, Te Riele (1955: 15) finds particularly pronounced in the Danaids a

> fanatisme déraissonable féminin, trait assez prononcé chez les Danaides. Mais d'autres qualités y sont également: une grande émotivité quand les périls menacent, mais fermeté quand ils sont là; la raffinement dans la persuasion, etc.

Kouretas' view that the Danaids' oedipal attachment to their father results in a "masculinity complex" fares little better from a psychoanalytic standpoint. Classical (Freudian) theory regularly ascribes the aetiology of such a neurosis either to identification with the father (as opposed to libidinal attachment) or to regression to a pre-oedipal state of attachment to the mother. According to Freud, the masculinity complex in women is not based on the oedipal situation, but is usually an alternate development, originating (like the oedipus complex) in acknowledgment of the fact of castration, but resulting in the assertion of masculinity and "the fantasy of being a man [which] in spite of everything often persists as a formative factor over long periods."[7]

Nowhere in the text can we see any evidence for masculine behavior on the part of the Danaids, nor is there any evidence of their desire to compete with men on a sexual or non-sexual level. While it must be admitted that phallic imagery recurs in the words of the Danaids (e.g., blood-smeared snakes, sword-like branches, etc.), this hardly indicates the wish to be a man. As the predominant imagery of the play as well as the mass murder which is the climactic action of the trilogy demonstrate, the Danaids are preoccupied not with acquiring the male organ but with the wound they have suffered and its possible recurrence; not with becoming men themselves, but rather with reducing men to their own mutilated state. For this reason phallic imagery appears not in connection with something desirable but as threatening danger, and the major patterns of imagery revolve around such metaphors as the picking of fruit, the shedding of blood, attacking snakes, walls threatened, and flowers which must be guarded. The sexual prospects of the Danaids threaten a re-animation of the original wound; when these future threats become present reality, the Danaids will be compelled to seek vengeance in a like manner, by beheading (i.e., castrating) their violators.[8] Only Hypermestra will be able (at least at first) to escape this circle of mutual violence, when she freely chooses a new situation constituted "neither by the blood of defloration transformed into a wound by an arrogant virility, nor the blood from wounds inflicted by women out of hatred for the male sex" (Sissa 1990: 133).

---

[7] Freud (1931) 230. For J. van Ophuijsen (1924) 47-48, the "idea of being a male" is "an idea based on identification with the father or the brother." For E. Jones (1927) 472, 468, identification with the father represents "denial of femininity," is "common to all forms of homosexuality," and "serves the function of keeping feminine wishes in repression." See also Lampl-de Groot (1928) 339.

[8] Although the Danaids lack masculine characteristics in Aeschylus, this is not true of all non-Aeschylean sources; e.g., the obviously phallic Danaids on a Palermo vase in Cook (1940), 400, fig. XXXVI.

Concerning the Danaids' association of sexuality with violent injury and the symbolic castration to which their fears will eventually lead them, note the following remarks by a professedly anti-Freudian female psychiatrist: "Normally, bleeding means damage or injury. It is an extraordinary jump for women to accept the idea that bleeding means health. Therefore fears of having been ripped (raped?) in the vulnerable body interior are not unusual in young girls who have had no preparation for menstruation," "The girl's inhibitions have several origins. More obviously, she is afraid of personal and social rejection; less obviously, not being suffused with a high sexual drive she has difficulty in perceiving vaginal sex as pleasurable and confounds sex with blood, mutilation, pain, penetration, and pregnancy," "I think it probable that penis envy in neurotic girls is less a function of sexual impulses than of aggressive impulses, with a concomitant desire for castration of the boy", Bardwick (1971) 49,52,13.

A LACANIAN VIEW

The prominence of phallic imagery in the *Suppliants* would seem to invite analysis by the phallocentric theories of Jacques Lacan, but here we confront an apparent problem of Lacanian theory. The problem — how can Lacan's masculinist notion of the oedipus complex be applied to the female oedipus complex? — restates, in a way, a central problem in attempting to analyze the psychology of the *Suppliants*: what can we know of female psychology in a culture reported to us almost entirely by men? The answer to the second problem is clear if not entirely satisfactory: as Winkler says, knowledge of "Greek women's representations of their own experience ... is possible in two ways, individually through a female author [this means Sappho] and collectively via the religious rites conducted exclusively by women" (1990: 12). We will return to the latter possibility at the end of this essay. As for the question of applying Lacan's phallocentric ideas to the situation of the Danaids, the real question is not *how* we could do this but rather *why* we would want to do it. Nevertheless, for those readers interested in Lacanian perspectives, the psychological situation of the Danaids could be interpreted as follows.

For Lacan the primary symbol of the (male) child's oedipal desire is the phallus: "ce qui resurgit dans l'inconscient du sujet c'est le désir de l'Autre, soit le phallus désiré par la Mère" (1966c: 733). The moment when desire is signified by the phallus, however, is also the moment when a new mediator appears, the symbolic Father, since "la signification du phallus, avons-nous dit, doit être evoquée dans l'imaginaire du sujet par la métaphore paternelle" (1966a: 557). Since desire is the Other's desire, and since the child now learns (and represses) that only the father can satisfy the mother's desire for the phallus, desire becomes the repressed desire to be what the father is and to have what the father has. The symbolic Father now appears as promulgator of the law of prohibition, and the child, by repressing the phallus as signifier of his desire, acquires both an unconscious (in which the phallic signifier suffers continual displacement along signifying chains) and a superego (the internalization of paternal prohibition). Thereby the child inherits the law of prohibition and takes his place in what Lacan calls the symbolic order: he will someday be a father himself and, although he may never be the phallus for his mother, he will someday be the phallus for a woman who represents the mother, the woman who "dans la dialectique phallocentrique ... représente l'Autre absolu" (1966c: 732).

We do not need Lacan's mystifying references to Symbolic, Real, and Imaginary registers to see how the Danaids might fit into a "phallocentric dialectic." If we assume, with Lacan, that the originary desire is the mother's desire to have the phallus, then the female child's desire, formed by identification with the mother (Io), is also to have the phallus of the father (Danaos). Because it must be repressed, this desire is displaced along a metaphoric series (Pelasgos, Zeus) until it reaches the wedding night; at this point Hypermestra (like Io, eventually) is able to take her place in the social order and to accomplish the transformation from a girl who desires her father to a woman who loves another man. For the other Danaids this conclusion must await the footrace that brings them husbands. Thus the female oedipus complex, from a Lacanian viewpoint, turns out in fact to be simpler and more straightforward than that of the boy. Lacan's major thesis, "Si le désir de la mère *est* le phallus, l'enfant veut être le phallus pour le satisfaire" (If the mother's desire *is* the phallus, the child wishes to be the phallus in order to satisfy it, 1966b: 693), is easily transferred from boy to girl: whereas the boy's desire, based on that of the mother, is to *be* the phallus she desires, the girl's desire, also based on that of the mother, is to *have* the phallus she desires. The critical difference is between being and having.

DANAOS AND HIS DAUGHTERS

Denial of a masculinity complex in the Danaids does not necessitate rejection of an unresolved oedipus complex as well.[9] On the contrary, the Danaids typify the oedipal situation: because of their excessive attachment to their father and their identification with a mother-substitute, they are unable to love other men and are therefore consumed by an incapacitating anxiety concerning sex and marriage.

One of Freud's earliest statements could serve as a clinical description of the Danaids' behavior and its causes:

> It is in the world of ideas, however, that the choice of an object is accomplished at first; and the sexual life of maturing youth is almost entirely restricted to indulging in fantasies, that is, in ideas that are not destined to be carried into effect. In these fantasies the infantile tendencies invariably emerge once more, but this time with intensified pressure from somatic sources. Among these tendencies the first place is taken with uniform frequency by the child's sexual impulses towards its parents, which are as a rule already differentiated owing to the attraction of the opposite sex — the son being drawn towards his mother and the daughter towards her father. At the same time as these plainly incestuous fantasies are overcome and repudiated, one of the most significant, but also one of the most painful psychical achievements of the pubertal period is completed: detachment from parental authority, a process that alone makes possible the opposition, which is so important for the progress of civilization, between the new generation and the old. At every stage in the course of development through which all human beings ought by rights to pass, a certain number are held back; so there are some who have never got over their parents' authority and have withdrawn their affection

---

[9] For early psychoanalytic theory, every female oedipus complex must remain to some extent unresolved: Freud (1931) 230, Lampl-de Groot (1928) 337.

from them either incompletely or not at all. They are mostly girls who, to the delight of their parents, have persisted in all their childish love far beyond puberty. It is most instructive to find that it is precisely these girls who in their later marriage lack the capacity to give their husbands what is due to them; they make cold wives and remain sexually anaesthetic. We learn from this that sexual love and what appears to be non-sexual love for parents are fed from the same sources; the latter, that is to say, merely corresponds to an infantile fixation of the libido (1905: 225-227, cf. Freud 1918: 203 and Yates 1930: 173).

Development of this interpretation requires analysis of two key issues: the relationship of the Danaids to their father Danaos, and their relationship to their ancestress Io. Although the Danaids' relationship with their father appears to lack the typical oedipal wishes present in normal development, it might be possible to find a trace of libidinal cathexis in the extreme dependence of the girls on their father. This dependence, however, seems to exist much more in what the Danaids say than in what they do. Although they address their father as πατὴρ καὶ βούλαρχος καὶ στασίαρχος ('father, advisor, and leader', 11-12), and as πατέρ᾽ εὐθαρσῆ Δαναόν, πρόνοον καὶ βούλαρχον ('father Danaos, brave and wise advisor', 969-970), in actual fact the girls themselves are left to their own resources in the major confrontations of the play. Upon the entrance of Pelasgos, king of Argos, Danaos, who up to this point has been voluble enough, becomes a mute character and remains so until the issue has been decided and the king is preparing to leave (a silence of 257 lines). Subsequently, after he himself has seen the arrival of the Egyptian ships, he gives his daughters rather specious advice about the difficulties involved in landing a fleet, and with that goes off to the city, leaving them defenseless.[10]

Garvie, after rejecting views which imply that Aeschylus was forced (by incompetence, inexperience, or the exigencies of nascent tragedy) to characterize Danaos as he does, suggests that "it is possible that the second actor was already so much an accepted stage convention that Aeschylus could not dispense with his presence for this play. Danaos moreover was provided by the myth, and could hardly be omitted from any treatment of the story" (1969: 136). As Kitto said, in discussing the belief that the tragic poet is sooner or later forced by the mythological data to write not what he wishes but what he must, "This myth about Myth should be exploded. It does us little credit, since all the evidence points the other way, and it renders us no service beyond that of exempting us from taking seriously all that we find in a play" (1966: 29).

Garvie goes on to explain the role of Danaos as a result of the exchange of function:

---

[10] The arguments supporting Wilamowitz' description of Danaos as an "Annex seiner Töchter" are summarized by Garvie (1969) 127.

> In making the Chorus the protagonist of the *Suppliants* Aeschylus has had to curtail the actor's part. But at the same time he has compensated him by giving him some of the functions of the normal tragic chorus. From the point of view of the plot Danaos may be superfluous, and his words may not be profound. But nowhere is he irrelevant or incompetently handled (1969: 138).

More satisfactory results might perhaps be gained from an analysis of Danaos' role in terms of the oedipal hypothesis advanced earlier. At first glance, the apparent irrelevance of Danaos seems to weigh against an overwhelming oedipal attachment on the part of his daughters, despite Kouretas' assertion that there is evidence of a counter-oedipal complex in Danaos' "violente réaction coléreuse" (1957: 601). This seems certainly true of Danaos, but the presence of a counter-oedipal complex in a parent does not at all necessitate the presence of its converse, an oedipal complex in a child. A solution to the problem of the Danaids' relationship with their father depends, I believe, on two important considerations: the pivotal role of fantasy in neurotic behavior, and the significance of Zeus in the *Suppliants*.

A major change in Freud's thought was his discovery that the stories told to him by his female patients about paternal seduction, all of which he had previously accepted as literal truth, were for the most part constructions of fantasy (Freud 1925: 34-35, 1931: 238, 1933: 120). From the point of view of the daughter, what matters in any case is not the real father but the fantasized father. Psychoanalytically, Danaos is precisely "superfluous" to the Danaids' neurotic fear of sexuality, since fantasy replaces reality in the neurotic situation. The Danaos of the play is real, but as such he does not figure in the fantasies of his daughters, since fantasy is by definition the distortion of reality. As Freud says:

> One must never allow oneself to be misled into applying the standards of reality to repressed psychical structures, and on that account, perhaps, into undervaluing the importance of fantasies in the formations of symptoms on the ground that they are not actualities, or into tracing a neurotic sense of guilt back to some other source because there is no evidence that any actual crime has been committed. One is bound to employ the currency that is in use in the country one is exploring — in our case a neurotic currency (1911: 225).

Garvie's statement that Danaos is "superfluous" but not "irrelevant" turns out to be right after all. Danaos is relevant because he is the father upon whom the Danaids are tragically fixated; he is superfluous because in their fantasy his place has been taken by Zeus.

DANAOS AND ZEUS

Garvie notes that "Zeus, upon whom everything depends, makes his appearance in the first word of the play" (1969: 70, n.4). This is indeed important, but its full significance lies in the fact that the phrase which responds to Ζεὺς μέν in the first line is Δαναὸς δέ (11).[11] This parallelism informs the entire play; the oedipal attachment of the Danaids is to the image of Danaos projected in fantasy, Zeus as omnipotent father and lover.[12]

The Danaids twice refer to Zeus as πατήρ (139,592), and twice they use the vocative πάτερ to refer ambivalently to either Danaos or Zeus (811,885). For Zeus to be referred to or addressed as father is not, of course, unique to the *Suppliants*, but the role of Zeus as double of Danaos is emphasized in the ambivalence of the two instances in which the chorus directly invokes him. After Danaos has revealed the arrival of the Aigyptids, his terrified daughters immediately call upon him as πάτερ (734) and repeat the vocative three more times in the brief kommos which follows (738,748,756). At this point Danaos leaves, but the Danaids continue their song of fear in a stasimon (776-824).

In the third strophe they again call upon πάτερ:

> ἔπιδε, πάτερ,
> βίαια μὴ φίλοις ὁρῶν
> ὄμμασιν ἐνδίκως·
> σεβίζου δ' ἱκέτας σέθεν,
> γαιάοχε παγκρατὲς Ζεῦ.

> See, father,
> looking upon violence
> with eyes justly hostile.
> Honor your suppliants,
> omnipotent protector, Zeus. (811-816)

The context and especially the postponed vocative Ζεῦ seem to indicate that πάτερ refers here primarily to Zeus, secondarily to the absent Danaos. An analogous situation occurs in the strophe 885-892, where the Danaids call upon πάτερ (885) and the strophe ends with the vocative Ζεῦ. The ambivalent reference of πάτερ in these two passages is in sharp contrast

---

[11] Metrically, line 11 follows a line which is paroemiac and ends in a full stop. As a result, line 11 stands in virtually antistrophic response to line 1. Syntactically, Ζεὺς μέν ... Δαναὸς δέ is a typical μέν ... δέ construction. Although a δέ intervenes in line 4, it is used absolutely, as the Scholiast saw: δίαν δὲ] ὁ δὲ ἀντὶ τοῦ γάρ.

[12] The word "Zeus" occurs 45 times in the *Suppliants* by far the greatest frequency in the extant plays of Aeschylus, with the predictable exception of the (perhaps non-Aeschylean) *Prometheus* (59). The figures for the other plays are *Persians* 5, *Septem* 19, *Agamemnon* 24, *Choephori* 13, *Eumenides* 22.

with the practice of Aeschylus in other occurrences of the vocative πάτερ. In none of the twenty-nine instances (all but five in the *Suppliants* or *Choephori*) is there the slightest possibility of ambiguity, except in the two just mentioned. The word πάτερ is regularly either followed or preceded immediately by the name of the person addressed, unless the vocative refers to the speaker's human father. The only exception (other than *Suppliants* 811 and 885) is *Suppliants* 480, but in this case the possibility of ambiguity is removed by the explanatory phrase τῶνδε παρθένων. Thus we must either assume that πάτερ refers in both instances to Zeus (which no editor or translator is willing to do), or we must accept the ambiguity as intentional.

Zeus appears in the *Suppliants* in several modes. His principal dramatic role, as Ζεὺς μὲν ἀφίκτωρ (1) indicates, is that of protector of the weak suppliant. He is also characterized as savior (26), avenger (645-646), and just judge (402-406), as "the protector of the weak, the avenger of the wronged, and a towering symbol of the ultimate triumph of justice in the world" (Golden 1962: 101). More important for our purposes are the various formulations, both abstract and concrete, which describe Zeus' higher nature, those characteristics which are not demanded by the predicament of the Danaids in this play as frightened and helpless suppliants. His role is described as one of absolute power and sovereignty; he is 'Lord of lords, most blessed of the blessed, and most efficacious power' (524-526), without whom nothing is accomplished for men (823-824; cf. *Agamemnon* 1487). He is omniscient (139) and his thought becomes deed as quickly as that of others becomes speech (598-599). Everything is effortless (ἄπονον, 100); "as he sits, he accomplishes his will in a mysterious way from the holy throne itself" (101-103).

The effortless omnipotence of Zeus (or of any supreme deity) is, of course, a common phenomenon. From a psychoanalytic point of view it is derived from the universal and inevitable disillusion of the infantile perception of parental power as unlimited. As Freud says:

> When the growing individual finds that he is destined to remain a child forever, that he can never do without protection against strange superior powers, he lends those powers the features belonging to the figure of his father; he creates for himself the Gods whom he dreads, whom he seeks to propitiate, and whom he nevertheless entrusts with his own protection (1927: 24).

In the *Suppliants* however, the transition from father to god is not a subsequent effect of the oedipus complex, but is rather an effort to maintain the complex while repressing its incestuous aspect; it is a matter not of the religious development of the race, but of the individual's erotic projection. As Dodds notes, in his discussion of the place of Zeus in Greek culture, "It was natural to project on to the heavenly Father those curious mixed feelings about the human one which the child dared not acknowledge even to himself" (1951: 48).

In either case, the omnipotence of the divine Father is a result of the child's view of her own father, not only because the parent must in fact seem omnipotent to the child, but also because, in the oedipal situation, the child transfers to the new love-object the same fantasies she had entertained about herself during that earlier period when, sheltered from reality, she had conceived the "dream of narcissistic omnipotence in a world of love and pleasure" (Brown 1959: 113). This transference represents, in Jones' words, "a substitute for the primary narcissism and feeling of omnipotence which the child is unable to sustain in the face of experience, a failure which is largely contributed to by the presence of the obviously powerful Father" (1923: 355).

DANAOS AND PELASGOS

The question of omnipotence occurs again in the attitude of the Danaids toward Pelasgos, king of Argos. Most critics have been puzzled by the discrepancy between this attitude and Pelasgos' apparent inability to act without the consent of his citizens. The position of Pelasgos, regarded by one critic (Diamontopoulos 1957) as an anachronism which reveals the true date of the play, is seen by another as "the center of [Aeschylus'] thinking in this play, as it certainly is the center of its tragic feeling" (Kitto 1961: 10). The existential dilemma of Pelasgos notwithstanding, we should not neglect the way in which his role, like those of Danaos and Zeus, must be seen in terms of the fantasies of the Danaids. The crucial passage is as follows:

Βα.   ἐγὼ δ' ἂν οὐ κραίνοιμ' ὑπόσχεσιν πάρος,
        ἀστοῖς δὲ πᾶσι τῶνδε κοινώσας πέρι.
Χο.   σύ τοι πόλις, σὺ δὲ τὸ δήμιον·
        πρύτανις ἄκριτος ὤν,
        κρατύνεις βωμόν, ἑστίαν χθονός,
        μονοψήφοισι νεύμασιν σέθεν,
        μονοσκήπτροισι δ' ἐν θρόνοις χρέος
        πᾶν ἐπικραίνεις· ἄγος φυλάσσου.

King: But I would fulfill no promise before
          I have shared these matters with all the citizens.
Chorus: But you are the city, you are the people.
          The ruler is not judged.
          You rule the altar and hearth of the land, by the command of your
          solitary vote;[13]
          from the throne with solitary scepter

---

[13] LSJ, s.v. μονόψηφος, attributes the phrase μονοψήφοισι νεύμασιν to Zeus, a Freudian slip!

you meet every need; beware of pollution. (368-375)

The deference of Pelasgos to his citizenry need not be regarded as a gross anachronism, "totally irrelevant in any mythological situation" (Forrest 1960: 240). As Lloyd-Jones says, popular assemblies, as well as respect for the wishes of the people, are found in the *Iliad* and "Aeschylus' allusions to the power of the assembly are perfectly consonant with this state of affairs."[14]

The Danaids evidently regard the rule of Pelasgos over his kingdom as similar to the rule of Zeus over the world.[15] In their eyes he is as omnipotent in his own sphere as Zeus in his. There is no authority higher than Pelasgos (371); likewise, there is no one above Zeus (595-597). For both, absolute rule is exercised from the throne itself (374, 103). In the fantasy of the Danaids, Pelasgos, like Zeus, enjoys the omnipotence of the oedipal father. In this context, his inability to act without the consent of his people demonstrates the opposition of reality to fantasy. As Méautis remarks, the Danaids "have lost their sense of, and contact with, reality" (1936: 61). In the language of psychoanalysis, the Danaids transfer to both rulers the omnipotence of the oedipal father, an omnipotence which remains "the overvaluation of mental processes as compared with reality."[16]

The connection of Pelasgos with Danaos perhaps indicates the meaning of Danaos' silence during the confrontation between king and chorus; in the presence of a father-substitute, Danaos is again superfluous. For the same reason, the Danaids' most impressive praises of Zeus occur when Danaos is absent (86-103,[17] 524-427, 590-599, 811-824). After his long silence (234-489), Danaos' first words to Pelasgos represent the opposition of reality to the identification of himself with the king which has been made in the eyes of the Danaids: "the nature of my shape is not similar to yours" (496). Thereupon he leaves, and the Danaids immediately look to Pelasgos as they had previously looked to their father: "How should I act?" (505). Pelasgos gives them directions which they follow explicitly. Then, like Danaos, he too leaves, saying, "Your father will not for a long time desert you" (516). Again, reality interrupts the identification of king and father,[18] but who is the father who will soon return? With the king and Danaos gone, the

---

[14] Lloyd-Jones (1964) 359. Rose (1957) 40-41 attributes the Danaids' beliefs to the fact that they "know only of absolute kings, and suppose this is one of them; if it were so, naturally the sole responsibility would rest on him." On the other hand, Smyth (1924) 43 sees the Danaids as representative of an Hellenic culture and opposed to barbarian beliefs and customs.

[15] Rose (1957) 41 sees a possibility of this in νεύμασιν.

[16] Freud (1913) 87. The equation father = king = god is a basic constituent of Freud's analysis of myth, dreams, cultural phenomena, and even neurotic symptoms. See, for especially relevant instances, Freud (1909) 241, (1919) 262, (1928a) 171, (1928b) 187, also Rank (1952) 78, n.78 and Rank and Sachs (1964) 84.

[17] Danaos may have accompanied the choros in the parados, or he may have come with them but has not yet spoken.

[18] The δέ of 517 effectively removes any ambiguity possible in πατήρ (516).

Danaids begin the invocation of Zeus: "Lord of lords, most blessed of the blessed, etc." (524-526). In the first antistrophe, they call upon Zeus as the lover of Io, and in the second strophe they refer to Io as their "mother" (539). After an account of the ordeals of Io, the stasimon returns to Zeus as father and begetter (592) and ends, as it began, with praise of Zeus as the greatest of gods, effortlessly omnipotent (595-599).

THE ROLE OF IO

The fact that Zeus was the lover of Io is, of course, the ultimate cause of the entire action of the play and is present throughout, either explicitly or implicitly. As R. Murray points out, "At times Zeus is approached in general terms in his varied but more traditional aspects; more frequently, he is invoked as Io's lover and savior, or as ancestor of the Danaids" (1958: 19).

If Zeus is a substitute for the oedipal father, how does Io, a rather remote ancestress,[19] fit into the oedipal situation? By the same process of projection whereby the oedipal father was connected with Zeus, Io becomes, in the structure of the play and in the minds of the Danaids, their fantasy mother. She, the object of their substitute father's love, becomes in their fantasy a substitute for the never-mentioned real mother. Instead of being an obstacle to such an identification, the gulf of generations separating Io from the Danaids enables them fully to identify themselves and their situation with her, thereby avoiding the risk and taboo of attempting to usurp the mother's place in the father's affection.[20]

The Danaids themselves indicate in a key passage both their identification with Io and the representation of Io as fantasized mother. After Danaos and Pelasgos have left them (503, 523), the Danaids' thoughts immediately turn, as we have seen, to Zeus. The initial strophe of the stasimon (524-530) demonstrates well how an intense oedipal attachment precludes the growth of love for other men. No mere mortal can hope to compare with the over-valuation of the oedipal father, an over-valuation in fantasy which is necessary if incestuous wishes are to be kept in a state of repression. For a man to attempt to usurp the position of one who is "Lord of lords, most blessed of the blessed" is truly an act of hybris, and the Danaids call upon Zeus to avert from them the ἀνδρῶν ὕβριν (528). The 'hybris of men' is for the Danaids not a particular flaw of the Aigyptids, but rather the necessary attribute of anyone who would dare to threaten the position of the cherished

---

[19] Io is the great-great-great-grandmother of the Danaids, by their own reckoning (313-321).

[20] Rank and Sachs (1964) 44-45 discuss the manner in which incestuous myths tend to be distorted by the splitting of characters and the multiplication of generations, whether through a single creative act or through a long and gradual process under the impact of cultural and ethical advancement.

father.[21] ἀνδρῶν (528) is contrasted with γυναικῶν (531); this leads to a particular woman, Io, the ancestress beloved of Zeus, φιλίας προγόνου γυναικός (533). At this point the Danaids move from the past to the present in which the past is reincarnate, and reveal the fantasy in which Io is their mother and they are Io:

παλαιὸν δ᾽ εἰς ἴχνος μετέσταν,
ματέρος ἀνθονόμους ἐπωπάς,
λειμῶνα βούχιλον, ἔνθεν Ἰὼ
    οἴστρῳ ἐρεσσομένα
    φεύγει ἁμαρτίνοος...

I have crossed over to the ancient path,
where my mother ate flowers and watched,
the rich meadow, from which Io
    driven by the gad-fly
    flees distraught... (538-542)

The Danaids now see themselves as standing in the foot-prints of their mother Io. Her situation, which they are doomed to repeat, is, as the imagery suggests, the rejection of female sexuality in the presence of threatening masculinity. The phallic meaning of stinging, piercing insects such as the gad-fly or bee is unmistakable (Brophy 1962: 426), and the symbolizing of the female sexual organs by flowers, gardens, meadows, etc., is virtually a cultural universal. οἴστρος (gad-fly) is a word regularly used by the tragedians to mean lust, passion, frenzy, and the stinging gadfly which pursues Io is clearly the symbol of Zeus' sexual intentions. λειμῶν (meadow) is another recurrent sexual symbol (Segal 1965: 163, n. 21), denoting specifically the female genitals (e.g., Euripides' *Cyclops* 171). It is significant that while the Danaids picture themselves fleeing the meadow of their sexuality as did Io, they fail to recognize that which is betrayed by their words, that the ultimate salvation of Io takes place in a λειμῶνα χιονόβοσκον ("a meadow nourished by snow", 559). The release of Io from her sufferings is accomplished when she is impregnated by that from which she fled, and in the place from which she fled.

The connection of flowers with the female genitals, especially in a state of virginity, is found in many languages and cultures, in both myths and dreams (Freud 1916-1917: 158). An example which seems particularly pertinent to the *Suppliants* is Freud's description of a young woman whose recurrent dreams about flowers signified the "fear of being deflowered" and "an over-valuation of her virginity" (1900: 377). Similar feelings are revealed in the Danaids' prayer that "the flower of youth be not plucked"

---

[21] The remarks of Lattimore (1964) 81-82, n.24, seem to me to miss the point. More relevant to the Aigyptids, at least in the eyes of the Danaids, is the description of hubris as "masculine pride and phallic self-satisfaction, even exhibitionism" (Slater 1968: 45).

(663). Ostensibly this is an allusion to the war which they pray will never engulf Argos, but the connection with their own war and with their own preoccupation with flowers is clear.[22]

In an earlier passage the Danaids were likewise led from thoughts of an omnipotent and omniscient father (139) to the protection of their virginity and the role of Io, who again is referred to not as ancestress but as mother:

> σπέρμα σεμνᾶς μέγα ματρός, εὐνᾶς
> ἀνδρῶν, ἒ ἔ,
> ἄγαμον ἀδάματον ἐκφυγεῖν.

> May the great seed of a holy mother,
> escaping the beds of men,
> remain unmarried and inviolate. (141-143)

In the initial strophe of the tragedy, the Danaids also speak of Io's fondness for flowers (ἀνθονομούσας, "flower-browsing", 43);[23] in the antistrophe they again refer to Io as mother:

> ὄντ' ἐπιλεξαμένα,
> νῦν ἐν ποιονόμοις
> ματρὸς ἀρχαίας τόποις τῶν
> πρόσθε πόνων μνασαμένα
> τά τε νῦν ἐπιδείξω
> πιστὰ τεκμήρια γαιανόμοις

> Invoking him, Epaphos,
> now in the browsing
> places of mother long ago,
> recalling former sufferings,
> now I will show
> faithful proofs to those who inhabit this land (49-54)

In this passage ματρὸς is ambiguous, since it may refer to either the Danaids or Epaphos (ὄντ' 49).[24] The ambiguity is consistent with the projection of Zeus as the oedipal father and of Io as the oedipal mother. The child of Zeus and Io is also the child of the fantasized parents of the Danaids and therefore equivalent to the Danaids themselves. The identification of the Danaids with Epaphos, ambiguously suggested at 51, is strengthened when the Danaids call upon Zeus not to dishonor the "child of the cow" (170-171). As Murray says,

---

[22] See Whittle (1964) for discussions of the importance of Io's "flowery diet" (27) and the use of flowers as a means of identification between the Danaids and Io (26-27).

[23] For the reading ἀνθονομούσας, see Whittle (1964) 24-29. Surely it is the sexual connotation of flowers which makes their gathering the standard occupation of the ravished maidens of antiquity, a custom noted in Dale (1967) 82, n. 244.

[24] Murray (1958) 69 thinks it refers to the Danaids, while Rose (1957) 20 thinks it refers to Epaphos.

Literally, of course, the child of the cow is Epaphos; however, the chorus appears to be intensifying its sense of identification with the ancestral line, since any dishonor to Epaphos is in this case figurative, and the phrase is only a circumlocution for dishonor to the Danaids themselves. Increasingly they think of themselves as "children of the cow" (1958: 24).

The Danaids' also refer to themselves as σπέρματ' εὐτέκνου βοός ("seed of a fruitful cow", 275; cf. 141, 151), and on one occasion describe themselves as a heifer (350-353). Both identifications made by the Danaids, that with Io and that with Epaphos, are explicable in light of the importance attached by psychoanalytic theory to the girl's identification with her mother (Lampl-de Groot 1928: 330) and to her desire to have a child that is a double of herself (Brown 1959: 127).

In the fantasy of the Danaids, the relationship between Zeus, the father they love, and Io, the mother with whom they identify, is clear enough — Zeus is the lover and savior of Io — but two factors in the relationship are particularly significant: the miraculous conception of Epaphos and the tortured wanderings of Io.

The rescue of Io and the conception of Epaphos are accomplished not by an explicit sexual act but by the breath and touch of Zeus (lines 17, 44, 535, 576-577, 1066-1067). The divine child, with whom the Danaids also identify themselves, is conceived immaculately. The frequent occurrence of immaculate conception in myth and religion (cf. Jesus in Christian myth or Quetzalcoatl in Aztec myth) stems ultimately from the child's refusal to believe that the mother is not a virgin (Jones 1923: 357). This refusal may be due to the over-valuation of the pre oedipal mother, to the infantile sadistic perception of intercourse (Bonaparte 1966: 132-134), or to the oedipal situation in which the child wishes to preserve the parent of the opposite sex for itself. In the event that the female child in the oedipal situation intensely identifies with the mother, intolerable tension may develop. On the one hand, she wishes to have the father to herself and to deny the mother sexual access to the father; on the other hand, vicarious satisfaction of her own desires may be attained through identification with the mother as sexual object of the father. This tension is portrayed in the *Suppliants* through the ambiguity surrounding the virginity of Io and through the non-sexual conception of Epaphos, the divine child who must be born as the child the Danaids are to receive from the father. Because the tension must accept both possibilities, the tortured wanderings of Io are both the punishment for her sexual relationship with the father (Wayne 1951: 216) and also the projection by the Danaids of their own incestuous guilt feelings (Freud 1917). Significantly, it is not Zeus, as in the *Prometheus* but Hera who is the chief agent of Io's suffering. Murray remarks cryptically that "Hera is, moreover, only an aspect of the deity" (1958: 57, n.3) but Hera is surely that aspect of the oedipal and pre-oedipal mother which forbids and punishes infantile desires.

THE PSYCHOLOGY OF THE *SUPPLIANTS*

The main points of this psychoanalytic interpretation of the *Suppliants* and the answers that are provided by it to the play's traditional problems may be summarized as follows, before going on to see how it affects our understanding of the entire Danaid trilogy:

1.   The *Suppliants* is a complex elaboration in dramatic form of two common mythical situations: the father who denies prospective suitors access to his desirable daughter, and the maiden who flees in fear from any sexual encounter.

2.   Because of this incestuous attachment to their father, the Danaids are unable to love other men and view potential usurpers of Danaos' position as violent rapists.

3.   The incestuous fantasy is concealed (and managed) by the Danaids through a series of substitutions in which Danaos is replaced by Pelasgos and Zeus, the play's two figures of paternal power and dominance (just as myths and cultures regularly project the father's authority onto kings and gods).

4.   Just as their father is replaced, ultimately, by Zeus in the Danaids' fantasy, their unnamed mothers are replaced by their ancestress Io, whom Zeus loved, whom the Danaids refer to as "mother," and with whom they identify.

5.   The Danaids' aversion to marriage is not caused by the violence and repulsiveness of the sons of Aigyptos, but itself causes the mixture of fear and hatred with which they regard their cousins. The aversion itself is doubly determined: on one hand they are saving themselves for the father they love; on the other hand their hysterical fear of sex is a common attribute of the ravished maidens of myth and has its modern counterpart in the typical anxieties which prospective sexual activity produces in an adolescent girl.

6.   Critics have uniformly complained of the "wooden" characterization of Danaos, especially his long awkward silences, his inept advice, and his abrupt departure when the Egyptians appear. While the play was thought to be primitive, these "faults" could be explained by reference to Aeschylus' inexperience in handling a second actor, but such explanations will no longer do. Danaos is a father who has been replaced by Pelasgos and Zeus in his daughters' fantasy; his silence or absence while the Danaids argue with Pelasgos or pray to Zeus is a sign that he has been replaced, whereas his presence, required to reveal the core of the fantasy, is nevertheless an embarrassment. His fatuous speeches are a reminder of the infantile nature

of the fantasy, and his jealous concern for his daughters' virginity (even at the end of the play, when he seems to see the men of Argos as an equal threat) indicates his complicity in their fixation.

7. The absolute authority which the Danaids attribute to Pelasgos, at variance with his actual role as a constitutional monarch who needs the consent of his people, nevertheless conforms with his status in the Danaids' fantasy as a replacement for the omnipotent oedipal father.

8. Of all Greek tragedies the *Suppliants* contains the most expansive and absolute statements of the omnipotence and omniscience of Zeus. This is probably not, as some have thought, a monotheistic theological statement by Aeschylus. It is a statement by the Danaids of the qualities invested in the father of childhood and now transferred to the deity. The replacement of Danaos by Zeus is an unconscious effort by the Danaids to maintain their oedipal fixation while at the same time suppressing its incestuous aspect.

9. Although Io is their great-great-great-grandmother, the Danaids clearly identify her both with their mother(s) and with themselves. They repeatedly call her mother, but they also find in her a double of themselves, both actually and wishfully. The situation is contradictory they view Io both as a woman who, like them, renounced sexuality in the face of threatening masculinity, and also as a mother who was loved by the father but contradiction is the ordinary discourse of the unconscious. Io's tortured wanderings are both her punishment for keeping the father to herself and a projection by the Danaids of their own incestuous guilt.

10. The immaculate conception of Epaphos follows from the roles of Io and Zeus as fantasized mother and father. The Danaids deny authentic sexuality to this relationship because they wish to have the father for themselves and to deny the mother sexual access to him; at the same time they strengthen their own identification with Io by assigning her to a state of quasi-virginity.

THE PSYCHOLOGY OF THE DANAID TRILOGY

Bound by a compulsive repetition of the past and an obsessive attachment to their father (an attachment which can only be intensified by the series of substitutions it goes through), the Danaids exemplify the abdication of individual will by members of a group (the choros as protagonist). The necessary step to individuation and maturity is a sexual initiative, the transformation of a girl in love with her father into a woman able to love other men, and this step will be taken by Hypermestra.

For both Freud and Aeschylus, an essential and continuing task of man is the struggle to free oneself from the past, in a way that is not self-mutilating but liberating. In the Danaids' relationship with Io, their equation of the mother of fantasy with the ancestress of the race, we see a portrayal of the grip in which a person is held by the past, whether the individual past that begins with birth or the supra-individual past that includes everything which can still affect the present. As Freud wrote, "the human individual has to devote himself to the great task of detaching himself from his parents, and not until that task is achieved can he cease to be a child and become a member of the social community" (1916-1917: 337).

In the final play of the trilogy, the Danaids' unitary fantasy of themselves as living out the determined repetition of the passion of Io a fantasy which "is not just a memory, but the hallucinatory re-animation of memory, a mode of self-delusion substituting the past for the present" (Brown 1959: 164) is shattered by Hypermestra, who frees herself from the collective neurosis, liberates repressed Eros, and emerges as an individual (Winnington-Ingram 1961: 146-147, 151). The reason for Hypermestra's action is given in the *Prometheus*:

μίαν δὲ παίδων ἵμερος θέλξει τὸ μὴ
κτεῖναι σύνευνον

But desire will charm one of the girls from killing her bed-partner. (865-866)

Much energy has been expended in the debate over whether παίδων refers to μίαν or ἵμερος.[25] There is no reason, however, to excise the ambiguity which Aeschylus put into the phrase, Hypermestra desires both children and her new husband. Her refusal to obey her father symbolizes her inner freedom from the father who restricts love as well as from the desire to have a child from the father. While her sisters continue bound to the compulsive repetition of the past and their pathological subjection to their father, Hypermestra is freed from the burden of her own past and that of her race. The child she desires and the love she feels are no longer products of fantasy, but for the first time are firmly situated in reality. As the one sizable extant fragment of the *Danaids* indicates, the Eros which wins over Hypermestra is no private illusion; it is the universal reality which "compels the earth to undergo marriage" and which ensures the generation and sustenance of all life (Fr. 125 M). It is through the liberation of this Eros in her own life that Hypermestra is enabled to escape the illusions of the group, its tendency "constantly to give what is unreal precedence over what is real" (Freud 1921: 80). At the same time, emergence from the bondage of infantile sexuality brings with it the realization of her own individuality, as her love for Lynkeus makes it possible for her to break away from the group. In Freud's words, "two people coming together for the purpose of sexual satisfaction are making a demonstration against the herd instinct, the group feeling" (1921: 140).

---

[25] For the various arguments, see Garvie (1969) 225-226. It sometimes seems in this dispute that the virtue of Hypermestra depends on παίδων modifying ἵμερος.

This notion of the climactic struggle to be free from the burden of the past is clearly a dominant characteristic of Aeschylean tragedy. The conclusions of the Danaid trilogy and of the *Prometheia* may well have asserted on a cosmic level the *Oresteia*'s dramatization of mankind's perennial task of overcoming the personal, familial, and political past. As Dodds said "the liberation of the individual from the bonds of clan and family is one of the major achievements of Greek rationalism" (1951: 34). But this liberation is not simply a negation of the past. The past is ambiguous in its effect and so also is that which breaks the hold of the past and forms the future. In a vision that went beyond morality, Aeschylus saw that on every level, from the psychic to the cosmic, the hope and shape of the future was contained in the effort to overcome the past. Because all possibilities are ultimately rooted in the past, the focus of the struggle contains a necessary ambivalence: whether the outcome will be beneficial or not depends on how the weight of the past is experienced and confronted in the present, whether it is allowed to carry everything with it to destruction or is transformed as the basis of a new life.

In the Danaid trilogy, the transition from past to future is centered on the transfer of love from father to husband. Eros, which appears everywhere else in the plays of Aeschylus as irrational and destructive, appears in the trilogy first as completely indeterminate, then as a tentative alternative to the Danaids' fanatic chastity, finally as the vindication of Hypermestra. In the first instance (521), Eros is the desire of the Danaids for the undefined object of their prayers, presumably that they will be successful in obtaining help from the citizens of Argos. In the second (1042), the Erotes are connected with Aphrodite in the servant girls' warning to the Danaids that marriage is the natural lot of women. In the third instance, from the *Danaids*, it is Eros which compels the earth to marry the sky, a universal sanction of Hypermestra's choice. The phrasing in the first and third instances is virtually identical, with one important exception:

τῶν σ' ἔρως ἔχει τυχεῖν *Suppliants* 521

ἔρως δὲ Γαῖαν λαμβάνει γάμου τ]υ[χ]ε[ῖν, fr. 125M

In the former, the object of Eros is the indefinite τῶν; in the latter, it is γάμου (marriage).

The tragedy of the Danaids is that they separate themselves from the universal love which alone can do what Danaos, Pelasgos, and even Zeus cannot do, that is, rescue from their self-imposed isolation the φυγάδες περίδρομοι, the fugitives in flight from themselves. The Danaids can no more easily cut themselves off from men than Zeus in the *Prometheus* can cut himself off from mortals; love is as necessary for them as compassionate reason is for him. This does not mean that Zeus will necessarily change, nor does it mean that the Danaids will change. An evolution which allows no alternatives would negate the ambivalence of the force which makes change possible and would reduce the future to a pre-ordained outcome. The emphasis lies squarely on the openness of possibilities, whether to repeat the past or to transform the future. In the ambiguity of great power, great resources, or great emotions, even those possibilities which appear as opposites are contained. The Eumenides are still the Erinyes, and where Eros is weak (or the destructive Eros holds sway), death and strife are strong; but the hope and expectation of Aeschylus may well have been the same as that of Freud, "that the other of the two 'Heavenly Powers,' eternal Eros, will make an effort to assert himself in the struggle with his equally immortal adversary" (1930: 145).

AESCHYLUS AND FEMALE PSYCHOLOGY

If we grant that Freud is correct at least in his belief that a prolonged overinvolvement of father and daughter may inhibit the daughter's ability to love other men, the correspondence between this theory and the situation of the Danaids in the *Suppliants* raises the question of how Aeschylus could write so revealingly and (from a psychoanalytic viewpoint) correctly about female psychology? An obvious answer would be that this ability is part of what makes an artist great, that Aeschylus, like Shakespeare, was not limited to the perspective of his gender. To escape this limitation may be difficult, but it certainly is not impossible, any more than it is impossible for a homosexual dramatist to write about heterosexual psychology or for a white novelist to write about black psychology or for a female poet to write about male psychology.

At the same time it must be admitted that anything we now say about women's feelings or thinking or psychology in ancient Greece is largely analogy, since (with the notable exception of Sappho) all of our sources are male:

> beyond the dominant ideology of the male, which purports to account for society in its totality, there existed ... another social reality constructed by women in which not only their own role and nature, but also those of men, might have been construed in a significantly different fashion ... but the evidence for it is not recoverable (Just 1989: 3).

Thus another answer might be that Aeschylus is not portraying female psychology at all, but rather male psychology, that what he says about the Danaids and their predicament is from a male viewpoint. Their predicament, after all, is not original with Aeschylus but is found in the body of myth which was the source of almost all Greek tragedy and which almost always represents a male viewpoint.

According to this line of reasoning the Danaid myth is an example of one of the most common patterns in Greek myth, the story of a daughter whose father does not want her to marry and therefore sets up apparently insurmountable obstacles in the way of her prospective suitors. While this pattern is ubiquitous in Greek myth, it is especially frequent in Argive myth, particularly in versions connecting it with conflict between brothers (who are often twins). The closest parallel to the Danaid story, in fact, concerns the rivalry of the Danaid Hypermestra's twin grandsons Akrisios and Proitos; Akrisios, like Danaos, does not want his daughter Danae to marry anyone, but his brother Proitos is in love with her. In the case of Aigyptos this desire is displaced onto the desire of his sons to marry the daughters of Danaos, and Danaos meanwhile manifests the usual characteristics of the mythic father who will not allow his daughter(s) to marry because he wants to keep her for himself. The closest parallels are with Oinomaos, father of Hippodameia, and Akrisios, father of Danae. Like Oinomaos, who "was in love with her himself" (Apollodoros, *Epitome* 2.4), Danaos refuses to let his daughter marry, receives an oracle warning of disaster if he does, contrives the death of the suitors, and even stages a version of the traditional suitors' race. Like Akrisios Danaos refuses to let his daughters marry because he receives a cautionary prophecy and locks up his daughter Hypermestra under guard, just as Akrisios does with Danae. The parallel between Danaos and Akrisios extends even further, since both myths are based on a conflict between twins over sexual possession of the daughter(s) of one of them. In the first myth Danaos strives to preserve his daughters' virginity, while Aigyptos, through the representation of his sons, attempts to win sexual possession of them; in the second Akrisios seeks to keep his daughter Danae inviolate, while his brother Proitos (without any displacement of desire onto sons) in one version manages to seduce Danae despite his brother's prohibition.

The psychology of this type of myth is indeed oedipal, but it is that of the male oedipus complex, in which the son wants to have the sole possession of his mother's attention and affection and sees his father as the jealous and possessive prohibitor of his wishes. The Danaids (like Danae, Hippodameia, Alkestis, Iole, etc.) are the forbidden objects of desire, kept unmarried by a dominant and powerful father until the right hero appears (in the Danaid myth this would be Lynkeus). Virtually every element in the Danaid version finds a parallel elsewhere; decapitation is also the fate of the unsuccessful suitors of Hippodameia, and death at the hands of the desired daughter comes to the suitors of Atalanta as to the husbands of the Danaids.

And yet, even if we grant that the basic structure of the story (with its built-in psychological component) pre-existed the version of Aeschylus, nevertheless it is in Aeschylus' version that we first find emphasized those elements which seem to reflect the fantasies of a daughter rather than of a son and it is precisely these elements (the role of Danaos and his connection with the portrayals of Zeus and Pelasgos, the identification of the Danaids with Io and Epaphos) which have posed great problems for critics. The genius of Aeschylus, it seems, has been to take a familiar collection of motifs in a given structure, then reverse the usual situation by viewing it through the eyes of the oedipal daughter.

THE PSYCHOLOGY OF INITIATION RITUAL

For those still unwilling, however, to grant that the man Aeschylus could compose a drama based on the psychology of women, there remains another possible, if undemonstrable, explanation of Aeschylus' "feminine" sensitivity in elaborating the identifications of the Danaids with Io and of Danaos with Pelasgos and Zeus. Perhaps these aspects of the drama were not invented by Aeschylus but rather derived from lost versions of the story connected with girls' initiation rituals.

We know next to nothing about what the Danaid story was like prior to its treatment by Aeschylus. Our earlier sources consist of a few meager fragments from the Hesiodic *Catalogue of Women* and two lines from the epic *Danais* both probably composed in the 6th century (West 1985: 136, but see Bernal 1987: 97 for an earlier dating of the *Danais*). Nevertheless a strong argument has recently been made by K. Dowden that the Danaid myth, like the genealogically related myths of Io and the daughters of Proitos, belongs to a large set of narratives which "correspond to the passage rites from maidenhood to the status of married women" (Dowden 1989: 4). In this interpretation the Danaids represent an age-group, the "daughters of the Danaoi tribe" (Dowden 1989: 157), a choros of fifty girls who in ritual performance enact first the rejection of marriage (flight from the suitors and their murder) and then acceptance of marriage (Hypermestra and the foot-race arranged for the other Danaids). Dowden's analysis is totally innocent of psychology, and yet a maiden-to-matron initiation exactly fits the psychoanalytic interpretation I have tried to make. Freud, Aeschylus, and initiation-theory all come together in the idea of breaking with the past so that society and individual can successfully advance. For Freud, as we saw earlier, the renunciation of oedipal fantasies in puberty is necessary in order to achieve "detachment from parental authority, a process that alone makes possible the opposition, which is so important for the progress of civiliza-tion, between the new generation and the old" (1905: 226). For Aeschylus, the same idea of escaping from and transforming the past so that a new and better future can be achieved is the central theme of the *Oresteia* and almost certainly of the *Prometheia* and Danaid-trilogy as well. And what better myth could there be in which to find this theme encapsulated than one connected with initiation and the transformation of a girl enclosed by her family and the past into a woman entering the future and her role in the social order?

It would seem to be precisely this kind of myth which could provide Aeschylus with the pattern elaborated in the *Suppliants*. We might reasonably expect that the hypothetical initiation myth would concern a girl whose attachment to her father (and mother) must be released, as well as a father whose proprietary claim on his daughter must be ended. We might also expect that this attachment be extended to king and god as well, just as Zeus appears in the exemplary myth of Io as god, king, and their representatives figure in the wide-spread practice of the *ius primae noctis*. And finally we might expect that the choros of Danaid maidens, in accordance with the basic principle of ritual to repeat a momentous and paradigmatic past event, would enact in identificatory repetition the triumphant ordeal of Io.

The Danaid trilogy was produced along with a satyr-drama, the *Amymone* whose plot probably was similar to the version of Apollodoros (2.1.4-5): Danaos sent his daughters to look for water; one of them, Amymone, threw a spear at a deer and happened to hit a sleeping satyr, who was aroused and desired to have intercourse with her; when she cried out, Poseidon appeared and the satyr fled; so Amymone slept with Poseidon, he showed her the springs at Lerna, and she became the mother of the illustrious Nauplios. For Dowden, "Amymone is an exceptional Danaid, a named individual who ... has nothing to do with the story of the fifty Danaids who flee the Egyptians" (1989: 151). It is true that Amymone presumably does not figure in the plot of the trilogy. Still it is clear that she is the double of the other named Danaid, Hypermestra, in that both of them come to regard sexuality, which they had first rejected, as something desirable (and the same must be true, ultimately, of the other Danaids as well). In fact the plot of the *Amymone* reflects in miniature the story of the trilogy, and could also have served as the myth of an initiation rite: the satyr may be compared to the sons of Aigyptos, lustful beasts in the eyes of the Danaids, and Poseidon, Amymone's rescuer and lover, is equivalent to his brother Zeus and the other paternal figures to whom the Danaids appeal for protection and ultimately for love.

Even the phallocentric discourse of Lacan fits into this picture. If the original desire of the Danaids to have the phallus of the father is eventually replaced by a new desire to have the phallus of a husband, the same transformation is the specific goal of the hypothetical initiation rite. And this transformation is the line of demarcation between the world of the family which must be left behind and the social order which, in fact, is constituted by this transformation. The central theme of Lacan and that of the initiation rite are the same: the exchange of women in society is parallel to, and dependent on, the exchange of the phallus within the family.

les femmes dans le réel servent, ne leur en déplaise, d'objets pour les échanges qu'ordonnent les structures élémentaires de la parenté ... tandis que ce qui se transmet parallèlement dans l'ordre symbolique, c'est le phallus (1966a: 565).

BIBLIOGRAPHY

References to Freud's works are cited by year, title, and volume number in *The Standard Edition of the Complete Psychological Works of Sigmund Freud*, ed. J. Strachey, A. Freud, A. Strachey, and A. Tyson. 24 vol. (London: 1964-1973). The text of Aeschylus used and cited is that of Gilbert Murray, *OCT* 2nd ed. (1955).

Bardwick J. (1971) *The Psychology of Women* (New York: 1971).
Bernal M. (1987) *Black Athena* vol. I, (New Brunswick: 1987).
Bonaparte M. (1966) "Passivity, Masochism and Femininity", in *Psychoanalysis and Female Sexuality*, ed. H.M. Ruitenbeek (New Haven: 1966).
Brophy B. (1962) *Black Ship to Hell* (London: 1962).
Brown N. (1959) *Life Against Death* (New York: 1959).
Cook A. (1940) *Zeus*, vol. III (Cambridge: 1940).
Dale A. (1967) *Euripides' Helena* (Oxford: 1967).
Devereux G. (1976) *Dreams in Greek Tragedy* (Berkeley: 1976).
Diamontopoulos A. (1957) "The Danaid Trilogy of Aeschylus", *Journal of Hellenic Studies* 77 (1957) 220-229.
Dodds E. (1951) *The Greeks and the Irrational* (Berkeley: 1951).
Dowden K. (1989) *Death and the Maiden* (London: 1989).
Forrest W. (1960) "Themistocles and Argos", *Classical Quarterly* 10 (1960) 221-241.
Freud S. (1900) *The Interpretation of Dreams* IV-V.
—— (1905) "Three Essays on the Theory of Sexuality", VII.
—— (1909) "Family Romances", IX.
—— (1911) "Formulations on the Two Principles of Mental Functioning", XXI.
—— (1913) *Totem and Taboo*, XIII.
—— (1916-1917) *Introductory Lectures on Psycho-Analysis*, XV-XVI.
—— (1917) "A Metapsychological Supplement to the Theory of Dreams", XIV.
—— (1918) "The Taboo of Virginity", XI.
—— (1919) "Preface to Reik, *Ritual: Psychoanalytic Studies*", XVII.
—— (1921) *Group Psychology and the Analysis of the Ego*, XVIII.
—— (1925) "An Autobiographical Study", XX.
—— (1927) *The Future of an Illusion*, XXI.
—— (1928a) "A Religious Experience", XXI.
—— (1928b) "Dostoevsky and Parricide," XXI.
—— (1930) *Civilization and its Discontents*, XXI.
—— (1931) "Female Sexuality", XXI.
—— (1933) *New Introductory Lectures*, XXII.
Garvie A. (1969) *Aeschylus' Supplices: Play and Trilogy* (Cambridge: 1969).
Golden L. (1962) *In Praise of Prometheus* (Chapel Hill: 1962).
Jones E. (1923) "The Madonna's Conception through the Ear", *Essays in Applied Psychoanalysis* (London: 1923).
—— (1927) "The Early Development of Female Sexuality", *International Journal of Psychoanalysis* 8 (1927) 459-472.
Just R. (1989) *Women in Athenian Law and Life* (London: 1989).
Kitto H. (1961) *Greek Tragedy* (London: ³1961).
—— (1966) *Poesis* (Berkeley: 1966).
Kouretas D. (1957) "Application de la psychanalyse à la mythologie: la névrose sexuelle des Danaides d'après les 'Suppliantes' d'Eschyle", *Revue française de Psychanalyse* 21 (1957) 597-602.
Lacan J. (1966a) "D'une question préliminaire à tout traitement possible de la psychose", *Ecrits* (Paris: 1966) 531-583.
—— (1966b) "La signification du phallus", *Ecrits* (Paris: 1966) 685-695.

—— (1966c) "Propos directifs pour un Congrès sur la sexualité feminine", *Ecrits* (Paris: 1966) 725-736.

Lampl-de Groot J. (1928) "The Evolution of the Oedipus Complex in Women," *International Journal of Psycho-Analysis* 9 (1928) 332-345.

Lattimore R. (1964) *Story Patterns in Greek Tragedy* (Ann Arbor: 1964).

Lesky A. (1954) "Die Datierung der *Hiketiden* und der Tragiker Mesatos", *Hermes* 82 (1954) 1-13.

Lloyd-Jones H. (1964) "The 'Supplices' of Aeschylus: the New Date and Old Problems", *L'Antiquité Classique* 33 (1964) 356-374.

Méautis G. (1936) *Eschyle et la Trilogie* (Paris: 1936).

Murray G. (1930) *Aeschylus: The Suppliant Women* (London: 1930).

Murray R. (1958) *The Motif of Io in Aeschylus' Suppliants* (Princeton: 1958).

Rank O. (1952) *The Myth of the Birth of the Hero*, trans. Robbins and S.E. Jelliffe (New York: 1952).

Rank O. and Sachs H. (1964) "The Significance of Psychoanalysis for the Humanities", in *Psychoanalysis as an Art and a Science*, ed. Slochower (Detroit: 1964).

Rose H. (1957) *A Commentary on the Surviving Plays of Aeschylus* (Amsterdam: 1957).

Segal C. "The Tragedy of the *Hippolytus*: The Waters of Ocean and the Untouched Meadow", *Harvard Studies in Classical Philology* 70 (1965) 117-169.

Sissa G. (1990) *Greek Virginity*, trans. A. Goldhammer (Cambridge: 1990).

Slater P. (1968) *The Glory of Hera* (Boston: 1968).

Smyth H. (1924) *Aeschylean Tragedy* (Berkeley: 1924).

te Riele G. (1955) *Les femmes chez Eschyle* (Groningen: 1955).

Thass-Thienemann T. (1967) *The Subconscious Language* (New York: 1967).

van Ophuijsen J. (1924) "Contributions to the Masculinity Complex in Women", *International Journal of Psycho-Analysis* 5 (1924) 39-49.

Wayne R. (1951) "Prometheus and Christ" in *Psychoanalysis and the Social Sciences*, vol. III (New York: 1951).

West M. (1985) *The Hesiodic Catalogue of Women* (Oxford: 1985).

Whittle E. (1964) "Two Notes on Aeschylus *Supplices*", *Classical Quarterly* 14 (1964) 24-31.

Winkler J. (1990) *The Constraints of Desire* (New York: 1990).

Winnington-Ingram R. (1961) "The Danaid Trilogy of Aeschylus", *Journal of Hellenic Studies* 61 (1961) 141-152.

Yates S. (1930) "An Investigation of the Psychological Factors in Virginity and Ritual Defloration", *International Journal of Psycho-Analysis* 11 (1930) 167-184.

ELEKTRA'S *KLEOS APHTHITON*: SOPHOKLES INTO OPERA

BY

MARIANNE MCDONALD

Introduction. Theoretical Exposition: Opera as Classical Nachleben and Interpretative Tool

Sophokles' Elektra is a heroine in the Homeric tradition, and she has truly gained the *kleos aphthiton* (κλέος ἄφθιτον), the "immortal fame," so beloved by Achilles. Different ages resonate this fame differently, but in opera it is as clear as ever. It leads to more understanding and appreciation of the Sophoklean original at the same time that it creates a new work of art.

Modern performances of ancient Greek tragedy involve us in a complicated system of what Aristotle calls δέσις and λύσις, "tying" and "untying." We see the conjunction of the ancient and the modern as we see ourselves in the ancient characters. Our individual problems may be insoluble, but we appreciate their resemblance to the problems others have always had, and thereby lift ourselves out of our own limited self-relevance and onto a higher plane of experience and suffering. It is *katharsis* squared, because superficially we seem to have even less in common with Agamemnon, Klytemnestra and Elektra than the original Greek audience did — we do not believe in their gods; we do not live in small, integrated city-states; we do not share their values and aspirations — but for this very reason, our response, as a modern audience, may be even more profound than that of the original audience two and one-half millennia ago in the Theatre of Dionysos.

If the modern performance is not just a translation of the original Greek text presented in spoken form by actors on a stage, but rather an operatic adaptation, with music and dance supplementing the text, then our experience is again enriched and elevated. Ancient Greek tragedy was originally presented in alternating passages of spoken and sung verbal exchanges: generally, the action moves forward in the dialogue sections spoken by the actors, and the chorus then provides commentary and meditation in their lyrics, which were accompanied by the flute, and choreographed.

At the end of the 16th century in Florence, a group, or *Camerata*, formalized ideas of Giovanni de' Bardi and Vincenzo Galilei (following the philologist Girolamo Mei) about ancient Greek music, and applied these

ideas to texts accompanied by music.[1] Expanded musical versions of Greek
drama with its rich mythology constituted our first operas. We remember
Nietzsche's famous study on tragedy as derived from music, *Die Geburt der
Tragödie aus dem Geiste der Musik*.[2] It is our loss that we do not have the
music that accompanied ancient drama so that we could know how abstract,
programmatic, lyrical, or percussive the music actually was.[3] Nevertheless,
music accompanied drama, and opera reinstates the prominence of music.
By altering verbal texts and adding musical commentary, modern opera
gives us new insights into the ancient plays.

We see the obvious analogy with ancient tragedy in the operas by Mozart
since he divides his libretto between arias and recitatives: the action moves
forward in the recitatives, and we learn from the characters in their arias
how they feel about these developments. A verbal text set to music is by
nature more abstract and more philosophical — indeed, more idealized —
than a simple spoken utterance. As Nietzsche said, speaking of Schopenhauer, "He conceded to music a character and an origin different from all
the other arts, because, unlike them, it is not a copy of the phenomenon, but
an immediate copy of the will itself, and therefore complements *everything
physical in the world*, and every phenomenon by representing *what is
metaphysical*, the thing in itself."[4] Again, it is further from our own
everyday experience and we receive it differently. A musical setting
simultaneously invites us into the character's own peculiar emotional range
and universalizes these emotions.

I maintain that these two dimensions — the profound response of the
modern audience to the seemingly alien matter of ancient Greek tragedy, and
the elevating and universalizing effect of music — make the experience of
a modern opera based on Greek tragedy an extraordinarily demanding and
rewarding one. I might run the risk of sounding like Wagner in his
theoretical writings, i.e. pompous and prescriptive, but the *Elektra* by
Richard Strauss and a few other masterpieces of that genre involve us in an
almost religious ritual: we worship not some god, or even some philosophi-

---

[1] "At the end of the sixteenth century a small group of aristocratic intelligentsia ... [had] the
avowed intention ... to reproduce as far as possible the combination of words and music which
together made up Greek theatre," Harewood (1987) 3. See also Sadie (1989) 15-16.

[2] See Silk and Stern (1990). There is an interesting discussion of this work and its relation
to opera in Lindenberger (1985).

[3] For a summary of what we know about ancient Greek music, see Barker (1989); he quotes
Plutarch and Aristophanes to show how the ancients viewed the difference between the three
major playwrights of Greek tragedy: "Aeschylus is noted for his grave simplicity, Sophocles
... for his elegant and full-bodied sweetness, and Euripides for his delicate fancy, dismissed as
airy trifles by Aristophanes, but much admired in his own time and later," (1989) I. 62-3.
Barker also speaks of the origin of tragedy, citing Aristotle: "The origins of the drama lie in
the forms that were essentially choral song and dance," I. 62. This reflects Aristotle's view that
tragedy was linked with the dithyramb in origin. See also Commoti (1989).

[4] Nietzsche (1967) 100.

cal concept, but rather the rarified and clarified essence of human emotion. We hear ourselves in elevated song.

Music itself is a new critical tool which can aid in interpreting historical periods and social issues. Theodor Adorno applied Hegelian classifications to music, which Edward Said in his brilliant *Musical Elaborations* has rejected, opting for "an alternative based on a geographical or spatial idea that is truer to the diversity and spread of human activity."[5] We see a movement from Adorno's abstractions to the particular.

Michael Ewans argues for the use of opera to interpret classics: "The opera successfully transmutes a τραγῳδία of the late fifth century B.C. into a *tragödie* of our own century ... with the images of the ancient drama and the modern reflecting each other in mutual admiration."[6] He interprets Elektra as created by Sophokles and Strauss, together with his librettist Hugo von Hofmannsthal, as, in the one case, "corrupted by her desire for vengeance to a level of savagery at least as low as that of the original criminals," and, in the other, "the sole rebel against a decaying, dictatorial system of monarchy so entrenched that, in fighting against it for human values, she loses them herself and is destroyed from within."[7]

Bryan Gilliam also shows how the music enhances interpretation. He cites Strauss in his informative and sensitive study of Strauss's *Elektra*, saying "that his musical setting both intensified the dramaturgy, especially through 'the force of its climaxes', and structural unity."[8]

Catherine Clément and Susan McClary give feminist readings to music, with tonality and masculine cadences seen as tools to tame the atonal chromatic female.[9] Each shows that rigid musical forms can reflect the rigidity of societies and countries that created them.

---

[5] Said (1991) xviii.

[6] Ewans (1984) 151-2. Although his work is invaluable, I find he reduces Aischylos' complexity, for instance, in saying, "In Wagner's trilogy the final resolution of the dilemmas, which become more entrenched as the cycle unfolds, comes not — as in Aischylos — from the calm judgement of Athena, goddess of wisdom incarnate, but from the furious anger of a woman scorned: Brunnhilde learns the wisdom needed to resolve the action of the *Ring* not through the power of reason but through her sufferings and jealousy, after Siegfried has betrayed her," Ewans (1984) 139. I feel this is a misreading of Aischylos, who claimed that one learned through suffering, and this was the violent grace afforded man by the gods (*Ag.* 176-83). And for a sensitive reading of the problematic ending of the *Oresteia*, which is hardly resolved by "the calm judgement of Athena," see Rosenmeyer (1982).

[7] Ewans (1984) 151 and 137. He claims, "As conceived by Strauss, Elektra truly has an Elektra complex," (145). I say she has more autonomy, as I shall argue in my text.

[8] Gilliam (1991) 104-5, quoting Schuh (1953) 154. Gilliam is also essential reading for those who wish to know the aetiology of Strauss's composition of the *Elektra*. His bibliography is to be recommended for those interested in the latest, and also some of the older and most important works, on Strauss's *Elektra*.

[9] Clément (1988). Many of Clément's ideas are echoed, varied and sometimes more subtly defined by McClary (1991). McClary wrote the introduction to Clément's book.

Catherine Clément has written of opera as the undoing of women. She is consistent in her application of this theory to Strauss's opera *Elektra*, and she interprets the character Elektra narrowly as the instrument of two males: her father Agamemnon and her brother Orestes. According to Clément, Elektra, as her mother before her, simply carries out phallocratic dictates, and, "The dawn rising over Mycenae is the dawn of our repression."[10] These views are echoed by Specht and Overhoff, so that, "Elektra seems no more than a vessel to contain mourning, the mirror that reflects Agamemnon: he is the 'true hero' of the opera."[11]

Susan McClary would like to call Elektra's death madness, but I think this undercuts the heroism of her climactic dance.[12] Since Foucault, madness has been increasingly seen as difficult to define. Who defines it and what are the underlying epistemological or political premises of the definition? When bombing of certain countries is called a defense of freedom, but bombing by others acts of terrorism, one sees the power wielded by rhetoric.

I think the time is ripe for feminist interpretations of predominantly male-dominated art forms, but a disservice is rendered both artists and women when these interpretations contribute to a new restrictive code in which female characters are not allowed the freedom of the males. It seems to me perverse that a man can die in glory or as a result of passion, as Ajax does, or Werther, Tristan, Romeo, Siegfried, while women are deprived of this defining and passionate gesture because of the dictates of a new political correctness. A comparable criticism applied to the male would say all of these characters (except Ajax, who is quite explicit in rejecting female dominance, or even influence, from Athena to Tekmessa) died or committed suicide mainly as a result of being dominated by female characters.

I would like to suggest a different reading, one that would empower Elektra again with the autonomy and yearning for freedom that Sophokles originally gave her. I claim Elektra acts in a complex way to bring about the goals of her particular passions, and, like Clément and Ewans, I shall use the modern opera as my critical tool for elucidating Sophokles' controversial heroine, whose significance Heiner Müller thinks is important for under-

---

[10] In addition she claims, "From crime to crime ... the family history is perpetuated. It can come to an end later only though the intervention of men and the invention of law ... The women, the survivors, fight one another, each one the bearer of a man ... the mother, dead ... with her the historic undoing and defeat of femininity begins ... The victorious woman, the one who defends the father's power, will, with her vengeance, have betrayed the cause of women," Clément (1988) 76-7.

[11] See Abbate (1989) 111. She cites elucidating statements by Overhoff (1978) and Specht (1921).

[12] "The chromatic excess of the madwoman became even more intense with Elektra ...," Clément (1988) 101.

standing the present: "In the century of Orestes and Elektra that's rising, *Oedipus* will be a comedy."[13]

The *Elektra* by Sophokles can be better understood if read against modern times and in particular against the opera by Strauss and Hofmannsthal; this Medusa is best apprehended in the reflection afforded us by the later version. Critical theory shows that the *Nachleben* of a work in its own way creates a new work which is not only a unique work of art for its own time, but allows a critical reevaluation of the ancient work. This complicated history of revival and recreation is traced, for instance, in the first chapter of George Steiner's *Antigones: How the Antigone Legend Has Endured in Western Literature, Art, and Thought*, besides being the prominent theme of my *Euripides in Cinema: The Heart Made Visible* and *Ancient Sun, Modern Light: Greek Drama on the Modern Stage.*[14]

Teilhard de Chardin said, "The universe as we know it is a joint product of the observer and the observed." The Heisenberg principle also shows how the observer can alter the observed in the act of observing. This applies to later interpretations of the classics. There is no longer a Sophoklean *Elektra* per se, but rather a complex configuration that is a cultural lightning rod for the time, country and creator that choose to recreate it.

I shall try to sort out some of the strands and show how Sophokles and Strauss/Hofmannsthal set up a dialectic between past and present that helps mutual definition. In both Elektra manifests a heroism and concern for the *genos* (clan) which sets up a rich resonance for understanding our own times.

I think Sophokles' Elektra is a valid heroine in her own right, dominated only by her own passionate choices. She kills in the service of freedom and in Strauss's version freely dances to death at the climax of her career. In this opera she, like Achilles, prefers a short life with glory to a long life of no consequence. She escapes the agony of life, following her Sophoklean precedent: "I see the dead do not suffer" (*El.* 1170). Sophokles in his *Oidipous at Kolonos* also has his chorus comment on the inadvisability of an overlong life, quoting a maxim frequently used to illustrate Greek pessimism:

Never to have lived is best, ancient writers say;
Never to have drawn the breath of life, never to have looked into the eye of day;
The second best's a gay goodnight and quickly turn away.[15]

---

[13] Müller (1984) 29.
[14] See Steiner (1984) and McDonald (1983 and 1991).
[15] Translation in Yeats (1940) 223.

Sophokles' *Elektra* has yielded perhaps the most controversial interpretations of any of the ancient Greek tragedies, except Euripides' *Bacchae*.[16] The interpretations range from seeing in Sophokles an endorsement of the vengeance depicted as in Homer, to seeing the brother and sister as an avenging duo, monsters who effect a mixture of matricide and merriment.[17] Many modern interpretations see Elektra as a character between these extremes: she represents both the civilized incentives leading to justice and of the darker drives of human nature which actually delights in murder.[18] This is also the "structuralist" position, which sets up and sometimes synthesizes polar opposites in an uneasy equilibrium.

My view of *Elektra*, both in Sophokles and Strauss, is more positive than negative. Strauss and Hofmannsthal distill and vary the information about Elektra so that she appears truly heroic. Like other Sophoklean heroes, she has alienating characteristics and commits anti-social acts, but nevertheless achieves the acme of human fulfillment through passion.[19] We never like this Sophoklean heroine, but we must admire her. She is a late romantic superwoman modelled on the heroic figures of Victor Hugo, Ibsen and Nietzsche.

---

[16] The following is a typical reaction towards this play: "Sophokles' *Elektra* has posed innumerable problems for critics and remains the Sophoklean play that most resists a standard or 'canonical' reading," Kitzinger (1991) 298. Kitzinger concentrates primarily on the play's dramatic necessity, partially effected by the "speech act" of the extended lie about Orestes' death. She sees the play as a conflict between *logos* and *ergon* ending negatively "in an all too telling silence," (1991) 327. The Strauss/Hofmannsthal opera eliminates the speech by the Paidagogos in favor of an ariatic exchange between Orestes and Elektra. The "Trugrede" becomes "Singspiel," culminating in a heroic *ergon*.

[17] For the "Homeric," positive interpretation see e.g., Whitman (1951); Adams (1957); Linforth (1963); for the negative response, see Kells, saying of Sophokles' *Elektra*, "The play is a continuous exercise in dramatic irony," and, "Electra" is "herself a Fury ... straining to catch her mother's dying cries, hissing in her venom (1410f), gloating in hideous triumph" (1973) 11. See also Sheppard (1918), (1927a) and (1927b). Murray's view is that this drama shows a "combination of matricide and good spirits" (1914) II.vi Introduction to *Electra*. For a general bibliography on the varying positions, see Segal (1981) 461, n.3. Another good summary of positions which refutes the interpretation of the play as ironic, and is thus critical of what Orestes and Elektra do, is Szlezak (1981). He points out that R. Dawe athetized the last words by Orestes and the chorus which endorse the act of killing transgressors, and the freedom gained thereby (1981) 4. He claims that Sophokles in this play shows Orestes and Elektra "helping friends and harming enemies" according to the ancient tradition. Grene says, "The *Electra* is perhaps the best-constructed and most unpleasant play that Sophocles wrote," (1992) II. 336.

[18] See Segal (1981). For a variation of this interpretation, see also Blundell (1989) 183, and the interesting chapter by Winnington-Ingram (1980) 217-247.

[19] This is the hero so well described by Knox (1966) 56: "The thing that distinguishes nearly all of them is their irreconcilable temper: the greatness of their passion brought them into conflict with men and even with the gods, and rather than accept the slightest diminution of that high esteem their pride demanded, they were ready to kill and die."

THE CLASSICAL BACKGROUND

Three of Aischylos' seven surviving plays deal with the legend of Orestes; his *Oresteia* is named after the hero. In the second play, the *Choephoroi*, Aischylos gives us a dutiful and religiously oriented Elektra, who carries out the will of Zeus, ratifying the values of the *polis*; the darker Erinyes are enlisted in the service of the clan-culture as the Eumenides. Aischylos' position assimilates the values of the old aristocracy to the new *polis*, at the same time as religion is used to shore up the traditional values of the old clans. Their power will reside in the Areopagos, and Orestes is seen to endorse the values of the old nobility by representing and carrying out the interests of the father. Through the establishment of a law court, vengeance in the future will be contained in the civilizing framework of the *polis*. Aischylos shows us the problematics of killing with the conflicting rights involved. Klytemnestra, the victim of clan warfare, has powerful arguments on her side.

Nine of Euripides' nineteen surviving plays deal with the family of Elektra and Orestes. Euripides does not reflect the values of the clan, nor those of the city, but rather concentrates on the individual. Demoting the house and the *polis*, he enters into internal space; his discourse is enacted within the individual. He shows us a psychologically unbalanced Elektra, distraught that she is deprived of her inheritance (*El.* 1088-1090),[20] a relatively sympathetic Klytemnestra and almost defensible Aigisthos, with more right on their side than the vicious and neurotic children that kill them.

In three of his surviving plays Sophokles mentions the family of Atreus (*Ajax, Philoktetes, Elektra*), but only one speaks of the vengeance of Orestes and Elektra. In his *Elektra*, Sophokles gives us an Elektra who is not as much concerned about her inheritance (452, 457, 960) as she is about effecting her personal justice, including that of the *genos*, and in this context where tyrants rule, the exercise of clan justice takes on the dimension of the exercise of freedom. This latter is the emphasis now. We see the development from Aischylos, whereby Elektra is now a representative of the *genos* fighting, as Antigone did, for the values of the family. But she also frees the *polis* from tyrants, a popular anachronistic theme that Sophokles adopts. In this version Klytemnestra and Aigisthos are despicable in their abuses.

---

[20] Cacoyannis found Euripides' Elektra so unappealing that, in his film based on Euripides' play (1961), he portrayed an essentially Sophoklean Elektra. See McDonald (1983) 283. I am surprised that Easterling (1989), in giving background for this opera, hardly indicates that the three representations by Aischylos, Sophokles and Euripides show us three different heroines. From Easterling's title and exposition one might believe that there *was* a consistent story. The dissonances among the three versions might be interpreted as cacophony by some, but at least they should be acknowledged.

In a certain sense Elektra, like other Sophoklean heroes, shows more Homeric values than those of the new *polis*. The *genos* counts for more. Like Achilles, she is a woman of deeds rather than words, and is even impatient with the deceptions Orestes must practice for their mutual safety. When her mother is mortally struck, she shouts, "Strike again." She recommends that Aigisthos' body be tossed to the animals (she obviously had not seen the *Antigone*). This is not an ordinary woman. Sophokles uses Chrysothemis, her compromising sister, as a foil to this heroine, much as he uses Ismene with Antigone.

STRAUSS/HOFMANNSTHAL'S ELEKTRA

Sophokles is the most dramatic of these three tragedians, and the most successful at pleasing the Athenian public. He is the main source of Hofmannsthal's drama, and when Strauss saw Hofmannsthal's play, he was overwhelmed by its magic, kindled by the ancient model. We shall look closely at how opera generally — and specifically this musical masterpiece — helps us understand the intent of the original master.

Strauss and Hofmannsthal added 19th century intensification to Sophokles' themes, not only interpreting the ancient author well, but interpreting convincingly the psychological drives: Schopenhauer's — and in this opera Nietzsche's — philosophy of will is coupled with Freud's death drive. The heroine denies the role socially assigned her and commits herself to serving a larger purpose which both fulfills and destroys her. She is a model for all freedom-fighters. The day after the victory of the revolution may be a source of new tragedy; we compare the days following the French revolution and heed the warnings of Frantz Fanon, but today is clearly a victory to be celebrated, because freedom is worth any price.[21] The later opera shows us the richness of Sophokles' message which is still blazingly effective. Many ancient tragedies *are* opera in their extravagance and show us the height of human achievement in realizing an ideal. The price one pays for this is obvious. If one chooses to be Elektra, one cannot be Chrysothemis.

Both in the opera and the play, Elektra combines Homeric *arete* ("virtue," "courage") with concern for a *polis* which should be governed by qualified people. *Arete* in her case also represents the ideals of the *genos* and she considers herself the true heir of Agamemnon. Following Aischylean and Aristotelian biology, Elektra's and Orestes' blood line comes only from the father. Klytemnestra was the receptacle in which the seed was sown and subsequently incubated. Strauss/Hofmannsthal's opera shows a loyalty which reflects this genetic tie, and in fact shows much that goes beyond loyalty

---

[21] See Fanon, particularly the chapter on "The Pitfalls of National Consciousness," (1963) 148-206.

and could be called incest. The opera dispenses with the speech by the Paidagogos describing Orestes' death, or the sight of Elektra holding an urn which supposedly contains her brother's ashes, to focus intensely on Sophokles' exchange, here in ariatic form, between Elektra and her brother when he reveals himself to her. This is certainly a love duet.

Strauss is quite programmatic in his music, and we can hear the orchestra imitating dogs barking, horses neighing and galloping, and even more abstract concepts such as the brilliance of crystals (when Klytemnestra appears wearing them as amulets to ward off evil, discussed below). He also uses the leitmotif — notably themes associated with Agamemnon and Orestes — and sometimes the same theme for both of them, as if Orestes were a type of avatar, or reincarnation (Musical Examples A and B). One might say that the music is another character, and also adds commentary to the text. When we hear Agamemnon's theme, even when there is no verbal allusion in the libretto to him, we are overwhelmed by his presence and the way he shapes the drama. He is both present and absent, providing Derridean différence. We hear his trace in the music.

GÖTZ FRIEDRICH'S PRODUCTION OF
STRAUSS/HOFMANNSTHAL'S ELEKTRA

I shall now look at some of the details of the opera by Strauss and Hofmannsthal as interpreted by Götz Friedrich. I have chosen Friedrich's version of Strauss's *Elektra* done in 1982, because it is an outstanding performance and readily available on video cassette. Friedrich has also done the *Salomé* (1974) which Strauss had performed in 1905; the *Elektra* was first performed four years later. In both operas Friedrich used the same actor and actress (Hans Beirer and Astrid Varney) to play the leading couples: Herodes and Herodias in one, and Aegisth and Klytämnestra in the other. Both "daughters" figure as the leads and both dance themselves to death, one figuratively and the other literally. Both die, having learned much from their mothers. Teresa Stratas, who has been called the most talented operatic actress in the world today, lives up to that reputation in the role of Salomé. Leonie Rysanek also executes a *tour de force* with her powerful voice in her role as Elektra.

When Friedrich's *Elektra* begins, we see a strange set in which the palace resembles what might be called Beirut Modern: a concrete house which looks more like military barracks than a palace, with scattered rubble, caves and passage-ways in front. The contrast is between order and chaos, civilized and uncivilized, and in this resembles the set of Brian Friel's *Dancing at Lughnasa*, which shows the interior of a cottage set beside a field filled with wild grass and flowers. By the end of both dramas one sees the lines blurred and the separation questioned.

Early on in the opera, the civilized rulers are seen to act savagely. A black girl is brutally whipped for defending Elektra. None of the rulers, nor the elite of the court, is black, so Friedrich gives us some additional political commentary, reinforcing the idea of imperial oppression and Elektra as freedom-fighter. The contemporary audience must identify Elektra with all those anti-imperialists in Ireland and Palestine who sacrifice themselves for freedom.[22]

In Friedrich's version, Elektra prays at Agamemnon's tomb. Agamemnon's statue is broken, and she carries his stone head as she executes a dizzying dance, with its triple rhythms an anticipation of her final frenetic waltz (Musical Example C). She thrusts the head between her legs, leaving no doubt about her incestuous devotion. Agamemnon appears as a ghost when she sings; when she first sees Agamemnon he has no wound, but the next time he appears with a bloody gash in his forehead, after Friedrich visually has reenacted his death at Klytemnestra's hands, a vivid reminiscence of Sophokles' play (see *El.* 8-11, 92-99, etc.).

Hofmannsthal's Elektra talks of blood sacrifices to her father: one hundred throats to be cut, and horses and dogs included in the sacrifice. We see her as her mother's heir: Sophokles' Klytemnestra had a monthly sacrifice of sheep to celebrate the day she slew Agamemnon (*El.* 277-281). Hofmannsthal shows us instead Elektra's fantasy of victims slaughtered to honor her father, and then the orgy of blood that Klytemnestra performs to quell her dreams.

Hofmannsthal's Elektra calls Chrysothemis "the daughter of my mother, the daughter of Klytemnestra," varying the comment by Sophokles' Elektra that it is frightful that she, the daughter of such a father, would forget him and concern herself only with her mother, called disparagingly "she who bore you" (*El.* 342). Sophokles has invented Chrysothemis to contrast with the more determined sister: the heroic and the noble vs. the one who "makes do." We appreciate Elektra's defiance all the more by seeing Chrysothemis' compromises.

In both the play and the opera, Chrysothemis dreams of a life including marriage and children. This leads to her endorsement by many later commentators as the "sane" character by comparison with Elektra; they say she is in the "right," and even the mouthpiece of Sophokles.[23] I would not do Sophokles such a disservice. Elektra sneers at what she considers ignoble concerns, but this heroism can also be alienating. We remember what

---

[22] See Said (1993), who widens the notion of imperialism and brilliantly delineates the link of culture with the tools the conquerors use to dominate.

[23] "Sophoclean scholars have, almost to a man, concluded that Chrysothemis, though weak, is fundamentally right." Whitman (1951) 156. I think Whitman's comment is exaggerated. Chrysothemis is conventional, and advocates what is safe for the status quo, but hardly "right" in a Platonic sense.

Antigone says about her brother Polyneikes: a husband or child can be replaced, but with father and mother dead, a brother is irreplaceable (*Ant.* 909-12). Goethe and others have been offended by these lines, and would like to consider them interpolations by an inferior hand. These are the defenders of Chrysothemis. Elektra, on the other hand, defends irreplaceable blood ties and her *genos*.

Hofmannsthal and Strauss show Klytemnestra conducting a propitiatory sacrifice, and consenting to consult with Elektra in hopes of alleviating her nightmares. Friedrich's Klytemnestra's flesh wobbles as she moves; she has a deathly pallor, presumably from nightly orgies, followed by long days of sleep and minimal exposure to the sun. She oozes decadence. Elektra tells her mother that only the proper sacrifice is needed to dispel her dreams. She plays with her mother mercilessly, revealing at last that her mother herself is the required victim. Sophokles' Chrysothemis describes the dream that Klytemnestra has had (*El.* 417-423): Agamemnon returns and takes his scepter back from Aigisthos. He plants it and a large tree grows from it and covers Mykenai. Hofmannsthal instead deals with the undefinable. The nightmare consists of a nameless horror:

... Und doch kriecht zwischen Tag und Nacht,
wenn ich mit öffnen Augen lieg', ein Etwas
hin über mich. Es ist kein Wort, es ist
kein Schmerz, es drückt mich nicht, es würgt mich nicht.
Nichts ist es, nicht einmal ein Alp, und dennoch,
es ist so fürchterlich, dass meine Seele
sich wünscht, erhängt zu sein ...[24]

As I lie, between day and night, with open eyes,
something crawls over me. It is wordless, painless; it
neither presses me, nor chokes me. It is nothing, not
even a nightmare, and yet it is so horrible that my
soul longs for hanging ...

Sophokles deals with the specific fear, Hofmannsthal with the ineffable. The dissonances reflect the state of Klytemnestra's restless soul (Musical Example D). Elektra's reply in C major suits her clear and guiltless response and is an anticipation of the final victorious chord in C major which concludes the opera (Musical Example E).

Klytemnestra uses crystals to ward off her dreams. The gods are not on the side of the tyrants: superstition and nightmare prevail, so crystals are necessary for casting spells. Klytemnestra claims she is hung with stones and each has a special power that one can harness if one knows how to use them. The flutes play fast triplets over 4/4 time, and the harp plays glissando chords with the strings giving a pizzicato accompaniment just off the major

---

[24] Hofmannsthal (1990) 59-61. The translation is mine.

beats followed by rests (Musical Example F). Not only does this suggest crystals, but the magic they entail. The dissonance occurring off the beat and alternating with silence is disconcerting and once again the music suggests the inarticulate.

Elektra and Orestes carry out the will of the gods, explicitly in Sophokles (*El.* 35-50), implicitly in Strauss/Hofmannsthal, but Klytemnestra must resort to pagan magic. We shall see by the end of the opera Elektra and Orestes will pray to the Christian God through suggestive music and invocations which remind one of the liturgy. The contrast of Elektra's harmonic sequences vs. Klytemnestra's dissonances lets the nonverbal replace the verbal and the music defines the indefinable. Elektra triumphs in the music: the proper God and the proper keys are on her side.

As Elektra concludes her baiting of her mother, the maids enter and whisper something in Klytemnestra's ear. Klytemnestra leaves laughing and makes menacing gestures as she looks down on Elektra from a window. She laughs again. We have not witnessed the debate between mother and daughter as in Sophokles. Once again a predominantly rational exchange has been transformed into the emotional one. The Sophoklean Elektra concludes that she has learned crime from her mother the criminal (*El.* 621). It is hard for us to see any crime, even a verbal one, in Hofmannsthal's Elektra, because the tyrants she eliminates are so obviously monsters. She is instrumental in killing her mother, but she does so in self-defense, and to liberate the city.

The dramatic irony in Sophokles' *Elektra* hearing of her brother's death, and fondling the urn in which she thinks his ashes have been encased, is transformed into Elektra's deceptive play with her mother, setting her up as the required victim to end her nightmares. Hofmannsthal concentrates more on the characterization of Klytemnestra here as an evil, haunted woman, and we are allowed both textually and musically to see and hear the world of nightmare.

Sophokles' Klytemnestra has a moment where her motherly concern, albeit brief, appears. After the Paidagogos tells her that Orestes is dead, she says, "O Zeus, should I call this fortunate? It is horrible, yet for the best. How sad it is that I must save my life through things that pain me" (*El.* 766-68). She may be a woman who wants to live, but she is still a mother mourning the loss of her child. Hofmannsthal will not allow us to see this softness in Klytemnestra.

Friedrich emphasizes physical interactions between the characters, or between the characters and inanimate objects. For instance, Elektra caresses Agamemnon's stone head, and anyone who has seen Friedrich's *Salomé* will recall how Salomé caressed John the Baptist's head in a similar way. Freud and Philip Slater would hardly miss the phallic significance.[25] Both Salomé and Elektra express a forbidden, obsessive love. Klytemnestra also caresses Elektra's breasts as she asks her advice about her dreams, and Herodias does the same with Salomé in another context. Later Elektra caresses Chrysothemis' breasts so violently that the latter has to push her away. Incest here has many variations. Another reference to the power of the *genos*?

Sophoklean irony is at play when Chrysothemis tells Elektra she thinks that Orestes has come back, just after Elektra has been told that he is dead. Hofmannsthal has Chrysothemis tell Elektra that messengers have come announcing Orestes' death. Elektra tries to convince her to help her kill Klytemnestra and Aigisthos. She refuses and flees Elektra's mental and physical pressure.

In Friedrich's opera, Orestes enters as if he were the ghost of Agamemnon — shrouded in dark, wearing a helmet. His eeriness suggests the ghost of Hamlet's father, and vengeance will also be his message. As Orestes reveals himself, the music is bleakly haunting, reminiscent of both the Agamemnon and Orestes themes. These change into a romantic duet as Elektra and Orestes sing of their love for each other, and Elektra makes him pledge not to leave her. The musical theme here is reminiscent of *Tod und Verklärung*, written nearly twenty years earlier. As the man described in this tone poem is transfigured by his death, so is Elektra by the arrival of Orestes, who will also be the one to signal her death when she is fulfilled by vengeance (Musical Examples G and H). Both melodic phrases are built on the descent of a perfect interval. Both the death in *Tod und Verklärung* and Elektra's are marked by the ominous clang of the Chinese bass gong and both convey triumph by the use of C major.

After the celebration of Orestes' arrival, the gods are mentioned and invoked. The duet becomes a *makarismos*: "blest is he ...". The *makarismos* was generally a song of praise for the bride and bridegroom, or for the dead. Euripides often uses the *makarismos* in an ironic way in his plays, seemingly as praise for the living, but in fact directed towards someone who

---

[25] Slater cites Freud on "turning to stone as a symbolic erection," (1968) 321, but then refutes this observation by saying, "The symbol of turning to stone captures not only the response of the moment — the frozen hypnotic staring — and the conjoined feelings, but also the more long-range adjustment to these: impotence, frigidity, anesthesia. We know, from clinical studies, how frequently these outcomes are associated with early incestuous arousal" (1968) 322. Earlier it is asked, "But why is the head used as such a symbol? Freud's interpretation employs the concept of 'displacement upwards' — the prudish substitution of a 'higher' more cerebral body part for a 'lower' one," p. 319. This symbolism has resonance for our two operas: since Salomé's love is not incestuous, she can fondle an actual head (albeit dead), but Elektra must restrict herself to the stone head. There are obvious objections to all this and our explanation may be much simpler. A head may often stand for a person's identity, and in particular, in Homer, the dead spirit: Circe tells Odysseus to invoke the strengthless heads of the dead: νεκύων ἀμενηνὰ κάρηνα (*Od.* 10.521).

will be dead by the end of the play.[26] In Strauss's opera it is also used ironically, as part of a love duet between brother and sister, when the two prepare for murder. Their symbolic marriage will be achieved through the ritual of vengeance and Elektra sings this *makarismos*, which besides expressing her love, serves as a paean for victory:

Der ist selig, der seine Tat zu tun kommt,
selig der, der ihn ersehnt,
selig, der ihn erschaut.
Selig, wer ihn erkennt,
selig, wer ihn berührt.
Selig, wer ihm das Beil aus der Erde grabt,
selig, wer ihm die Fackel hält,
selig, selig, wer ihm öffnet die Tür.[27]

Blessed is he who comes to perform his deed,
blessed is the one who longs for him,
blessed who sees him,
blessed who recognizes him,
blessed who touches him.
Blessed who digs up the axe for him,
blessed the one who holds the torch for him,
blessed who opens the door for him.

This blasphemous yet evocative litany is well greeted by the Paidagogos, who asks if the two are mad, since a sound might set off the alarm. This is also in Sophokles, and gives us a moment of *opera buffa* in a long *opera seria*. The incantation is equivalent to the prayers uttered in Aischylos' *Choephoroi* (246ff. and passim), besides being reminiscent of prayers used in the Catholic mass. Here in Hofmannsthal's ritualistic text, Apollo is joined by Christ, and religion endorses the revolutionary coup.

The entire opera can be read along the lines of the mass with Introit, Offertory, Communion and Alleluia. Victims are offered to quell Klytemnestra's dreams. It is said another victim will bring her nightmares to an end. She will be the victim, the *agnus* offered to the *deus*. The blood of the victims is turned into the wine of vengeance. After the sacrifice Elektra dances her alleluia, and the ritual ends: *ite missa est*. Elektra goes through her own death and transfiguration.

The ritual continues in the opera following Klytemnestra's death as Aigisthos is lured to his death by Elektra dancing. She accompanies him into the house as a bacchant would, with a blazing torch and dance. Aigisthos

---

[26] For the general use of the *makarismos*, and also its ironic use in the plays of Euripides, see McDonald (1978) 171-74.

[27] Hofmannsthal (1990) 105. This litany is reminiscent of the Catholic mass, which Thomas Murphy in his *Sanctuary Lamp* used along with the *Oresteia* to color his own theme of vengeance and resolution, see McDonald (1991) 171-85.

screams out, "Is there no one to hear me?" Elektra answers from outside the palace, "Agamemnon does," and we hear a loud triumphant version of the Agamemnon theme. The rain that began the opera starts again to pour in a jouissance appropriate for Elektra's final dance to celebrate her marriage with death.

Earlier rain was linked with blood in the text and in the music. As Elektra cries to her father about her vengeance and the victorious rite to follow in which blood will be shed to atone for the original bloody murder:

Von den Sternen stürzt alle Zeit herab,
so wird das Blut aus hundert Kehlen stürzen
auf dein Grab! So wie aus umgeworfnen Krugen
wird's aus den gebundnen Mördern fliessen.[28]

As all time rains down from the stars, so will
the blood of a hundred throats rain down onto your grave.
As from overturned pitchers, so will the blood
flow from the bound murderers.

This is Hofmannsthal's and Strauss's echo of Aischylos' Klytemnestra: after she has killed Agamemnon, she rejoices in the dew of Agamemnon's blood, as the earth rejoices in rain at the time when blossoms are born (*Ag.* 1390-92). The music is reminiscent of the motif for rain that Beethoven used in movement two of his Pastoral Symphony; there continuous triplets in the second violins and violas suggest a running brook (Musical Example I). Bryan Gilliam points out that blood in Elektra's opening scene "serves a threefold purpose — as a reference to Agamemnon's violent death, to the sacrificial blood that will avenge that death, and to the blood relation between Agamemnon and his children."[29] This blood is the blood of the *genos*, and its demands are Elektra's imperative.

We can also see some symbolism in the triplets which we have just shown are often used to suggest water, or perhaps even the pervasive triple time that characterizes Elektra's passionate dances. This tripartite musical imagery could allude to both the divine trinity and the human (Agamemnon/Elektra/Orestes). As wine in the Catholic Mass is transubstantiated into the blood of Christ, so here the water that pervades the scenery and text is translated into the blood of the murderers.

This modern trope not only adds resonance to the past, but is another endorsement of the rightness of the act of vengeance, as Sophokles tells us. There are bloody aspects to any mass or to any revolution, but at the moment of sacrifice there can be a magic space in which, as Seamus Heaney

---

[28] Hofmannsthal (1990) 41.
[29] Gilliam (1991) 27.

says, "The longed-for tidal wave /Of Justice can rise up /And hope and history rhyme."[30]

Friedrich stages the murders for us, and we see them both with mirrors replicating the bloody images. Blood flows down the palace walls outside. Blood flows as freely as the rain, and Elektra dances in both. The blood of her triumphant vengeance replaces her menstrual blood: her vengeance and fulfillment are her marriage and child.

Sophokles' Aigisthos and Orestes bandy grim words about as Orestes orders him within the palace. In Hofmannsthal's version Elektra is solely responsible for delivering Aigisthos to Orestes waiting within. We do not have the ironic scene in Sophokles, where Aigisthos sees a body and thinks it is Orestes', but finds it is Klytemnestra's — a grim reworking of the trick on Elektra who had to hold her brother's "death urn." In Hofmannsthal's version there are no mistakes, and little irony.

Sophokles has Orestes say to Aigisthos that it would be good if criminals were executed swiftly, then there would be less crime (*El.* 1505-8). No such moralizing from Orestes in Hofmannsthal's text. Orestes disappears into the house when he enters to slay his mother, and is only glimpsed through a window. He has no more to say. Nor do we have the chorus' affirmation of freedom (*El.* 1508-10). Hofmannsthal has given triumphant, poetic and passionate words to Elektra. She dominates the stage. It is she who enacts her personal freedom, which coincides with the *polis'* freedom, in her final frenzied waltz.

As Chrysothemis announces victory to the transfigured Elektra, the latter goes into a strange aria, claiming that she herself is the music of victory, and she knows that she must lead the dance, but ocean weighs her down. She claims she enacts the will of the gods. She sowed darkness and gathered in joy. She was a corpse, but now is the fire of life, and her flame consumes the world's darkness. Her face is paler than the moon. (We remember this pallor was Klytemnestra's, so Elektra has in a sense become a transfigured doublet of her mother.) If someone looks at her, he must know death, or be consumed with joy. Elektra asks Chrysothemis if she sees the light coming from her. She is the moon. Chrysothemis speaks of regained love, now that her brother is here. Elektra says love kills. She says for those who have such joy, one can only be quiet and dance. Then she dances and falls into a death-trance. Chrysothemis' last words are cries to Orestes. Elektra, "the Elektral," "the bedless one," will not marry the living, but like Antigone, will go as a bride to the dead.[31] She is married to death in her triumph and the whole opera has been her *makarismos*.

---

[30] Heaney (1990) 77.

[31] "Electra (with the derivation of her name from a- and lektron) is first mentioned by Xanthus, of whom we know nothing except that he was a lyric poet and earlier than Stesichorus," Denniston (1968) x.

The opera gives us a reading of Sophokles which through alterations intensifies the core of the drama. It is a genuine new creation, which also sheds light on the ancient work. The modern reworking creates and reflects new trends: this Elektra is Freud's wildest dream come true, the perfect model for the Elektra complex. She has a single-minded loyalty to her father.

EVIDENCE FROM SOPHOKLES FOR STRAUSS/HOFMANNSTHAL'S HEROIC INTERPRETATION: A CLASSIC'S DYNAMIC NACHLEBEN

I shall now recapitulate the evidence from Sophokles' play itself for this reading of Elektra as a noble heroine, devoted to her father and the *genos*, even to the point of incestuous suggestions. Although the ancient text rarely confronts the modern version in most *Nachleben* studies, in this case it is interesting to see how fundamentally Strauss/Hofmannsthal's version is faithful to the theme of the *genos* in their new, psychologically expanded, and interpretively rich, version.

In Sophokles we find reference after reference to the father: "All night I mourn my father and lie alone on my bed" (*El.* 92-5). She claims she is the only one of the house to mourn (100). She prays to various gods to watch over those who die unjustly and also punish those who violate the marriage bed. She cries out, "Revenge my father's murder." Marriage and murder are linked as they will be later (110-116). Elektra, the unwed (ἀνύμφευτος), weeps all the years and longs for Orestes (164-172). She blames the murderers for despising the dead (234-35). She speaks of avenging justice, the blood justice owed one's kin (ἀντιφόνους δίκας: 248).

Elektra calls herself a noble woman (εὐγενὴς γυνή) who looks over her violated father's home (257-58). She says she hates her mother because her mother forces her to live with her father's murderers (261-64). She sees Aigisthos sitting on her father's throne, wearing her father's robes, and lying with her father's wife.[32]

Instance after instance can be listed to show Elektra's devotion to her father. Klytemnestra scolds her for her devotion to her father (*El.* 289-90).

---

[32] Gilliam has written an invaluable book, but occasionally seems wrong about Greek tragedy. E.g., he says Sophokles "makes it clear that Clytemnestra's greatest transgression in Electra's eyes, was the fact that she now shared Agamemnon's bed with the accomplice," (1991) 29. This was Euripides' emphasis and Hofmannsthal took it over into his play. Gilliam was misled by Hofmannsthal in this case. Sophokles' Elektra is quite clear that the murder of her father by her mother is the greatest reason for her hating her mother: she begins her *agon* (verbal debate) by saying "If you say 'I murdered your father,' who could say anything more vile." So also Gilliam claims, "Sophocles' Clytemnestra is a character not tormented by dreams of Orestes..." (1991) 30. This ignores the unsettling dream that Klytemnestra had and urgently seeks to propitiate. Elektra immediately realizes that Orestes was behind this dream (*El.* 459-60).

Elektra calls her father "noble" (ἄριστος: 366), and Chrysothemis "base" (κακή: 367): by betraying her father she has betrayed her kin (φίλους: 368). Elektra refuses the name of mother for Klytemnestra, and calls her instead mistress/master (δεσπότιν: 597).

Elektra shows this same noble love for one's kin to her brother Orestes. She claims his death has slain her (El. 808). She sees herself as deprived of both father and brother. She speaks of the noble and royal blood she shares with her brother, both sprung from a noble father (858-59). She asks Chrysothemis to join her in her noble deed of slaying their father's murderers, saying words comparable to Ajax's (S. Aj. 473-80), namely that to live basely is a base thing for nobles (El. 989), and later its reverse, that even without Orestes, she would have either lived nobly or died nobly (καλῶς: 1320-1). This is the ancient cry of the genos, that noble deeds and noble blood go together. Elektra says also that they would show piety and win good fame (εὔκλειαν: 973ff., 984ff.) by such a brave act. Many have noted Elektra's nobility, e.g., Whitman, who claimed, "Elektra wears her torment as a badge of her nobility, the one proof that she is still a princess."[33]

When Orestes reveals himself, she addresses him in terms of their race and blood (El. 1232ff.). She speaks of him in terms of pleasure, and prays he will never be removed from her. Orestes goes into the palace, describing it as a place of ancient wealth (1393). One hears Klytemnestra ask for pity for her who bore the child, but this only underlines the fact that the father was the one who generated them, and again the genos prevails (Κλ. ὦ τέκνον τέκνον, οἴκτιρε τὴν τεκοῦσαν. Ηλ. ἀλλ' οὐκ ἐκ σέθεν ᾠκτίρεθ' οὗτος ὁ γεννήσας πατήρ: 1410-12). Vater über alles. The chorus reminds them they are still in the polis, but makes reference to the race (ὦ πόλις, ὦ γενεὰ τάλαινα: 1413).

The chorus praise the offspring for achieving freedom, and these words conclude the play: ὦ σπέρμ' Ἀτρέως ... δι' ἐλευθερίας: 1508-10).

The children have freed the city from the tyrants who have abused their power. Words describing the acts of tyrants abound (e.g., 254 ff., 520-2, 664: πρέπει γὰρ ὡς τύραννος εἰσορᾶν, 'She looks quite the tyrant,' said of Klytemnestra).

OPERA FOR INTERPRETING THE CLASSICS: CONCLUSION

Strauss and Hofmannsthal, as presented by Friedrich, transfer devotion to the genos clearly into the incestuous arena, and music contributes to the sensuality, besides underlining the heroic act. We remember that Aigisthos' own loyalty to his genos may have been intensified by fact that he was

---

[33] Whitman (1951) 165.

conceived in the incestuous union between his father Thyestes and his daughter Pelopeia. Incest is only suggested in this opera, but it is clear that vengeance is something due the beloved. Elektra dies for her brother and father as Antigone died for her brother in a type of mock marriage, which Elektra celebrated in dance, in the final perverse *makarismos*. The dance makes physical the love implied in the text. Love in her case will kill, as it killed in the past ("Liebe tötet" = Elektra's *Liebestod*). Strauss's Elektra claims the light and music emanate from her: "Ob ich die Musik nicht höre? Sie kommt doch aus mir ... Seht ihr das Licht, dass von mir ausgeht?" She is fulfilled by her vengeance and death as Chrysothemis will be in exogamy. Strauss's Elektra will remain intimately and symbolically endogamous. Segal corroborates this: "Elektra exemplifies interiority carried to its extreme," and further, "Elektra's commitment to death over life is a condition not only of her soul but of her whole universe."[34] The music affirms the triumph of Elektra's death with an E-flat minor chord violently thrust into C major, the last chord of the opera (Musical Example E).

Gilliam has an excellent analysis of the keys and themes that Strauss explicitly selected to suggest the complex concatenation of what we associate with the characters and their motives, feelings and circumstance in this opera. The key of E major, the key of Elektra's dance, is typically used "to express Dionysian, passionate, or even erotic sensations in music, hence the use of E as tonal centre for Don Juan."[35] Agamemnon's death is in C minor, as E flat minor conveys Elektra's death. It is most appropriate for Elektra's triumphal dance to be in a major variation of E, and for the entire opera to resolve in C major, the musical affirmation of Agamemnon's death avenged. Gilliam points out other uses Strauss made of C major to convey a type of triumph at the end of a work, namely "evoking the ultimate restoration of the soul in the coda of *Tod und Verklärung*; the perfection of nature in *Also Sprach Zarathustra*; the restoration of sexual harmony at the end of *Die Frau ohne Schatten*; and the final chorus of *Der Friedenstag*, where opposing armies are reconciled at the end of the Thirty Years War."[36] Since this final chord is a major version of the minor chord associated with Agamemnon's death, here is the ultimate victory of the *genos* which Elektra joyously affirms in her bacchic dance. Ancient and modern religious associations, coupled with musical suggestions show us an Elektra transfigured in death, and transubstantiated into music. She is "the music while the music lasts."

Clément and McClary might say this is hardly the politically correct thing to do, to eliminate a female heroine in this way. They lump Elektra with

---

[34] Segal (1981) 257 and 249. It might not be out of place at this point to quote the second law of thermodynamics: "For a closed system, entropy is either constant or increasing."

[35] Hofmannsthal (1990) 68.

[36] Hofmannsthal (1990) 227.

Tosca, Mélisande, and the heroine of *Erwartung* singing her mad chro-
matics. I rather agree with Abbate who sees Elektra as more than this: we
both "hear the opera's voices."[37]

Sophokles and Strauss/Hofmannsthal give Elektra unique victories. For
her to kill the tyrants is essential for freedom, both her own and the city's.
Certain abuses call for retaliation. Even Elektra's death echoes the motif of
freedom. Is life with Pylades to be preferred? Elektra's dance of death is a
celebration at the peak of her life and power, her *aristeia*. She did not go
gently, but danced into that good night, because her words and feet "had
forked lightning."[38]

BIBLIOGRAPHY

Abbate C. (1989) "Elektra's Voice: Music and Language in Strauss's Opera", in Puffett (1989).
Adams S.M. (1957) *Sophocles the Playwright*, *Phoenix* supp. 3 (Toronto: 1957).
Barker A. (1989) *Greek Musical Writings*: I. *The Musician and his Art* (1984; rpt. Cambridge:
    1989), and II. *Harmonic and Acoustic Theory* (Cambridge: 1989).
Blundell M. (1989) *Helping Friends and Harming Enemies: A Study in Sophocles and Greek
    Ethics* (Cambridge: 1989).
Clément C. (1988) *Opera, or The Undoing of Women*, trans. B. Wing (Minnesota: 1988).
Commoti G. (1989) *Music in Greek and Roman Culture*, trans. R. Munson (Baltimore: 1989).
Del Mar N. (1986) Richard Strauss: *A Critical Commentary on his Life and Works*, I (1962; rpt.
    Ithaca, N.Y.: 1986).
Denniston J.D. *(1968) Euripides:* Electra (1939; rpt. Oxford: 1968).
Easterling P.E. (1989) "Elektra's Story", in Puffett (1989) 10-16.
Ewans M. (1982) *Wagner and Aeschylus: The Ring and the Oresteia* (London: 1982).
—— (1984) "Elektra: Sophokles, Von Hofmannsthal, Strauss", *Ramus* 13.2 (1984) 135-54.
Fanon F. (1963) *The Wretched of the Earth*, trans. C. Farrington (New York: 1963).
Gilliam B. (1991) *Richard Strauss's Elektra* (Oxford: 1991).
Grene D. and Lattimore R. (eds) (1992) *The Complete Greek Tragedies* II (1942; rpt. Chicago:
    1992).
Harewood The Earl of (ed.) (1987) *The Definitive Kobbe's Opera Book* (1919; rpt. with corr.
    New York: 1987).
Heaney S. (1990) *The Cure at Troy: A Version of Sophocles' Philoctetes* (London: 1990).

---

[37] "The protean Elektra of this reading is a far cry from the empty vessel, the woman without
access to deed or action, envisaged by some critics (those, it must be said, who are deaf to the
opera's voices, reading words alone)," Puffett (1989) 127. Roger W. Oliver has two main
criticisms of Clément's unrelenting "diatribe against the victimization of women in opera":
"First, it is impossible, even within the librettos themselves, to make the schematic death is bad,
life is good dichotomy underlying her assumptions ... Isn't there a nobility and even heroic
quality to Butterfly's death that will never be available to Pinkerton? ... In equating strength and
power and survival with virtue, Clément is going against the grain of many of the operas she
discusses," (1992) 41.

[38] Thanks first to John Sullivan and Irene de Jong for careful editing. Thanks also to Thomas
MacCary for his invaluable suggestions. Then I thank Albert Liu, Bridget McDonald and
Thomas Rosenmeyer for their help with this paper. Karen Elaine pointed out the influence of
Tod und Verklärung, and Beethoven's *Pastorale*, and added to the musical interpretations.
Archer Martin has also contributed useful research.

Hofmannsthal H. von (1990) *Libretto for Richard Strauss's Elektra* (Middlesex England: 1990).
John N. (1988) *Richard Strauss: Salomé/Elektra*, English National Opera and The Royal Opera Guide Series, 37 (London: 1988).
Kells J.H. (1973) *Sophocles: Electra* (Cambridge: 1973).
Kitzinger R. (1991) "Why Mourning Becomes Elektra", *Classical Antiquity* 10 (1991) 298-327.
Knox B. (1966) *The Heroic Temper: Studies in Sophoclean Tragedy* (Berkeley: 1966).
Lindenberger H. (1985) *Opera: The Extravagant Art* (1984; rpt. Ithaca, N.Y.: 1985).
Linforth I.M. (1963) "Electra's Day in the Tragedy of Sophocles", *University of California Publications in Classical Philology* 19 (1963) 89-126.
McClary S. (1991) *Feminine Endings: Music Gender and Sexuality* (Minnesota: 1991).
McDonald M. (1978) *Terms for Happiness in Euripides* (Göttingen: 1978).
—— (1983) *Euripides in Cinema: The Heart Made Visible* (1983; rpt. Boston: 1991).
—— (1991) *Ancient Sun Modern Light: Greek Drama on the Modern Stage* (New York: 1991).
Müller H. (1984) *Projection 1975 in Hamletmachine and Other Texts for the Stage*, ed. C. Weber (New York: 1984).
Murray G. (ed.) (1914) *The Plays of Euripides* (London: 1914) II. Introduction to *Electra*, v-ix.
Nietzsche F. (1967) *The Birth of Tragedy and The Case of Wagner*, trans. W. Kaufmann (New York: 1967).
Oliver R.W. (1992) "The Mystique of Opera", *Performing Arts Journal* 14.41.2 (1992) 32-42.
Overhoff K. (1978) *Die Elektra-Partitur von Richard Strauss: Ein Lehrbuch für die Technik der dramatischen Komposition* (Salzburg: 1978).
Pearson A.C. (1971) *Sophoclis Fabulae* (1924; rpt. Oxford: 1971).
Puffett D. (ed.) (1989) *Richard Strauss: Elektra, Cambridge Opera Handbooks* (Cambridge: 1989).
Rosenmeyer T.G. (1982) *The Art of Aeschylus* (Berkeley: 1982).
Sadie S. (1989) *The New Grove Handbooks in Music: History of Opera* (London: 1989).
Said E. (1991) *Musical Elaborations* (New York: 1991).
—— (1993) *Culture and Imperialism* (New York: 1993).
Schuh R. (ed.) (1953) *Richard Strauss, Recollections and Reflections*, trans. L.J. Lawrence (London: 1953).
Segal C. (1981) *Tragedy and Civilization: An Interpretation of Sophocles* (Cambridge: 1981).
Segar K. (1988) "Hofmannsthal's 'Elektra': From Drama to Libretto", in John (1988) 55-62.
Szlezak T.A. (1981) "Sophokles' *Elektra* und das Problem des ironischen Dramas", *Museum Helveticum* 38.1 (1981) 1-21.
Sheppard J.T. (1918) "The Tragedy of *Electra*, According to Sophocles", *Classical Quarterly* 12 (1918) 80-88.
—— (1927a) "*Electra*: A Defense of Sophocles", *Classical Review* 41 (1927) 2-9.
—— (1927b) "*Electra* Again", *Classical Review* 41 (1927b) 163-65.
Silk M.S. and Stern J.P. (1990) *Nietzsche on Tragedy* (1981; rpt. Cambridge: 1990).
Slater P. (1968) *The Glory of Hera: Greek Mythology and the Greek Family* (Boston: 1968).
Specht R. (1921) *Richard Strauss und sein Werk*, Vols. 1 and 2 (Leipzig: 1921).
Steiner G. (1984) *Antigones: How the Antigone Legend Has Endured in Western Literature, Art and Thought* (Oxford: 1984).
Strauss R. (1967) *Richard Strauss's Elektra: An Opera in One Act, Conductor's Score*, 1908 (Miami-Florida: 1967).
—— (1979) *Richard Strauss's Tod und Verklärung, Conductor's Score* (New York: 1979).
Whitman C.H. (1951) *Sophocles: A Study of Heroic Humanism* (Boston: 1951).
Winnington-Ingram R. P. (1980) *Sophocles: An Interpretation* (Cambridge: 1980).
Wintle C. (1988) "Elektra and the 'Elektra Complex'", in John (1988) 63-79.
Yeats W.B. (1940) *The Collected Poems of W.B. Yeats* (1903; rpt. New York: 1940).

Musical Examples

A. Strauss (1967) 26 (abbreviation by Karen Elaine):

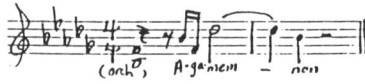

B. Del Mar (1986) 308.

C. Strauss (1967) 42 (abbreviation by Karen Elaine):

D. Del Mar (1986) I 312.

E. Puffett (1989) 104.

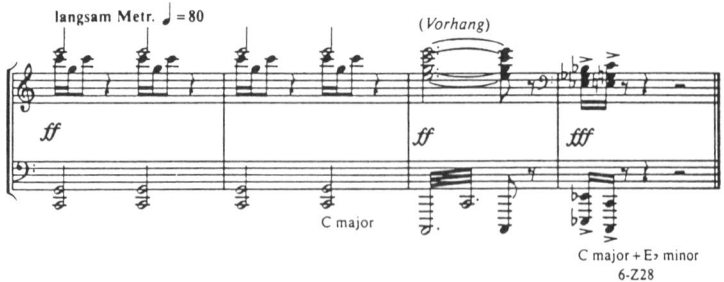

F. Strauss (1967) 119.

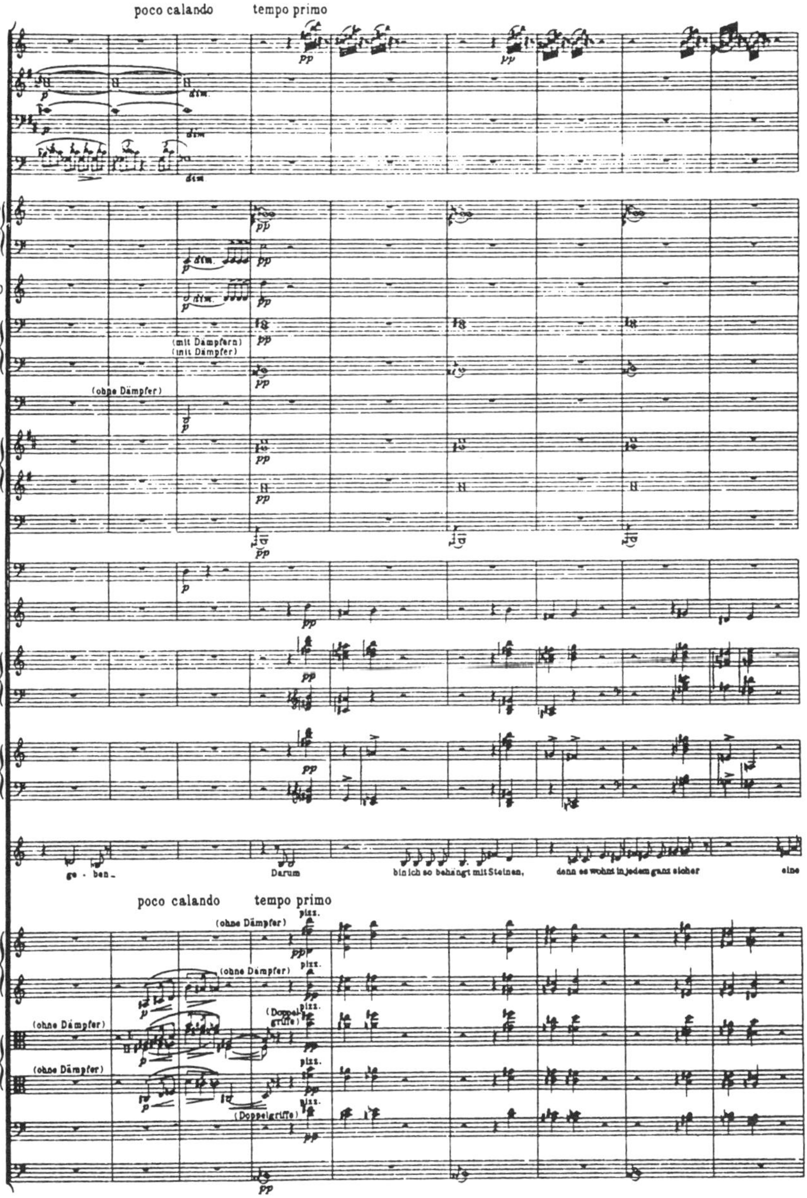

G. Strauss (1979) 106 (*Töd und Verklärung*; abbreviation by Karen Elaine)

H. Strauss (1967) 272-75, 4 measures after 149a to 153 a (abbreviation by Karen Elaine):

I. Strauss (1967) 33 (abbreviation by Karen Elaine):

SIMONIDES' ODE TO SCOPAS IN CONTEXTS*

BY

GLENN W. MOST

INTERPRETATION AND CONTEXT

How do texts come to generate interpretations? Under what circumstances, and by what mechanisms, can a text challenge people in such a way that they end up finding no more appropriate response than to interpret it? The Greeks themselves were fascinated from earliest times by those forms of discourse for which a challenge to interpretation was a central component of the original intention and for which therefore successful and unsuccessful responses could usually be distinguished unambiguously: for example oracles (whose extraordinary prominence in early Greek literature and history is well known[1]), maxims (already attached at an early period to the greatest sages, as fruit and explanation of their success[2]), laws (the privileged form in ancient Greece for attempts to control social behavior[3]), and riddles (at least some Greeks were even capable of believing that Homer had died because of his inability to solve one rather silly one[4]). On the other hand, the Greeks were more reluctant to theorize about (though not to

---

* This article is a revised version of a lecture delivered in various forms between December 1988 and February 1989 at the Wissenschaftskolleg in (West) Berlin, at the annual convention of the American Philological Association on a panel entitled "The Challenge of the Text," and at the Université de Lille. My praise goes to my hosts and audiences for their criticism and discussion, and in particular to André Laks. Any blame attaching to the conclusions and errors presented here remains my own.

[1] The lord whose oracle is at Delphi utters pronouncements for which interpretation is neither unnecessary (οὔτε λέγει) nor impossible (οὔτε κρύπτει), but which can be interpreted successfully or unsuccessfully (σημαίνει). Heraclitus' fragment (22 B 93 Diels-Kranz), itself a quasi-oracle, combines a riddle which can (apparently) be solved easily (which lord has an oracle at Delphi? but then again, what is a lord?) with an enigma which cannot be reduced to any single answer (what precisely does σημαίνει mean?).

[2] In this case the correct interpretation which the text challenges its recipient to adopt involves not so much a verbal formulation enunciated once as rather a pattern of behavior followed throughout one's life.

[3] Singly and in groups, laws already tend to be attached to the seven sages; throughout Greek philosophy, most notably in the Platonic tradition, they continue to represent the noblest achievement of the philosopher.

[4] *Vita Homeri Plutarchi* 61-71, *Vita* IV.17-22, V.35-47, VI.56-61 Allen; for variants cf. *Certamen Homeri et Hesiodi* 323-333 and *Vita Herodotea* 492-506 Allen (≈ Suda s.v. "Ομηρος 530.12-531.1 Adler). See the useful collection of material in Schultz (1914) 62-125.

generate) the far more perplexing challenges posed by a second, much larger category of texts (let us call them "literary texts"), those which were not originally intended as challenges at all, or at least not as they later seemed, and to which no single response can ever claim full and exclusive legitimacy. Hermeneutics is a Greek word, but not, at least until quite late, a Greek scholarly discipline.[5] And if, as I have suggested elsewhere,[6] one reason for the relative lack of ancient theoretical interest in the perplexities to which this latter category of texts give rise was Plato's forceful opposition to any attempt to develop a non-philosophical method for dealing with them, then it becomes all the more interesting that the problems which can be encountered in such texts are so well illustrated by Plato himself, in the episode in the *Protagoras* in which Protagoras presents Simonides' ode to Scopas as a challenge to Socrates, and Socrates attempts to meet that challenge.

Protagoras begins by asserting that the most important part of education for a man consists in learning to be clever (δεινός) with regard to poetry: that is, to be capable of understanding the statements that the poets have made rightly or wrongly, to tell these apart, and to explain them when asked (338E-339A). He then introduces into the discussion a poem Socrates admits he knows well, Simonides' ode to Scopas. According to Protagoras, the matter at issue is the same as that in their whole disputation, ἀρετή, merely transferred (μετενηνεγμένον) now to the domain of poetry (339A). Socrates acknowledges that he considers the poem well made and that he could not do so if it turned out that Simonides contradicted himself in it (339B). Thereupon Protagoras, who has already quoted the poem's opening, ἄνδρ' ἀγαθὸν μὲν ἀλαθέως γενέσθαι | χαλεπὸν χερσίν τε καὶ ποσὶ καὶ νόωι | τετράγωνον ἄνευ ψόγου τετυγμένον ("It is hard to become a man truly noble, in hands and feet and mind, fashioned foursquare without reproach," 339B), introduces another passage from somewhat later: οὐδέ μοι ἐμμελέως τὸ Πιττάκειον | νέμεται, καίτοι σοφοῦ παρὰ φωτὸς εἰ- | ρημένον· χαλεπὸν φάτ' ἐσθλὸν ἔμμεναι ("Nor do I think that the word of Pittacus was said harmoniously, although said by a wise man. He said that it is hard to be noble," 339C).[7] Once Protagoras has explained that it is self-contradictory to assert some proposition and then to attack someone for asserting it (339C-D), the audience roars approval and Socrates feels as though he has almost been knocked out (339D-E). He tries to buy time by enlisting Prodicus' help twice, first in establishing a contrast between becoming and

---

[5] I have argued this general point in more detail in Most (1984) and (1986).

[6] See especially Most (1986), where this point is argued with regard both to the fragments and testimonia of the Sophists and to Plato's dialogues.

[7] I use the text of the poem printed as fragment 542 in Page (1962) 282-3. For the sake of convenience, all translations of the poem, unless otherwise indicated, are taken, slightly modified, from Bowra (1961) 341-8.

being (340B-D), then in claiming that by "hard" Simonides had really meant "bad" (341A-C). Protagoras has no difficulty pointing out the futility of both attempts, and Socrates drops them without demur (340D-E; 341D). In the meantime, however, Socrates has managed to prepare a more ambitious, and in certain regards a more serious, answer. This falls into two parts. It begins with a circumstantial disquisition on Crete and Sparta as the true homes of Greek philosophy, as reflected later in the maxims of Pittacus and the other sages, and attributes to Simonides the intention of trying to achieve glory for himself by criticizing Pittacus' celebrated saying (342A-C). Socrates then goes on to examine the poem in sequence from beginning to end, interpreting it line by line in the light of that presumed intention (342C-347A).

Protagoras' challenge is addressed simultaneously to Socrates and to Simonides: if the poet cannot be acquitted of the charge of being self-contradictory, the philosopher too will be convicted of insufficient δεινότης in matters poetic and consequently in education. Socrates must defend himself, but the only way he can do so is by rescuing Simonides. Protagoras' polemic strategy is to propose the two passages for consideration without any regard to possible contexts for them: he resolutely ignores not only the poem's *external* context, that is, the circumstances under which it was originally performed (though he is quite aware that it was addressed to Scopas[8]), but also its *internal* context, consisting of the other utterances within the poem surrounding the ones he cites (though of course he knows that both passages come from the same poem[9]). As a result, the two sentences he quotes seem to float like monads, pure citations quite free of any determinate attachments, and to collide with one another in unmediated and windowless contradiction. It is surely not accidental that Protagoras introduces both passages with που, the vaguest of particles, in which gentlemanly contempt for pedantic niceties mixes with a genuine indifference to precision of context.

Once the diversionary preliminaries are out of the way, Socrates directs his counter-strategy precisely to the goal of supplying both kinds of context, external and internal[10] — his aim, as it were, is to specify both of Protagoras' που's. To be sure, Socrates' lecture on Doric philosophy may well strike us as being playful, both in its details and in its basic thesis. Nevertheless it provides an example of the *kind* of story which must be told by anyone who wants to integrate a text plausibly into a determinate external context. By establishing Pittacus' philosophical dignity, Socrates aims to vindicate Simonides' seriousness as well. Socrates transposes the

---

[8] This is made clear by the words with which he introduces his first quotation: λέγει γάρ που Σιμωνίδης πρὸς Σκόπαν, τὸν Κρέοντος υἱὸν τοῦ Θετταλοῦ, ὅτι... (339A).

[9] This is made clear by the words with which he introduces his second quotation: οἶσθα οὖν, ἔφη, ὅτι προιόντος τοῦ ᾄσματος λέγει που· (339C).

[10] See Gundert (1952) 72-3, 78-9. This crucial point is misunderstood in Scodel (1987) 30.

apparent contradiction within Simonides himself into a hypothetical one between Simonides and Pittacus, and, retrojecting into the past the metaphorical athletic contest between Protagoras and himself, imagines a similar athletic struggle between Simonides and Pittacus.[11] In this way the poet becomes one character engaged in animated dialogue with others, and a specific dramatic motivation can be identified for all his utterances. What unifies this fiction of complex dramatic interaction is Socrates' fundamental hypothesis of a central intention on the part of Simonides, underlying all the individual utterances.[12]

But such an imaginative construct is not likely to command assent unless it can be supported by further argument and persuasive evidence. This first, external context must therefore guide and be tested against the analysis of a second context, this time one which is internal to the text. The transition from the first to the second stage is explicitly asserted in Plato's dialogue,[13] while the verbal echoes between the general statement of Simonides' alleged intention, which concludes the discussion of the poem's putative external context, and the last sentence of the analysis of the internal context[14] not only formally close the ring-composition of Socrates' lengthy speech but also thematically assert the necessary methodological correlation of its two parts.

In its second section, Socrates pursues what he takes to be Simonides' intention step by step through his poem, using as many other phrases as he can identify as relevant internal context in order to confirm, illustrate, and modify his exegesis of the two passages with which Protagoras had challenged him. Notoriously, Socrates seems to leave out very little except for the passage intervening between the two phrases Protagoras quotes. Socrates had already justified his accepting Protagoras' dismissal of his second Prodican diversion by pointing out that the immediately following line proves that Simonides could not have meant "bad" by "hard."[15] So too, throughout the rest of his own extended interpretation, Socrates will cite each verse as internal context to cast light on what precedes it and to introduce what follows it.[16]

---

[11] The athletic terminology: ὥσπερει ὑπὸ ἀγαθοῦ πύκτου πληγείς (339E); εἰ καθέλοι τοῦτο τὸ ῥῆμα ὥσπερ εὐδοκιμοῦντα ἀθλητὴν καὶ περιγένοιτο αὐτοῦ (342C).

[12] See especially 343C: εἰς τοῦτο οὖν τὸ ῥῆμα καὶ τούτου ἕνεκα τούτῳ ἐπιβουλεύων κολοῦσαι αὐτὸ ἅπαν τὸ ᾆσμα πεποίηκεν, ὥς μοι φαίνεται.

[13] ἐπισκεψώμεθα δὴ αὐτὸ κοινῇ ἅπαντες, εἰ ἄρα ἐγὼ ἀληθῆ λέγω (343C).

[14] Cf. εἰς τοῦτο οὖν τὸ ῥῆμα καὶ τούτου ἕνεκα τούτῳ ἐπιβουλεύων κολοῦσαι αὐτὸ ἅπαν τὸ ᾆσμα πεποίηκεν, ὥς μοι φαίνεται (343C) and ταῦτά μοι δοκεῖ, ὦ Πρόδικε καὶ Πρωταγόρα, ἦν δ' ἐγώ, Σιμωνίδης διανοούμενος πεποιηκέναι τοῦτο τὸ ᾆσμα (347A).

[15] ἐπεὶ ὅτι γε Σιμωνίδης οὐ λέγει τὸ χαλεπὸν κακόν, μέγα τεκμήριόν ἐστιν εὐθὺς τὸ μετὰ τοῦτο ῥῆμα (341D-E).

[16] E.g., καὶ τὰ ἐπιόντα πάντα τούτῳ μαρτυρεῖ, ὅτι οὕτως εἴρηται (344B); λέγει γὰρ μετὰ τοῦτο ὀλίγα διελθών (344C); ταῦτά τε οὖν πάντα πρὸς τὸν Πιττακὸν εἴρηται, καὶ τὰ ἐπιόντα γε τοῦ ᾆσματος ἔτι μᾶλλον δηλοῖ (345C).

To be sure, the violence Socrates' interpretation inflicts upon the meaning and position of Simonides' words makes his exegesis of the poem no less implausible than his lecture on Doric philosophy. Moreover, his own subsequent rejection of discussions of poetry as analogous to the symposia of those unable to entertain one another with their own conversation (347Cf.) is a clear invitation to consider literary interpretation as a whole to be philosophically unserious. But the cogency of such an invitation would certainly be weakened if the only example of an extended interpretation the *Protagoras* supplied, namely Socrates', were obviously and irremediably flawed, for then it could not be excluded that some superior interpretation (potentially, the one Hippias offers, 347A-B) might still yield philosophically interesting results. The likelihood that, despite the many quirks in its details and conclusions, Socrates' analysis of Simonides' ode is intended by Plato to be serious, at least in certain regards,[17] is increased not only by Socrates' pedantic care to cite and explain practically every phrase in the poem, but also by his extracting from it doctrines we can recognize as important tenets of Plato's own philosophy.[18] From Plato's standpoint, the problem with Socrates' interpretation is not that it makes mistakes, but simply that it is an interpretation. For a non-Platonic analysis of the basic motives and mechanisms of literary interpretation, however, Socrates' exegesis may be considered paradigmatic. If, as Plato seems to suggest, Socrates' procedure of contextualization is not only just, but also inevitable, then the differences among various interpretations will be due to their different premises, modes of application, and degrees of expertise in deployment of that procedure, but not to its absence or presence or basic character.

This Platonic scene of a textual challenge consisting in context-free citation and of a response to the challenge formulated as a double contextualization, first external and then internal, may be considered representative of a whole class of problems that confront the philologist. For often the most perplexing difficulties are not posed by texts themselves, but by uncertainties concerning their contexts: one common way in which texts can become a challenge is that they become *decontextualized*, and efforts to meet this kind of challenge will usually consist in an attempt to *recontextualize* them.

Decontextualization can occur in several ways. It can be part of the author's intention: publication, for example, guarantees that a text will fall into the hands of people who have no idea of its original external context. On the other hand, even if a text was conceived entirely within the limits of a particular occasion, if it is literary it will exceed them and will invite future readers to contextualize it in new ways by applying it to situations the

---

[17] See Gundert (1952) 89-93 and Kleist (1880) 10-12, 29 n. 34.
[18] Especially the doctrine that no one errs willingly, 345Df. Gigon (1946) 143-5 argues unconvincingly that such doctrines should be ascribed not to Plato but to Aristippus.

author did not or could not foresee. With time, anyway, original external contexts tend to get lost and unintended recontextualizations to proliferate; indeed, in the case of ancient Greek and Latin literature, not only have specific circumstances been lost, but so too have whole cultures, within which those circumstances made at least certain meanings accessible which will now never be recovered. And even where the original context has not been lost, texts can be deliberately decontextualized so that they can be recontextualized within ideological systems which provide them with a new truth value, positive or negative (Plato's various discussions of Greek poetry offer numerous examples of this procedure).

In the most general terms, interpretation is nothing other than recontextualization, the elaboration of hypothetical external contexts within which problematic texts can be embedded in such a way that coherent and detailed analysis of them can derive their peculiarities from determinate features of these postulated contexts. As a general rule, the internal context provided by the text itself generates the external context (for the latter was invented only as a response to features of the former), but then goes on to provide a test for its viability (for at every moment the text can be measured against the imagined external context to determine to what degree the former can be derived from the latter), so that in practice the two kinds of context tend to be inter-dependent. There are many different varieties of external context which can be used for purposes of recontextualization: for example, the author's historical circumstances, the audience's, the author's psychology, the reader's, the text's genre, various systems of belief, and so on. The differences between schools of interpretation usually derive from differences in the type of external context they prefer to imagine, those between individual interpretations from differences of detail between specific hypothetical contexts.

Obviously, this is a risky procedure, no matter how cautiously it is performed: it trades in hypotheses which no evidence will ever be able finally to warrant. It is often thought that the securest form of external context is historical, for example that provided by the first audience; but in fact over-confidence on this score would be self-delusive. For the richer in detail the imagined historical context is, the more transparent its fictitiousness becomes, no matter how solid the documentary basis upon which it seems to rest (for such documents can never confirm a hypothesis, they can only permit it by not contradicting it). On the other hand, even a stubbornly formalist interpretative strategy, like New Criticism, operates on the basis of detailed premises, concerning the type of text involved and the type of intention and interest to be ascribed to author and audience, which constitute an external context that ought not to pass as self-evident. The fact that interpretation is ineluctably speculative is of course not at all a reason not to interpret, for no other, non-speculative way to discuss the meaning of texts is available; but it is at least a reason for self-doubt — that is, for methodological reflection.

In general, at least three principles and two canons of evidence tend to guide interpretation and at least in appearance (if not in reality) limit its risks. Most philologists seem to follow these rules more or less consistently (when they do not they are likely to be censured by the professional community); and it would be easy to show that all five are at work in Socrates' exegesis of Simonides. The three principles are all forms of the fundamental economic imperative, that a minimum of material resources and energy be used up in exchange for a maximum of gain. The first and most important one is *economy of consumption*: of two interpretations, the one that makes thriftier use of the text at hand, subsuming more of it as argumentative evidence and wasting less of it as irrelevant or counterproductive, is preferable. An interpretation which can account for only a small portion of the text is *prima facie* suspect (not, be it noted, necessarily false); an interpretation which can put the whole text into its service is *prima facie* attractive. The second principle is *economy of expense*: of two interpretations, the one that adds fewer *ad hoc* hypotheses to the necessary minimum is preferable. An interpretation which cannot dispense with particular hypotheses for which there is no evidence other than the plausibility of the general interpretation they are designed to reinforce is likewise suspect. The third principle is *economy of scope*: of two interpretations, the one that can be applied to a wider range of texts or problems beyond the one in question without yielding trivial results is preferable. A coherent interpretation of a text which results in that text's becoming anomalous within its author's œuvre, or its author anomalous within his culture, is suspect. The canons of evidence define the material upon which these principles tend to be exercised. The first is *parallelism*: a hypothesis' plausibility is thought to be strengthened by parallels and weakened by their lack. This is particularly important in the case of dead cultures: for here the absence of native speakers means we can only be certain that something is possible if it is attested as having been actual. But by the same token, the fact that a dead culture is transmitted only fragmentarily means we can be quite certain that many parallels which once existed for a usage have since been lost and are probably unrecoverable for us. Hence arises a paradox peculiar to those philological disciplines which are concerned with non-modern languages: on the one hand the sensible precept "Einmal ist keinmal," on the other hand the indisputable phenomenon of the *hapax legomenon*. The second canon, closely allied to the first, is *centripetality*: the closer to the text the parallel or other supportive evidence is, the greater its explanatory power is thought to be, closeness being determined with regard to an informally but widely acknowledged hierarchy of degrees of proximity. A parallel from the author's other works in the same genre will usually have more weight than a parallel from other works by the same author in different genres or by different authors in the same genre, but all will normally have more weight than a parallel from a different author in a different genre — to say nothing of a parallel from a completely different culture.

These principles and canons of evidence guide most interpretations, consciously or unconsciously, but neither alone nor together do they guarantee results which we can have any reason to believe will coincide with the truth of the matter. We may wish to think that they direct us towards what the author really intended or what his text really means, and it may even be the case that, psychologically, our activity as interpreters is largely dependent upon our belief that these principles really do work — they may function, in other words, rather like Kantian regulative ideals. But it seems better to regard them not in terms of the author and his text, to which they bear no obvious relation, but rather in terms of the interpretative community — that of professional philologists — which actually makes use of them. This is a community defined not only by the texts it reads but also by the way it reads them; and despite pluralism and polemics, the area of difference within it is far smaller than that of consensus. In that sense, it may be said that these rules are the methodological assumptions that structure the discourse of philology.

INTERPRETATION OF CONTEXTS

In the present context, Simonides' ode to Scopas is of interest not only because Socrates' discussion of the poem, to which we owe its fragmentary preservation, centrally problematizes the role of contexts in the interpretation of texts, but also because unresolved issues of external and internal context seem often to have haunted interpretations of the text. On the one hand, it was already recognized early in the nineteenth century that even though Socrates' exegesis could not provide a reliable guide to the meaning of Simonides' poem, wary criticism might still succeed in detaching the text of the poem from the context of Socrates' discussion of it; and in the course of that century generations of German scholars from Heyne through Wilamowitz gradually managed to establish a fairly reliable text of Simonides' ode.[19] Though controversy continues to simmer on points of detail,[20] the following text, that of Page, may be taken as representative of

---

[19] For brief sketches of the history of the problem and bibliographical references, see Aars (1888) 3-4, Gentili (1964) 278-80 and n. 1, Michelangeli (1896) 28-30, and Smyth (1900) 311. Michelangeli (1896) 22-27 provides a useful synopsis of the various texts proposed up to his time.

[20] A resolutely minority position with regard to the constitution of the text is assumed by Gentili (1964) 285-90 and 297-302.

a wide scholarly consensus which has scarcely changed since the publication
of Aars' study over a century ago:

ἄνδρ᾽ ἀγαθὸν μὲν ἀλαθέως γενέσθαι
χαλεπὸν χερσίν τε καὶ ποσὶ καὶ νόωι
        τετράγωνον ἄνευ ψόγου τετυγμένον·
      [
 5   [
      [
      [
      [
      [
10   [
      οὐδέ μοι ἐμμελέως τὸ Πιττάκειον
      νέμεται, καίτοι σοφοῦ παρὰ φωτὸς εἰ-
        ρημένον· χαλεπὸν φάτ᾽ ἐσθλὸν ἔμμεναι.
      θεὸς ἂν μόνος τοῦτ᾽ ἔχοι γέρας, ἄνδρα δ᾽ οὐκ
15   ἔστι μὴ οὐ κακὸν ἔμμεναι,
      ὃν ἀμήχανος συμφορὰ καθέληι·
      πράξας γὰρ εὖ πᾶς ἀνὴρ ἀγαθός,
      κακὸς δ᾽ εἰ κακῶς [
      [ἐπὶ πλεῖστον δὲ καὶ ἄριστοί εἰσιν
20   [οὓς ἂν οἱ θεοὶ φιλῶσιν.]
      τοὔνεκεν οὔ ποτ᾽ ἐγὼ τὸ μὴ γενέσθαι
      δυνατὸν διζήμενος κενεὰν ἐς ἄ-
        πρακτον ἐλπίδα μοῖραν αἰῶνος βαλέω,
      πανάμωμον ἄνθρωπον, εὐρυεδέος ὅσοι
25   καρπὸν αἰνύμεθα χθονός·
      ἐπὶ δ᾽ ὑμὶν εὑρὼν ἀπαγγελέω.
      πάντας δ᾽ ἐπαίνημι καὶ φιλέω,
      ἑκὼν ὅστις ἔρδηι
      μηδὲν αἰσχρόν· ἀνάγκαι
30   δ᾽ οὐδὲ θεοὶ μάχονται.
      [
      [
      [οὐκ εἰμὶ φιλόψογος, ἐπεὶ ἔμοιγε ἐξαρκεῖ
      [ὃς ἂν μὴ κακὸς ἦι] μηδ᾽ ἄγαν ἀπάλαμνος εἰ-
35   δώς γ᾽ ὀνησίπολιν δίκαν,
      ὑγιὴς ἀνήρ· οὐ †μὴν† ἐγὼ
      μωμήσομαι· τῶν γὰρ ἠλιθίων
      ἀπείρων γενέθλα.
      πάντα τοι καλά, τοῖσίν
40   τ᾽ αἰσχρὰ μὴ μέμεικται. (Fr. 542 PMG)

It is hard to become a man truly noble, in hands and feet and mind, fashioned
foursquare without reproach. [...]
Nor do I think that the word of Pittacus was said harmoniously, although said
by a wise man. He said that it is hard to be noble. God alone can have this
privilege, and man cannot but be base, whomsoever irresistible misfortune has

overtaken. For in good fortune every man is noble, and in bad fortune base, and for the most part they are the noblest whom the gods love.

Therefore shall I never, in a search for what cannot exist, waste my span of life in an empty, impracticable hope — the all-blameless man, among all of us who win the fruit of the broad-based earth. If I find him, I shall tell you the news. But I praise and love all, whosoever does nothing base of his own free will; but against necessity not even the gods fight.

I am no lover of carping. Sufficient for me is the man who is not base, nor too violent, if he has in his heart the justice which helps the city, a sound man; nor shall I blame him, for the generation of fools is past counting. All things are fair in which base things are not mingled. (trans. C.M. Bowra. slightly modified)

On the other hand, in two fundamental regards it has proved far harder to detach the interpretation of the poem from the context of Protagoras' introduction of it within the dialogue. The first, Protagoras' challenge to Socrates — that in the two passages Protagoras quotes Simonides seems to contradict himself — has long dominated scholarly discussion. This is odd, for the challenge, though seemingly adroit, in fact admits of a fairly straightforward solution.

The obvious strategy for dealing with Protagoras' problem, and the one adopted at least since the time of Plato, is to try to establish that the two propositions involved are actually not identical and hence cannot contradict one another after all. Let us reduce the two phrases to their semantic core and align them:

> (1-2)   ἀγαθόν   γενέσθαι   χαλεπόν.
> (13)   ἐσθλόν   ἔμμεναι   χαλεπόν.

Within which pair of seemingly like terms should the interpreter proclaim the existence of a conceptual difference stark enough to prevent the two propositions from collapsing into tautology? Both of the apparent candidates have been canvassed: neither has yielded satisfactory results. Socrates' own solution, to distinguish between γενέσθαι (1) as becoming and ἔμμεναι (13) as being (*Prot.* 343Ef.), has been followed by many scholars[21] and (despite Wilamowitz' vehement protest[22]) is not excluded in principle. Yet in the present case such a distinction necessarily fails, since it could only be maintained if it were terminologically consistent at least throughout the immediate internal context constituted by the rest of the poem. But Simonides goes on a few lines later to use ἔμμεναι (15) to mean not "be" but rather "become"[23] and γενέσθαι (21) to mean not so much "become"

---

[21] E.g., Aars (1888) 12; Blass (1872) 331; Campbell (1967) 386-7; des Places (1969) 239; Donlan (1969) 75; Gerber (1970) 321; Gundert (1952) 76, 83-4; Jurenka (1906) 867-9; Kegel (1962) 9-10; Woodbury (1953) 155-7.

[22] Wilamowitz-Moellendorff (1913) 165.

[23] Cf. Fränkel (1968) 73 n. 7.

as rather "exist." Similarly, Verdam's attempt to contrast ἀγαθός (1) and ἐσθλός (13)[24] founders on the fact that in line 17 Simonides uses ἀγαθός in a sense indistinguishable from that of ἐσθλός a few lines earlier.

Does this mean, then, that the two propositions are identical after all? Must we in despair simply accept Simonides' apparent self-contradiction as an allegedly characteristic feature of so-called archaic thought?[25] Or, alternatively, must we adopt Wilamowitz's suggestion that Simonides first quotes the maxim, imposed upon him as a topic for poetry by Scopas, and then goes on to reject it (although this view involves among other defects an impossible meaning for νέμεται [12])?[26] Fortunately, all escapes are not blocked. For two further features in these two passages remain to be considered: on the one hand, the determinants which Simonides adds to the first passage but which are lacking in the second one, the adverb ἀλαθέως and χερσίν τε καὶ ποσὶ καὶ νόωι τετράγωνον ἄνευ ψόγου τετυγμένον; and on the other hand, one other word in the semantic core of the two passages in question, χαλεπόν (2, 13). Strangely enough, both features seem hitherto to have been almost entirely neglected in this connection;[27] but it is only with their help that the puzzle can be resolved. χαλεπόν, to be sure, is the only word in these two phrases that occurs unchanged in both: but in itself it is capable of bearing two quite different meanings, encapsulated in the definition of Apollonius the Sophist, χαλεπόν· δύσεργον, ἀδύνατον.[28] As δύσεργον, χαλεπόν describes that which is hard to accomplish but capable nevertheless of being achieved, and is contrasted with "easy";[29] as ἀδύνατον, χαλεπόν describes that which no amount of effort can ever attain, and is contrasted with "possible." It is precisely the latter, euphemistic usage which is most common in ancient Greek anthropological generaliz-

---

[24] Verdam (1928) 308, followed by Donlan (1969) 81 and Woodbury (1953) 156.

[25] So e.g. Christ (1941) 15, Fränkel (1968) 72-4, and Scodel (1987) 36 n. 7. But the alleged involuntary discrepancies in such large-scale productions as the epics of Homer or Hesiod or the elegies of Solon cannot provide much help in explaining so blatant and deliberate a contradiction within scarcely ten lines in a small lyric ode. On the presumed illogicality of "archaic thought" in general, see especially Fränkel (1968) 40-96; for criticisms of this approach to early Greek poetry see Most (1985) 216-7.

[26] Wilamowitz-Moellendorff (1913) 166ff., who seems to have been misled by the fact that the lines in question are indeed quoted as a challenge — but by Protagoras in Plato's dialogue, not by Simonides in his poem.

[27] Schütrumpf (1987) 14-16 and Svenbro (1984) 127-33 seem to be the only scholars to have at least partially recognized the importance of the additional determinants. But Schütrumpf introduces a distinction between two different ideals of perfection (between moral quality and tenor of life) which is quite foreign to Simonides' poem, and Svenbro's attempt to resolve the apparent contradiction by understanding ἀλαθέως in line 1 as meaning "as revealed by poetry" requires giving the term an impossibly narrow meaning. And neither scholar sees the central ambiguity of χαλεπόν.

[28] Apoll. Soph. 166.31 Bekker. For other ancient acknowledgements of this ambiguity, see Schol. ad Hom. Il. 16.620; Hesych. and Suda s.v. χαλεπὰ τὰ καλά; Etym. Mag. 804.55.

[29] E.g., Hom. Od. 11.156, 19.189; Theognis 464.

ations on what human beings are capable of in contrast with the gods.[30]
Which meaning are we to attach to the word in its two appearances in this
poem? In the first passage, Simonides implies his own understanding of
Pittacus' saying (that is, that it is "impossible" to be good) by interpolating
into it a series of hyperbolic determinants (ἀλαθέως...χερσίν τε καὶ ποσὶ
καὶ νόωι τετράγωνον ἄνευ ψόγου τετυγμένον), and even though he does
not explicitly assert that by χαλεπόν he means "impossible" rather than just
"difficult," these determinants make his meaning quite clear; but when he
cites the proverb a second time, and this time does so much more accurate-
ly,[31] the absence of those determinants means that he can unambiguously
declare that, since this time the adjective means "difficult," therefore the
proposition containing it (in this meaning) is false (for it would only be true
if the adjective could bear no other meaning here than "impossible").[32]
This is nearly, but not quite, the same thing as saying, "It is hard to be a
good man — no, Pittacus is wrong, as a matter of fact it is impossible":[33]
for the witty sophistication with which Simonides chooses not only to cite
the proverb the first time in an improved form in which its meaning is
acceptable, but also to use the same predicate in both phrases, means that
what the second passage contradicts is really not the first one, but instead
only a one-sided misunderstanding of the first one (that which would have
taken χαλεπόν as merely δύσεργον). In short, according to Simonides, it is
not wrong to say, "It is hard to become a man truly noble, in hands and feet
and mind, fashioned foursquare without reproach," for here it is clear that
"hard" means "impossible"; but it is wrong to say, "It is hard to be noble,"
for here "hard" seems to mean merely "difficult." And, with the same wit,
Simonides exculpates Pittacus himself, "a wise man" (12): for at fault is not
the man so much as rather his verbal formulation, the "Pittacism" (τὸ
Πιττάκειον, 11). Words, even those spoken by wise men, can distort their
speakers' intentions: Pittacus' wisdom has been betrayed by his very own
celebrated utterance. What better proof could Simonides wish for his claim
that human success and failure depend not upon humans but upon the gods?

Thus Protagoras' explicit challenge to Socrates can be met fairly easily
by considerations concerning the internal context of the poem; these can

---

[30] E.g., Hom. Il. 16.620; Od. 10.305, 23.81, 184; H.Dem. 111; Pind. N. 10.72; Bacch. 5.94;
Solon 16.1 West; Theognis 1075.

[31] The exact terms of Pittacus' saying were usually reported as χαλεπὰ τὰ καλά: see
Paroem. Gr. 1.172, 462 and 2.89, 717 Leutsch-Schneidewin; and Hesych. and Suda s.v χαλεπὰ
τὰ καλά.

[32] In grammatical terms, the particle μέν in line 1 is picked up by the δέ of οὐδέ in line 11.
This seems to be the view suggested already at Prot. 343C-344A.

[33] So already Wilamowitz-Moellendorff (1913) 167 and especially Fränkel (1962) 352 and
(1968) 73, followed by Easterling (1974) 42 and Gundert (1952) 74.

then be supported by parallels from other ancient authors,[34] but are simple enough not to require us to imagine a determinate external context. On the other hand, far more confusion seems ultimately to have derived from Protagoras' second red herring, his assertion that what Simonides' poem is really about is ἀρετή.[35] Since Wilamowitz, an ethical reading of the poem has been dominant. This reading has many variants, and no two of its proponents agree on all its details, but perhaps it can be synthesized as follows:[36] In the first two strophes, Simonides begins by considering the aristocratic morality, characteristic of the Archaic period, which determined a man's worth by his social standing, his property and power, and his success in action. Simonides undermines this ethos by showing that, on its terms, human worth depends entirely on the gods and can change radically from one moment to the next so that, strictly speaking, it is not hard to be good, but impossible. Then, in the third strophe, the poet introduces his own alternative, a new morality based on conscience and intention, by declaring that he loves and praises all who do nothing shameful willingly. Finally, in the fourth strophe, he characterizes in more detail the positive model he advocates, stressing in particular those political virtues like justice which are potentially available to all citizens. Proponents of this reading celebrate Simonides' poem as a turning-point in the moral development of ancient Greece: here for the first time inner criteria of moral worth are substituted for external ones, democratic ideals for aristocratic ones, and attainable goals for absolute ones. For one scholar, "Simonides was in the van of ethical thought in his day";[37] for another, "he was an important innovator in the formulation of higher ethical thought";[38] for a third, "conscience as the primary source of morality is Simonides' gigantic contribution to the Greek, and also to the Western world."[39]

There is much to be said against this interpretation of Simonides' poem. Methodologically, the "trickle-down" theory of intellectual history, according to which the great ideas are invented by great men and communicated by

---

[34] Fränkel (1962) 352 n. 13 cites Sen. *Epist.* 22.13-5 for his view, which has affinities with the one proposed here; Easterling (1974) 42-3 adds Soph. *Ag.* 750ff. and *Trach.* 1ff.

[35] Or, more precisely, from a wide-spread confusion concerning the precise meaning of this assertion: for in fact Protagoras does not go on to discuss the content of the views about ἀρετή propounded by the poem, but rather the question of whether the poem is itself a good poem or not, inasmuch as the ἀρετή of a poem is not to contradict itself.

[36] For representative examples, see Babut (1975) 26-7, 52-7; Balasch (1967) 47-52; Bowra (1934) 231-9 and (1961) 327-36; Christ (1941) 21-5; des Places (1969) 240; Donlan (1969) 71-90; Fränkel (1962) 350-6; Gentili (1964) 290-5; Gundert (1952) 87; Kegel (1962) 13-27; Maschke (1926) 23-8; Pfeiffer (1929) 148; Reinhardt (1916) 129-31; Rohdich (1979) 122-5; Schütrumpf (1987) 19-22; Segal (1985) 223-4; Wilamowitz-Moellendorff (1913) 169-80; Woodbury (1953) 159-63.

[37] Bowra (1961) 327.

[38] Donlan (1969) 71.

[39] Balasch (1967) 47.

them to the toiling masses in crucial documents which just happen to have
been preserved for us, may conceivably be applicable to certain cases in
mathematics and the sciences (where progress depends upon the acquisition
of considerable preliminary knowledge), but seems *prima facie* most
unlikely when the matter at issue is the moral experience available to any
adult's inspection. Furthermore, in terms of the external context actually
furnished by the evolution of Greek moral thought, there is not a single
element in Simonides' poem for which scholars have not found parallels in
earlier Greek thought, from Homer to Dracon.[40]

But the decisive objection to this particular external recontextualization
of the ode is that it does not pass the test of point-by-point comparison with
the internal context of the ode itself. Thus (i) the opening of the poem
nowhere refers to the aristocratic archaic ethos of success and external
goods. The words χερσίν τε καὶ ποσὶ καὶ νόωι ("hands and feet and mind,"
2) seem intended to emphasize not so much socially acknowledged
achievements as rather the individual's own capacities, and they climax,
with νόωι, in a decidedly mentalist factor. (ii) The second strophe certainly
does not attack archaic morality — indeed, it programmatically confirms
views on human mutability and dependence upon the gods common in
Greek thought at least since the Homeric epics[41] — but on the other hand
it is just as clearly not intended to function as a *reductio*, provisionally
accepting the archaic ethos for the sake of argument only in order to show
the absurdities to which it leads. In point of fact, the second strophe is not
rejected in what follows but serves as an argumentative basis for the rest of
the poem. What is more, it is hard to see what sense to attribute to the
alleged claim in line 14 that only a god could be morally virtuous or attain
wealth and social prestige. (iii) But the most serious difficulties are raised
by the view that the third strophe proposes intentionality as a new basis for
moral thought. (a) First, Simonides' formulation is strikingly negative — he
does not say, "I approve of the man of good will," but rather "I approve of
the man who does nothing shameful willingly." (b) Second, his formulation
is immediately followed by a prominent concession to a category which is
called ἀνάγκη, "necessity" (29), and is left entirely unspecified. What is this
necessity acting under the constraint of which men can commit shameful
acts and yet not incur Simonides' censure? If Simonides were really
focusing attention upon issues of free will, compulsion, and responsibility,
we might expect him to clarify his meaning: but he does not. (c) Third, if
intention is the central innovation in the poem, it is odd that in the fourth
strophe Simonides no longer mentions it and apparently uses the same term,
κακός (34), which had occurred thrice in the second strophe, in the allegedly

---

[40] See particularly Dickie (1978) 24-32 and Parry (1965) 301-4; also Bowra (1934) 233-34
and (1961) 329-30, and Christ (1941) 18-20.
[41] See in general Fränkel (1968) 23-39.

archaic section of the poem (15, 18*bis*). (d) Fourth, and above all, the contrast between ἑκών and ἀνάγκη which organizes lines 27-30, so far from being an innovation on the part of Simonides, actually occurs frequently as early as the epics of Homer and Hesiod, in which people who do a bad thing ἑκόντες are considered to be more culpable, while those who do a bad thing not ἑκόντες are considered to be less culpable. For example, during the massacre of the suitors in *Odyssey* 22, the bard Phemius pleads that he should be spared on the grounds that he did not sing to the suitors ἑκών but yielded to their overpowering ἀνάγκη: whereupon Telemachus recommends mercy and Odysseus obeys.[42] Thus, if there is indeed any moral novelty in this section of the poem, it is not in the introduction of the category of intentionality but rather in the use to which that category is put: not being ἑκών not only exculpates someone for Simonides, it is now rewarded with the poet's friendship and praise. In other words, what had earlier been a *minimal* condition (sufficing only to free a defendant from severe penalties) is now a *maximal* condition (sufficing to guarantee high rewards). But the reasons for such a transformation remain entirely obscure. (iv) And finally, the view that the morality of the poem's conclusion is democratic seems scarcely compatible with Simonides' assertion that the number of fools is infinite (37-38); nor does the poet's reference to respect for justice (35) help at all to specify the particular kind of political system he is envisaging — for it is not only in a democracy that citizens can excercize justice, and from Hesiod through Pindar and down through the Roman and Byzantine periods, kings, tyrants, and emperors are all praised for observing the justice which makes cities flourish.

Some of these objections have been raised by the minority of scholars who have questioned the view that Simonides' poem is centrally addressed to moral issues.[43] Nevertheless, the philological community still seems to comprise a "moral" majority. No doubt this is partly due to a lingering influence exerted by Protagoras' assertion that the poem is really about ἀρετή, merely transferred to the domain of poetry. In other words, as it were, the context of the poem's transmission continues subliminally to shape the views of its general purpose long after it has been consciously discarded as an aid to understanding the meaning of its details. But Protagoras' claim could surely not have imposed itself upon anyone were it not that the poem

---

[42] ὡς ἐγὼ οὔ τι ἑκὼν ἐς σὸν δόμον οὐδὲ χατίζων | πωλεύμην μνηστῆρσιν ἀεισόμενος μετὰ δαῖτας, | ἀλλὰ πολὺ πλέονες καὶ κρείσσονες ἦγον ἀνάγκη (Hom. *Od.* 22.351-53); in response Telemachus calls Phemius ἀναίτιος (356). For other examples, see Hom. *Il.* 6.523, 13.234, 23.585; Hes. *Th.* 232, *Erg.* 282. On free will and compulsion in Homer see Maschke (1926) 4-7. For the view that τὸ ἀκούσιον is forgiveable, see e.g. Soph. *Trach.* 727-28; *TrGF* 80.1-2; Thuc. 3.40.1; Antiphon *Orat.* 5.92, *Tetral.* 3.1.6; Aristot. *EN* 3.1.1109b30ff., *EE* 2.8. 1225a21ff.

[43] See especially Dickie (1978) 21-3 and Jurenka (1906) 865-7. Adkins (1960) 165-7, 196-7, 355-9 criticizes this particular moral reading but remains trapped in other moral concerns.

itself is obviously full of apparently moral terms: ἀγαθός (1, 17), ἐσθλός (13), κακός (15, 18, 34), ἄριστοι (19), αἰσχρόν (29, 40), and καλόν (39). Do not these words virtually compel some sort of moral reading?

Not necessarily. The poem is also full of terms describing the activity of praising and blaming: ψόγος (3), πανάμωμος (24), ἐπαίνημι (27), φιλόψο-γος (33), and μωμήσομαι (37).[44] Now the presence of these latter terms need not be remarkable in itself. On the moral reading, Simonides first determines what is good and bad, and then goes on to praise the good and to blame the bad accordingly; first he makes a moral argument, then he draws from it the consequences for the kinds of discourse he will produce. But we have seen that the moral terminology of the poem does not seem to yield a coherent argument in ethical terms, but rather, from one section of the poem to another, it shifts freely among quite different varieties of ethical views without declaring allegiance to any particular one, and without progressing consistently in a single direction or even seeming to notice contradictions and discrepancies. It might be noted, moreover, that the language of praise and blame does not emerge only later in the poem than that of good and bad, but already appears in the opening sentence as the culminating term in the definition of the truly good man (ἄνευ ψόγου, "without reproach" 3).

It is a well-established hermeneutic precept that a poem that does not seem to work should be turned upside down, like a finely crafted Swiss watch, and shaken a couple of times to see what happens. Applying this sophisticated procedure to Simonides' ode reveals that it is possible not only to use ethical terms as a starting point in order to define discursive ones, but also to use discursive terms as a starting point in order to define ethical ones. Not only can "good" and "bad" designate primary qualities of persons which then justify praising or blaming them: alternatively, praise and blame can be primary activities which result in their objects being called good or bad. "Good" need not denote a moral substance, but simply "what is praised"; and conversely "bad" may mean nothing more than "what is blamed." This is how even Aristotle, for example, proceeds in his ethical treatises. To determine what is good or bad, he often asks what it is that people praise or blame; for example, the fact that they praise the mean indicates that it is good, the fact that they censure extremes means that they are bad.[45] Prima facie there is no reason to expect Simonides to employ a more sophisticated method of reflection in such matters than Aristotle does.

Simonides' ode to Scopas, then, is a poem not about ἀρετή — a word which does not appear anywhere in it — but about praise and blame. It does not ask what it is that makes a man good or bad, but instead what kind of

---

[44] This has been noticed by Crotty (1982) 33-34.

[45] E.g., Arist. EE 3.7.1, 8, 10; 8.3.4; MM 1.2.1-2, 5.1-2, 22.2-3, 23.1-2; DVV 1.1, 8.3-4. On the ways Aristotle makes use of ἔνδοξα in moral and rhetorical inquiry, see Most (1993a).

man should be praised or blamed.[46] Substituting, in the interpretation of the poem, "praiseworthy" for words like "good" and "blameworthy" for words like "bad" makes the contradictions and confusions which arose from the substantivization of its moral vocabulary simply vanish. (i) Simonides begins by declaring in the first strophe that it is hard to find someone who cannot be blamed in any regard whatsoever: he adopts Pittacus' maxim, but transforms it not only by reinforcing it but also by specifying climactically that it involves freedom from blame (ἄνευ ψόγου, "without reproach" 3).[47] (ii) In the second strophe he goes on to say that to be fully free of blame is impossible for a human and possible only for a god, since among men praise and blame are dependent upon success and failure, and these in turn are in the lap of the gods. Those humans are praised most whom the gods love — as Theognis puts it in a striking parallel, ὃν δὲ θεοὶ τιμῶσιν, ὁ καὶ μωμεύμενος αἰνεῖ, "Whom the gods honor, even the fault-finder praises."[48] (iii) "Therefore," Simonides continues in the third and fourth strophes, "I shall not waste my time looking for a man whom no one blames, for none such could possibly exist; instead, I for my part shall praise whoever does not commit a shameful deed of his own free will (of course, if he does so under the compulsion of necessity, that is another matter), whoever is not blameworthy nor excessively violent and who respects the laws of his city — for the number of people who deserve censure as not even satisfying these criteria is infinite. In short, I shall praise whatever is free of shameful elements."

For this line of thought, which prohibits the eventuality of censure by appeal to the power of necessity and goes so far as to term the result not merely acceptable but even καλόν ("fair"), a fragment of Pindar offers a remarkably close parallel. Xenophon of Corinth had promised to devote a hundred temple prostitutes to the cult of Aphrodite if he received the goddess' favor; now, having gained his wish, he fulfils his vow and commissions Pindar to compose a poem for this peculiar occasion. In the surviving fragment, Pindar writes, "To you, maidens, he made it possible without criticism (ἄνευθ' ἐπαγορίας) to pluck the fruit of soft youth on lovely beds; for under necessity all is fine (σὺν δ' ἀνάγκᾳ πᾶν καλόν)."[49] We might well imagine that some people would want to blame the girls for

---

[46] Crotty (1982) 39 and now Carson (1992) 120 argue along generally similar lines.

[47] That the first strophe went on to name Scopas explicitly is rendered virtually certain by generic considerations and by the fact that Protagoras and Socrates know that the poem was addressed to him; see Aars (1888) 9 and Blass (1872) 329. But what else this first strophe contained we can only guess. Perhaps Simonides went on, after beginning "It is hard to find someone who cannot be blamed in any regard whatsoever," to add, "And you, Scopas, with your full experience of the world know this very well" (so Christ [1941] 15) or even "And so even you, Scopas, have been criticized by a few people."

[48] Theognis 169.

[49] Pindar Frag. 122 Snell-Maehler.

their sexual promiscuity and Xenophon for offering them. But Pindar's appeal to the necessity of religious obligations, admitted by everyone, not only exculpates them all but even makes the whole rather odd situation fine and praiseworthy. Indeed, Pindar's phrase πᾶν καλόν is so similar verbally to Simonides' words πάντα καλά that it is worth wondering whether Pindar might be consciously echoing Simonides' ode, or, perhaps more likely, whether both might be drawing independently upon some popular proverb.[50]

This much can be derived from a close examination of the internal context of the poem. But the result has at least two odd features. The first is the marked emphasis, from beginning to end, upon the impossibility of finding anyone at all who cannot be blamed for at least something. The second is the curious transformation of what had traditionally been a minimal condition into a maximal one, the awarding of highest praise not to the man who performs heroic exploits but rather to the one who commits no shameful deed except under the compulsion of necessity. What kind of external context can be hypothesized to account for these peculiarities? We have seen that an external contextualization in terms of the development of Greek moral thought is unconvincing. Perhaps a more concretely historical one in terms of the poem's original situation of performance might prove more productive. About Simonides we know that he was a professional poet of praise, hired to compose encomiastic poetry in various genres at the expense, and in honor, of patrons who were certainly distinguished by power and wealth but not necessarily by a high ethical standard.[51] As Socrates himself puts it in the course of his discussion of this poem in the *Protagoras*, "And often, I suppose, Simonides thought that he too had praised and eulogized some tyrant or some other such person, not of his own free will but under constraint" (346B).[52] About Scopas we know that Phainias, a Peripatetic who wrote a historical work entitled Τυράννων ἀναίρεσις ἐκ τιμωρίας ("The Murder of Tyrants for Revenge"), included him in this work and described him as a heavy drinker.[53] To be sure, Phainias was writing about two centuries after Scopas and we should be wary of jumping to the conclusion, on the sole basis of his testimony, that Scopas was a brutal

---

[50] Vernant (1979) places the phrase in a wider context, perhaps too much so.

[51] On Simonides and praise poetry for hire, see especially Detienne (1964) and Svenbro (1984) 125-45.

[52] πολλάκις δέ, οἶμαι, καὶ Σιμωνίδης ἡγήσατο καὶ αὐτὸς ἢ τύραννον ἢ ἄλλον τινὰ τῶν τοιούτων ἐπαινέσαι καὶ ἐγκωμιάσαι οὐχ ἑκών, ἀλλ᾽ ἀναγκαζόμενος (346B). The facts that Socrates uses the observation to support a quite implausible interpretation of the word ἑκών in Simonides and that he deliberately speaks vaguely and generally about tyrants rather than specifically about Scopas does not in the least lessen the importance of this neglected passage for the interpretation of this poem.

[53] Athen. *Deipn.* 10.438C = Phain. Frag. 14 Wehrli. Already Aristotle collected examples of tyrants who fell τιμωρίας χάριν (*Pol.* 5.10.1311a25ff.).

alcoholic who was assassinated by one of his indignant subjects in retaliation for some violent outrage (though of course he may well have been). But whether or not Phainias' allegation was historically true, its very existence suffices to prove that during at least part of the period between Scopas' and Phainias' lifetimes Scopas was blamed by some people (certainly Phainias, probably his sources or informants), and there is no reason to disbelieve that Scopas had also been blamed by some people during Simonides' lifetime as well. For these oddities in the poem to make sense, we do not need to suppose that Scopas had committed some specific crime of which Simonides was aware (though of course this remains possible), but only that Simonides knew that some people criticized Scopas, or even that Simonides could assume that it was likely that a man of Scopas' power would have detractors. For the words Simonides uses in line 27, ἐπαίνημι καὶ φιλέω ("I praise and love"), are technical terms used in the language of epinician poetry specifically to describe the relation of the poet to his patron.[54] Clearly it is this relation which is the central subject matter of Simonides' ode. So far from proclaiming the virtues of democracy, it actually provides an apology for tyranny. Scopas may be blamed by some: but then again, who is not? Simonides will gladly accept the patronage of a man who only commits shameful deeds when he is compelled to do so by necessity — but what tyrant has not invoked the excuse of necessity to justify the most reprehensible acts? In praising a patron criticized by some, Simonides is saying in effect, "Let us not expect the impossible. Nobody is perfect. At least Scopas has never done anything shameful unless he had to (and hence it was not shameful: and this plea excuses even the gods); for the rest he is not excessively violent and respects the laws of the city, and if I wanted to criticize there are lots of foolish people who do not even achieve this much I could blame."

Thus the aptest social and generic context for Simonides' poem is not a philosophical discussion of virtue and vice but the symposiastic exercise of praise and blame.[55] The poem itself is best seen not as a moral treatise designed to analyze what makes a man good or bad, but rather as the theoretical reflection of a practitioner of encomiastic poetry upon his poetic practice, designed to determine what kind of patron is the proper subject for encomium.[56] Since at the same time the poem seeks to justify the choice of Scopas as an appropriate object for praise, it manages to combine a theorization of encomium with the practical performance of an actual

---

[54] For ἐπαίνημι cf. Pind. O. 13.2; P. 2.67, 10.69; N. 5.19; fr. 43.4; Bacch. fr. 56. For φιλέω cf. Pind. P. 1.60, 92, 2.83, 4.29, 10.66; N. 3.76; Parth. 1.11.

[55] On the symposium as the institutional framework for much of early Greek monodic poetry, see Bowie (1986), Vetta (1983), Most (1982), Murray (1990), Rösler (1980).

[56] Among modern scholars, Dickie (1978) 21-2, 32 and Schütrumpf (1987) 22-23 come closest to this view. See also Crotty (1982) 33-40 and now Carson (1992) 114, 120.

encomium of Scopas. But therein lies a difficulty. For in effect Simonides
was trying to use one and the same poem to convey two rather different
messages to two quite different audiences: on the one hand to Scopas, whose
commission he had accepted and who could expect to be praised extrava-
gantly; and on the other hand to professional colleagues and a pan-Hellenic
audience (including other potential patrons), who might well blame him for
praising Scopas. He must balance his poem upon a razor's edge of tact if it
is not to fall into one or the other of opposite kinds of failure. Scopas
certainly was ἀγαθός in the sense of enjoying considerable wealth and
power, but he is not very likely to have been ἀγαθός in the sense of being
a paragon of moral virtue. Simonides must deploy a systematic ambiguity
between the two meanings of this term and of others if he is to hope to
satisfy both kinds of audiences.

Sufficient proof that his text ultimately succeeds in avoiding the
symmetrical pitfalls of an unambiguous declaration of allegiance to the one
set of meanings (success) or to the other (virtue) is provided by the
perplexity of generations of classical scholars who have tried in vain to pin
it down. But can we be sure that Simonides achieved success with both of
his contemporary audiences? With regard to his non-Thessalian readership,
the fact that his poem became famous in Greece is indicated by Protagoras'
choice of it for his controversy with Socrates and by the familiarity with
which they both discuss it from memory.[57] But what of Simonides' patron?
Might not Scopas have deemed the encomium half-hearted, or suspected his
poet of praising him with faint damns?[58] We cannot be sure. For if, on the
one hand, Scopas and his court were indeed sophisticated and enlightened,
an encomium like this may not have been offensive. Many Greeks thought
it better to be envied than pitied, and a ruler, if he wished, could choose to
read Simonides' poem as a hymn both to the magnitude of his power and
to the enlightened use to which he puts it. After all, Simonides asserts that
only a god could achieve greater success than a man like Scopas has, and
he supports this assertion by an appeal to many of the most traditional
elements of Greek popular morality. On the other hand, numerous testimonia
report that Simonides said he could not fool the Thessalians because they
were too stupid, or that Scopas refused to pay money he owed Simonides
for a different poem he had commissioned but was dissatisfied with, or more

---

[57] See especially 339B.
[58] So e.g. Flach (1884) 635 ("Man muß gestehn, dass niemals ein Fürst in vorsichtigerer
Weise in Schutz genommen ist und in beschränkterer Weise Lob erhalten hat") and Gundert
(1952) 86.

generally that the Scopadai were avaricious.[59] Perhaps, then, Scopas was not so pleased with Simonides' encomium after all.

This is of course only a hypothesis: but it has at least the virtues of accounting for the poem's oddities and of being supported both by parallels from contemporary Greek literature[60] and by what we know about Simonides and can guess about Scopas. If it is accepted provisionally as plausible, the result is curious: interpretations of the poem along more or less similar lines dominated throughout the nineteenth century, while the moral reading our century has favored seems never to have occurred to anyone before Wilamowitz. In the nineteenth century, the constitution of the text was still far from secure, but its interpretation had achieved results remarkably similar to those proposed here. There is, however, this important difference: older scholars sought some particular referent, some specific outrage which Scopas had actually committed and to which this poem was covertly alluding (thereby laying themselves open to the objection that Simonides must have been an extremely tactless encomiast if his eulogy was really a concealed accusation), while the present study argues in terms of a more generalized ideological system involving power and discourse, praise and blame. In the nineteenth century most scholars agreed that Scopas must have been unpopular: they were uncertain only about precisely what crime he had committed to become so unpopular.[61] It was Wilamowitz's influential article which both finally provided an apparently reliable text for the poem and liquidated the traditional interpretation of it in terms of Scopas' unpopularity as a "groundless assumption," substituting for it the (equally groundless) moral reading in which intention comes to replace archaic morality.[62] After Wilamowitz, most scholars went on to print an acceptable text but to burden it with an implausible interpretation, freeing the text of Simonides from the context of the *Protagoras*, while locking its meaning into the context of Protagoras' and Socrates' discussion of ἀρετή.

Just as the right text does not entail a plausible interpretation, so too a faulty text need not preclude one. Sometimes, the text may be less important than the contexts against which it is set.

---

[59] Respectively, (a) Plut. *De aud. poet.* 15D; (b) Callim. Fr. 68 Pf., Cic. *De nat. deor.* 2.86. 352, Quintil. *Inst. orat.* 11.2.12ff.; (c) Plut. *Cato mai.* 18, *De cupid. devit.* 527C. Van Groningen (1948) 2-7 suggests on the basis of the first of these passages that Simonides' Thessalian poems had no myths; but this strange view rests upon a misunderstanding of the term ἀπάτη.

[60] Most notably Pindar's Second Pythian Ode, on which see Most (1985) 101-32.

[61] E.g., Aars (1888) 13; Apelt (1922) 132 n. 102; Bergk (1882) 385-6; Bertram (1885) 55; Flach (1884) 635; Jurenka (1906) 869, 874-5; Madvig (1875) 413; Michelangeli (1896) 10-11; Müller (1875) 354; Sauppe (1857) xx; Schneidewin (1835) xv, xxviii, and 21-22, and (1839) 379; Smyth (1900) 311-2; Taylor (1960) 253 and n. 1.

[62] Wilamowitz-Moellendorff (1913) 169.

CONTEXTS OF INTERPRETATION

It is hard to explain the recent popularity of the so-called New Historicism in Anglo-American modern language studies except as an exaggerated reaction to some of the exaggerations of Deconstruction, which preceded and accompanied it. Deconstruction, for its part, had succeeded in supplanting New Criticism and imposing itself not only by virtue of its intrinsic merits and by a particularly felicitous starting-position within American academic politics, but also because in certain crucial regards it could be seen to satisfy some of the very same criteria which New Criticism had established as valid over the course of several decades. Both critical approaches practised especially refined and subtle varieties of close reading in preference to external contextualizations (history, biography, psychology, etc.). Both focused upon a relatively small canon of great works (for the most part Romantic and so-called pre- and post-Romantic), and both tended to discover within these works structures of paradox and irony. This continuity of taste and method subtended, permitted, and to a certain extent defused the differences between the two methods: Deconstruction's enlargement of the canon to include not only lyric poetry but also great novels and works of philosophy (for the most part, again, Romantic and so-called pre- and post-Romantic), and its reinterpretation of repetition no longer as a sign and instrument of organic closure, but instead as an uncontrolled symptom of the obsessive failure to attain closure. If New Criticism had thought it could dispense once and for all with the category of intention, Deconstruction discovered itself compulsively returning over and over again to its starting point in the problematization of that very same category.

As happens so often in intellectual history, New Historicism moved to usurp Deconstruction's dominance by rehearsing some of the same strategies which Deconstruction had applied with such success against New Criticism. If Deconstruction had enlarged the canon to include fiction and philosophy, New Historicism went on to include virtually any text whatsoever, not disdaining historiography (understood as just one more text) and public and private documents, or even advertising and the artifacts of popular culture. Now, however, the category of literariness, which had fortified the bastion of New Criticism's and Deconstruction's smaller canon, would clearly no longer do. Instead, the concept of ideology had to be deployed so as to bridge the differences between literary and non-literary texts. The real but secondary differences in method between the two schools were well illustrated by those which separated their two French inspirers: if Derrida represented one extreme of programmatically syntagmatic or metonymic exploration of purely internal contextualizations, leaping nimbly from one part of a text to another without seeming to trouble himself to explain his method or to seek external warrants for his claims, Foucault championed entirely paradigmatic or metaphorical studies of largely external contextualizations, jumping agilely from a passage in one text to one in another, and then to others linked with one another only by their all belonging to the same generously defined period. Beneath the undeniable differences lay an unacknowledged similarity: both methods derived their impetus, their fascination, and their limitation from the determined refusal to attempt systematically to integrate with one another internal and external recontextualizations. Indeed, even in their preferred objects of study, polemic concealed consensus. Deconstruction and Derrida focused on the impossibility of authenticity, consciousness, and representation, to be sure, while New Historicism and Foucault pursued the themes of sexuality, power, and marginalization; but what fascinated both were the failed attempts to establish autonomy and control, the dissonances and ruptures within and between discourses, the crises of a subjectivity conceived not as individual but as general or social. Thus it was that those who were dissatisfied with what they considered Deconstruction's esoteric aestheticism could come to celebrate New Historicism's apparent commitment to political issues. Yet they would find the transition from the one school to the other made surprisingly painless by their underlying similarities.

Now that the wave of New Historicism has already crested in modern language studies, leaving the jetsam of Cultural Studies stranded on the shores of numerous English and Comparative Literature departments in the United States, it can be expected to begin to wash sooner or later upon Classics as well — indeed, in the recent writings of a few remarkably prescient classical scholars, this has already happened.[63] Such is the state of classical scholarship that this will bring not only disadvantages. Classics is still often burdened by an astonishingly unsophisticated view of the relation between ancient literature and ancient history: on the one side words, on the other things; on the one hand individual subjectivities and poetic refinements, on the other institutional constraints and the brutalities of power. Ancient historians are too often seen not as authors of one more problematic (and in many regards fictional) text, but as the immediate and transparent expression of the way things were, as purveyors of a self-evident historical truth which can then be used to resolve the challenges posed by literature; while ancient poets are too often examined only from the perspective of their connection to specific political events, as though the inevitable obscurity of such connections were the only or most interesting of the difficulties they pose. In this regard as in others, the wide-spread institutional division between departments of classical philology and departments of ancient history represents a betrayal of Wolf's ideal of "Altertumswissenschaft."[64]

---

[63] Comparing Winkler (1985) and (1989) clearly reveals two stages in this transition. Some further examples are to be found in Selden and Hexter (1992).

[64] On the origins and meaning of this ideal, see Most (1993b).

Perhaps the New Historicism will shake matters up. To be sure, it may fade away fairly quickly itself, for it is unlikely to be able to resist for long the elementary truth that interpretation involves systematic recourse to both internal and external contextualizations, cooperating with one another as constant checks and confirmations. In the meantime it may do some good; at the very least, it should serve to undermine facile oppositions between history and literature. Not only Simonides' ode to Scopas, but many other ancient poetic texts, may end up benefiting by being put into historical contexts which are highly specific, not because they are made up exclusively of particular identifiable political or personal events, but instead because they form complex and dynamic ideological structures. In the present case, the contrasts between a Thessalian landed feudal dynast and an island-born but pan-Hellenically ambitious enlightened poet, between the controlled exploitation of commissioned praise and the eruptive possibilities of unfettered blame, between traditional admiration of success and power on the one hand and of moral virtue on the other, create a unique set of contradictions and imbalances within the general system of relations between power and discourse in late sixth-century Greece. Simonides' poem is not only a response to a particular historical situation which we shall never fully recover: it is also the medium in which a larger and more complex historical context theorizes itself, bringing to consciousness and to eloquent expression its richly self-contradictory identity. Small wonder, then, that Simonides chose to begin his ode with Pittacus' proverb: for in his subtle attempt to unfold the ambiguity of χαλεπόν — is it hard to be good, or is it impossible? — are concentrated many of the contradictions of his whole culture.

BIBLIOGRAPHY

Aars J. (1888) "Das Gedicht des Simonides in Platons *Protagoras*", *Christiana Videnskabs-Selskabs Forhandlinger* 5 (1888).
Adkins A.W.H. (1960) *Merit and Responsibility. A Study in Greek Values* (Oxford: 1960).
Apelt O. (1922) *Platons Dialog Protagoras* (Leipzig: ²1922).
Babut D. (1975) "Simonide Moraliste", *Revue des Études Grecques* 88 (1975) 20-62.
Balasch M. (1967) "Sófocles y Simónides", *Boletin des Instituto de Estudios Helenicos (Barcelona, Facoldade de Filosofia)* 1 (1967) 45-63.
Bergk T. (1882) *Poetae Lyrici Graeci. 3: Poetas Melicos continens* (Leipzig: ⁴1882).
Bertram H. (1885) *Platons Protagoras für den Schulgebrauch erklärt* (Gotha: 1885).
Blass F. (1872) "Das Simonideische Gedicht im *Protagoras* des Platon", *Rheinisches Museum* 27 (1872) 326-32.
Bowie E.L. (1986) "Early Greek Elegy, Symposium, and Public Festival", *Journal of Hellenic Studies* 106 (1986) 13-35.
Bowra C.M. (1934) "Simonides and Scopas", *Classical Philology* 29 (1934) 230-9.
—— (1961) *Greek Lyric Poetry* (Oxford: ²1961).
Campbell D.A. (1967) *Greek Lyric Poetry: A Selection* (London: 1967).
Carson A. (1992) "How Not to Read a Poem: Unmixing Simonides from *Protagoras*", *Classical Philology* 87 (1992) 110-30.
Christ G. (1941). *Simonidesstudien* (Freiburg: 1941).

Crotty K. (1982) *Song and Action: The Victory Odes of Pindar* (Baltimore-London: 1982).

des Places E. (1969) "Simonide et Socrate dans le «Protagoras» de Platon", *Les Études Classiques* 37 (1969) 236-44.

Detienne M. (1964) "Simonide de Céos ou la sécularisation de la poèsie", *Revue des Études Grecques* 77 (1964) 405-19.

Dickie M. (1978) "The Argument and Form of Simonides 542 *PMG*", *Harvard Studies in Classical Philology* 82 (1978) 21-33.

Donlan W. (1969) "Simonides, Fr. 4D and *P. Oxy.* 2432", *Transactions of the American Philological Association* 100 (1969) 71-95.

Easterling P.E. (1974) "Alcman 58 and Simonides 37", *Proceedings of the Cambridge Philological Association* 200 (1974) 37-43.

Flach H. (1884) *Geschichte der griechischen Lyrik nach den Quellen dargestellt* (Tübingen: 1884).

Fränkel H. (1962) *Dichtung und Philosophie des frühen Griechentums. Eine Geschichte der griechischen Epik, Lyrik und Prosa bis zur Mitte des fünften Jahrhunderts* (Munich: ³1962).

—— (1968) *Wege und Formen frühgriechischen Denkens. Literarische und philosophiegeschichtliche Studien*, ed. F. Tietze (Munich: 1968).

Gentili B. (1964) "Studi su Simonide. II: Simonide e Platone", *Maia* 16 (1964) 278-306.

Gerber D.E. (1970) *Euterpe. An Anthology of Early Greek Lyric, Elegiac, and Iambic Poetry* (Amsterdam: 1970).

Gigon O. (1946) "Studien zu Platons *Protagoras*", in *Phyllobolia für Peter von der Mühll zum 60. Geburtstag...*, ed. O. Gigon, K. Meuli, W. Theiler, F. Wehrli, and B. Wyss (Basel: 1946) 91-152.

Gundert H. (1952) "Die Simonides-Interpretation in Platons *Protagoras*", in *EPMHNEIA. Festschrift O. Regenbogen...* (Heidelberg: 1952) 71-93.

Jurenka H. (1906) "Des Simonides Siegeslied auf Skopas in Platons *Protagoras*", *Zeitschrift für die österreichischen Gymnasien* 57 (1906) 865-75.

Kegel W.J.H.F. (1962) *Simonides* (Groningen: 1962).

Kleist H.v. (1880) "Die methodologische bedeutung des platonischen dialogs *Protagoras*", *Philologus* 39 (1880) 1-32.

Madvig J.N. (1875) "Exegetische Bemerkungen. 2: Platons *Protagoras* 346B. Das Gedicht des Simonides auf den Skopas", in *Kleine philologische Schriften* (Leipzig: 1875).

Maschke R. (1926) *Die Willenslehre im griechischen Recht* (Berlin: 1926).

Michelangeli L.A. (1896) *Frammenti della melica greca da Terpandro a Bacchilide* (Bologna: 1896).

Most G.W. (1982) "Greek Lyric Poets", in *Ancient Writers: Greece and Rome*, ed. T.J. Luce (New York: 1982) 1.75-98.

—— (1984) "Rhetorik und Hermeneutik: Zur Konstitution der Neuzeitlichkeit", *Antike und Abendland* 30 (1984) 62-79.

—— (1985) *The Measures of Praise: Structure and Function in Pindar's Second Pythian and Seventh Nemean Odes* (Göttingen: 1985).

—— (1986) "Sophistique et herméneutique," in *Positions de la Sophistique. Colloque de Cérisy*, ed. B. Cassin (Paris: 1986) 233-45.

—— (1993a) "The Uses of ἔνδοξα: Philosophy and Rhetoric in the *Rhetoric*," in *Symposium Aristotelicum 1990: Aristotle on Rhetoric and Philosophy*, ed. D.J. Furley and A. Nehamas (Princeton: 1993).

—— (1993b) "Literature and Classical Scholarship in the Eighteenth Century," in *The Cambridge History of Literary Criticism*, Vol. 4, ed. H.B. Nisbet and C. Rawson (Cambridge: 1993).

Müller K.O. (1875) *Geschichte der griechischen Literatur bis auf das Zeitalter Alexander's*, Vol. 1 (Stuttgart: ³1875).

Murray O. ed. (1990) *Sympotica: a Symposium on the Symposion* (Oxford: 1990).

Page D.L. (1962) *Poetae Melici Graeci* (Oxford: 1962).

Parry H. (1965) "An Interpretation of Simonides 4 (Diehl)", *Transactions of the American Philological Association* 96 (1965) 297-320.

Pfeiffer R. (1929) "Gottheit und Individuum in der frühgriechischen Lyrik", *Philologus* 84 (1929) 137-52.

Reinhardt K. (1916) *Parmenides und die Geschichte der griechischen Philosophie* (Bonn: 1916).

Rösler W. (1980) *Dichter und Gruppe. Eine Untersuchung zu den Bedingungen und zur historischen Funktion früher griechischer Lyrik am Beispiel Alkaios* (Munich: 1980).

Rohdich H. (1979) "Das verspottete Jenseits", *Rheinisches Museum für Philologie* 122 (1979) 119-30.

Sauppe H. (1857) *Platons Ausgewählte Dialogen. 2: Protagoras* (Berlin: 1857).

Schneidewin F.G. (1835) *Simonidis Cei Carminum Reliquiae* (Braunschweig: 1835).

—— (1839) *Delectus Poetarum Iambicorum et Melicorum Graecorum* (Göttingen: 1839).

Schütrumpf E. (1987) "Simonides an Skopas (542 PMG)", *Würzburger Jahrbücher* 13 (1987) 11-23.

Schultz W. (1914) "Rätsel", in *RE* II.1.A (Stuttgart: 1914) 62-125.

Scodel R. (1987) "Literary Interpretation in Plato's *Protagoras*", *Ancient Philosophy* 6 (1987) 25-37.

Segal C. (1985) "Choral Lyric in the Fifth Century," in *The Cambridge History of Classical Literature. I: Greek Literature*, ed. by P.E. Easterling and B.M.W. Knox (Cambridge: 1985).

Selden D. and Hexter R. ed. (1992) *Innovations of Antiquity* (New York: 1992).

Smyth H.W. (1900) *Greek Melic Poets* (London: 1900).

Svenbro J. (1984) *La parola e il marmo. Alle origini della poetica greca* (Turin: 1984).

Taylor, A.E. (1960) *Plato. The Man and his Work* (London: ⁷1960).

van Groningen B.A. (1948) "Simonide et les Thessaliens", *Mnemosyne* 1 (1948) 1-7.

Verdam H.D. (1928) "De carmine Simonideo, quod interpretatur Plato in Protagora dialogo", *Mnemosyne* 56 (1928) 299-310.

Vernant J.P. (1979) "πάντα καλά d'Homère à Simonide", *Annali della Scuola Normale Superiore di Pisa, Classe di lettere e filosofia* 3:9 (1979) 1365-74.

Vetta M. (1983) *Poesia e simposio nella Grecia antica. Guida storica* (Rome-Bari: 1983).

Wilamowitz-Moellendorff U. v. (1913) *Sappho und Simonides. Untersuchungen über griechische Lyriker* (Berlin: 1913).

Winkler J.J. (1985) *Auctor & Actor. A Narratological Reading of Apuleius's The Golden Ass* (Berkeley-Los Angeles-London: 1985).

—— (1989) *Constraints of Desire: The Anthropology of Sex and Gender in Ancient Greece* (New York: 1989).

Woodbury L. (1953) "Simonides on ἀρετή", *Transactions of the American Philological Association* 84 (1953) 135-63.

INTERTEXTUALITY AND THEOCRITUS 13

BY

A. MARIA VAN ERP TAALMAN KIP

INTRODUCTION: INTERTEXTUALITY

The term intertextuality derives from Julia Kristeva, according to whom every text is "a permutation of texts, an intertextuality: in the space of a given text, several utterances, taken from other texts, intersect and neutralize one another" (1980: 36). And elsewhere she describes the phenomenon as follows: "any text is constructed as a mosaic of quotations; any text is the absorption and transformation of another. The notion of *intertextuality* replaces that of intersubjectivity, and poetic language is read as at least double" (1980: 66).

The term has gained a firm foothold since the appearance of Kristeva's book, but that is not to say that all critics use it in the same way she does, or even share her views. To Kristeva intertextuality is the conditio sine qua non of *every* written or spoken text and she quickly dropped the term when others began to use it in a sense not meant by her — "le sens banal de 'critique des sources' d'un texte" (1974: 59).

Although my discussion will centre on Theocritus' poem, and not on the theory of intertextuality, a few preliminary remarks are in order. It is customary today to distinguish between a broad and a restricted concept of intertextuality and these different concepts entail rather different views on fundamental issues: the status of the author, the work and the reader.[1] Kristeva virtually abolished the role of the author. Her concept of intertextuality is, as Pfister says, "the text-theoretical lever with which she, in the context of a marxist-freudian deconstruction of subjectivity, wants to disrupt the bourgeois concept of an autonomous subject who wants to convey something. The author of the text thereby becomes the mere playground of the intertextual game, whereas the production shifts to the text itself" (1985: 8).[2]

---

[1] For a general survey of opinions, see Mertens and Beekman (1990) 1-24, and Pfister (1985).

[2] "Der texttheoretische Hebel, mit dem sie im Kontext einer marxistisch-freudianischen Dekonstruktion der Subjektivität den bürgerlichen Begriff eines autonomen und intentionalen Subjekts aus den Angeln heben will. Der Autor eines Textes wird damit zum blossen Projektionsraum des intertextuellen Spiels, während die Produktivität auf den Text selber

To Barthes, whose views are akin to Kristeva's, the absence of the author is the hallmark of literature. He distinguishes between 'work' and 'Text': the Text is enthroned, while the work is considered an object of consumption (1986: 62). The author, he says, "is reputed to be the father and the owner of his work; ... the Text on the other hand is read without the Father's inscription" (61). Elsewhere he argues that: "literature (it would be better, from now on, to say *writing*), by refusing to assign to the text (and to the world-as-text) a "secret", i.e. an ultimate meaning, liberates an activity we may call countertheological, properly revolutionary, for to refuse to halt meaning is finally to refuse God and his hypostases, reason, science, the law" (54).

In the view of both Kristeva and Barthes everything is — or ought to be — up to the reader, and the text does not — or ought not to — imply a meaning. At the other end of the spectrum we find those critics who reinstate the author and even the author's intention. According to Broich, for instance, intertextuality occurs "when an author in composing his text not only is aware of using other texts but also expects his recipient to recognise that the relation between the text he is reading and other texts is intended by the author and that it is important for the understanding of this text. Thus intertextuality in this more restricted sense presupposes the successful realisation of a very specific communication process, where not only the author *and* the reader are aware of the intertextuality of a text but where also both partners in the communication process take into account the other's awareness" (1985: 31).[3]

Many critics engaged in the interpretation of a separate poem or novel tend towards a more restricted concept of intertextuality, such as that of Broich. That is to say, they do not consider the reader supreme, and do not deny the text a meaning to be sought by the reader. Moreover, as a rule the ideological overtones of Kristeva and Barthes are lacking. However, it is not surprising that objections are often raised to the notion of the 'author's intention'. In his stimulating work, Claes puts it as follows: "It is often suggested that the reader must try to discover the author's intention. Such a method leads almost inevitably to psychologising, whereby the text as it stands is reduced to a more original 'text': the intention of its author. This is quite a presumptuous undertaking: surely we cannot look into the author's

---

übergeht."

   [3] "Wenn ein Autor bei der Abfassung seines Textes sich nicht nur der Verwendung anderer Texte bewusst ist, sondern auch vom Rezipienten erwartet, dass er diese Beziehung zwischen seinem Text und anderen Texten als vom Autor intendiert und als wichtig für das Verständnis seines Textes erkennt. Intertextualität in diesem engeren Sinn setzt also das Gelingen eines ganz bestimmten Kommunikationsprozesses voraus, bei dem nicht nur Autor *und* Leser sich der Intertextualität eines Textes bewusst sind, sondern bei dem jeder der beiden Partner des Kommunikationsvorgangs darüber hinaus auch das Intertextualitätsbewusstsein seines Partners miteinkalkuliert." Cf. Pfister (1985) 27, and Schulte-Middelich (1985) 206.

head? Does the author himself always know his intentions? And are these intentions always realised in his work?" (1988: 59; the translation is mine). The implied answer to these questions is obviously 'no', and of course it is not advisable to search for a more original text as described by Claes; no such text exists, and we would simply be creating a text of our own. Nevertheless, Claes, too, is unwilling to give the reader plenary powers. Not *all* the readers' associations are relevant to a work's intertextuality, and not *all* interpretations are equally valid. But how are we to judge?

Claes does not offer any clear solution, and perhaps there is none. However, we should at least try not to contradict the author's intention. In a number of cases we know what he did *not* intend; thus he does not refer to texts that did not yet exist in his time or could not possibly be known to him. We can be quite sure that Theocritus does not refer to Vergil or the New Testament or Chinese poetry.

Elsewhere in his book Claes returns to this problem, stating again that the author's intention cannot be a determining factor. "Cryptomnesia", he says, "the unconscious remembrance of details, is a common phenomenon. It is, for instance, quite possible that an author, within a culture so deeply imbued with Christianity as is ours, unknowingly introduces a number of biblical allusions" (1988: 132). This is possible indeed, although unconscious remembrance need not play a part. An author may use a well-known expression, without realising that it is derived from the Bible. He may say for example 'give a stone for bread' without thinking for a moment of *Matthew* 7.9. In such cases the author's intention is absent, but the reader cannot be sure and it may be difficult to decide whether such a reference should be taken into account or ignored. However, the rest of the work may be of help. If there are other clearer references to the Bible, we cannot go far wrong if we assume that also the questionable one was meant the same way.

Broich's restricted definition of intertextuality is intended primarily to rule out the notion of 'influence': "A text, for example, may have been influenced by other texts, while the author is not aware of this influence or does not consider the perception of this influence by the reader a requirement for the adequate understanding of his text" (1985: 31-32).[4] The reader may note such an influence, but although it may play a part in his evaluation, it does not enable him to achieve a more thorough interpretation. Nor is plagiarism covered by Broich's definition, since a plagiarising author does *not* intend the reader to detect the text(s) behind his text.

One may well ask whether intertextuality in its more restricted sense presents us with an approach to literature that is really new. Is it not in

---

[4] "So kann z.B. ein Text durch andere Texte beeinflusst sein, ohne dass der Autor sich dieses Einflusses bewusst ist oder ohne dass er die Erkenntnis dieses Einflusses durch den Leser als Voraussetzung für das adäquate Verständnis seines Textes ansieht."

effect a specious term for a well-known practice — old wine in a new bottle? Classical scholars in particular may be inclined to ask this question and to answer it in the affirmative. Nevertheless, the introduction of the term and the amount of discussion it prompted have undoubtedly focused attention on a number of relevant issues. In what way does the author incorporate the work of a forerunner (the 'praetext') in his own text? How does the reader become aware of the presence of the praetext? And, in particular, what are the function and the effect of the praetext in its new context? I shall deal with the last question in connection with Theocritus' *Idyll* 13, and a few general observations will be made on the other two.

An author may refer to a literary genre without referring to any particular text. Aristophanes' 'tragic' lines, for example, are not always related to a definite passage from tragedy; nevertheless, by their wording and metrical rigour they refer to the tragic genre as a whole. Likewise, the mere choice of a certain metre may conjure up a body of texts composed in this same metre. But in instances like these the praetext is not a definite work which is present, wholly or in part, in the background of the new text.

When a work as a whole is meant to refer to another work, the author may indicate this to his readers in various ways. He may do so, for example, by means of the title of his work, by the names he gives to his characters, or by introducing the praetext as an object of interest to his characters.[5] In a number of cases such indications will alert even a reader who does not know the praetext(s), simply by making him feel that there is something that he cannot quite grasp. He may then go in search of clues. But if he feels that the text is completely comprehensible to him, the signals will fail to reach him, clear though they may seem to a reader who does know the praetext.

The same can be said with regard to references to a definite line or passage from a praetext. Such a reference may be so obvious that no reader can miss it. The following lines from Eliot's *The Waste Land* are a classic example:

> *Poi s'ascose nel foco che gli affina*
> *Quando fiam uti Chelidon* — O swallow swallow
> *Le Prince d'Aquitaine à la tour abolie*

Since Eliot is quoting Dante, the *Pervigilium Veneris* and Gérard de Nerval in the original languages, and since the quotations are printed in italics, the reader will be in no doubt. Moreover, since Eliot has added notes to his poem, the reader can locate the quotations and examine them in their original context. Armed with the necessary knowledge, he may then return to *The Waste Land*, to ponder their presence there.

---

[5] A number of instances, especially concerning the novel, will be found in Broich (1985) 35-46.

However, the above example, classic though it may be, is most extreme and therefore not particularly illuminating. If the praetext is in a foreign language, authors will often translate their quotations or use an existing translation. Moreover, in most cases we are not concerned with verbal quotations of any length. The author may vary the praetext, add to it or summarize it, or merely allude to it by means of some significant words. And more often than not these quotations or allusions are not clearly marked off but rather woven into the pattern of their new context. In *Idyll* 2, 106-110, Theocritus is unmistakably referring to Sappho's fr. 31, but the reader who is not familiar with this poem will not be aware of this and will not have the feeling that something has escaped him.

In discussing the relationship between the *Aeneid* and the Homeric poems, Lyne shows how Vergil 'helps' his readers. He notes for example "the striking verbal similarity of Aeneas' opening situation to Odysseus' in *Od.* 5: it signals the presence of Odysseus behind the figure of Aeneas — inviting us to compare and contrast, and to ask questions" (1987: 103-104). But of course, this striking verbal similarity is only of help to the reader who has a thorough knowledge of the *Odyssey*: "The reader is supposed to know the source material and the significance it had in its own setting, and bring that knowledge to bear when he reads the new construction". (102) Nevertheless, if one were to read Vergil without knowing Homer, the *Aeneid* would not be incomprehensible. But it would certainly not be understood completely; one has to know the praetext "soll das Sinnpotential des Textes ausgeschöpft werden" (Pfister 1985: 23).

Now Vergil could be sure of his readers, for they undoubtedly knew their Homer. But a modern author cannot always be that sure. His reading public is much more scattered and may be spread over several continents. Literary education is far less uniform than it was in antiquity and a reader cannot possibly carry with him the cultural baggage of every single author. He may very well enjoy a novel or a poem without recognising the importance of its intertextuality, and in such a case the communication between author and reader is only partially successful. Critical scholarship may be of help here, but no small demands are made on the reader: the more he has read, the more he will understand.

ANCIENT GREEK INTERTEXTUALITY. THE HYLAS STORY

Joseph Schöpp (1985: 333) posits that intertextuality is preferably demonstrated on the basis of postmodern texts: "In texts like these authors are quoting intensively and compulsively, such as is customary especially in the last stage of a culture; a stage in which creativity manifests itself first of all in reverting to the preceding".[6] In the following sentence he refers to this as "alexandrinische Praxis". There is a measure of truth in this: Alexandrian, or rather Hellenistic, poetry sought to break new paths without entirely abandoning tradition, creating something new by varying the old. Thus it is understandable that intertextuality should play a role of some importance in the work of these poets. We can be certain about their authorial intention, while they, for their part, could be certain that they would be understood by their readers. Writing for a highly erudite in-crowd, they knew that their allusions and the way they played with literary tradition would not be lost on them.

When studying the Hellenistic poets we must realise that part of the intertextuality may ecape us, for the simple reason that much of Greek literature that was known to them has been lost to us. And when we turn to Theocritus' *Idyll* 13, the epyllion about Hylas and Heracles, the written tradition faces us us with another problem: the fact that we often do not know with certainty when a particular Greek work 'appeared'.

The actual source of the Hylas story is unknown. Strabo describes (12.4.3) a ritual in which the citizens of Cios took to the hills and called on Hylas, since Heracles had charged them never to give up the search. The Hellenistic poets may have been inspired by this local tradition, but according to the scholion accompanying *Argonautica* 1355-7, the Laconian epicist Cinaethon had already told the story: ὅτι δὲ Κιανοὶ ... ὤμοσαν μὴ λήξειν ζητοῦντες Ὕλαν ... Κιναίθων ἱστορεῖ ἐν Ἡρακλείᾳ. Today, however, Cinaethon is such a shadowy figure that we can say with certainty only that the story appeared (or reappeared) in the third century, and from then on seems to have had a great deal of appeal for many authors.[7]

It is not certain that Callimachus ever wrote a poem about Hylas, and even assuming that he did, we have no way of knowing how he dealt with the theme.[8] We do, however, have the version by Apollonius, and it is here that our problems begin. It is abundantly clear that there is a relationship between Theocritus' poem and *Argonautica* 1.1207-1372, but we have absolutely no criterion for determining which text came first. Theories have been put forward, but these are based on esthetic and thus subjective

---

[6] "In solchen Texten wird nämlich mit einer Intensität und Zwanghaftigkeit zitiert, wie dies vor allem in kulturellen Spätzeiten üblich ist, in denen Kreativität sich zuallererst im Rückgriff auf Vorgängiges manifestiert."

[7] We know that Hylas appeared in the work of Nicander. In Latin literature we meet him in the poetry of Propertius (1.20) and Valerius Flaccus (*Arg.* 3.487-597). Vergil (*Georgica* 3.6) makes it clear that the theme was very popular: *cui non dictus Hylas puer* ...?

[8] The scholiast of Apollonius (ad *Arg.* 1.1207) finds fault with the poet because Hylas is carrying a woman's jar: πιθανώτερον δὲ ἦν ἀμφορέα εἰπεῖν, ὡς Καλλίμαχος. This remark seems to suggest that Callimachus did write about Hylas, but Pfeiffer does not consider this decisive proof: *de quolibet iuvene vel viro dixisse potest* (see fr. 596 in his edition of Callimachus).

considerations. Those who opt for Theocritus (such as Gow) say that he 'improved upon' Apollonius, and for that reason must have come later. Those who prefer Apollonius (such as Köhnken) hold that the reverse is true. The discussion has gotten no further than this type of speculative argumentation, and as long as there are no external data on which to base a standpoint, the problem will remain insoluble.

As we have seen, it is an indisputable fact that here one poet is drawing on the work of the other. But if we continue to use the criterion of authorial intention, then an intertextual relationship with Apollonius' epic can only exist if Theocritus reacted to the *Argonautica* and not vice versa. For this reason, in my discussion of the 13th *Idyll* I will disregard the Apollonius passage, and confine myself to those authors who clearly preceded Theocritus. Even with this restriction, there will be no shortage of material.

THEOCRITUS' HYLAS. IDYLL 13

Theocritus presents the theme of his poem — Eros — in the initial verses, which are addressed to Nicias: the god plays a role not only in their own lives, indeed, not only in the lives of mortals. To illustrate this fact, he then introduces Heracles. There are those who say that the section addressed to Nicias continues up to and including v. 15, and that the actual story does not start until 16.[9] However, I do not believe that the line can be that finely drawn, given that ἀλλ' at the beginning of 16 forms a link with the opening words of 10: χωρὶς δ'οὐδέποκ' ἧς, 'and he never parted from him'. We would do better to confine ourselves to the assertion that once Heracles has been introduced, the direct link with the addressee is dropped.

Heracles is presented to the readers as 'Amphitryon's son with the heart of bronze, he who resisted the raging lion' (5-6). These words are unmistakably epically coloured, if only by virtue of τὸν λῖν. This word for 'lion' occurs several times in the *Iliad*, and once in the pseudo Hesiodic *Shield of Heracles* (172), reappearing only in Antimachus. χαλκεοκάρδιος is a different story. Compound adjectives beginning with χαλκο- or χαλκεο- often appear in the *Iliad*, but there they refer to the weapons of the combatants, and not to their hearts.[10] Gow's reference to ἦτορ χάλκεον (2.490) is hardly relevant, since here the poet is speaking of his own heart: without the support of the Muses he would not be able to list the Greek warriors, even if he possessed a χάλκεον ἦτορ. This is the only time that χάλκεος or χάλκειος is used by Homer in relation to the heart or the mind,

---

[9] So for example Pretagostini (1984) 92.
[10] χαλκεοθώρηξ (*Il.* 4.448; 8.62), χαλκεοχίτων (*Il.* 1.371; 2.47 *et alibi*), χαλκοκορυστής (*Il.* 5.699; 6.199 *et alibi*), χαλκοπάρῃος (*Il.* 12.183; 17.294; 20.397), χαλκοκνῆμις (*Il.* 7.41). In one case the voice is said to be of bronze: χαλκεόφωνος (*Il.* 5.785).

but he does use σιδήρεος, 'iron', in this way. Achilles, says the dying Hector, has a σιδήρεος θυμός (22.357), a 'heart of iron', and Penelope has, according to Odysseus, a σιδήρεον ἦτορ (*Od.* 23.172). This does not indicate that somebody is courageous, but rather relentless and merciless; in *Od.* 5.191 Calypso contrasts a θυμὸς σιδήρεος with a θυμὸς ἐλεήμων, a 'compassionate mind'. Likewise σιδηρόφρων, which appears twice in Aeschylus, is a negative qualification.[11] Theocritus may well have coined the adjective χαλκεοκάρδιος, thus evoking associations with epic poetry and at the same time creating a certain ambiguity. Is Heracles characterised only as a hero or, to some extent, as a brute as well? In any case, the heart of bronze has its weak spot: Heracles ἤρατο παιδός (6), 'was in love with a boy'.

Theocritus examines two aspects of the relationship between Heracles and Hylas. First we are told that Heracles is planning to groom his sweet ἐρώμενος, 'the boy with the braid of hair', to be as great a hero as he is himself. And second, we learn that Heracles never left his side, neither in the afternoon, nor the morning, nor the evening.

It is worthwhile to consider here the manner in which Theocritus describes these three parts of the day. First there is the afternoon: οὔτ' εἰ μέσον ἆμαρ ὄροιτο (10), 'not when noon had set in'; according to Dover, this part of the day is "expressed plainly". But is it? ὄρνυμι is preeminently an epic verb and the word combination μέσον ἦμαρ is used in a similar way in the *Iliad*: in the enumeration of the three parts of the day.[12] Before killing Lycaon Achilles says to him:

ἔσσεται ἢ ἠὼς ἢ δείλη ἢ μέσον ἦμαρ
ὁππότε τις καὶ ἐμεῖο Ἄρη ἐκ θυμὸν ἔληται

(21.111-112)

('There shall come a dawn or eve or midday, when my life too shall some man take in battle.'

Transl. A.T. Murray)

It does not seem too far-fetched to suppose that Theocritus' μέσον ἆμαρ derives from 21.111 and that, as Gutzwiller (1981: 21) says, the lines 10b-13 are an 'expansion' of this line.[13] But if we accept this, another question

---

[11] Gow refers not only to χάλκεον ἦτορ but also to σιδηρόφρων: "χαλκεοκάρδιος = σιδηρόφρων, having an ἦτορ χάλκεον (*Il.* 2.490)". But since there is hardly any similarity between the poet's heart of bronze and the 'iron mind' of all those who do not pity Prometheus (A. *Pr.* 244), the reader is none the wiser.

[12] The use of the Homeric ἦμαρ (or ἆμαρ) is not in itself remarkable, since Theocritus uses it regularly and for an obvious reason: the metrical structure of ἡμέρα is poorly suited to the hexameter; ἀμέρα is found only in 29.7, a poem that is written in another metre. Forms of ὄρνυμι, however, are rare in the *Idylls*; there is only ὦρσεν in 24,15 and ἐπῶρσαν in 24,82.

[13] Cf. Campbell (1990) 115, note 3: "an elaborate reworking, in ascending tricolon form, of *Il.* 21.111".

presents itself. Theocritus is alluding here to one of the most impressive and most solemn passages of the *Iliad* and the contrast between the original context and the new one could not be greater. Homer's Achilles speaks of the inevitable moment of death: Patroclus has died, he himself will die, so why not Lycaon? Theocritus describes the daily life of two inseparable lovers. Does he intend this contrast merely to underline the distance between the *Iliad* and his own poetry? Or does he, by evoking the thought of death, also suggest what will become of Heracles' love? Even inseparable lovers are parted by death, and although Hylas does not die in the normal sense of the word, he does depart from normal life and is lost to Heracles. The allusion may have been meant in this way, but I am not altogether sure.

Next, the morning is described: οὔθ᾽ ὁπόχ᾽ ἁ λεύκιππος ἀνατρέχοι ἐς Διὸς ᾽Αώς ('nor when Dawn with her white horses rushed upwards to Zeus' palace'; 11), but following this highly poetic description (λεύκιππος is also found in the 'grande lyrique'; Bacchylides fr. 20 c 22) we are transported to a totally different world. In describing the evening, Theocritus uses the image of a mother hen who flaps her wings as a sign that it is time for her chicks to take to the roost for the night (12-13).[14] Gow comments: "The homely picture of the hen settling for the night and the chickens about to follow her to roost has charm, but it consorts somewhat oddly both with its heroic setting and with the chariot of Dawn in the preceding line." He seems to think this is somewhat awkward of the poet, while it is precisely this kind of contrast which Theocritus is striving for. In this poem he brings together worlds that are incompatible with one another, and so he does in this passage. His description negates the sublimity of the preceding line, while at the same time he adopts a slightly mocking view of the superhero Heracles. There is, after all, a certain parallel to be drawn between Heracles' unceasing paternal exertions and those of the mother hen keeping a vigilant eye on her chicks.[15] Moreover, as we shall see later on in the poem, it is towards the fall of night that Heracles loses his beloved Hylas.

In a single extended sentence (vv. 16-24) the poet describes the gathering of the Argonauts, and underlines the wonderful qualities of the Argo by sketching its successful voyage to Colchis. In these verses a number of words and word combinations are reminiscent of the language of the epic. Thus we find προλελεγμένοι (18) in *Il.* 13.689, in the same — almost unique — meaning. In πασᾶν ἐκ πολίων (18) there is a variation of πολλέων ἐκ πόλιων (2.131; 9.544, likewise at the beginning of the verse), while μέγα λαῖτμα, the 'great gulf', appears seven times in the *Odyssey*.

---

[14] In this description ἐπ᾽ αἰθαλόεντι πετευρῷ ('on the smoke-stained perch') may be, as Gutzwiller (1981: 21) says, a humorous variation on Hesiod's αἰθαλόεντα κεραυνόν (*Th.* 72, 504, 707, 854).

[15] Cf. Gutzwiller (1981) 21: "Heracles is not in truth behaving as a father-hero, but as a mother-hen."

The adjective εὔεδρος (21) clearly refers to the epic εὔσελμος or ἐΰσελμος. But the passage is not entirely without its surprises. In v. 19 the poet calls Heracles ταλαεργός, 'bearing or enduring labour' in the version of LSJ. This, too, is an epic word, but can hardly serve to make Heracles more impressive, for in Homer, as well as in Hesiod, it is used exclusively for mules.

When the season to sail has come, this is again described in three ways (25-6). First the poet refers to the rise of the Pleiades, "an epic-celestial sign", according to Mastronarde (1968: 280). But then we are again in a rural landscape: 'at the time when the outer edges of the domains nourish the young lamb'; this is followed by the third reference: τετραμμένου εἴαρος ἤδη, 'when spring has already turned into summer'. The collocation ἆμος (25) ... τᾶμος (27) is reminiscent of Hesiod's *Erga* (see, for instance, 414-420; 582-585), while θεῖος ἄωτος ἡρώων (27-28), 'the divine flower of the heroes', is without a doubt a reference to Pindar's 4th *Pythian Ode*, in which the Argonauts are called ναυτᾶν ἄωτος (188). Through this Pindaric association the glorious heroism of the Argonauts is emphasized, while, on the other hand, there may be a tinge of irony in ναυτιλίας μιμνάσκετο, 'besought themselves of the sea voyage'. In any case, the phrasing does not suggest that they had been eagerly looking forward to their heroic enterprise.

Once the Argonauts arrive in Cios, Theocritus abruptly places them in an unmistakably pastoral atmosphere. The end of the verse δαῖτα πένοντο is Homeric, but as it is used there (*Od.* 2.322) to refer to the suitors who are preparing a meal in the palace of Odysseus, it calls up no heroic associations. In true bucolic style, the Argonauts spread out upon the ground a bed of plants, having cut sedge and galingale for that purpose. In the midst of this bucolic scene Hylas goes off to fetch water. Again there is explicit mention of his hair, but now by means of the standard Homeric epitheton of Menelaus: Ὕλας ὁ ξανθός (36), 'the fair Hylas'. For an instant we associate the boy with the Homeric hero, but Hylas is decidedly no warrior, although he is in the company of warriors. He is handsome and desirable, but also passive and defenceless.

The spring which Hylas finds is surrounded by plants: the description of the place has been included in Motte's list of the 'love landscapes' of Greek literature.[16] The nymphs are called δειναὶ θεαί, 'formidable goddesses', just as in the *Odyssey* Athena, Calypso and Circe are referred to as δεινὴ θεός. While they have ἀπαλαὶ φρένες (48), 'tender hearts', they are nevertheless to be feared, not least by Hylas: they have only to grab his hand and he falls straight into the water.

---

[16] See pp. 208-211. On p. 213: "Tout se passe comme si les Grecs ne pouvaient se représenter idéalement l'unité amoureuse sans que surgisse en leur esprit l'image d'un espace verdoyant, ...".

Theocritus uses the words ταὶ δ'ἐν χερὶ πᾶσαι ἔφυσαν (47) to describe this gesture, clearly a variation of ἕν τ'ἄρα οἱ φῦ χειρὶ, the Homeric formula for a handshake, invariably followed by: ἔπος τ'ἔφατ' ἐκ τ' ὀνόμαζε(ν). In Homer it is almost always used to indicate a friendly gesture of greeting, but here, according to Mastronarde (1968: 279, note 9), "the phrase is shifted to a forceful seizure (Eust. 1424-38 gives the clinging of an octopus as one of several associations of ἐμφῦναι; such a connotation might add a sinister note here.)". Yet I doubt whether this is meant as a "forceful seizure". Hylas is not a powerful man, and as he 'held out his jug in the direction of the water' (46) he was in a position in which it is not easy to hold one's balance; the nymphs seem to have no difficulty in carrying out their plan.

There is one case in which the Homeric handshake is not particularly friendly. Antinous grasps Telemachus' hand, and holds onto it during the entire eighteen verses of what is in effect a quite hostile conversation between them. Telemachus ultimately withdraws (σπάσατ') his hand from that of the other (Od. 2.302-321). In two cases there is an erotic context. In Od. 8.291 the formulary verse is preliminary to Ares' proposition to Aphrodite about sharing her bed. In Od. 11.247 Poseidon clasps the hand of Tyro, when he takes his leave of her with the announcement that within the year she will give birth to twins. But in principle the handclasp has no erotic connotations whatsoever. Hecuba presses the hand of Hector (Il. 6.253), and Thetis that of Achilles (Il. 19.7) when she finds him weeping. Perhaps all these combined associations were precisely what Theocritus was aiming for. For although we are told that the nymphs are quite beside themselves with love (48 49a), once they have captured Hylas, they take him upon their knees and comfort him (53-54) as if he were their child. The role of Heracles, who brought him up as a father would have done, now seems to have been taken over by three mothers. The fact that in Theocritus' poem the second half of the formulary verse is absent may serve to underline the mysterious nature of these events. Not a word is spoken.

In vv. 48-49a the love of the nymphs is described as follows: πασάων γὰρ ἔρως ἁπαλὰς φρένας ἐξεφόβησεν Ἀργείῳ ἐπὶ παιδί ('for love of the Argive boy had frightened the tender hearts of them all'). Although this is not a specific reference to Homer or any other author, and strictly speaking there is no question of intertextuality, I would like to look more closely at the verb ἐξεφόβησεν. This, too, Gow finds "odd", pointing out that here Apollonius uses πτοιέω: τῆς δὲ φρένας ἐπτοίησεν Κύπρις (Arg. 1.1232-3). But why then is ἐκφοβέω odd? Initially πτοιέω means 'to frighten'; in Homer φοβέω means 'to drive away', and later on again 'to frighten'. The difference is, however, that πτοιέω had already been used by Sappho (31.6) and Alcaeus (283.3) to convey overwhelming emotions of love, and the metaphor had probably lost some of its force by the time Apollonius used it. Theocritus was apparently reaching for a verb with a comparable meaning, but one that — as far as we know — had not yet been employed to describe the power of Eros. Thus in a manner of speaking he has transported (ἐκ)φοβέω from the field of battle to the field of love, just as in later passages he calls up other, more direct, associations with the battle-field.[17]

When Hylas falls into the water, this is compared to a falling star. In Gow's view this comparison is "perhaps suggested by *Il.* 4.75, where Athena's descent from Olympus to earth is compared to a shooting star sent ἢ ναύτῃσι τέρας ἠὲ στρατῷ εὐρέι λαῶν." Mastronarde maintains that in that case "Hylas is humorously substituted for Athena" (1968: 279, note 9). We might add that here, as well as in *Iliad* 4, there is a comment forthcoming from the characters who observe the phenomenon. In the *Iliad* the soldiers wonder what is going to happen (ὧδε δέ τις εἴπεσκεν ..., 81), while in the case of Theocritus a sailor urges his mates to prepare to sail (ναύτας δέ τις εἶπεν ..., 51). Here, however, the sailor's words are part of the comparison, although there is a mysterious association with the main narrative, since the Argonauts are also ready to sail, in spite of the fact that it is close to midnight (68).[18]

Campbell (1990: 115) is certainly correct when he says that Theocritus also evokes a simile that appears in the *Iliad*, both in 13.389-91 and in 16.482-4:

ἤριπε δ᾽, ὡς ὅτε τις δρῦς ἤριπεν ἢ ἀχερωίς
ἠὲ πίτυς βλωθρή, τήν τ᾽ οὔρεσι τέκτονες ἄνδρες
ἐξέταμον πελέκεσσι νεήκεσι νήιον εἶναι.

('and he fell, as an oak falls or a poplar or a tall pine, that among the mountains shipwrights fell with wetted axes to be a ship's timber.')

In 13 it is the death of Asius which is described in this manner, while in 16 it is the death of Sarpedon; both have fought bravely on the battlefield, but have succumbed to the violence. A variation of this simile appears in *The Shield of Heracles*, 421-2:

ἤριπε δ᾽ ὡς ὅτε τις δρῦς ἤριπεν ἢ ὅτε πεύκη
ἠλίβατος πληγεῖσα Διὸς ψολόεντι κεραυνῷ.

('and Cycnus fell as an oak falls or a lofty pine that is stricken by the lurid thunderbolt of Zeus'

Transl. Hugh G. Evelyn-White)

---

[17] Cf. *Idyll* 2.137, where Eros frightens away the bride from her bedroom.
[18] Cf. Campbell (1990) 115-116; however, his explanation of the Argonauts' departure at midnight (viz. that they fear a surprise attack because Hylas has not returned; 116) is too rationalistic for my taste. Real men, in real life, would perhaps behave this way, but that is no reason to introduce such behaviour into the poem.

Here it is Cycnus, the violent son of Ares, who falls victim to his opponent, and the opponent is Heracles, who makes him fall like the Nymphs make Hylas fall. But Hylas is no brutish warrior like Cycnus, nor a noble hero like Sarpedon, and the Nymphs need no strength. They simply grasp his hand and he is immediately drawn down into the water, without even token resistance. Hylas is not dead — he is in fact immortal (72) — but he is cut off for good from human existence, and from the heroic life which Heracles had dreamt of for him.[19]

While Hylas weeps in the lap of the nymphs, Heracles goes off in search of him, armed with the traditional instruments of his heroism, the bow and the club. The first thing he does is to call to him (58-9a):

τρὶς μὲν Ὕλαν ἄυσεν, ὅσον βαθὺς ἤρυγε λαιμός·
τρὶς δ᾽ἄρ᾽ ὁ παῖς ὑπάκουσεν, ...

('Thrice he shouted 'Hylas', as loud as his deep throat could roar, and thrice the boy answered, ...')

This is an obvious variation on *Il.* 11.462-3:

τρὶς μὲν ἔπειτ᾽ ἤυσεν, ὅσον κεφαλὴ χάδε φωτός,
τρὶς δ᾽ἄιεν ἰάχοντος Ἀρηίφιλος Μενέλαος.

('Thrice shouted he then loud as a man's head can shout, and thrice did Menelaus, dear to Ares, hear his call')

Here it is Odysseus who, when cornered on the battlefield, calls on his comrades in arms to come to his aid; Menelaus hears him and together with Aiax runs to free him. Heracles, however, is not calling to a comrade-in-arms, but to a beloved. In the world of heroes he can take on any adversary, but here he has lost his way in a world in which neither weapons nor the overpowering volume of his shouts are of any effect. Hylas replies, but his voice is muffled by the water, and Heracles cannot tell where the voice is coming from. He has been bested by three tenderhearted nymphs.

The epic mode is continued in the lion comparison which follows, where an ὠμοφάγος λίς ('a carnivorous lion'; cf. for the adjective *Il.* 5.782; 7,256; 15.592) hears the sound of a hind, and runs to the meal awaiting him. This points up the incongruity of the preceding passage. Hylas is not Heracles' prey, but as Mastronarde (1968: 277) remarks, the "natural connotations of weakness and tenderness" associated with the hind are likewise characteristic of Hylas. Not only are the means which Heracles uses to regain his beloved

---

[19] Gutzwiller (1981: 26-27) compares the description of Hylas' 'abduction' with the opening passage of the Homeric Hymn to Demeter. Both Hylas and Persephone encounter danger in a lovely meadow while reaching to take a desired object. If indeed the Hymn is alluded to, Hylas is simultaneously contrasted with a warrior and compared with a girl.

totally inadequate, but the beloved himself is an unsuitable match for the hero.

Although we are not told that Heracles rushes off in the direction of the noise, we may infer from the comparison that he does so. The failure of this endeavour remains entirely implicit. But Heracles perseveres, and continues his search, braving 'untrodden thorn bushes' (64). Hylas has disappeared into his *locus amoenus*, but nature is hostile to Heracles. He also forgets his 'calling': τὰ δ᾽ Ἰάσονος ὕστερα πάντ᾽ ἦς (67), 'and all Jason's interests were pushed into the background'. And the description of his search concludes with a reference to the god whom no one can escape: χαλεπὸς γὰρ ἔσω θεὸς ἧπαρ ἄμυσσεν (71), 'for a tormenting god was rending his heart'.

The first of the four final verses is devoted to the beauty and immortality of Hylas. The other three refer to Heracles: 'But the heroes mocked Heracles, because he had deserted the ship and had withdrawn from the Argo with its thirty rowing benches, and on foot had arrived at the Colchians and the inhospitable Phasis' (73-75). In the translation given here, the final line is also part of the mocking words of the Argonauts. Others prefer to see this last verse as standing on its own: 'but on foot he reached the Colchians and the inhospitable Phasis'. According to this interpretation Heracles is rehabilitated in the closing line, as his desertion is quite made up for by his fabulous walk.

Although his arguments are not equally valid, Gow is certainly right in rejecting this second explanation. In my view, his first argument, viz. the fact that the Greek does not permit us to take the closing line (75) as an independent sentence, is decisive. If Heracles' arrival were meant to nullify the mockery of the Argonauts, there would be a clear-cut contrast between l.75 and ll.73-4, as in Edmonds' translation in the Loeb edition: 'Nevertheless he made the inhospitable land of the Colchians afoot'. However, there is in the Greek not the slightest indication of a 'nevertheless' and such a translation is clearly mistaken. Heracles' arrival on foot is in no way marked off from the mockery of his desertion.[20]

CONCLUSION

Many scholars past and present have gone in search of the "message" that Theocritus has for Nicias. According to Wilamowitz (1906: 177), this poem is "eine Apologie der Knabenliebe": Heracles temporarily neglects his

---

[20] Cf. Bonnanno (1986) 33. Gow points out that an emphasising pronoun might have done the job, e.g. πεζᾷ ὃ δ᾽ ἐς ... Mastronarde (1968: 288, n. 33) states that "the deciding argument should derive from sense", meaning his own interpretation. He considers Gow's arguments unconvincing, but he only refutes the one argument that really cuts no ice and disregards the others.

mission, but in the end it all works out, and he rejoins the heroes. This is Theocritus' way of defending himself against the criticism which Nicias voiced concerning his love life. In Webster's view (1964: 85), this *Idyll* was intended to console Nicias, but he adds that the last verse contains a hint for Nicias "that however much he indulges in love-affairs he will have to return to his ordinary life as a doctor in the end" (86).[21] Pretagostini elaborates on the idea of a consolatory poem. Nicias, he posits, is grieving over a broken relationship, and Theocritus is trying to console him. Nicias' ἐρώμενος has outgrown this phase in his life and has moved on to the role of ἐραστής in a heterosexual relationship; the Hylas story demonstrates that this is part of the inevitable course of events. This also explains the presence of the three nymphs: he has reached the age at which a young man becomes attractive to women in general.[22]

Assertions of this type concerning the amorous relationships of Theocritus and Nicias are little more than speculations, and fail to address the essence of the poem itself. An essential element in this *Idyll* is the fact that the love of Heracles for Hylas is unsuited to his heroic status as a result of which he is confronted with a world which is not his own, and which he cannot enter. And in this confrontation it is he who is the loser. Hylas accompanies the heroes as Heracles' ἐρώμενος, although he does not seem to be truly at home among them. And the one time he is separated from his ἐραστής, he inspires love in that other world as well, and in this way becomes a helpless victim.

Heracles' traditional weapons and his unbridled and potentially violent activity are pointless in the service of this unheroic quest. They are useless against the weak, mysterious and yet dangerous beings who, surrounded by the plants of their lush meadow, make their home in the water. The confrontation with this other world gently mocks and undermines his heroism and, to some extent, epic poetry itself. Here I am expressly *not* thinking of Homer, but rather of the epic poetry imitative of Homer written in Theocritus' own day.[23]

And now we turn once more to intertextuality and its function in this poem. As we have seen, in this epyllion it is above all the epic genre, and the Homeric epic in particular, to which Theocritus is referring. In some cases it is a question of a single word, a — presumably — made-up word

---

[21] Cf. Walker (1980) 102, who even remarks: "Theocritus was right: Nicias got married and settled down as a doctor in his native Miletus (cf. *Idyll* XXVIII)". But how do we know about the chronological relation between *Idyll* 13 and Nicias' settling down as a doctor?

[22] Mastronarde, although not sharing the views of Petragostini, does think of a kind of *rite de passage*: "Hylas ... is pulled into the water, becomes immortal, and will (by implication) graduate to the active role of male lover of females" (1968: 275). But it is, indeed, by implication. Theocritus' final image of him does little to suggest it.

[23] Cf. Mastronarde (1968) 288: "Theocritus' *Idyll* 13 questions the value of the traditional conception of the epic and the heroic in contemporary literature".

with epic overtones, such as χαλκεοκάρδιος, or an epic word placed in an
unexpected context (ταλαεργός). In the case of the comparison with the
falling star, the key words κατήριπε ... ὡς ὅτε ... ἤριπεν are sufficient to
call up the image of an Homeric comparison, but with a totally different
content. The lion comparison bears the stamp of Homer. There are no literal
quotations of any length, and this was obviously intentional. V. 58 offers
clear enough proof of this. Theocritus not only replaced ἔπειτ' by Ὕλαν,
but also varied the second half of the verse, so that the reference, while
unmistakable, also bears the stamp of originality.

The role of intertextuality in the 13th *Idyll* has to some extent become
clear in the course of the present discussion. The references almost
invariably serve to emphasize the clash between the two worlds of the poem.
χαλκεοκάρδιος is in ironic contrast to ἤρατο παιδός, while ταλαεργός casts
an ironic shadow over the hero. When Hylas falls into the water we are
reminded of the death of Sarpedon or Cycnus. When Heracles calls out for
his beloved, we are reminded of Odysseus' cries on the battlefield, and when
he hears Hylas' voice, the comparison with the lion again calls to mind the
Homeric battlefield. The contrast between the original and the new context
accentuates the contrast between the heroic world and the world into which
Hylas disappears.

Intertextuality, it has been said, is capable of being both affirmative and
innovative: "it appears as a historical crypt, that is, as formation of cultural
ideology; and it shows up as a tactical device for critical deconstruction. In
the first role, it seems a prison; in the second, an escape key".[24] And
Pfister comments on these words: "It is true that these opposite functions,
founded on the opposite relation of repetition and difference, always
manifest themselves simultaneously, but the domination of the one or the
other function is determinative for the intertextuality of a particular period.
In classicism, for example, the conservative function, which confirms the
established codes and systems, is dominant, while in modernism, equally full
of intertextuality, the opposite function of destabilization and innovation has
the upper hand" (1985: 22).[25] How does Theocritus fit into this dichotomy?

Theocritus does not take a stand against Homer and other predecessors,
but he does realise that it is impossible to continue in the same way. He
refers to their work without rejecting it, but he does point up the distance

---

[24] V.B. Leich *Deconstructive Criticism: An Advanced Introduction* (London 1983) 110;
quoted by Pfister (1985) 22.
[25] "Diese beiden gegenläufigen Funktionen, die auf den gegenläufigen Relationen von
Repetition und Differenz beruhen, sind zwar wohl immer gleichzeitig gegeben, die Dominanz
der einen oder der anderen Funktion macht jedoch die historische Spezifik der Intertextualität
in einer bestimmten Epoche aus. Im Klassizismus z.B. dominiert die konservative, die
vorgegebene Codes und Systeme affirmierende Funktion, im ebenfalls hochintertextuellen
Modernismus dagegen die entgegengesetzte Funktion der Destabilisierung und der Innovation."

which separates his own work from theirs.[26] The result is a fascinating and original poem, of which Tennyson is alleged to have said: "I should be content to die if I had written anything equal to this."

BIBLIOGRAPHY

Barthes R. (1986) *Le bruisement de la langue* (Paris 1984); I quote the English translation by Richard Howard: *The Rustle of Language* (Oxford: 1986). *The Death of the Author* (49-55) was first published in 1968; *From Work to Text* (56-68) in 1971.

Bonnanno M.G. (1986) "Sul finale dell' Ila: Theocritus XIII 73-75", *Quaderni Urbinati di Cultura Classica* 24 (1986) 29-36.

Broich U. and Pfister M. (eds.) (1985) *Intertextualität. Formen, Funktionen, anglistische Fallstudien* (Tübingen: 1985).

Broich U. (1985) "Formen der Markierung von Intertextualität", in Broich and Pfister (1985) 312-47.

Campbell M. (1990) "Theocritus Thirteen", in *Owls to Athens. Essays on Classical Subjects Presented to Sir Kenneth Dover*, ed. E.M. Craik (Oxford: 1990) 113-119.

Claes P. (1988) *Echo's Echo's. De kunst van de allusie* (Amsterdam: 1988).

Dover K.J. (1971) *Theocritus. Select Poems* (London: 1971).

Gow A.S.F. (1952) *Theocritus* (Cambridge: ²1952).

Gutzwiller K.J. (1981) *Studies in the Hellenistic Epyllion* (Meisenheim am Glan: 1981).

Köhnken A. (1965) *Apollonios Rhodios und Theokrit* (Göttingen: 1965).

Kristeva J. (1980) Σημειωτική: *Recherches pour une sémanalyse* (Paris: 1969); I quote the English translation in *Desire in Language. A Semiotic Approach to Literature and Art*, ed. L.S. Roudiez (Oxford: 1980). Translated by T. Gora, A. Jardine and L.S. Roudiez.

——— (1974) *La Révolution du langage poétique* (Paris: 1974).

Lyne R.O.A.M. (1987) *Further Voices in Vergil's Aeneid* (Oxford: 1987).

Mastronarde D.J. (1968) "Theocritus *Idyll* 13: Love and the Hero", *Transactions and Proceedings of the American Philological Association* 99 (1968) 273-290.

Mertens A. and Beekman K. (eds.) (1990) *Intertekstualiteit in theorie en praktijk* (Dordrecht: 1990).

Motte A. (1973) *Prairies et Jardins de la Grèce antique* (Brussel: 1973).

Pfister M. (1985) "Konzepte der Intertextualität", in Broich and Pfister (1985) 1-30.

Pretagostini R. (1984) *Ricerche sulla Poesia Alessandrina* (Rome: 1984).

Schöpp J.C. (1985) "Endmeshed in endtanglements": *Intertextualität in Donald Barthelmes The Dead Father*, in Broich and Pfister (1985) 332-348.

Schulte-Middelich B. (1985) "Funktionen intertextueller Textkonstitution", in Broich and Pfister (1985) 197-242.

Walker S.F. (1980) *Theocritus* (Boston: 1980).

Webster T.B.L. (1964) *Hellenistic Poetry and Art* (London: 1964).

Wilamowitz-Moellendorff U. von (1906) *Die Textgeschichte der Griechischen Bukoliker* (Berlin: 1906).

---

[26] To a certain extent this might be said of all the *Idylls* that are written in dactylic hexameters: the metre itself refers to the epic genre, though of course to Hesiod as well. But in the epyllia subject and language bring the confrontation more clearly to the fore.

SPEECH-ACTS AND *SPRACHSPIELE*:
MAKING PEACE IN PLAUTUS*

BY

RIP COHEN

When, in Plato's *Republic* (607d-608a), Philosophy anticipates the return of Poetry, pictured as a banished beloved intent on rekindling their affair, the imagined encounter echoes two kinds of utterance represented in classical love poetry: a lover's request to be taken back after a rupture, and a response to such a request. If poetics thus serves to keep poetry in exile, Plato (willy-nilly) provides early evidence for (what we might call) a poetic genre, the negotiation of peace between parted (or merely quarrelling) lovers. Here I shall examine three Plautine examples and try to nudge Philosophy and Poetry back together again.

No theory can provide a set of rules that would enable us to determine the force of an utterance in a complex classical love poem, nor, for that matter, of many utterances in natural language.[1] Interpretation, whether of natural or poetic utterances,[2] is not a science. But some general framework may help in the reading of classical love poetry. It is not enough to understand the meaning of words (surely they cannot be understood out of context) and the syntax and morphology of the language in question. Meaning, in so far as it can be determined at all, is a product of utterances, conceived of in

---

* Professor Alva Walter Bennett insisted in his classes at the University of California in the early 1970's that to understand a classical poem one has to figure out who is saying what to whom, under what circumstances, to what end, and stressed the importance of the social, historical and cultural context, the relative prestige of speaker and addressee, and so on. Thus, the concept of genre advocated here owes much to an oral tradition I was privileged to receive and does not derive from work in the various fields (philosophy of language, pragmatics, sociolinguistics, sociology of language, ethnography of speech, social psychology, etc.) which have developed similar approaches to natural language, even if that bibliography may be adduced in support. I would also like to thank Professor Peter Bing, of Emory University, who forced me to defend at such length (in the introduction to *Games of Venus*) my interpretation of Theognis 371-372 and who argued (with learning, wit, and often overtaxed patience) with me about nearly every poem and fragment on my list. This is for them.

[1] Wittgenstein (1953) passim and (1969) 139-140, 559. [All references to Wittgenstein refer to paragraph or section numbers, not pages.]

[2] Cf. Steiner (1984) on arguments among the Russian formalists and members of the Prague Linguistic Circle over possible criteria for such a distinction. And see also Petrey (1990) 70-85 for a discussion (with some bibliography) of the applicability of speech act theory to literary texts. Bakhtin (1986) stresses the interplay between speech genres and literary genres.

their entirety, and the force of utterances, including stylistic variation, is relative to the circumstances of their use, the conventions of the society, the relationship existing between speaker and addressee, and so on.[3]

In philosophy and linguistic pragmatics, the meaning or force of utterances has been a focus of incandescent debate, but this has hardly ignited classical poetics. Still, the notion of poetic genre, in the narrow sense in which this word has been simmering in Classics,[4] begs many of the same questions.

Given the immense bibliography on poetic genres (in different languages and periods), I should stress that genre in this narrow sense is not determined by form but by the force of the utterance. In this sense, love poetry is not a genre, nor is lyric, elegy, epigram and so on. Nor, obviously, are tragedy and comedy. Rather, genres are kinds of utterance, such as saying hello or goodbye or happy birthday, wooing or renouncing a lover, praising an athletic victor or mourning the dead. It is this notion of genre that may be compared with two key concepts in the philosophy of language.

One is the concept of the *speech-act*, a term coined by J.L. Austin (1980). He holds that many (or most, if not all) human utterances do something, perform an act, and that in such utterances we can identify a basic *illocutionary* force. In other words: in saying x, a speaker does y. For example, in saying, "I'd like to be alone now," she was asking me to leave. Roughly speaking, the illocutionary force of an utterance is the thrust of what is said.

Wittgenstein's concept of the *Sprachspiel* (often translated as "language-game") is also meant to stress that speech is inextricably linked to activity, but he insists that it is impossible to define a *Sprachspiel*. One can only provide examples.[5] Some scholars in linguistic pragmatics believe that

---

[3] Wittgenstein (1953) 337, 489, 525-534, 588, 663. Part 2.IX-XI; Austin (1980) 73-74, 76-77. 115, 138. Cf. Levinson (1979) and Bakhtin (1986). Sociolinguistics, pragmatics, the ethnography of speech, the sociology of language, social psychology, and social semiotics agree on this point.

[4] Cairns (1972), but the tradition extends back to earlier studies, such as that of the *paraclausithuron* (Copley 1956). Bundy (1962), in essence, identifies Pindar's epinician odes as a genre on pragmatic criteria. For a recent example, see Winkler (1990) 73, 85-93, 95-97 on the *agoge*.

[5] Wittgenstein (1953) 65-89, esp. 71: "Und gerade so erklärt man etwa, was ein Spiel ist. Man gibt Beispiele und will, dass sie in einem gewissen Sinn verstanden werden. — Aber mit diesem Ausdruck meine ich nicht: er solle nun in diesen Beispiele das Gemeinsame sehen, welches ich — aus irgend einem Grunde — nicht aussprechen konnte. Sondern: er solle diese Beispiele nun in bestimmter Weise *verwenden*. Das Exemplifizieren ist hier nicht ein *indirektes* Mittel der Erklärung, — in Ermanglung eines Bessern. Denn, missverstanden kann auch jede allgemeine Erklärung werden. *So* spielen wir eben das Spiel. (Ich meine das Sprachspiel mit dem Wort 'Spiel'.)".

Wittgenstein's approach, with its greater flexibility, is to be preferred to that of Austin.[6]

In some cases the kernel of a genre identified by classical scholars seems to correspond to a basic illocutionary force. For instance: in the *syntaktikon*, a departing traveler says good-bye; in the *paraklausithyron* a locked-out lover asks to be let in; in the *renuntiatio amoris*, someone renounces love or a lover.

Whereas Austin thinks the kinds of illocutionary force can be listed and attempts "some general preliminary classification", Wittgenstein stresses that the *Sprachspiele* in natural language are innumerable, and change over time.[7] By comparison, the number of kinds of utterance in classical love poetry seems quite small. Though this may be due partly to the limits of the extant corpus, it probably reflects the tendency of classical love poetry to imitate utterances that perform a significant move within the history of an affair, and it is this set of moves that is limited.

Though the kind of utterance may be transparent in many poems (and we do not need, for example, the name *propemptikon* to see that in certain poems someone bids farewell to a departing traveller), it is often purposely disguised or hidden by the poet, and the failure to find it may lead to confusion and misguided "interpretations."

In classical love poetry the force of an utterance may be more specific than that of any of the illocutionary forces identified by Austin. Asking for kisses (as in Catullus 5) is not on Austin's list, but I dare say Wittgenstein would have considered it a *Sprachspiel*. Thus, though the kernel of a genre may correspond to a speech-act, it need not. And what we must find is that kernel, whatever it is, however expressed.

Since there is no generally accepted term for the "kernel" of a genre, I shall follow Wittgenstein's metaphor and call it the *move*.[8] Referring

---

[6] Levinson (1983) 280-282. It should be noted that some of the examples of *Sprachspiele* given by Wittgenstein (1953) 23, e.g. beg, thank, curse, greet, pray, are also in the list given by Austin (1980) 153-63.

[7] Austin (1980) 150; Wittgenstein (1953) 23, (1969) 65, 94-99, 256. Quintilian (*Institutio Oratoria* 3.4.3) astutely recognizes that utterances perform many functions, and (though he declines to classify them as rhetorical genres) provides a list of examples which anticipate the concepts of *Sprachspiele* and speech-acts. Cf. Bakhtin (1986): "... Each separate utterance is individual, of course, but each sphere in which language is used develops its own *relatively stables types* of these utterances. These we may call *speech genres*. The wealth and diversity of speech genres are boundless because the various possibilities of human activity are inexhaustible, and because each sphere of activity contains an entire repertoire of speech genres which differentiate and grow as the particular sphere develops and becomes more complex. Special emphasis should be placed on the extreme *heterogeneity* of speech genres (oral and written) ..."

[8] In Bing and Cohen (1991) 20-50 it was dubbed the *speech-action*, but *move* seems more in keeping not only with Wittgenstein's arguments, but also with his repeated use of the analogy of a chess game. (As Harris [1988 *passim*] points out, this analogy was also a favorite with

specifically, then, to the corpus of Greek and Latin love poetry from Archilochus to Ovid, I would say that a genre is a kind of utterance, and that each kind of utterance makes a move. Though some literary theorists might equate the move with the speech-act,[9] we shall have to see how well Austin's concept bears up under the stress of Plautine dialogue.

A poem may represent several kinds of utterance, each with its own move. Cairns (1972) seems to assume that if there are two genres in a poem, one will be dominant (the other, in his terms, will be *included*), but this solution sidesteps the problem by ignoring the evidence.[10] Such poems must be analyzed individually, to determine the relationship between moves.[11]

The offer of reconciliation, for instance, may be found alone. Likewise, the response to such an offer can appear by itself, though in such cases the offer will be lurking in some form, whether narrated, cited, mentioned, referred to, anticipated or merely presupposed. Elsewhere, however, offer and response are represented together (Horace *Odes* 3.9 is a perfect example, but cf. also Propertius 3.6 and 4.8).

Conversation analysts call such phenomena *adjacency pairs*, "the kind of paired utterances of which question-answer, greeting-greeting, offer-acceptance, apology-minimization, etc., are prototypical".[12] If we accept this term, and consider the adjacency pair *offer/response* or *request/response* (as they function in erotic peace-negotiations) a genre, we would then be left with half a genre for the cases where one appears alone.

If we agree that every classical love poem represents at least one move, any reading of a poem that sees none or allegedly detects a move not

---

Saussure.) *Move* has entered the lexicon of pragmatics, sometimes as a synonym for speech-act, sometimes as an "interactional move" — a "functional unit" — in a conversation. Goffman (1976), taking his cue from Wittgenstein, introduced the term (in a biting critique of speech-acts and adjacency pairs). Cf. Levinson (1983) 288-290, 303, 310-311 and the references there.

[9] Levinson (1983) 278-283 turns back to Wittgenstein, after a thorough critique of speech-acts, but the concept is accepted without hesitation by many literary theorists. Cf. Petrey (1990) and references there.

[10] In some complicated cases we may find an interweaving of moves and so of genres. An excellent example of this is the First Cologne Epode of Archilochus, where a seduction is woven into a dialogue consisting of an offer of reconciliation, delivered by a girl on behalf of her sister, and a response to that offer. See Bing and Cohen (1991) 46-49 for an analysis of this controversial fragment. See also Slings in Bremer e.a. (1987).

[11] Theocritus 1 is a prime example of a poem with many moves, see Bing and Cohen (1991) 144, note 6.

[12] Levinson (1983) 303.

elsewhere exemplified would immediately be suspect.[13] Theognis 371-372 is a case in point.

Μή μ' ἀέκοντα βίῃ κεντῶν ὑπ' ἄμαξαν ἔλαυνε
εἰς φιλότητα λίην, Κύρνε, προσελκόμενος.

Don't try to push me to the wagon, pricking hard, I won't go,
Kyrnos, though you draw me all too deeply into your love.

This utterance probably represents the rejection by a lover of a beloved's attempt to rekindle an affair, and not the rejection of an attempt to initiate one. The decisive argument, for me at least, is that whereas we can point to other examples in classical poetry of the former move, we have none of the latter.[14]

The concept of a move may, then, be useful in the analysis of classical love poetry, but there are several problems: (1) By what criteria do we identify the move in an utterance? (2) How do we decide whether two similar but apparently differing utterances represent the same move or two distinct but related moves? (3) What is the relation between identifying a move and naming it? Doesn't the name, whether a word or a phrase, bring us back to the problem of interpreting the meaning of an utterance (our name)? Won't other utterances then qualify or fail to qualify as examples of the same move, depending on our name and how we interpret it?

---

[13] It can be asked whether it is not conceivable that only a single example of a genre has survived in the extant corpus of classical love poetry. This remains to be seen. Wittgenstein, I think, would say that a *Sprachspiel* cannot be played only once (1953) 199: "Es kann nicht ein einziges Mal nur ein Mensch einer Regel gefolgt sein." Such an utterance would not be recognizable, and so would not be intelligible, certainly not to an audience. Two interlocutors might be able to invent and make use of a kind of utterance on a single occasion, but this could hardly be used in a literary text, whether intended for a live audience or for readers, since they could not be expected to recognize it. Jauss (1982) writes: "Just as there is no act of verbal communication that is not related to a general, socially or situationally conditioned norm or convention, it is also unimaginable that a literary work set itself into an informational vacuum, without indicating a specific situation of understanding. To this extent, every work belongs to a genre — whereby I mean neither more nor less than that for each work a preconstituted horizon of expectation must be ready at hand (this can also be understood as a relationship of "rules of the game" [*Zusammenhang von Spielregeln*]) to orient the reader's (public's) understanding and enable a qualifying reception."

[14] See Bing and Cohen (1991) 30-35. Rejections of offers of reconciliation are represented in all three scenes of Plautus I shall be examining, as well as in: Archilochus P. Colon. 7511 = SLG 478 (cf. Bing and Cohen [1991] 46-49); Theognis 599-602, 1249-1252; Callimachus Pf. 44; Theocritus 6.32-33 (and one may be referred to in Theocritus 1.83,85 [cf. Bing and Cohen (1991) 144, note 6]); Terence, *Eunuchus* 49; Catullus 11, (and possibly 107 and 109, both bitterly ironic in my view); Virgil, *Aeneid* 469-474 (Aeneas may not be trying to rekindle the affair, but he is apologizing for considerable injury done to a beloved, and Dido's response is silence, then flight); Propertius 3.25.5. Ovid *Remedia Amoris* 689 advises those who have renounced not to let themselves be won back by tears (vv.601-782 provide "specific precepts to prevent [love's] renewal" and 673-692 deal with how to handle a chance encounter — see Henderson (1979) xxi and his notes on these sections).

The decision to identify an utterance as constituting a certain move presupposes familiarity with that move. In interpreting a poem we must act as judges and ask whether, in saying *x*, the speaker was doing *y* (for example, rejecting an offer of reconciliation). Of course there will be problems. Even in our own experience, though we can recognize the moves in erotic discourse, we may sometimes be uncertain precisely what force an utterance carries. Still, both in natural language and in Roman Comedy, context, background information and subsequent actions and utterances tend to resolve such difficulties. It is in the shorter forms of poetry, where we have no such help, that it may be hard to detect the move and even harder to provide persuasive arguments to defend our reading. This is why the study of moves in classical love poetry might well begin with Plautus.

As to the second question, on where we draw the line between similar but distinct and different but similar moves, we can only adduce examples and give reasons for our decision. The classification will be grounded in experience, not logic. We need description, not theory.[15]

The closely related problem of naming has been treated by linguists in relation to the theory of speech-acts.[16] A repertoire of names (or phrases) denoting moves will reflect our criteria and influence subsequent classification. "Saying no" to a request for amorous favors might be considered a speech-act but (as we saw in Theognis 371-372) there is a significant difference between "saying no" to the the first advance and "saying no" to a request for reconciliation. Or consider the speech-act that we might call "asking to be let in." The phrase "may I come in," uttered on my first visit to the home of a woman with whom I have no amorous relationship, would not have the same force (pragmatic or emotional) as the same phrase uttered to the same woman on the same doorstep when I have come on an unannounced visit after a lengthy affair long since over. Neither the location nor the phrase would be a sufficient criterion for determining the force of the utterance. The move must be judged by evaluating the "total speech-situation."

Now I shall turn to three scenes of Plautus (*Amphitruo* 898-945, *Cistellaria* 449-527, *Poenulus* 353-405) which represent an offer of (or request for) amorous reconciliation and a response (or responses). There we can study in context phenomena such as indirectness in the making of a move and the use of different speech-acts to perform the same move, and reassess some of the problems raised above.

---

[15] Cf. Jauss (1982) 80: "[Genres] cannot be deduced or defined, but only historically determined, delimited and described.", and 93: "The modern theory of genres can proceed only descriptively and not by definition."

[16] E.g. Downes (1984) 348-349.

AMPHITRUO 898-945

When the play opens, Juppiter is inside the home of Amphitruo making love with his wife, Alcumena. To this end, he has assumed Amphitruo's form and brought along Mercury in the guise of Amphitruo's servant, Sosia. After a double night (which the king of the gods has conveniently arranged), he emerges from the house, bids Alcumena a fond farewell, and leaves (499-545). Then the real Amphitruo, who has just waged a successful war, returns home with the real Sosia (654-681) and is greeted by his wife with a surprised "Back so soon?" (682ff.). After a great deal of comic confusion and mutual recrimination Amphitruo sets off with Sosia to find a witness to confirm his story. Alcumena, left alone, is furious at her husband for the insults he has cast at her. It is at this point that Juppiter comes back and tries to make up with her.

This is the fullest representation of amorous reconciliation in Roman Comedy. Before it begins, we are given a description of the mood of each participant; then we hear the discourses of each during the scene, including a formulaic version of the request for forgiveness, and both possible responses (negative and positive) to the request; and, immediately after the scene itself, in the interchange between Juppiter and Sosia, we get some metalinguistic description of what has just gone on. In these respects, we could hardly have ordered up a better example.

On the other hand, there are many complications: Juppiter is not Alcumena's husband; Alcumena is mad at Amphitruo, but her wrath is directed toward Juppiter; it was Juppiter she spent the night with, but Amphitruo who insulted her and stomped off; when Juppiter, pretending to be Amphitruo, swears an oath that invokes the wrath of Juppiter against Amphitruo if he (Juppiter) is lying, this is, in Austin's terms, an "unhappy" speech-act. To be "happy", a performative (a strictly formulaic speech-act) must meet certain conditions, among them, "the particular persons and circumstances in a given case must be appropriate for the invocation of the particular procedure invoked."[17] These twists, if they undermine the scene's

---

[17] Austin (1980) 14-15 provides a scheme of "felicity conditions" which "are necessary for the smooth or 'happy' functioning of a performative (or at least of a highly developed explicit performative)." The first (A. 1) of these states that "There must exist an accepted conventional procedure having a certain conventional effect, that procedure to include the uttering of certain words by certain persons in certain circumstances." The second condition (A. 2) is cited in the text. Furthermore "(B. 1) The procedure must be executed by all participants both correctly and (B. 2) completely" and "(G. 1) Where, as often, the procedure is designed for use by persons having certain thoughts or feelings, or for the inauguration of certain consequential conduct on the part of any participant, then a person participating in and so invoking the procedure must in fact have those thoughts or feelings, and the participants must intend so to conduct themselves, and further (G. 2) must actually so conduct themselves subsequently." Austin devotes lectures II-IV to felicity conditions and "infelicities" and the whole matter has been much debated. Cf. Searle (1969, 1979) and the critique in Levinson (1983) 238-241, who

paradigmatic value, add to its comic effect and offer material for pragmatic analysis.

Before our scene begins Juppiter announces (873-875) that he will now take on the form of Amphitruo again and wreak further havoc. Then Alcumena delivers the following monologue:

> ALC. Durare nequeo in aedibus. ita me probri,
> stupri, dedecoris a viro argutam meo!
> ea quae sunt facta infecta ut reddat clamitat,
> quae neque sunt facta neque ego in me admisi arguit;
> atque id me susque deque esse habituram putat.
> non edepol faciam, neque me perpetiar probri
> falso insimulatam, quin ego illum aut deseram
> aut satis faciat mi ille atque adiuret insuper,
> nolle esse dicta quae in me insontem protulit.

> ALC. I can't stay in this house, accused like that
> by my husband of shame, dishonor and disgrace.
> What's done he insists be undone
> and accuses me of what I didn't and couldn't do
> and thinks that I'll just shrug it all off.
> I certainly won't, and I won't let myself
> be falsely accused of disgrace. I'll either leave him
> or he'll apologize and swear over and above
> that I'm guiltless and he wishes he hadn't said those things.

(882-90)

Thus we know her mood, her intentions, and the prerequisites she has set for reconciliation. Juppiter, who hears all this (whether or not he is omniscient, he is on stage), then tells us what he intends to do:

> IVPP. Faciundum est mi illud, fieri quod illaec postulat
> si me illam amantem sese studeam recipere,
> quando ego quod feci, id factum Amphitruoni offuit
> atque illi dudum meus amor negotium
> insonti exhibuit, nunc autem insonti mihi
> illius ira in hanc et male dicta expetent.

> IVPP. I must do what she demands done
> if I want her to receive me as her lover;
> since what I did hurt Amphitruo
> and my passion just now gave him problems
> though he was guiltless, now I, though guiltless,
> will bear the brunt of her wrath and harsh words.

(891-6)

---

observes (238, note 9) that "in general, students are well advised to turn back to Austin's often more subtle treatment of the isssues."

At this point (897-898) Alcumena sees Juppiter and the encounter begins. To understand their dialogue we must draw on information about setting, situation, social, linguistic and cultural conventions, the prior relationship between participants,[18] and their intentions. Otherwise, what could we make of Juppiter's opening remark: *Te volo, uxor, conloqui. / quo te avortisti?* ("Wife, I want to speak with you. Why do you turn away?" 898-899). Speech-act theory would be hard-pressed to tell us how it functions in this context (is it a declaration of intent, a summons, an order?), but a few concepts from conversation analysis may help.[19]

Participants in a conversation take turns, but an adjacency pair need not be realized in a single pair of turns. Between the first and second part of an adjacency pair there may be an *insertion sequence*, a series of intervening turns (theoretically open ended). The second position in an adjacency pair might therefore occupy the fourth turn. For example:

(Turn 1) A: Will you come over?
(Turn 2) B: Did you read the Wittgenstein?
(Turn 3) A: Yes.
(Turn 4) B: Okay, I'll be right there.

Here a second adjacency pair (turns 2 and 3) is inserted between the invitation in turn 1 and the acceptance in turn 4. Furthermore, a request (or invitation or offer, etc.) may be preceded by a *pre-request* (or pre-invitation, and so on):

(Turn 1) A: Are you busy tonight?
(Turn 2) B: No.
(Turn 3) A: Would you like to come over?
(Turn 4) B: I'd love to.

Such *pre-sequences* are part of *preference-organization*. Levinson (1983) 307 explains:

> not all the potential second parts to a first part of an adjacency pair are of equal standing: there is a ranking operating over the alternatives such that there is at least one preferred and one dispreferred category of response. It must be pointed out immediately that the notion of *preference* is not a psychological one, in the sense that it does not refer to speakers' or hearers' individual preferences. Rather it is a structural notion that corresponds closely to the linguistic concept of markedness. In essence, preferred seconds are unmarked — they occur as

---

[18] Of course in this case, the prior relationship between the participants is complex, since for Alcumena this includes both her relationship with Amphitruo, with whom she has just had a bitter argument (659-854), and her relationship with the disguised Juppiter, with whom she had spent a long and presumably pleasant night (cf. 473-474) followed by a loving farewell (499-545).

[19] The ensuing exposition is based on Levinson (1983).

structurally simpler turns; in contrast dispreferred seconds are marked by various kinds of structural complexity. Thus dispreferred seconds are typically delivered: (a) after some significant delay; (b) with some preface marking their dispreferred status ...; (c) with some acount of why the preferred second cannot be performed.

Thus, in a basic four turn structure with a pre-sequence, the first turn checks out "whether some precondition obtains for the action to be performed" in the third turn. The second turn is "an answer indicating that the precondition obtains, often with a question or request to proceed" to the third turn. And the fourth turn is a response to the third. And, naturally:

> Request refusals are dispreferred: therefore ... to be avoided if possible. One major reason for utilizing a pre-request is then that it allows the producer to check out whether a request is likely to succeed, and if not to avoid one in order to avoid its subsequent dispreferred response, namely a rejection.

Though this may seem like going far afield merely to seek disquietude, it has an immediate application. For in our scene the utterance "I want to talk with you" is a pre-request in an attempt to make peace. And while the speech-act theorist cannot detect any morpho-syntactic or lexical indications in the phrase *te volo, uxor, conloqui* that mark its "indirect illocutionary force," the conversation analyst could point out that if the wife responds by saying "Of course, darling, I'm so sorry about what happened," we would witness a "collapse of the four position sequence into the two-position sequence consisting of a position 1 turn followed by a position 4 turn."

Alcumena does not answer at once; she turns away. We may call this either delay (one of the ways in which dispreferred seconds are marked) or a silence which nevertheless occupies Alcumena's turn in the conversation and so will be construed as a response.[20] Thereupon Juppiter asks, "Why do you turn away?" — a second overture of peace, since it implies that she should at least face him and hear what he has to say. The first step in any peace process is for the warring parties to listen to one another.

When she answers *Ita ingenium meumst: / inimicos semper osa sum optuerier* ("That's the way I am: I loathe looking at enemies" 899-900), she is not describing her character or normal behavior, but implying that he is an enemy, and so affirming that a "state of war" exists between them. Juppiter picks this up: *Heia autem inimicos?* ("Oh, so it's enemies, then, is it?"). Nor is this merely a metalinguistic comment. He is asking her not to treat him as an enemy, giving her another chance to make peace at the

---

[20] Levinson (1983) 329, commenting on the function of silence in another context, writes that "silence has no features of its own: all the different significances attributed to it must have their sources in the structural expectations engendered by the surrounding talk. So sequential expectations are not only capable of making something out of nothing, but also of constructing many different kinds of significance out of the sheer absence of talk. If conversational organization can map 'meaning' onto silence, it can also map situated significance onto utterances — and in fact can be shown to regularly do so."

beginning of the negotiations. She won't: *Sic est, vera praedico; / nisi etiam hoc falso dici insimulaturus es* ("That's right, I'm telling it like it is; unless you're going to tell me that even this is a lie"). In referring to what Amphitruo said to her (736, 762, 813, 818-819, 836, 838), the accusations (that she was lying when she said she had lain with *him* the night before) which she wants retracted with oaths, she is beginning to lay out her (tough) bargaining position. Juppiter comments: *Nimis iracunda es* ("You're really angry"). To be angry at a lover need not imply a rupture, but the switch from "being angry" to "not being angry" can be tantamount to making peace.[21] His observation acknowledges the state of war, and we infer from Alcumena's next words that he tries to calm her wrath by touching her, offering peace by a gesture.[22]

> ALC. Potin ut abstineas manum?
> nam certo, si sis sanus aut sapias satis,
> quam tu impudicam esse arbitrere et praedices,
> cum ea tu sermonem nec ioco nec serio
> tibi habeas, nisi sis stultior stultissimo.

> ALC. Could you take your hands off me?
> Because, if you were sane or bright enough
> you wouldn't talk, in earnest or in game,
> with a woman you think and call unchaste
> unless you were dumber than the dumbest.

(903-6)

The expression "take your hands off me" could carry a different force in another context; here it signifies the rejection of yet another peace overture. And by referring once more to Amphitruo's accusation that she has been *impudica*, Alcumena is again calling for a retraction. In verbal retaliation for those insults, she ventures one of her own, calling Juppiter "dumber than the dumbest". Since his overtures and pre-requests have been useless, Juppiter must retract what he didn't say:

> Si dixi, nihilo magis es, neque ego esse arbitor,
> et id huc revorti uti me purgarem tibi.
> nam numquam quicquam meo animo fuit aegrius,
> quam postquam audivi ted esse iratam mihi.
> cur dixisti? inquies. ego expediam tibi.
> non edepol quo te esse impudicam crederem;
> verum periclitatus sum animum tuom,
> quid faceres et quo pacto id ferre induceres.

---

[21] Both in this scene and in the one we shall be looking at from the *Poenulus*, peace is made when the woman says she is not angry (here, at v. 937; in *Poenulus*, at v.404).

[22] It may be characteristic of many moves in classical love poetry that they can also be enacted by a gesture. Cf. Levinson (1983) 281 and the references cited there.

equidem ioco illa dixeram dudum tibi,
ridiculi causa. vel hunc rogato Sosiam.

If I said it, that doesn't make you that, nor do I think you're that
and I've come back to apologize to you,
because nothing has ever made me suffer more
than when I learned that you were angry with me.
'Why did you say it?' you'll ask. I'll tell you.
Not, certainly, because I believed you were unchaste;
I was testing your fibre,
to see what you'd do, how you'd handle it.
Yes, I said those things just now as a game,
a kind of practical joke. Why just ask Sosia here.

                                                                    (908-17)

Alcumena won't accept this, doesn't offer the preferred response. Instead,
she counters by daring him to carry out the "threat" Amphitruo had made
in 848-851:

ALC. Quin huc adducis meum cognatum Naucratem,
testem quem dudum te adducturum dixeras,
te huc non venisse?

ALC. Why don't you bring here my kinsman Naucrates,
whom you said before you'd bring as a witness
that you hadn't come here.

                                                                    (918-20)

Not wanting to produce a witness for the prosecution, Juppiter clings to his
excuse: *Si quid dictum est per iocum, / non aequom est id te serio
praevortier* ("If something's been said as a joke, it's not fair for you to take
it seriously" 920-921); but Alcumena will not yield: *Ego illud scio quam
doluerit cordi meo* ("I know how deeply that pained my heart" 922); so he
must get to his divine knees: *Per dexteram tuam te, Alcumena, oro obsecro,
/ da mihi hanc veniam, ignosce, irata ne sies* ("By your right hand,
Alcumena, I beg and beseech you, forgive me, pardon me, don't be angry"
923-924).

This is the basic move made by Juppiter in this scene (and it should be
noted that it refers to and is probably accompanied by a gesture — the
taking of her right hand — which symbolizes the move). He has abandoned
pre-requests, conciliatory gestures and explanations, and formally begs to be
pardoned. Austin would call this a speech-act, and Juppiter's language here
is lexically and morpho-syntactically formulaic. Two verbs of beseeching in
the first person present indicative active *(oro obsecro)* introduce the request,
articulated by three verbs which are morphologically or semantically
imperatives, though here these imperatives beg (rather than order) the
addressee to perform the indicated acts *(da ... ignosce ... ne sies)*. But it is
only in context that we can know what the speaker is asking forgiveness for,

and what he means to gain by being forgiven. So the specific move — the request for amorous reconciliation — cannot be determined by the phrasing, however formulaic. Moreover, though from Alcumena's point of view the request is "happy" (since she believes she is speaking with her husband), the utterance obviously does not fulfill the necessary felicity conditions set down by Austin.

The pragmatic confusion, so crucial to the comic effect of the scene, shows considerable metalinguistic sophistication on the part of the poet, and presumes that the audience can appreciate the turns wrung on a well known speech-act (or speech event[23] or *Sprachspiel*). One of the funnier aspects was probably that Juppiter, whatever his position in the cosmic hierarchy, must beg a mortal woman to take him back. This inversion of roles in the distribution of power is pressed home here, since Juppiter is acting out the role of a repentant husband begging for pardon and Alcumena holds the power to grant or withhold it. She begins by insisting on her innocence, and thus on the injustice done to her by Amphitruo's accusations.

ALC. Ego istaec feci verba virtute irrita;
nunc, quando factis me impudicis abstini,
ab impudicis dictis avorti volo.

ALC. I made those words of yours meaningless by my virtue;
now, since I've kept from shameful acts,
I wish to keep from shameful words.

(925-7)

Then she responds directly to his request: *valeas, tibi habeas res tuas, reddas meas* ("Goodbye, you may take your things, give me back mine" 928).[24] This phrase, as we know from the *Twelve Tables*, uses the legal language of divorce.[25] Uttering the words *tuas res tibi habeto* (or *agito*) constituted a *repudium* (divorce). Thus in the turn where we might have

---

[23] This term, which seems to have been introduced by Hymes (1972), is widely used in the ethnography of speech. Cf. Downes (1984) 255ff. for an introduction. The speech event contains 15 components which can be summarized in 8 compartments: Situation, particiants, ends, act sequences, key (tone, manner, etc.), instrumentalities (spoken or written speech, choice of dialect or language), norms (of interpretation and interaction), and "genre." But among the examples of "genre" is a poem!

[24] On the force of the subjunctives in this verse, cf. Lindsay (1907) 64: "To disentangle the various threads of which the Latin Subj. is composed is not easy. [...] In *Amph.* 928 *valeas, tibi habeas res tuas, reddas meas*, the three Subjunctives would, if they occurred in separate sentences, be classified as Optative, Permissive and Imperative respectively. But the crudeness of such a distinction is evident when we find them together in the same line."

[25] Cicero, *Phil.* 2.28.69: *Illam mimam suas res sibi habere iussit, ex XII Tabulis*, claves ademit *exegit. Quam porro spectatus civis, quam probatus cuius ex omni vita nihil est honestius quam quod cum mima fecit divortium*. The example of utterances that *ipso facto* constitute a divorce in some cultures is used by Austin (1980) 27 and has become a favorite. Cf. Petrey (1990) 9.

expected the second part of the adjacency pair request/response, Alcumena
first denies the validity of the words which Juppiter has retracted, and then
(as far as she is concerned) divorces him on the spot (an "unhappy"
divorce!): an oblique if very emphatic refusal to shed her anger and forgive
him. To drive home the firmness of her decision, she indirectly declares her
intention to leave at once: *iuben mi ire comites?* ("Will you tell someone to
accompany me?" 929). The force of this question is clear in context.

Juppiter refuses to accept her answer and ignores her request: *Sanan es?*
("Are you out of your mind?"); but she insists *Si non iubes, / ibo egomet;
comitem mihi Pudicitiam duxero* ("If you won't, I'll go alone; I'll take my
honor with me as an escort" 929-930), again referring to Amphitruo's
unkind words, which Juppiter (in his role as her husband) has yet to retract,
as he has yet to swear the oath he knows is prerequisite to peace. Faced
with such stubborn resistance to his pleas, and seeing her (probably) turn to
leave, Juppiter must act quickly.

> IVPP. Mane, arbitratu tuo ius iurandum dabo,
> me meam pudicam esse uxorem arbitrarier.
> id ego si fallo, tum te, summe Iuppiter,
> quaeso, Amphitruoni ut semper iratus sies.

> IVPP. Wait! since you want me to, I'll swear
> that I believe my wife is chaste.
> And if I lie, then I beg you, O highest Juppiter,
> always to be angry at Amphitruo.

                                                                    (931-4)

The oath ought not be classified (as it would be by Austin) merely as an
oath. It has a function: to persuade Alcumena to forgive him. And however
dire it may seem to her, this oath is an inside joke between Juppiter (and
hence, Plautus) and the audience. For Alcumena, *meam* refers to her, and
Amphitruoni to the man she hears speaking before her; for Juppiter and the
audience, *meam* may well refer to Juno, and *Amphitruoni*, rather than being
a substitute for *mihi*, stresses the comic "infelicity" of the oath. Juppiter
calls down his own wrath on the hapless Amphitruo. For Alcumena, the
wrath of Juppiter could well mean death for her husband; and if the god is
chuckling to himself and the audience laughing aloud, she is moved by the
apparent severity of the oath, and at once puts in a word on her interlocutor's behalf: *A, propitius sit potius* ("May he be propitious instead!").
Juppiter assents, and seeing that she is both moved and distressed by the
danger to which her interlocutor has seemingly exposed himself, he takes
advantage and repeats his request:

> IVPP. Confido fore;
> nam ius iurandum verum te advorsum dedi.
> iam nunc irata non es?

> IVPP. I trust he will be;
> for the oath I've sworn to you is true.
> Now are you no longer angry?"

(935-7)

This time the request is articulated as a question. "I beg you, forgive me, don't be angry" has become "So then you're not angry any more?" — but the move is no less clear. Juppiter's posture is no longer so pleading, because he now expects a positive response. He gets it: *Non sum* ("I'm not"). We should recall that "preferred (and thus unmarked) seconds to different and unrelated adjacency pair first parts have less material than dispreferreds (marked seconds)".[26] In contrast to her prior, complex, dispreferred responses, Alcumena utters the preferred response here with utmost simplicity. In saying *non sum* she simultaneously declares that she is no longer angry (and so forgives him) and makes peace (*pax facta est* says Juppiter just below, at v.965). Content (and relishing the expected results of this outcome), Juppiter indulges in a bit of *erotodidaxis*:

> IVPP. Bene facis;
> nam in hominum aetate multa eveniunt huius modi:
> capiunt voluptates, capiunt rursum miserias;
> irae interveniunt, redeunt rursum in gratiam.
> verum irae si quae forte eveniunt huius modi
> inter eos, rursum si reventum in gratiam est,
> bis tanto amici sunt inter se quam prius.

> IVPP. That's good.
> For in the life of men many such things happen:
> they get pleasure, then they get woe;
> anger crops up, then they're reconciled.
> But if any such anger should crop up
> between them, if then they're reconciled again,
> they're twice as much in love as they were before.

(937-43)

This passage (whose sense echoes — directly or indirectly — throughout European literature[27]) provides some metalanguage describing what has just taken place. The phrase *redire in gratiam* 940, 942) means "to make up,"

---

[26] Levinson (1983) 333.

[27] Cf. Terence, *Eunuchus*. 59-61, Plutarch, *Amat.* 764c for similar statements (which must have been proverbial). In English we might just cite Shakespeare's Sonnet 119:

> O benefit of ill, now I find true
> That better is, by evil still made better.
> And ruin'd love when it is built anew
> Growes fairer than at first, more strong, far greater.

"to be reconciled." One criterion for identifying a speech-act or move is that there exist in natural language a way of describing it.[28]

Alcumena, even as she yields, adds a final reprimand:

ALC. Primum cavisse oportuit ne diceres
verum eadem si isdem purgas mi, patiunda sunt.

ALC. You shouldn't have said it in the first place,
but since with those words you atone for it,
    I'll have to let it pass.

                               (944-5)

Jupiter does not respond directly to this, but instead orders that preparations be made for him to fulfill the vows he (as Amphitruo) had taken when he prayed for his safe return home (946-948). Alcumena says she will take care of it (949) and Juppiter tells her to summon Sosia, who should summon Blepharo (the helmsman of their ship) to lunch. In short, now that the peace negotiations have been successfully concluded, Juppiter reassumes his role as man of the house, giving one order after another, and each of them could be called a speech-act. Whatever the function of each, these are moves in a new game and so mark the end — in this scene — of the complex *Sprachspiel* we are studying.

In the next scene (III,3), Sosia questions Juppiter (whom he takes to be Amphitruo) about what has happened in the meantime: *Iam pax est inter vos duos? / nam quia vos tranquillos video, gaudeo et volup est mihi* ("Is there peace now between you two? For since I see you both calmed down, I'm glad and it's a joy for me too" 957-958). Explaining that, like a good slave, he's sad when his master is sad, happy when he is happy (959-961), he asks again: *sed age responde: iam vos rediistis in concordiam?* ("But come on, answer, have you already made up?" 962). Juppiter, although Sosia saw Amphitruo in a real rage, sticks to the story he has used with Alcumena: *Derides, qui scis haec dudum me dixisse per iocum* ("You're kidding, you know I said those things before as a joke" 963). Sosia is incredulous: *An id ioco dixisti? equidem serio ac vero ratus* ("You said it as a joke? I sure thought it was in earnest and serious" 964). Juppiter sidesteps the problem, pragmatically tricky, and merely says: *Habui expurigationem; pax facta est* ("I've apologized; we've made peace" 965).

Here we find some more metalanguage describing erotic reconciliation: *pacem inter vos esse* (957), *redire in concordiam* (963), *expurigationem habere* (965, corresponding to *purgare*, used by Alcumena in v.945), and *pacem fieri* (965). These, together with *redire/revenire in gratiam* (940, 942) provide us with a small lexicon of words and phrases referring to apologizing, making peace, being in a state of peace, and so on.

---

[28] Cf. Levinson (1983) 368 and the references given there.

Peace-making is mentioned elsewhere in this play in a variety of contexts, beginning with Mercury's retrospectively punning assertion in the prologue (32): *propterea pace advenio et pacem ad vos affero* ("And so I come in peace, and I bring you peace"). Some of these expressions refer to peace-negotiations between enemies at war (208-209, 257), some are figurative but non-erotic (389, 391, 396, 1127), while two others (outside the scene we have been examining) refer to negotiations between warring lovers. These two are especially important. At vv.474-5 Mercury, explaining the plot to the audience, says that "finally Juppiter will lead the couple back to their former harmony" *(denique Alcumenam Iuppiter / rediget antiquam coniugi in concordiam)*. And at the end of the play, as foretold, his machinations now all but ended, Juppiter appears *ex machina* (1131) and tells the bewildered husband: *tu cum Alcumena uxore antiquam in gratiam / redi* ("you return to your former harmony with your wife Alcumena" 1141-1142). Amphitruo promises to do so (1144-1145), and the spectators are urged to applaud (1146). The comedy ends, then, on the theme of erotic reconciliation. The scene of peace-making between Juppiter and Alcumena occupies a central place in the play's structure,[29] is prefigured by earlier references to peace-making, and looks forward to the final reconciliation between the real Amphitruo and his peace-beridden wife.

CISTELLARIA 449-527

From the first scene of *Cistellaria* (1-119) we gather: that Selenium is in love with Alcesimarchus (87); that he has sworn to marry her (98-99); that he is now being obliged by his father to wed another woman, a relative of his from Lemnos (99-100); that Melaenis, Selenium's "mother," is angry at her because, despite the boy's treachery, she has not left him and returned home. Selenium explains all this to her friend Gymnasium (whose inebriated mother and manager, Syra, listens in) because Melaenis has insisted she go home and she needs someone to look after the house for three days (104-105). Gymnasium agrees to do her this favor, and Selenium asks her please not to be rough on Alcesimarchus when he returns (from a stay out in the country at his father's villa, 225-226), because she still loves him (107-110).

The scene we shall be looking at occurs in one of the sections of the comedy badly marred by lacunae. But this unfortunate circumstance allows us to demonstrate once again the crucial role context plays in determining the force of utterances. If we had nothing more of the play than the following fragment,[30] what could we make of it?

---

[29] A safe assertion, I think, despite the lacuna beginning at v.1034.

[30] I take the text from Leo (1895), who prints *fraterculum* in 452 but suggests *puerculum* in his apparatus. Cf. the editions of Lindsay (1910) and Ernout (1961). This is not the place to

SEL. Molestus es.
ALC. Meae issula sua <aede>s egent. ad me <sine ducam>.
        SEL. Aufer manum.
ALC. Germana mea sororcula. SEL. Repudio te fraterculum.
ALC. Tum tu igitur, mea matercula. MEL. Repudio te puerculum.
ALC. Obsecro te SEL. Valeas. ALC. Vt sinas SEL. Nil moror. ALC. Expurigare
me.
SEL. < > ALC. Sine dicam. MEL. Satis sapit mihi tuis periuriis.
*   at nunc non potest. ALC. Supplicium polliceri volo.
SEL. At mi aps te accipere non libet. ALC. Em omnia
patior iure infelix. SEL. Volup est neque tis misereri decet.
quamquam hominem *
                verba dare   *
non illa   *   qui frangant foedera
                eos   *

SEL. You're a pain.
ALC. My <house> misses its darling. <Let me take you> to my home.
SEL. Take your hands off me.
ALC. My darling sister. SEL. You're no darling brother of mine.
ALC. Then you, my darling mother. MEL. You're no darling boy of mine.
ALC. I beg you...SEL. Buzz off. ALC. ...to let me...
    SEL. I don't care. ALC. ...apologize.
ALC. Let me speak. SEL. I've had enough of your lies
*   but now it's impossible. ALC. I wan't to promise attonement.
SEL. But I don't feel like accepting it. ALC. Ai! it's only right
that I be wracked by every torment. SEL. I'm glad, and it
    would be wrong to pity you.
Although a man *
        *empty words *
not those things (?) *
            men who break faith
        them

(449-61)

At most we could say that Alcesimarchus is trying to apologize and
Selenium won't listen. Note that *Meae issula sua aedes egent. ad me <sine
ducam>* ("My house misses its darling. <Let me take you> to my home"),
which would provide key information, is a restoration based partly on the
available context.[31] Yet we can be certain that this interchange represents
offers of reconciliation and negative responses to those offers, because an
earlier conversation between Alcesimarchus and a slave (here designated as
T for *tertius*, that is, third slave) has mercifully survived (there is a lacuna
shortly before it, and two folia missing immediately after):

---

consider proposed emendations.
[31] All that remains is apparently *meau.ssula sua....segent ad me*..........

T. Cave sis cum Amore tu unquam bellum sumpseris.
ALC. Quid faciam? T. Ad matrem eius devenias domum,
expurges, iures, ores blande per precem
eamque exores ne tibi suscenseat.
ALC. Expurigabo hercle omnia ad raucam ravim.

T. Make sure you never get into a war with love.
ALC. What should I do? T. Go to her mother's home,
apologize, swear, beg suavely in prayer
and persuade her not to be mad at you.
ALC. I'll apologize for everything until I'm husky hoarse.

(300-5)

Thus, in saying *molestus es* ("you're a pain" 449) Selenium is already rejecting Alcesimarchus' peace overtures. And when he tells her that his houses misses its darling (if the emendation is correct) he is broaching the subject. By responding *aufer manum* ("take your hands off me") she again rebuffs his implied offer. He then calls her *germana mea sororcula* ("my darling sister"), and the affectionate vocative may be considered a pre-request. Her curt response *repudio te fraterculum* ("You're no darling brother of mine") rejects the overture, so he turns to Melaenis (the girl's "mother"), tries the same tactic and meets a similar rebuff. Then follows the overlapping exchange at v.453. Selenium interrupts him twice, contravening the normal rules of turn-taking,[32] but he manages (in three turns) to get out "I beg you ... to let me ... apologize." Her interruptions ("buzz off" and "I don't care") lead him (after another interruption, illegible but no doubt cool) to say: *sine dicam* ("let me speak" 454). This request to be allowed to speak, if not precisely equivalent to an offer, is here a request to be allowed to proffer one. Since she can anticipate what he is likely to say, her response functions as yet another refusal to make up: *satis sapit mihi tuis periuriis* ("I've had enough of your lies"). And the same can be said of the next exchange:[33]

ALC.   supplicium polliceri volo
SEL.   At mi aps te accipere non libet.

ALC.   I want to promise atonement.
SEL.   But I don't feel like accepting it.

(455-6)

---

[32] Cf. Levinson (1983) 319: "... there are overlaps allowed (and thus their location and nature predicted) by the rules, and overlaps that contravene the rules *(interruptions)*."

[33] *OLD* s.v. *supplicium* notes that in Sallust, *Iugurtha* 46.2 the word is "*applied to a peace-offering brought by an envoy.*"

In each of these exchanges Alcesimarchus offers peace, or some part of a discourse supporting a peace proposal, or merely asks to be allowed to make one, and Selenium (or, in v.452, Melaenis, on her behalf) refuses to listen.

Then the text breaks off. What is left suggests that she is accusing him of having lied to her (*verba dare ... qui frangant foedera* "empty words ... men who break faith"). When it picks up again Selenium has left the stage and Alcesimarchus is talking with Melaenis. He will not let her go until he has had a chance to state his case (464). "I beg you" *(obsecro)*, he says. "You beg in vain" *(At frustra obsecras)*, she replies (467). "I'll swear an oath" *(Dabo / ius iurandum)*, he protests (470-471). "But I'm weary now of your oath-swearing *(At ego nunc <ab> illo mihi <caveo> iure iurando tuo)*, she retorts (472). Melaenis reproaches him for his alleged engagement to the other girl, a rich Lemnian (479, 492-496), much better off than she and her "daughter". The argument continues:

> ALC. Di me perdant — MEL. Quodcumque optes, tibi velim contingere.
> ALC. Si illam uxorem duxero umquam, mihi quam despondit pater.
> MEL. Et me si umquam tibi uxorem filiam dedero meam.
> ALC. Patierin me periurare? MEL. Pol te aliquanto facilius
> quam me meamque rem perire et ludificari filiam
> alibi quaere ubi iuri iurando tuo satis sit subsidi
> hic apud nos iam, Alcesimarche, confregisti tesseram.

> ALC. May the gods destroy me... MEL. I hope what you wish for happens to you!
> ALC. ... if I ever marry that woman my father has engaged me to.
> MEL. And me, if I ever give you my daughter to wife.
> ALC. Will you let me perjure myself? MEL. Yes, much rather
> than let you wreck me and my affairs and make my daughter a laughing stock.
> Find another place where your swearing can help you.
> Here in our house, Alcesimarchus, you've shredded your ticket.

> (497-503)

In swearing that he will not marry the other girl, Alcesimarchus is in effect swearing that he intends to marry Selenium. Melaenis' counter-oath, if carried out, would make his oath false (unhappy, in Austin's terms), and he complains, but she is not moved. In telling him to look elsewhere (*alibi quaere* 501) for someone who will believe his oaths, she implies that she does not believe them. All these exhanges reenact the adjacency pair we are studying, yet each would appear to be a different speech-act.

And what would speech-act theory make of the utterance: "Here, at our house, you've broken your *tessera* (503)?[34] Social conventions and general

---

[34] A *tessera* is, among other things, a "(properly square or rectangular) token or voucher" and especially *(tessera hospitalis)* "a token divided between friends, so that by fitting the two pieces together they might recognize each other," but can also mean "a ticket qualifying the holder for some benefit" (*OLD* s.v.). Though *OLD* (s.v. *confringo*) glosses our phrase as "*destroyed our*

context are not sufficient to determine its specific force; its place in the structure of this conversation enables us to read it as a conclusive "no" to the request for peace. That Melaenis means it as conclusive can be confirmed by Alcesimarchus' desperate attempt to continue the conversation:

ALC. Face semel periclum. MEL. Feci saepe, quod factum queror.

ALC. Give it a try this one time.
MEL. I've often given it a try, and I'm sorry I did.
(504)

We can arguably infer from this exchange that she means to leave (or is already walking off the stage), and the directness and vehemence of his subsequent pleas would seem to support this inference.

ALC. Redde mi illam. MEL. Inter novam rem verbum usurpabo vetus.
quod dedi datum non vellem, quod relicuomst non dabo.
ALC. Non remissura es mihi illam? MEL. Pro me responsas tibi.
ALC. Non remittes? MEL. Scis iam dudum omnem meam sententiam.
ALC. Satin istuc tibi in corde certumst? MEL. Quin ego commentor quidem.

ALC. Send her back to me. MEL. I'll apply an old adage to a new situation:
What I gave, I wish I hadn't given. What's left I won't give.
ALC. You're not going to send her back?
MEL. You're answering yourself for me.
ALC. You won't send her back? MEL. You've long since learned my intention.
ALC. Have you really firmly decided that? MEL. Why, I'm not even thinking
about it any more.
(505-9)

Each of his utterances in this segment of the dialogue is an indirect request — delivered to a representative of the beloved — for reconciliation. Each is equivalent to a direct request such as "come back," but each is grammatically and lexically different. We find an imperative *(redde)*, a question with a periphrastic construction consisting of a future active participle plus a form of *esse (remissura es)*, another question, this time with a simple future *(remittes)*, and finally the follow-up question "Are you quite sure (that you will not send her back to me)?" Her responses are much more varied in form and content, but each one is a refusal to accede to his request.

Then, true to his promise (304) to swear until he is hoarse, he begins an oath, but confuses the genealogies of the gods he is invoking, and Melainis interrupts to correct them (512-516). He blames these slip-ups on her (517). "Go on" *(perge dicere* 517), she says. He responds, "Why don't *you* go on and speak, so I can know what you're going to decide" *(Anne etiam, ut quid consultura sis sciam, pergis eloqui?* 518). "I won't sent her back. That's

---

friendship," it could also be read as "you've destroyed the ticket (that entitled you to special privileges)."

final" (*Non remittam. definitumst* 519), she replies. This brief insertion sequence interrupts the oath but reiterates the adjacency pair. Then, after invoking Juno and Janus, he fumbles again before recovering: "I don't know what I want to say. Now I know. Yes, listen, woman, so you'll know what I mean to do" (*quid dicam nescio. / iam scio. immo, mulier, audi, meam ut scias sententiam* 520-521). In the middle of a "combination" in this chess game, he has momentarily forgotten his plan. He threatens mate:

> ALC. di me omnes, magni minuti, et etiam patellarii
> faxint, ne ego <dem vivae> vivos savium Selenio
> nisi ego teque tuamque † filiam meque hodie obtruncavero,
> poste autem cum primo luci cras nisi ambo occidero,
> et equidem hercle nisi pedatu tertio † omnis efflixero,
> nisi tu illam remittis ad me.

> ALC. May all the gods, big and small, and even the dish-gods
> keep me, while I live <from giving the living> Selenium a kiss
> if I don't slaughter you and your daughter and myself today
> and then tomorrow kill you both at the crack of dawn
> and also butcher you all in the third onslaught,[35]
> unless you send her back to me.

(522-8)

This oath functions — bizarrely — as a request for peace (the request is imbedded in *nisi tu illam remittis ad me* 527). The structure of the conversation, the nature of the *Sprachspiel*, and the context (both the plot of the comedy, and the fact that it is a comedy) allow the spectators (and readers) to grasp the force of these utterances.

A pragmatic analysis of this scene presents another problem. Selenium is upset because she has heard that Alcesimarchus is to be married to "another" girl (*ei nunc alia ducendast domum, / sua cognata Lemniensis, quae habitat hic in proxumo. / nam eum pater eius subegit* 99-101, cf. 195). But in fact *she* is that other girl whom he is to wed (600-630). So the peace negotiations would probably have been comic in part because some of the basic presuppositions underlying the quarrel are simply false. He swears he will never marry the other, apologizes for the plan, renounces it, and asks for forgiveness. Selenium declines to go back, and Melaenis refuses to send her back, all because of the other girl. All this is "unhappy" in Austin's terms, because the appropriate circumstances do not obtain. Yet all is acted out as though the situation (within the fictive world of the play) were what the characters incorrectly think it is.

---

[35] According to *OLD* (s.v.), *pedatus* or *pedatum* is apparently "one of three formal stages in presenting an ultimatum or sim." This appears to be its first documented occurrence, and the meaning is uncertain.

Reconciliation between the two does take place. After Melaenis has told Selenium the truth about her parentage, they (along with Halisca, an *ancilla*) enter (631) just as Alcesimarchus is apparently about to kill himself (though he may be feigning a suicide as a way of getting back his girl). Selenium hears him say *Recipe me ad te, Mors, amicum et benevolum* ("I am a friend who loves you, take me, O Death" 639) and rushes over to stop him. He welcomes her and decides to live on (*O Salute mea salus salubrior, / tu nunc, si ego volo seu nolo, sola me ut vivam facis* "O my salvation, more salubrious than salvation itself, only you now can make me live, whether I want to or not" 644-645), but will not speak with Melaenis (*Nil mecum tibi, mortuos tibi sum: hanc ut habeo certum est non ammittere* "I've nothing to do with you, I'm dead to you; since I have her, I'm not going to let her go" 646-647). They exit together, and Melaenis comments:

> MEL. Abiit, abstulit
> mulierem. ibo, persequar iam illum intro, ut haec ex me sciat
> eadem, si possum tranquillum facere ex irato mihi.

> MEL. He left, he took away
> the girl. I'll go, I'll follow him inside right now, so he can find out these
> same things and I'll see if I can soothe his anger towards me

> (650-2)

Peace has been made between Alcesimarchus and Selenium. But now, stung by Melaenis' repeated rebuffs in their prior peace-talks, Alcesimarchus is angry at *her*, and it is she who must try to make peace with him. This brief remark, in which Melaenis uses the lexicon of reconciliation, calls attention to the importance of peace-making in this play.

POENULUS 353-405

Agorastacoles is in love with Adelphasium. He and his slave, Milphio, have been watching her and Anterastilis, another meretrix, prepare to go to the shrine of Venus (210-329), and just as the girls are ready to leave, Agorastocles greets them and begins a conversation (330). He tries to detain them, pressing his suit with Adelphasium, but she rebuffs him (335). When he tries to embrace her, she tells him to stop (350). Agorastocoles then asks Milphio for help.

There is no radical rupture of the relationship, as in the *Amphitruo*, nor any jealousy over a rival, as in the *Cistellaria*. Adelphasium is *irata* because Agorastocles has not yet arranged to buy her freedom, and simply refuses to be detained by his amorous overtures. Nevertheless, there is a momentary interruption in the courtship, and he senses he must do something to soothe her wrath and win her back. In this sense, the situation bears certain similarities to that in the *Cistellaria*, but there most of the peace-negotiations are conducted by the boy with the girl's representative (her "mother"), whereas here Milphio, acting on behalf of Agorastocles, tries to get Adelphasium to forgive his master. The ensuing confusion, as we shall see, is due to the use of a substitute speaker in the peace-talks.

Let's look first at the exchange between the young master and his slave at the moment when Agorastocles asks him to intercede:

> AG. Cur mihi haec irata est? MI. Cur haec irata est tibi?
> cur ego id curem? namque istaec magis meast curatio?
> AG. Iam hercle tu peristi, nisi illam mihi tam tranquillam facis
> quae mare olimst, quom ibi alcedo pullos educit suos.
> MI. Quid faciam? AG. Exora, blandire, palpa. MI. Faciam sedulo.
> sed vide sis, ne tu oratorem hunc pugnis pectas postea.
> AG. Non faciam.

> AG. Why is she angry at me? MI. Why is she angry at you?
> Why should I care? I mean, what concern is that of mine?
> AG. By Hercules, you're dead if you don't make her as calm
> as the sea is when the halcyon is bringing forth its young.
> MI. What should I do? AG. Win her over, sweet-talk her, soothe her.
>   MI. I'll do it with zeal.
> But don't, please, afterwards, comb your spokesman with fists.
> AG. I won't.

>   (353-9)

Agorastocles' instructions to Milphio are explicit. Since she is *irata*, he must make her *tranquilla*. To effect this change, he must "sweet-talk" her (or "say sweet nothings" *blandiri*) and "soothe" or "stroke" her *(palpare)*. The ambiguity of *palpare* is important, since Milphio can understand it literally (meaning "stroke") or figuratively ("soothe"). He evidently takes it in the former sense: he says he will eagerly do as he is told, and asks that he not be beaten for having done so. No sooner has Milpio acceded to the request than Adelphasium begins to rail at Agorastocles for not keeping his word:

> AD. Non aequos in me es, sed morare et male facis.
> bene promittis multa ex multis: omnia incassum cadunt.
> liberare iuravisti me haud semel, sed centiens:
> dum te exspecto, neque ego usquam aliam mihi paravi copiam
> neque istuc usquam apparet; ita nunc servio nihilo minus.
> i, soror. apscede tu a me.

> AD. You're not fair to me, you keep delaying, I don't like it.
> You're good at promising lots of things on all sides, but nothing comes to anything.
> You've sworn not once but a hundred times to free me
> and while I've been waiting for you, I've never made myself available to anyone else

but that freedom doesn't appear; so I'm no less a slave.
Come on, sister. You, get away from me.

(359-64)

She ends her complaint by telling Anterastilis that they should leave (to go to the shrine of Venus), and when Agorastocles tries to approach (or block) her, she brushes him off. Both her utterances in v. 364 indirectly express her refusal to make peace. Agorastocles is desperate: *Perii. ecquid agis, Milphio?* ("I'm dead. Aren't you going to do something, Milphio?"). Milphio begins to sweet-talk Adelphasium:

MI. Mea voluptas, mea delicia, mea vita, mea amoenitas,
meus ocellus, meum labellum, mea salus, meum savium,
meum mel, meum cor, mea colustra, meus molliculus caseus —

MI. My joy, my delight, my life, my charmer,
my little eye, my lip, my salvation, my kiss,
my honey, my heart, my beestings, my soft little cheese ...

(365-7)

Whereat Agorastocles comments:

AG. Mene ego illaec patiar praesente dici? discrucior miser,
nisi ego illum iubeo quadrigis cursim ad carnificem rapi.

AG. Am I going to suffer those things to be said in my presence? I'll die wracked by pain
if I don't order him to be dragged headlong to the hangman by a four horse team.

(368-9)

Milphio, who has not heard this aside, proceeds:

MI. Noli, amabo, suscensere ero meo, causa mea.
ego faxo, si non irata es, ninnium pro te dabit
atque te faciet ut sis civis Attica atque libera.
quin adire sinis? quin tibi qui bene volunt, bene vis item?
si ante quid mentitust, nunciam dehinc erit verax tibi.
sine te exorem, sine prehendam auriculis, sine dem savium.

MI. For my sake, please don't be upset with my master.
I'll make sure, if you're not angry, that he'll give a lot for you,
and will make you an Athenian citizen, and free.
Why don't you let me get near you? Why don't you love those who love you?
If he's lied a bit before, from now on he'll be truthful to you.
Let me persuade you, let me touch your little ears, let me give you a kiss.

(370-5)

Although he is asking her to not be angry with his master, Milphio is also trying to make the physical gestures (get near her, touch her, kiss her) that the lover himself might properly attempt in order to bring about a reconciliation. Clearly, if the foregoing amorous vocatives were out of place and infuriated Agorastocles, these gestures can not be pragmatically transformed and are certain to enrage him even more. Meanwhile, Adelphasium rejects the peace offer and Milphio continues the negotiations.

> AD. Apscede hinc sis, sycophanta par ero. MI. At scin quo modo?
> iam hercle ego faciam ploratillum, nisi te facio propitiam,
> atque hic ne me verberetillum faciat, nisi te propitio,
> male formido: novi ego huius mores morosi malos.
> quam ob rem amabo, mea voluptas, sine te hoc exorarier.

> AD. Get away from here, please, swindler just like your master.
>   MI. Do you know on what terms?
> By Hercules, I'll have a bit of crying to do if you're not won over,
> and he'll be whipping me a bit, if I don't win you over,
> I'm afraid: I know this tough guy's bad temper.
> And so, please, my joy, let yourself be persuaded.

>   (376-80)

This speech, probably accompanied by further attempts to touch, stroke and kiss her, is too much for Agorastocles:

> AG. Non ego homo trioboli sum, nisi ego illi mastigiae
> exturbo oculos atque dentes. em voluptatem tibi,
> em mel, em cor, em labellum, em salutem, em savium.

> AG. I'm not worth three obols, if I don't tear
> the eyes and teeth out of that rascal. Take that! your "joy,"
> and that! "honey" and that! "little lip" and that! "salvation" and that! "kiss."

>   (381-3)

Milphio, who has presumably been getting flogged at every *em*, protests, since his master is breaking the promise he made at v.359. But Agorastocles continues echoing the litany of amorous vocatives (and even names one that Milphio has not used).[36]

> MI. Impias, ere, te: oratorem verberas. AG. Iam istoc magis:
> etiam ocellum addam et labellum et linguam. MI. Ecquid facies modi?

> MI. Master, you're staining yourself with impiety:
>   you're flogging your spokesman. AG. And that too!
> Something for "little eye," too, and for "lip" and for "tongue."
> MI. Done yet?

>   (384-5)

---

[36] Since *orare* in v.386 responds to *oratorem* in v.384, and since Milphio has not (in the transmitted text) included *lingua* among his terms of endearment, Leo and other editors have thought v.385 spurious.

In the exchange that follows, Agorastocles explains the reason for his fury, and gives more specific grammatical instructions on the method of persuasion to be used.

> AG. sicine ego te orare iussi? MI. Quo modo ergo orem? AG. Rogas?
> sic enim diceres, sceleste: huius voluptas, te opsecro,
> huius mel, huius cor, huius labellum, huius lingua, huius savium,
> huius delicia, huius salus amoena, huius festivitas:
> huius colustra, huius dulciculus caseus, mastigia,
> huius cor, huius studium, huius savium, mastigia.
> omnia illa, quae dicebas tua, esse ea memorares mea.

> AG. Is that how I told you to plead? MI. Then how should I be pleading?
> AG. You're asking? Well you should have spoken like this: "his joy, I beg you,
> his honey, his heart, his lip, his tongue, his kiss,
> his delight, his sweet salvation, his darling,
> his beestings, his sweet little cheese ..." rascal!
> "... his heart, his desire, his kiss ..." rascal!
> Everything that you said was yours you should have been calling mine.

> (386-91)

The essence of this outburst is that the spokesman cannot use amorous vocatives of the form "my ..." in trying to make peace between the lover and the beloved. These expressions, as Agorastocles points out, cannot be "happily" maintained with first person singular pronominal adjectives. Milphio then renews his attempt to persuade the girl, demonstrating how awkward, or ridiculous, it is to use "his ..." with a string of amorous vocatives.

> MI. Opsecro hercle te, voluptas huius atque odium meum,
> huius amica mammeata, mea inimica et malevola,
> oculus huius, lippitudo mea, mel huius, fel meum,
> ut tu huic irata ne sis aut, si id fieri non potest,
> capias restim ac te suspendas cum ero et vostra familia.
> nam mihi iam video propter te victitandum sorbilo,
> itaque iam quasi ostreatum tergum ulceribus gestito
> propter amorem vestrum.

> MI. By Hercules, I beseech you, his joy and my pain,
> his full-breasted friend, my ill-wishing enemy,
> his eye, my oozing of eyes, his honey, my bile,
> that you not be angry at him, or, if that can't be,
> that you get a rope and hang yourself, with my master and your family,
> because I see now that because of you I'll be subsisting on sips,
> and my back is striped like an oyster with wounds
> for your love's sake.

> (392-9)

The core of the request for peace has been only slightly changed: instead of *Noli, amabo, suscensere ero meo* (370) he says *obsecro te ... // ut tu huic irata ne sis* (392,395). Otherwise, the vocatives have been transformed into antonymic pairs, accompanied by "his" and "my" respectively, and if she doesn't want to make up, an alternative is offered: she can hang herself, Agorastocles, and her family. Clearly both these modifications are incompatible with a "felicitous" speech-act of the kind ordered by Agorastocle, and both are meant (by the playwright, but also by Milphio) to have a comic effect. Adelphasium gathers that the request for peace is now motivated by the slave's desire to avoid further punishment, and responds accordingly: *Amabo, men prohibere postulas / ne te verberet magis quam ne mendax me advorsum siet?* ("Please, do you think I can keep him from flogging you any more than from lying to me?" 399-400). At this point Anterastilis asks her to make peace for another reason: so that they can leave.

> ANT. Aliquid huic responde, amabo, commode, ne incommodus
> nobis sit. nam detinet nos de nostro negotio.
> ANT. Please say something agreeable to him, so he'll stop being disagreeable
> to us. He's keeping us from our business.

(401-2)

Agreeing with Anterastilis *(verum)*, she speaks directly to Agorastocles for the first time since v.364:

> AD. Verum. etiam tibi hanc ammitam noxiam unam, Agorastocles.
> non sum irata. AG. Non es? AD. Non sum.
>
> AD. True. Okay, I'll forgive you this one offense, Agorastocles.
> I'm not angry. AG. You're not? AD. I'm not.

(403-4)

ammitam expresses her intention to forgive; *non sum irata* ends the quarrel. As in the *Ampitruo*, this phrase, uttered in context, is an act (or a speech-act) of forgiveness and effects (or performs) the reconciliation. Agorastocles, perhaps incredulous (since he has just heard Milphio utter such an "unhappy" request on his behalf, and has probably not heard Anterastilis ask Adelphasium to say something nice to him so they can be off), asks for verification *(non es?)*, and *non sum* reiterates the act. He then asks for a kiss, allegedly as proof:

> AG. Da ergo, ut credam, savium.
> AD. Mox dabo, quom ab re divina rediero. AG. I ergo strenue.

> AG. Then give me a kiss, so I'll believe it.
> AD. I'll give you one as soon as I get back from the sacrifice. AG. Then go quickly.[37]
>
> (404-5)

The pragmatic complications in this scene demonstrate once again an understanding of linguistic phenomena such as speech-acts, felicity conditions, and pragmatic constraints on grammatical transformations. Milphio, in two formal attempts (365-367, 370 and 392-395) to make peace between his master and Adelphasium, uses a formula which includes amorous vocatives and a request that the beloved not be angry at the lover. The preferred response, when Adelphasium finally utters it (404) is "unmarked." And, comically, her forgiveness is motivated by concerns extrinsic to the amorous situation (namely, the desire to leave).

All the characters are aware of the game being played (or of the speech-event, or adjacency pair). Agorastocles asks Milphio to make peace for him, and Milphio knows how to go about this, even if he exceeds the limits of his mandate. When his master reprimands him and revises the instructions, Milphio humorously calls attention to the absurdity of the required transformations. Adelphasium knows how to reject and how to accept the offer of peace. And Anterastilis can tell when the game has come to an impasse and peace must be made so that they can get on with their business. All this means is that the playwright has created characters with the social and linguistic competence needed to carry on conversations, and that he and his characters have a metalinguistic understanding of the conventions that normally apply to *Sprachspiele*. In this they are no different from other human beings, except perhaps in the pervasive comic effect intended.

* * *

The negotiation of peace betweeen lovers lies at the heart of each of the three scenes of Plautus we have examined, and in each we have found a high degree of metalinguistic sophistication in the handling of these negotiations. In the *Amphitruo*, reconciliation plays a central role in the plot, and this is arguably true of the other two comedies as well, though I shall not press the point here.[38] Suffice it to say that three of the twenty extant

---

[37] "Go quickly" here implies "Come back soon (to kiss me)" so that "go" is equivalent to "come back" and once again the poet (or his model — in any event, the poetic tradition of Greek and Roman poetry) is playing games with speech-acts.

[38] I have already noted that in the *Cistellaria* as soon as peace is made between boy and girl, the girl's "mother" marches off to make peace between herself and the boy. In the *Poenulus* Agorastocles asks Milphio to forgive him at the beginning of the play (140-144), and before our scene begins, when Adelphasium says she is going off to propitiate Venus, Agorastocles asks, "Oh, is she angry then" (333-334). The comedy ends with a (non-amorous) request for forgiveness (1410-1413). In fact, in more than half of the extant plays of Plautus there is a request for forgiveness (and usually, though not always, a reconciliation of some kind) in the

plays of Plautus contain a scene constructed around a single adjacency pair: the offer of peace, and a response to that offer.[39]

<h2>REFLECTING</h2>

We began by considering the interrelated concepts of speech-act, *Sprachspiel*, and genre. Testing Austin's theory of speech-acts in three scenes of Plautus, we find that there are indeed direct, formulaic ways of doing something with utterances, for instance, asking for forgiveness. But there are also other ways of doing the same thing that can only be understood in context. And in these scenes, asking for forgiveness performs another function, that of trying to make peace with a beloved. Yet the offer to make up need not be articulated as a request for forgiveness (e.g. Alcesimarchus' dire oath). Finally, phenomena observed by modern linguists in the analysis of real conversations occur in these represented conversations (e.g. adjacency pairs, insertion sequences, pre-requests, marked unpreferred responses, unmarked preferred responses).

   The concept of a speech-act was originally meant to unthrone a dogma of logical positivism that held that a statement which is neither true nor false is meaningless. Wittgenstein's *Tractatus* (1922) was often cited to support this dogma, but he had meanwhile retracted, and the concept of *Sprachspiel* may be seen as a kind of atonement for his earlier sins. Both Wittgenstein (1953) and Austin insist, then, that we do many things with words other than make statements that can be judged true or false. But what are these things? How many of them are there? How do we isolate and identify them? Austin himself admitted that no grammatical or lexical criteria can necessarily determine the illocutionary force of an utterance, and later attempts to formalize such criteria have (predictably) failed. Wittgenstein foresaw this, though many linguists set spinning by speech-acts were slow

---

end lines. Cf. *Asinaria* 921ff.; *Aulularia* 739ff.; *Bacchides* 1164-5, 1185-6, 1199; *Casina* 1000ff.; *Curculio* 701; *Epidicus* 729ff.; *Mercator* 992, 996, 1012; *Mostellaria* 1129ff., 1155ff., 1162ff.; *Persa* 753ff.; *Pseudolus* 1329ff.; *Stichus* 729ff.; *Trinummus* 1164ff., 1184ff.; *Truculentus* 899ff.

[39] We might also note that at the end of Terence's *Phormio* Demipho asks Nausistrata to forgive her husband (for having led a double life with another woman): *verum iam, quando accusando fieri infectum non potest, / ignosce: orat confitetur purgat: quid vis amplius?* ("But now, since recrimination cannot undo what's done, forgive him: he begs, he confesses, he's sorry: what more do you want?") This request (1034-1035) is answered by a refusal to answer (1043-1045), at least for the moment: *immo ut meam iam scias sententiam, / neque ego ignosco neque promitto quicquam neque respondeo / priu' quam gnatum videro: eius iudicio permitto omnia: / quod is iubebit faciam.* ("No, so you know what I intend to do: I neither forgive nor promise anything nor will I even respond / until I see my son: if he agrees, I'll let it all pass: / I'll do what he tells me to"). So that one of the six extant plays of Terence all but ends with the same adjacency pair.

to catch up to him. In a sense, Wittgenstein saw that if there is a unit of meaning, it is *not* a linguistic unit.

The negotiation of peace between lovers is a complex *Sprachspiel* which can be analyzed as a series of moves in a game. In the scenes we have examined, offer and response occur together, though they may be separated by insertion sequences and other interruptions. Glancing briefly now at the corpus of Greek and Latin love poetry (in shorter forms) from Archilochus to Ovid, I would argue that in each of the following poems or fragments we find one move or the other (or both) represented, narrated, cited, anticipated, deprecated, mentioned, or referred to:[40]

Archilochus P. Colon 7511;
Sappho L-P 1, L-P 15 9-12;
Theognis 371-372, 599-602, 1249-1252, 579-584;
Anacreon P 400;
Callimachus Pf. 41 (G-P 4), Pf. 44 (G-P 9), Pf. 45 (G-P 10);
Theocritus 1, 6, 30;
The Grenfell Papyrus;
Meleager G-P 55 (= AP 12.147);
Anon. G-P 11 (= AP 12.79);
Catullus 11, 45, 107, 109;
Virgil *Eclogues* 10;
Horace *Odes* 3.9;
Tibullus 1.5;
Sulpicia =[Tibullus] 4.12 (= 3.18)
Propertius 1.18, 2.5, 2.13, 2.26a, 2.27, 3.6, 3.8, 3.20, 4.8;
Ovid *Amores* 2.19.15-16, 3.11.

The utterances used in this *Sprachspiel* may vary widely. Data documenting such utterances in natural language would presumably be difficult to obtain. Still, we may assume that anything from the simplest non-verbal gestures (one of the two ex-lovers appears at the door and is welcomed with an embrace) to a complex and extended series of negotiations may, under given circumstances, bring about a reconciliation. Much will depend on the causes, nature and duration of the separation (or other suspension of the amorous relationship), and on the relative position of the two individuals. Under what circumstances is peace being negotiated? Who holds the high ground? Who has strategic or tactical advantages? The moves used to ask for reconciliation and those employed to respond can include many that are not specific to this *Sprachspiel*. If one party has offended or hurt the other, an apology is presumably in order (as in Sulpicia). But if they have agreed to separate peaceably, we would expect other moves. The setting could also play a role. If one lover has been locked out, then "please let me in" would be tantamount to a request for reconciliation (as in the Grenfell Papyrus). The

---

[40] Discussions of some of these passages in Bing and Cohen (1991) passim.

moves may be few or many, predictable or unpredictable, brief and simple or long and complex. To know that a certain move counts as an offer or a response, we may have to be intimately familiar with the situation, the relationship, and details of the conversational conventions already established between the two individuals.

How does this apply to classical love poetry? We cannot necessarily identify a genre based on grammatical or lexical features of the move, even if some such features do seem closely associated with a given move. And the less context we have, the more difficult it may be to identify moves. Moreover, as I have suggested, disguising the move by expressing it indirectly, by irony, metaphor, or any number of "stylistic devices" seems to have been an important objective for most Greek and Latin love poets. To identify the move in a poem is not to "solve the problem of meaning", but merely to recognize the basic communicative force of a kind of utterance. Any analyst who misses, mistakes or overlooks the move is failing in one of his main responsibilities.

Hence the importance of studying a set of poems representing the same move and also of seeing that a given move may be made by a variety of speech-acts. A genre (if we are to use this word in speaking of classical love poetry) corresponds to a move and not necessarily to a speech-act. A move may be expressed by a variety of speech-acts, and the speech-act by which a move is articulated, even if it includes recognizable lexical elements, may undergo unpredictable if fully comprehensible morphological and syntactic transformations.

A comparative and historical pragmatics of the European love poem would do well to begin with Greek and Latin, but its scope must be much broader. It should describe — over time and across languages — who played what games, in what contexts, by what rules (however flexible), what moves were possible and how they were made. Making peace between lovers is one such game. It can be played silently in bed.[41] We have seen here that it can also be played with wit and pragmatic know-how on the Plautine stage.

---

[41] In the *Ars Amatoria* (2.433-466) Ovid prays to be the victim of a violent attack of (justified) jealousy, and advises his readers how to make peace quickly (I paraphrase): put your arms around her neck, and let her weep into your chest, give her kisses as she cries, give her the joys of Venus as she weeps (457-459): *pax erit; hoc uno soluitur ira modo* ("there will be peace; that's the only way wrath can be melted" 460). Once she's had her full of rage, take her to bed: she'll soften up (461-462). *illic depositis habitat Concordia telis, / illic, crede mihi, Gratia nata loco est* ("There, when the arms have been laid down, Harmony shall dwell; there, believe me, Forgiveness is born" 463-464). Note the language we have learned in Plautus: *pax, ira, concordia, gratia.*

BIBLIOGRAPHY

Austin J.L. (1980) *How to Do Things with Words* (Oxford: ^{2}1980).

—— (1970) *Philosophical Papers* (Oxford: 1970).

—— (1971) "Performative-Constative", in Searle (1971) 13-22.

Bakhtin M.M. (1986) "The Problem of Speech Genres", in *Speech Genres and Other Essays*, trans. V. McGee; ed. M. Holquist and C. Emerson (Austin: 1986).

Bing P. and Cohen R. (1991) *Games of Venus: an Anthology of Greek and Roman Erotic Verse from Sappho to Ovid* (New York-London: 1991).

Bremer J.M. and A.M. van Erp Taalman Kip and S.R. Slings (1987) *Some Recently Found Greek Poems* (*Mnemosyne* suppl. 99) (Leiden: 1987).

Brown P. and Levinson S. (1987) *Politeness* (Cambridge: 1987).

Bundy E. (1962) "Studia Pindarica", in *University of California Studies in Classical Philology* 18 (Berkeley-Los Angeles: 1962).

Cairns F. (1972) *Generic Composition in Greek and Roman Poetry* (Edinburgh: 1972).

—— (1979) "Self-Imitation within a Generic Framework. Ovid *Amores* 2.9 and 3.11 and the *Renuntiatio Amoris*", in West and Wooodman (1979) 121-141.

Cohen R. (1991) "Reymon Gonçalves: Taking Him Back", in *Estudos Portugueses: Homenagem a Luciana Stegagno Picchio* (Lisboa: 1991) 37-55.

Cole P. and Morgan J. (eds.) (1975) *Syntax and Semantics*, 3 vols. (Englewood Cliffs: 1975).

Comrie B. (1976) *Aspect: an Introduction to the Study of Verbal Aspect and Related Problems* (Cambridge: 1976).

Copley F.O. (1956) *Exclusus Amator: A Study in Latin Love Poetry* (Baltimore: 1956).

Cunningham I.C. (1987) *Herodas Mimiambi cum Appendice Fragmentorum Mimorum Papyraceorum* (Leipzig: 1987).

Downes W. (1984) *Language and Society* (London: 1984).

Elam K. (1980) *The Semiotics of Theatre and Drama* (London-New York: 1980).

Enk P.J. (1962) *Sex. Propertii Elegiarum Liber Secundus*, 2 vols. (Leyden: 1962).

Ernout A. (1961) *Plaute*, 5 vols. (Paris: 1961).

Fedeli P. (1985) *Properzio. Il Libro Terzo delle Elegie* (Bari: 1985).

Giglioli P.P. (ed.) (1972) *Language and Social Context* (Harmondsworth: 1972).

Goffman E. (1964) "The Neglected Situation", in *American Anthropologist* 66:6 (1962) 133-6.

—— (1976) "Replies and Responses", *Language and Society* 5 (1976) 257-313 (repr. in E. Goffman, *Forms of Talk* (Philadelphia: 1981) 5-77.

Gow A.S.F. (1952) *Theocritus*, 2 vols. (Cambridge: 1952).

Gow A.S.F. and Page D.L. (1965) *The Greek Anthology. Hellenistic Epigrams*, 2 vols. (Cambridge: 1965).

Grice H.P. (1975) "Logic and Conversation", in Cole and Morgan (1975) v.3, 41-58.

Griffin J. (1985) *Latin Poets and Roman Life* (London: 1985).

Gumperz J.J. (1977) "Sociocultural Knowledge in Conversational Inference", in Saville-Troike (1977) 191-211.

—— (1982) *Discourse Strategies* (Cambridge: 1982).

Gumperz J.J. and Hymes D.H. (eds.) (1972) *Directions in Sociolinguistics* (New York: 1972).

Harris R. (1988) *Language, Saussure and Wittgenstein: How to Play Games with Words* (London-New York: 1988).

Henderson A.A.R. (ed.) (1979) *P. Ovidi Nasonis Remedia Amoris* (Edinburgh: 1979).

Hernadi, P. (1972) *Beyond Genre: New Directions in Literary Classification* (Ithaca, N.Y.-London: 1972).

Hymes D.H. (1964) "Toward Ethnographies of Communication: The Analysis of Communicative Events", in *American Anthropologist* 66:6 (1962) 1-34 (rept. in Giglioli (1972) 21-44).

—— (ed.) (1964a) *Language in Culture and Society* (New York: 1964).

—— (1972) "Models of the Interaction of Language and Social Life", in Gumperz and Hymes (1972) 35-71.

—— (1974) *Foundations in Sociolinguistics: An Ethnographic Approach* (Philadelphia: 1974).
Jauss H.R. (1982) *Toward an Aesthetics of Reception* (Minneapolis: 1982).
Kauer R. and Lindsay W.M. (1926) *P. Terenti Afri Comoediae* (Oxford: 1926).
Leo F. (1895-6) *Plauti Comoediae*, 2 vols. (Berlin: 1895-6).
Levinson S. (1979) "Activity Types and Language", *Linguistics* 17 (1979) 365-399.
—— (1983) *Pragmatics* (Cambridge: 1983).
Lindsay, W.M. (1907) *Syntax of Plautus* (Oxford: 1907).
—— (1910) *Plautus*, 2 vols. (Oxford: 1910).
Lobel E. and Page D.L. (1955) *Poetarum Lesbiorum Fragmenta* (Oxford: 1955).
Lodge G. (1924-33) *Lexicon Plautinum*, 2 vols (Leipzig: 1924-33).
Lyons J. (1977) *Semantics*, 2 vols (London-New York): 1977).
—— (1981a) *Language and Linguistics* (Cambridge-Melbourne-New York: 1981).
—— (1981b) *Language, Meaning and Context* (London: 1981).
Malinowski B. (1923) "The Problem of Meaning in Primitive Languages", Supplement I to Ogden and Richards (1945).
Maurach G. (1988) *Der Poenulus des Plautus* (Heidelberg: 1988).
Morson G.S. (ed.) (1986) *Bakhtin: Essays and Dialogues on his Work* (Chicago: 1986).
Ogden C.K. and Richards I.A (1945) *The Meaning of Meaning* (London: [7]1945).
Ohman R. (1971) "Speech Acts and the Definition of Literature", in *Philosophy and Rhetoric* 4 (1971) 1-19.
Owen M.L. (1983) *Apologies and Remedial Exchanges: a Study of Language Use in Social Interaction* (Berlin-New York: 1983).
Page D.L. (1955) *Sappho and Alcaeus* (Oxford: 1955).
—— (1962) *Poetae Melici Graeci* (Oxford: 1962).
—— (1975) *Epigrammata Graeca* (Oxford: 1975).
Pinkster H. (1990) *Latin Syntax and Semantics* (London: 1990).
Pride J.B. and Holmes J. (eds.) (1972) *Sociolinguistics* (Harmondsworth: 1972).
Petrey, S. (1990) *Speech Acts and Literary Theory* (New York-London: 1990).
Pfeiffer R. (1941, 1953) *Callimachus*, 2 vols. (Oxford: 1941, 1953).
Powell J.U. (1925) *Collectanea Alexandrina* (Oxford: 1925).
Russell D.A. and Wilson N.G. (1981) *Menander Rhetor* (Oxford: 1981).
Saville-Troike M. (ed.) (1977) *Linguistics and Anthropology* (Washington: 1977).
—— (1989) *The Ethnography of Communication: an Introduction* (Oxford: [2]1989).
Schenkein J. (ed.) (1978) *Studies in the Organization of Conversational Interaction* (New York: 1978).
Searle J.R. (1969) *Speech Acts* (Cambridge: 1969).
—— (ed.) (1971) *Philosophy of Language* (Oxford: 1971).
Steiner P. (1984) *Russian Formalism: a Metapoetics* (Ithaca, N.Y.: 1984).
Todorov T. (1976) "The Origin of Genres", *New Literary History* 7, 1 (1976) 159-170.
—— (1981) *Michail Bakhtine: le principe dialogique suivi de Écrits du Cercle de Bakhtine* (Paris 1981). (Eng. tr. *Mikhail Bakhtin: The Dialogical Principle*, Minneapolis: 1984).
Vetta M. (1980) *Theognis. Elegiarum Liber Secundus* (Rome: 1980).
West D. and Woodman T. (eds.) (1979) *Creative Imitation and Latin Literature* (Cambridge: 1979).
Winkler J.J. (1990) *The Constraints of Desire: the Anthropology of Sex and Gender in Ancient Greece* (New York-London: 1990).
Wittgenstein L. (1922) *Tractatus Logico-Philosophicus* (London: 1922).
—— (1953) *Philosophische Untersuchungen* (Oxford: 1953).
—— (1967) *Zettel* (Oxford: 1967).
—— (1969) *Über Gewissheit* (Oxford: 1969).
—— (1969a) *Philosophische Grammatik* (Oxford: 1969).
—— (1969b) *Blue and Brown Books* (Oxford: 1969).
—— (1977) *Bemerkungen über die Farben* (Oxford: 1977).

—— (1978) *Bemerkungen über die Grundlagen der Mathematik* (Oxford: 1978).
—— (1979) *Tagebücher 1914-1916* (Oxford: ²1979).
—— (1980) *Bemerkungen über die Philosophie der Psychologie*, 2 vols. (Oxford: 1980).
—— (1980a) *Vermischte Bemerkungen* (Oxford: ²1980).

HISTORICIZING READING:
THE AESTHETICS OF RECEPTION AND HORACE'S 'SORACTE ODE'[1]

BY

RUURD R. NAUTA

In the valedictory lecture which Hans Robert Jauss delivered in 1987 at the University of Constance, he proclaimed that reception theory, which he had launched in his inaugural lecture in 1967, had met with such success that 'in retrospect it becomes incomprehensible that its problems have ever been problems at all'; a few moments later, he went as far as to speak of a 'paradigm shift'.[2] Even if it can be doubted whether Jauss was correct in applying Thomas S. Kuhn's account of the history of science to the history of literary studies,[3] there can be no doubt that reception theory is firmly established, at least in Germany, and that research on reception has become a routine activity of literary scholarship. One sign of the wide diffusion of reception theory is the abundance of introductions, surveys, anthologies, bibliographies and special issues of journals — and there are even protreptic articles addressed to classicists.[4]

What gives one pause, however, is a closer look at the publications I have just referred to. The German titles I listed in my note all date back to the 1970s, while the English titles, even though they are from the 1980s, do not report any newer developments. One gets the impression that reception theory came to a standstill more than a decade ago. This impression is confirmed when one considers the intellectual biographies of its two major

---

[1] This is a considerably revised and expanded version of an article published in Dutch as Nauta (1991).

[2] The inaugural lecture was published in its definitive version as "Literaturgeschichte als Provokation der Literaturwissenschaft" in Jauss (1970) 144-207. The valedictory lecture was published, together with a useful bibliography of Jauss's writings, as Jauss (1987); the quotations are from p. 5. Here as elsewhere the translations are my own.

[3] Cf. Kuhn (1970). Already in the very first phase of the elaboration of reception theory, Jauss had announced a 'paradigm shift': Jauss (1969); later, he put the term in the title of a review of his own work: Jauss (1983).

[4] Among all this material a few items stand out. Warning 1975 collects major theoretical contributions, Link (1976) pursues systematic and didactic aims, whereas Grimm (1977) offers theory, applications and seventy pages of bibliography; in English Holub (1984) may be recommended as an accessible, well-balanced and dispassionate introduction, with a good annotated bibliography. Opportunities for classical philology are discussed by Barner (1977) and P.L. Schmidt (1985).

representatives. Hans Robert Jauss brought out a massive synthesis of his work in 1982, but since then he has not significantly modified or extended his views.[5] Wolfgang Iser, who was Jauss's colleague at Constance, but has also taught in the USA, has moved from his analyses of the reading process in the 1970s to much wider issues of literary anthropology in the 1980s, now crowned by his new book.[6] At first sight this state of affairs would seem to fit in with Jauss's view of a 'paradigm shift': the 'revolution' being accomplished, we would now have reached a phase of 'normal science'. But such an account is clearly unsatisfactory, because the advent of reception theory has by no means put an end either to controversy in theory or to divergence in practice. On the contrary, even in Germany and indeed in Constance itself reception theory is in the process of being supplanted by various brands of 'post-structuralism'.[7] Should we then conclude that reception theory has not solved its problems as definitively as Jauss believed? If this question is firmly posed, there seems to be still room for more discussion of reception theory and its potential for classical philology.

But first a few points of terminology and demarcation have to be settled. It is customary to think of 'reception theory' as a cohesive body of thought in which Jauss and Iser have about equal shares;[8] yet Iser has emphatically declared that he did not offer a *Rezeptionstheorie*, but a *Wirkungstheorie*, by which he meant that he was concerned with response as pre-structured by the text *(Wirkung)*, not response as realized by the reader *(Rezeption)*.[9] Even if Iser is set apart, 'reception theory' still covers a wide array of approaches, including the flourishing empirical (sociological and psychological) study of reception, with which Jauss, however, will have nothing to do.[10] It is therefore useful to refer to his theories by a term of its own, and fortunately he himself has coined one: *Rezeptionsästhetik*, somewhat uneasily anglicized as 'aesthetics of reception'.[11] If one needs a label for Iser, one could follow general American practice and reckon him among the 'reader-response

<hr/>

[5] Jauss (1982); a first instalment had been published a few years earlier: Jauss (1977a).

[6] Compare Iser (1972) and (1976) with Iser (1991).

[7] Or so it appeared to me when I spent the academic year 1988-89 at the University of Constance, on a fellowship from the Netherlands Organization for Scientific Research (NWO); this support is hereby gratefully acknowledged.

[8] This is true of all the works mentioned in n. 4. Holub (1984) is careful not to merge Iser's thought with Jauss's, but still treats both men together as 'the major theorists' (chapter title) of 'reception theory' (book title).

[9] Iser (1976) 8.

[10] See Ibsch and Schram (eds.) (1987).

[11] I use the term for Jauss's work as a whole, although Jauss himself has not often spoken of *Rezeptionsästhetik* since 1973, but rather put his work under the heading of 'aesthetic experience and literary hermeneutics', the title of Jauss (1982).

critics', as long as one realizes that this is even more of a mixed bag than 'reception theory'.[12]

Separating Iser from Jauss brings up the question which of the two to select for discussion. Iser's work has the advantage of providing something of a method for studying concrete texts: one tries to describe how the text structures the experience of the reader as s/he goes along; examples of this kind of analysis in classical philology are already available.[13] In the case of Jauss, however, it is much less clear whether he offers a method, and if so, for what. But quite recently two American classicists independently (and in different ways) have held up the same text of Jauss as a model to be followed in the interpretation of Roman poetry.[14] Because this text is (I think) highly problematical and moreover not representative of Jauss's work as a whole, I felt that it might serve a useful purpose if I attempted an exposition of the 'aesthetics of reception' rather than discussing the more familiar 'reader-response criticism'.

LITERARY HISTORY

Jauss's main concern in his epoch-making lecture of 1967 is immediately apparent from its title, or rather from both of its titles: it was delivered as *Was heisst und zu welchem Ende studiert man Literaturgeschichte?* (with a glance at Schiller) and published as *Literaturgeschichte als Provokation der Literaturwissenschaft.*[15] At first sight paradoxically, Jauss proposed to renew literary scholarship not by having recourse to modern methods such as those of structuralism (then very much *en vogue*), but by returning to the old and obsolescent discipline of literary history. Jauss's reason for this move was his belief that literary history is called upon to account for three fundamental truths about literary works: that they are not timeless entities, but historical events; that they are not mere objects, but works of art; and that some works of the past are still part of our present experience of literature. Current literary history, Jauss argued, was unsatisfactory in these respects, because it was still under the spell of the two dominating tendencies of nineteenth-century scholarship: historicism, which refused to

---

[12] See Tompkins (1980), Suleiman and Crosman (1980) and Freund (1987). In all of these Iser (but not Jauss) is prominently present.

[13] See e.g. Pedrick and Rabinowitz (1986) and Slater (1990).

[14] Galinsky (1992) 8-11, Edmunds (1992). Galinsky refers to an earlier partial publication (in Fuhrmann, Jauss and Pannenberg (eds.) (1981) 473-81; cf. 472), Edmunds to an English translation of "Der poetische Text im Horizontwandel der Lektüre (Baudelaires Gedicht: 'Spleen II')" in Jauss (1982) 813-65.

[15] Schiller's famous inaugural lecture at Jena in 1789 was called *Was heisst und zu welchem Ende studiert man Universalgeschichte?*; on the sense of the allusion cf. Holub (1984) 53-54. I will quote Jauss's lecture from its final version in Jauss (1970) 144-207; parenthetical numbers in my main text will refer to this publication.

study the past from the perspective of the present, and positivism, which treated the literary work as a 'fact' to be 'explained' from its sources or from the biography of its author. As a reaction against positivism, *Geistes-geschichte* and *Traditionsforschung* had reinstated consideration of literature as art, but at the cost of neglecting its ties with the real world.[16] More promising than these traditional approaches are Marxism and Russian Formalism, which both have the advantage that they see the literary work as part of a historical process which is still continuing, so that past and present are connected. But Marxism views the history of literature as a mere 'reflection' of socio-economic history,[17] whereas Russian Formalism regards the two as completely independent. So Marxism fails to account for the aesthetic character of literature, Formalism for its historical character. How can we account for both?

Jauss's answer is: by devising a *Rezeptionsästhetik*, a theory of art which enables us to deal with the reception of literature by its audience. Traditional literary scholarship had focused either on the author or on the representation of reality or on the work itself, but had systematically ignored the audience. Yet it is the audience which decides on the aesthetic character of the work as well as on its place in history. In order to explain why this is so, Jauss introduces a term which has become as notorious as *Rezeptionsästhetik* itself: *Erwartungshorizont*, anglicized as 'horizon of expectation(s)'.

Unfortunately, Jauss is not very precise in his use of this term. One of the problems is that he seems to use it both with the subjective and with the objective genitive. Thus, when he speaks of 'the horizon of expectation of the audience' (182), the genitive is clearly subjective, but in 'the horizon of expectation of a text' (175), 'of a work' (177), or 'of literature' (202), the genitive is apparently objective. Yet it is not as clear-cut as that, because Jauss also speaks of 'the horizon of expectation ... which the author assumes in his audience' (177), adducing as examples works which evoke 'the horizon of expectation of their readers' (176) in order then to 'destroy' this horizon and go off in unexpected directions; in such cases the work has an expectation of the expectation of its audience, and this 'expected expecta-tion' can only be known by interpreting *the work itself*.[18] If the work is not that explicit, Jauss suggests that we can determine the 'horizon of expecta-tion' by looking at three factors: the norms of the genre to which the work belongs, the forms and themes of related works, and the opposition between

---

[16] In this context Jauss is particularly severe on Curtius (1948): see Jauss (1970) 153-54; similarly Jauss (1982) 687-88.

[17] It must be noted that Marxists have accused Jauss of simplifying their positions: see the summary of the discussion in Holub (1984) 121-34.

[18] Jauss had in fact first employed the notion of 'horizon of expectation' in his interpretation of the Old French *Roman de Renart*; see his own comments in Jauss (1970) 184, 200-02 and (1982) 690-94.

the poetical and the practical functions of language (173-77); in this case one also analyzes *the literary system*. Yet it should be obvious (even if Jauss fights shy of it) that if one wishes to give an accurate account of how a work acted on the expectations of its readers, hearers or spectators, one also has to describe *the audience*. Later, Jauss admitted this and tried to disentangle the various meanings of 'horizon of expectation'. He proposed to distinguish between a literary (or even 'intra-literary') horizon of expectation, inscribed in the work, and a social one, brought to the work by the reader.[19] Yet this still seems to conflate the subject and the object of the expectation: the work 'expects' not only literary, but also social attitudes in its readers, whereas these readers expect from the work the articulation not only of social, but also of literary norms. Once we have clarified this, we are in a position to specify which kind of 'horizon of expectation' Jauss in fact uses in his attempt to reconcile aesthetics and history: it is the horizon of expectation of the audience, comprising both the literary features of the work and the social implications of its contents.

To begin with aesthetics: originally Jauss believed that he could establish not only the aesthetic *character*, but even the aesthetic *value* of a literary work from the past with the help of the horizon of expectation: the greater the distance between the work and the expectations of its original audience, the more valuable he supposed the work to be (177-79). This one-sided and simplistic view was a typical product of the revolutionary spirit of the late 1960s, as Jauss soon realized, and in 1972 he delivered another public lecture at Constance, in which he openly repudiated his earlier 'aesthetics of negativity'; subsequently, he elaborated a theory of aesthetic experience which allowed literature (at least before the modern era) to affirm or to establish norms as well as to negate them.[20] On this amended view, the horizon of expectation no longer serves to determine aesthetic *value*; does it still serve to account for aesthetic *character*? This must seem doubtful, because a comparison of a literary work with the horizon of expectation of its audience necessarily focuses on the newness (or otherwise) of the aesthetic experience, not on the aesthetic experience itself. 'Negativity' has not been eliminated, because it is inherent in the concept of 'expectation'. We will meet with the same bias when we turn to Jauss's treatment of history.

It is important to realize that 'history' in Jauss has two meanings: chronological development (as against timelessness) and 'general' history (as against 'intra-literary' history). Correspondingly, when he wishes to give an account of the 'historical' character of literature, he has to explain two things: first, how literature evolves in time; second, how it partakes of what

---

[19] See Jauss (1975) 328, 337-39.

[20] The lecture was published as Jauss (1972); it contains *in nuce* the theory of aesthetic experience as presented at far greater length in Jauss (1977a) and finally in Jauss (1982) 17-359.

happens in the world at large. Both explanations employ the horizon of expectation. To begin with the second: here we can well see why it is essential that the horizon of expectation have a social component: only if that is granted, is it possible to explain how a *literary* work can act on the *social* expectations of its readers and thereby influence their attitudes and even their behaviour. The point is an important one, because it provides Jauss with his main argument in his quarrel with Marxism: whereas Marxists, he contends, describe literature as merely *abbildend*, he, with his notion of horizon of expectation, is able to describe it as *bildend* (199-207). Here too, Jauss primarily thinks of the horizon of expectation being 'broken through' *(durchbrochen)*, but one can correct this one-sidedness (in accordance with his later views) without compromising his claim: when expectations are confirmed or newly argued for or extended, that too can have an impact on social practice.

In Jauss's model of literary evolution, on the other hand, it is crucial that the horizon of expectation is indeed broken through: only when that happens does a 'change of horizon' *(Horizontwandel)* occur, which sets the historical process off in a new direction. Subsequent works now have to meet new expectations, with the consequence that they will be different, because authors are also readers and are also affected by the change of horizon. The new horizon will then be broken through in its turn, the works which follow will again be different, etc. In this case Jauss is aware that his model only accounts for innovation as such, but cannot explain in what the innovation consists: why the horizon is broken through in this specific way and not in another. To make up for this deficiency, Jauss supplements his model (perhaps not quite consistently) with 'the historical logic of question and answer' (189-92, 198),[21] according to which a work leaves its audience with a problem, to which a new work then provides a solution, leaving the audience with yet another problem, etc.; if we recognize what the questions were, we can also understand the solutions. Thus the process of change of horizon takes place through the alternation of question and answer, and as this process continues into our own day, it mediates the past with the present.

The literary history here designed by Jauss has for its avowed aim 'to understand the historical succession of literary works' (169) and tries to achieve that aim by linking the works through their receptions: instead of a sequence work — work — work, etc., we get a sequence work — reception — work — reception — work, etc. This is a definite improvement, but cannot yet account for a further feature of the reception of literary works,

---

[21] Jauss refers to various publications by Hans Blumenberg, but takes the expression 'the logic of question and answer' from Hans-Georg Gadamer, who in his turn took it from R.G. Collingwood: see Gadamer (1986) 375-84 (351-60 in older editions). Elsewhere, Jauss refers directly back to Gadamer; this will be discussed below.

also discussed by Jauss. A literary work has its reception not just at the moment of its original appearance, when it acts on the horizon of expectation of its first audience (or 'solves' their 'problems'), but also at later periods of time, when it can still (or again) influence the historical process; or to put it from another perspective: a new literary work reacts not only to the reception of the immediately preceding work, but also to the reception of such older works as still affect literary consciousness. So it seems that the work — reception — work model needs to be supplemented by an account of later receptions, which would however destroy the simplicity and practicability of the model. If one wishes to put Jauss's suggestions into practice, one obviously needs to renounce the lofty ambition of describing 'the historical succession of literary works' and satisfy oneself with studying the connections among a few works only.

One possibility is to write the history of a *genre*. A genre is a historical series of works, but if we wish to describe how and why each work in the series differs from its predecessors, we cannot be content with just comparing the works, but need to take account of the receptions of these works. At each point in the series, the reception of the works thus far has created an expectation as to what a work in the genre should be like; a new work, if it is to be accepted as belonging to the genre, must conform to these expectations. But if this new work makes a contribution of its own (as will happen), its reception will modify the generic expectation, causing a revision of the reception of the earlier works. This new situation will then again be changed by a following work, etc.[22] A history of a genre along these lines is feasible if the genre is more or less clearly circumscribed and does not contain too many works, as is the case with most genres of ancient literature. With genres such as tragedy or the (modern) novel, however, it is difficult to imagine how a Jaussian history could be written.

Jauss's own practical work has mainly consisted in studies of the connection between two works only, in which he has tried to show that the second work provided an answer to questions posed by the first. From the pairs chosen by Jauss it is again apparent that literary history cannot limit itself to the chronological succession of works: the pairs not only belong to different periods, but even to different languages (Rousseau's *Nouvelle Héloïse* and Goethe's *Werther*, Goethe's and Valéry's *Faust*, etc.).[23] This type of research is of course also familiar from studies on the *Nachleben* of

---

[22] Jauss has given his views on genre in "Theorie der Gattungen und Literatur des Mittelalters", first published in 1972 and reprinted in Jauss (1977b); for a fuller exposition and an application to ancient bucolic see Nauta (1990).

[23] These studies have been incorporated in Jauss (1982); see 505-33 for Valéry and Goethe, 585-653 for Goethe and Rousseau; also 534-84 on the dramas about Amphitryo by Plautus, Molière and Kleist (a series of three works this time) and 704-52 on the dramas about Iphigeneia by Goethe and Racine.

the classics; its subject is sometimes known as 'productive reception'.[24]
Jauss distinguishes himself by his emphasis on question and answer, but it
should be noted that in these studies he no longer speaks of the 'historical
logic', but of the 'hermeneutics' of question and answer: his primary aim
has shifted from history to interpretation. He wants to understand a work by
studying how it reacts to an earlier work.

One further step is to abandon diachrony altogether and to concentrate on
the synchronic interaction between an individual work and the horizon of
expectation of its original audience. This entails falling back into the
historicism which reception aesthetics set out to overcome, but nevertheless
the focus on the audience has a few advantages over the old historicism.[25]
First, the object of study is now the *communication* between author, work
and audience, not merely the production of the work by its author. Second,
this attention to communication leads to a consideration of the *functions* of
the work for its audience: did the work affirm or deny existing norms, did
it strengthen or undermine group solidarity, did it offer entertainment or did
it provoke thought or even action? — such questions can indeed offer a
meaningful perspective on the relation between literature and (general)
history.[26] Finally, practitioners of this kind of research are more
hermeneutically aware, because they no longer pretend to offer 'the'
interpretation of the past work, but only a reconstruction of the meaning the
work had for its original audience. Such a hermeneutical position does not,
however, question that it is possible to give an objective description of the
work as well of the horizon of expectation of the original audience:
otherwise, how could one describe the interaction of the two? Indeed, Jauss
himself argues at length that the horizon of expectation is *objektivierbar*
(173-77). Yet elsewhere in his lecture he seems to deny with equal emphasis
that objective historical knowledge is possible. At this point (if not earlier)
we become aware that there is a third gravitational centre in Jauss's text
besides aesthetics and history: hermeneutics.

Jauss develops his hermeneutics not so much in the context of the work
— reception — work model as in the context of another model, which one
might call the work — reception — reception model: a work of the past is
connected with the present not only by 'the historical succession of literary
works' (169), but also by 'the chain of receptions' (170) of the work itself;
in this chain our own reception is the latest (but not the last) link. According

---

[24] See e.g. Barner (1973).

[25] What I here call (by implication) a 'new historicism' is something different from the
American 'New Historicism' (cf. e.g. Veeser 1989); but there are, I think, possibilities of
contact.

[26] This approach is sometimes known as *Funktionsgeschichte*; within classical philology, it
has been especially successful in the study of archaic Greek lyric: see e.g. Rösler (1980) and
(1984), where the term is discussed at 188 with n. 33. On Horace there is Mauch (1986). For
further discussion and application to Latin literature, see Nauta (1987) and (1994).

to Jauss this implies that our reception can never be privileged over other receptions: even if we are philologists or historians, we cannot attain immediate access to the work we study, but only an access mediated by the preceding *Rezeptionsgeschichte*, of which we are ineluctably a part (168-73, 183-89). To describe what happens in this 'history of reception' Jauss again uses the metaphor of the horizon: whereas in the first model a work acted on a 'horizon of expectation', and, if it was sufficiently new, could bring about a 'change of horizon', in the second model a 'fusion of horizons' *(Horizontverschmelzung)* takes place, in which the horizon of the readers 'fuses' with the horizon of the work. Here the work has its own horizon from the start, and to this extent Jauss's later division of the horizon of expectation into one of the work and one of the audience can be seen as a harmonization of his two notions of horizon. Yet the two notions derive from different intellectual traditions, as Jauss's own references betray: he notes that the 'horizon of expectation' plays a role in the scientific methodology of Karl R. Popper (201-02),[27] whereas for the 'fusion of horizons' he acknowledges his indebtedness to the anti-methodological hermeneutics of Hans-Georg Gadamer (185-89).[28] Gadamer is also the source for 'the logic of question and answer', which we have already encountered as a principle of historical development, and which is here introduced as an instrument of hermeneutics: to understand a text from the past is to understand the question to which it was an answer. Yet, as Jauss remarks, 'Gadamer demonstrates that the reconstructed question can no longer stand in its own horizon, because this horizon is always already encompassed by the horizon of our present'; this implies that 'the historical question needs to pass into *(übergehen in)* the question that the tradition is for us' (185).[29] According to this hermeneutics, therefore, there can be no objective historical reconstruction of the horizon of a work or of the horizon of its audience. Yet we have seen that Jauss aimed at just such a reconstruction and argued that it was feasible. This tension in Jauss' thinking between

---

[27] Jauss refers to an article (in German) of 1964, which had originally appeared in 1949; this seems to be the first occurrence of *Erwartungshorizont* in Popper, who may have taken the term from Karl Mannheim's *Mensch und Gesellschaft* (1935), the English edition of which he extensively criticized in *The Poverty of Historicism*. Yet neither Popper nor Mannheim seems to have been Jauss's source. The term was apparently coined by Husserl: it occurs in the 1923 and the 1928 indices to the first book of the *Ideen* (though not, as far as I can ascertain, in the passages to which these indices refer) and in the 1929 Paris lectures (*Husserliana*, vol. 1, p. 19). But Jauss knew Husserl only indirectly (174, n. 71, 178, n. 77; also (1982) 665-67), and the two concepts of horizon are very different; cf. Anz 1976. See generally the *Historisches Wörterbuch der Philosophie* 3 (1974), s.v. "Horizont" (esp. 1194-1206).

[28] See Gadamer (1986) 305-12 (284-90). The concept of *Wirkungsgeschichte*, developed by Gadamer in these pages, is at the back of Jauss's *Rezeptionsgeschichte*. For 'the logic of question and answer' see above, n. 21.

[29] Jauss partly paraphrases, partly quotes Gadamer (1986) 379-80 (356).

what one could call an 'objectivist' and a 'subjectivist' position we will encounter again.

More than the work — reception — work model, the work — reception — reception model has stimulated diachronic research, because in this case the material can be clearly delimited; moreover such research can link up with philological traditions which, even if marginal, are well-established. Since the 1970s there has been a boom in studies carrying titles or subtitles of the type 'the reception of author X (in period Y or in culture Z)', but these studies hardly ever propose to bring out the historical determination of our own reception as a product of earlier receptions (which is impossible in any case if period Y does not continue into the present or if culture Z is not our own). The hermeneutic dimension is absent,[30] and the bottles now labeled 'reception' contain old wines, which used to be called 'the *Nachleben* (or *Fortleben*) of X', 'the influence of X', 'the heritage of X', etc.[31] Yet, as in the case of research into the horizon of expectation of the original audience, the focus on reception can lead to progress in comparison with conventional approaches because of attention now paid to the *interaction* of the work and the audience, in this case later audiences.

On the other hand, studies do exist in which the history of the reception of a work is indeed undertaken in order to clarify the researcher's own hermeneutic consciousness. Jauss himself provided a 'paradigm' (as he called it) in an article on Goethe's *Iphigenie*, first published in 1973.[32] The paradigm is not one of literary history, but of interpretation: Jauss speaks of a *rezeptionsgeschichtliche Deutung* and a *rezeptionsästhetische Interpretation* (738; cf. 704-07). Reception is involved in two ways: as the reception *of* the *Iphigenie* and as the reception *by* the *Iphigenie*, viz. of Racine's *Iphigénie*, the work which according to Jauss posed the question to which Goethe's play was the answer. The original 'horizon of question and answer' (707) is linked to our own questions and answers by the history of the reception of the play (705-06). Thus the two aspects of reception are combined, but the combination is perhaps not as easy as it seems. Jauss's discussion of the history of the reception of Goethe's play is marked by a

---

[30] Note how Gadamer (1986) 305-06 (284-85) emphasized that he did not plead for *Wirkungsgeschichte* as a discipline, but as hermeneutic self-consciousness. Jauss, however, lists examples of the 'rezeptionsgeschichtliche Methode' (183 with n. 91); cf. also Jauss (1975) 326-27.

[31] On this tradition see Stückrath (1979), esp. 132, n. 22 on the change in terminology. Examples concerning classical authors are given by Barner (1977) 514-15 and P.L. Schmidt (1985) 76, n. 27. The new history of Latin literature by von Albrecht (1992) systematically lists such studies in separate sections on "Fortwirken" (not "Rezeption"!); cf. e.g. at 581, n. 4 the titles listed for Horace.

[32] This article was incorporated in Jauss (1982) 704-52; the characterization as a 'paradigm' occurs in the "Nachwort" at 738, 742 and elsewhere. Henceforward, bracketed page-numbers in my main text will refer to Jauss (1982).

curious dialectic: His initial motivation is to show that our own reception is always historically situated, that we are always inevitably *in* the *Rezeptionsgeschichte*; yet in the course of his research into the historical determinants of the earlier receptions, he develops a confidence that we, now forewarned, can avoid historical determination, that we can get *out of* the *Rezeptionsgeschichte*. Thus, he argues that the earlier receptions have 'covered up the historically original meaning' (705), whereas his own interpretation is not 'a mere concession to the tastes of the present time' (as one might be tempted to think in view of its stress on 'liberation'), but retrieves 'the lost character' of the work (728). The history of reception is here no more than the traditional *Geschichte der Forschung*, undertaken for heuristic, pedagogical and rhetorical reasons: to find out what the problems are, to show why others have erred, and to set off in greater splendour one's own solution. It seems as if Jauss does not provide any new 'paradigm' of interpretation, but merely couches traditional philological practice in a Gadamerian vocabulary. A number of years later, however, he made another attempt at designing his own hermeneutics, in the article which I mentioned at the beginning, and to which I now turn.

INTERPRETATION

In "Der poetische Text im Horizontwandel der Lektüre (Baudelaires Gedicht: 'Spleen II')" from 1979-80[33] Jauss distinguishes three 'readings', which are 'phenomenologically' successive (814), though not, as he admits, in practice. These are an 'aesthetically perceptual', a 'retrospectively explicating' and a 'historical' reading (813), in which we recognize the three dimensions of aesthetics, hermeneutics and history. It would be incorrect, however, to limit the term 'hermeneutical' to the second reading: rather, Jauss's enterprise as such is hermeneutical, and 'explication' *(Auslegung)* is only one moment in the total hermeneutical process (813-14). The key term 'horizon' and its compound 'change of horizon' also recur, now coupled with 'of reading' (already in the title). Jauss describes the first and the second reading as occurring within a 'horizon', so that a 'change of horizon' takes place in the transition from the first reading to the second (820). Not, however, in the transition from the second reading to the third, because the third is not in fact a 'reading', but a study of the history of the reception of the text; in this context, 'horizon' still refers to the horizon of a historical audience, and 'change of horizon' to the modification of that horizon effected by the reception of the text (846). The 'fusion of horizons' is now absent, which signalizes, as we will see later on, a conscious departure from Gadamer. Yet

---

[33] The article was incorporated in Jauss (1982) 813-65 (at 813 the title is misprinted as 'Horizont*en*wandel'); the date of writing is given as 1980 at 813, n. 1 and as 1979 at 819.

Jauss claims that his tripartition itself is directly derived from Gadamer (to whom the original article was dedicated).

Jauss refers to those passages of *Wahrheit und Methode* in which Gadamer takes up the eighteenth-century doctrine of the three *subtilitates*: the *subtilitas intelligendi* or *Verstehen*, the *subtilitas explicandi* or *Auslegung* and the *subtilitas applicandi* or *Anwendung*, which I will translate as 'understanding', 'explication' and 'application'.[34] According to Gadamer, the hermeneutics of Romanticism had already demonstrated that understanding and explication are two sides of the same coin; he now argues that application is also part of this unity, because 'in understanding there always takes place something like an application of the text ... to the present situation of the interpreter'. One divergence between Jauss and Gadamer is immediately obvious: Jauss's historical reading does not correspond to Gadamer's application; it is not even the history of this application, because it also comprises the history of the 'aesthetic' and 'explicative' moments. More fundamentally, for Gadamer understanding, explication and application are inseparable aspects of understanding *the same thing*, whereas in Jauss each successive reading understands *something different*, something which could not be understood in the preceding reading. This becomes particularly clear in Jauss's treatment of understanding and explication, which in Gadamer, after Schleiermacher, are related as 'speaking aloud' is related to 'speaking inwardly'.[35]

In Jauss, the 'understanding' reading is also called 'aesthetic' and (with something of a *figura etymologica*) 'perceptual'. 'Perception', according to Jauss, is a linear process in time, and his first reading is tantamount to a 'reader-response' analysis of the experiences 'the reader' has when going through the text (indeed Iser is invoked: 820). When the reading process has reached its end, the 'form' of the text has been 'fulfilled', but not yet its 'meaning': for that to happen, the retrospection of the second reading is required (820, 837). This differential treatment of form and meaning must seem questionable, because the perception of formal features involves retrospection just as well: even a simple rhyme cannot be recognized as such without a memory of what has gone before (Jauss unwittingly acknowledges as much when he slips into phrases like 'looking back' (827, 831) in the course of his first reading). It would seem a truer description that form and meaning are *both* constituted by the interaction of anticipation and retrospection. Moreover, the reduction of the 'aesthetic' to a linear process must be criticized: the aesthetic experience of a poem (in the sense of the experience of a poem as art) may for some readers consist in the 'dynamic'

---

[34] Gadamer (1986) 312-16 (290-95); the quotation in the next sentence is from 313 (291). These pages were the starting-point for Fuhrmann, Jauss and Pannenberg (eds.) (1981), in which Jauss originally published the first section of his article (cf. n. 14).

[35] See Gadamer (1986) 188 (172-73), with the quotation from Schleiermacher in n. 15.

enactment or re-enactment of its first perception, but for other readers it may consist in a more 'static' contemplation which requires the first perception to be completed. This differentiation between readers brings up the question of the status of 'the reader'.

Jauss does not engage in a typology of implied, informed, ideal or superreaders (apart from rejecting the latter), but puts himself 'into the role of a reader with the educational horizon *(Bildungshorizont)* of our present day' (819). One could ask how homogeneous that horizon is (a question which also arises about Jauss's earlier dealings with 'the' horizon of 'the' audience), but here I would like to draw attention to another issue. Jauss undertakes 'to suspend for the moment his competence in literary history and in the language' (819) and indeed, in reading a poem by Baudelaire entitled "Spleen", he elaborately tries *not* to know anything about the meaning of 'spleen' or about the role of that word in Baudelaire's work, and even contrives to ignore that in *Les Fleurs du Mal* the poem stands together with three others also called "Spleen" (825-26). His impulse seems to be not so much to evade the hermeneutic circle (about which he does not talk) as to keep the 'aesthetic perception' as pure and as absolute as possible. In other words: Jauss's first reader (and his second to some degree) is an unredeemed practitioner of *werkimmanente Interpretation*, refusing to acknowledge that his reading is set in a historical horizon of previous knowledge and existing commitments. If we now expect Jauss to point this out and analyze the expectations and presuppositions which went into the making of his reader's 'progressive horizon of aesthetic perception' (825) or of his 'retrospective horizon of explicative understanding' (836), we will be disappointed: since Jauss has decided to identify himself with his reader, he must share both this reader's horizon and his attempt to forget all about it. Jauss does not even explain why he selected this particular poem in the first place: apparently because he had just presented his interpretation of it at a scholarly conference.[36] In this case Jauss himself overlooks that a reading is always set in some horizon, some framework within which it is a meaningful activity, and that published readings (like his own) are usually set in the framework of academic debate between scholars who have strong investments in the interpretations they propose.

Now Jauss does analyze the history of the reception of the poem, but only in the third reading, after his interpretation is already finished. This obscures the fact that the interpretation has been strongly guided by the history of the reception. In theory Jauss of course admits this (824), but his failure to feed back the third reading into the first and second (and the second into the first) conveys a false suggestion about the reading process. The demand to

---

[36] See Jauss (1989b) 186-88 for the interpretation and 166, n. * for the conference and its date (1978).

make literary hermeneutics truly literary (814) cannot be met by simply
putting an 'aesthetic' reading 'first'.

The third reading is the one which is most obviously continuous with the
original project of the aesthetics of reception. Jauss begins by reconstructing
the 'horizon of expectation' (813, 847, 849, 853) of the original audience
and by showing how Baudelaire took up a 'contrary position' to it (853).
We are very close here to the *Provokation*, which culminated in a discussion
of the lawsuit brought against Flaubert for *Madame Bovary* in 1857; the
very same year, of course, saw Baudelaire put on trial for *Les Fleurs du Mal*
(847-48). This trial did not particularly address the second "Spleen" poem,
which confronts Jauss with a difficulty that he duly notes: receptions of
Baudelaire for a long time did not take the form of interpretations (847).
The texts Jauss can find are (in chronological sequence) a few essayistic
(and even novelistic) treatments of *Les Fleurs du Mal* as a whole, then two
monographs from 1953 in which the second "Spleen" poem gets a few
pages, and then three articles from the 1970s which are specifically devoted
to this poem (848-65). Apparently the practice of reading itself (at least the
practice of writing about reading) has changed in the course of history. This
would seem to pose a challenge to *Rezeptionsgeschichte*, but Jauss does not
rise to it. Instead, he treats all texts as if they were interpretations competing
with his own, and dispenses praise and (mostly) blame, just as he had done
in the article on Goethe's *Iphigenie*. His criterium is 'the intention of the
poem' (863) as he had established it in his first and second readings and in
the earlier part of the third reading, that concerned with the reconstruction
of the historical horizon of the text. Jauss seems to believe that his first and
second readings give him access to 'the intentionality of the text' (816), but
in spite of this claim, these readings do not offer a new hermeneutics (apart
from being distinguished from each other). It is in the context of the third
reading that Jauss makes his own contribution: we will gain access to 'the
meaning intended by the author' (703) if in the third reading we carry out
a *Horizontabhebung*, a 'setting off of horizons' (821-22).

The term *Horizontabhebung* derives from the same context in Gadamer
as *Horizontverschmelzung*, which Jauss had adopted in the *Provokation*, but
now significantly abandons.[37] In Gadamer, both terms are intimately linked:
when we wish to understand a text from the past, we cannot naively
assimilate its otherness, but we have to 'set off' its horizon from our own,
only then to 'fuse' both horizons in the act of understanding. This is closely
connected with Gadamer's insistence on application: understanding what the

---

[37] See the reference in n. 28. Gadamer does not use the noun *Horizontabhebung*, but he does
use the verb *abheben* with the object *Horizont(e)*. Jauss introduced *Horizontabhebung* in the
"Spleen" essay at 821-22, then returned to it in the "Einleitung" to the third part of Jauss (1982)
at 657-58 and 666-69; cf. also Jauss (1989a) 203 (where it is translated as 'differentiation of
horizons').

text says is the same as understanding what it says *to me*. We have seen that Jauss, in spite of his assertions to the contrary, does not integrate application in this way, so that for him the 'setting off of horizons' is no longer a necessary preliminary to understanding, but is in itself a way of understanding; the object of this understanding is the historical meaning of the text, separated from its application to the present. Yet Jauss's views on reception forbid him to identify this historical meaning with 'the' meaning of the text; he notes that one would 'fall back into historicism' if one could not turn the question "what did the text say?" into the question "what does the text say to me and what do I say to the text?" (822). The formulation is almost the same as the one quoted above from the *Provokation*, where, due to the fusion of horizons, the two questions 'passed into' *(übergehen in)* each other in the sense of becoming identical; here, where the 'setting off of horizons' keeps the questions distinct, one cannot quite see what 'turn into' *(überführen in)* could mean. Again, the problem seems to be that Jauss wishes to remain faithful to a Gadamerian hermeneutics while at the same time straining away from it.

If we ask what the "Spleen" article can contribute to philology, we come to the same conclusions, I think, as we reached earlier about the *Provokation*. Jauss's ideas about the horizon of expectation of the original audience and of later audiences usefully encourage consideration of the communication process as a whole, including function, and do not lack the hermeneutical self-awareness which nowadays one is entitled to demand of *any* approach. But a specifically Jaussian hermeneutics does not exist. Jauss tried to find a form of understanding that would be 'historical' without being 'historicist', but failed, because he did not reconcile the Gadamerian and the historicist elements in his position. Yet it is precisely his promise of offering the best of both worlds that has allured his readers.

HISTORICIZING READING

In 1992 Lowell Edmunds published his book *From a Sabine Jar*,[38] in which 'Jauss's method is applied in an experimental spirit to the reading of an ode of Horace' (x); however, Edmunds deviates from Jauss in several significant ways, of which I will discuss only two: his handling of historical evidence and his exclusion of the history of scholarship from the third reading. The ode chosen by Edmunds is 1.9, often dubbed 'the Soracte Ode', after the mountain mentioned in the second line:[39]

---

[38] Edmunds (1992); parenthetical page-references in my main text will henceforth refer to this work.

[39] Since Edmunds polemicizes against this 'title' (see 65-74), I emphasize that I use it only as a conventional designation, without prejudicing my interpretation of the ode.

I Vides ut alta stet niue candidum
  Soracte, nec iam sustineant onus
   siluae laborantes geluque
    flumina constiterint acuto?

II Dissolue frigus ligna super foco   5
  large reponens atque benignius
   deprome quadrimum Sabina,
    o Thaliarche, merum diota.

III Permitte diuis cetera, qui simul
  strauere uentos aequore feruido   10
   deproeliantis, nec cupressi
    nec ueteres agitantur orni.

IV Quid sit futurum cras fuge quaerere et
  quem Fors dierum cumque dabit lucro
   appone, nec dulcis amores   15
    sperne puer neque tu choreas,

V donec uirenti canities abest
  morosa. Nunc et Campus et areae
   lenesque sub noctem susurri
    composita repetantur hora,   20

VI nunc et latentis proditor intimo
  gratus puellae risus ab angulo
   pignusque dereptum lacertis
    aut digito male pertinaci.

(I) Do you see how Soracte stands white with high-piled snow, and the labouring woods no longer sustain their burden, and the streams have frozen to sharp ice? (II) Dissolve the cold: put logs on the hearth in large measure and more generously draw off the four-year-old wine, Thaliarchus, from its Sabine jar. (III) Leave everything else to the gods: as soon as they have laid low the winds battling on the tossing sea, neither the cypresses are shaken nor the old ash-trees. (IV) Forbear to ask what will happen tomorrow, and whatever day Fortune will give you, set it down as gain, and do not spurn the pleasures of love nor dancing while you are young, (V) as long as your green youth is untouched by sulky whiteness. Now seek the Campus and the squares and soft whisperings before nightfall at the appointed hour, (VI) now seek the welcome laughter of a girl which betrays her as she hides in a secret corner, and the pledge pulled off from her arms or her scarcely resisting finger.

This ode, written more than two thousand years ago in a language now long extinct, stands at a far greater historical distance from the modern reader than Baudelaire's "Spleen" poem, written in the previous century in a language that is still spoken in more or less the same form. With Horace it is even more apparent than with Baudelaire that understanding is impossible without historical knowledge (including historical knowledge of the language). It is therefore natural that Edmunds is much concerned about how to distribute this requisite historical knowledge over his three readings. In theory, he 'suspends detailed historical information' (3) in the first reading, undertakes 'historical and philological research' (24) in the second reading, but only 'within the aesthetic perspective of the first' (25), whereas his third reading is 'strictly historical' (25). But because he uses 'standard grammars, commentaries, and dictionaries' (3) in the first reading, that reading recognizes Horace's imitation of Alcaeus, fr. 338 Voigt (4-5, 9-11), argues from the (mistaken) view that 'Roman houses did not have the kind of windows from which a landscape could be observed' (8),[40] and is knowledgeable about the habitats of trees in ancient Italy (13). The second reading then tries to find out what associations 'the Romans' (25) connected with Mt. Soracte (25-27) and with the name 'Thaliarchus' (32-33), questions which are discussed in the standard commentaries just as well, but not, in these cases, to Edmunds's satisfaction. No commentary, however, has detected the references to Lucretius that Edmunds believes the poem to make, and for that reason, apparently, these are discussed in the third reading (59-65). This third reading 'attempts to establish the horizon of expectation of the ode's original audience' (41), but of course the audience's recognition of Alcaeus belongs in that horizon just as much as their (alleged) recognition of Lucretius (cf. 59-60), together with the associations of trees, of Mt. Soracte and of the name 'Thaliarchus'. What this suggests is that even in his first and second readings Edmunds was engaged in reconstructing the horizon of expectation of the Roman audience, in establishing how *they* would have understood the poem (he himself speaks of the 'code' shared by the poet and his readers: 4, 16, etc.). That Edmunds does not recognize this seems to be due to the lingering influence of New Criticism, with its puritanical attitude toward history (just as in Jauss we recognized the unacknowledged presence of *werkimmanente Interpretation*). This suspicion is corroborated by the observation that Edmunds pretends to read the poem in isolation: he discusses the eight poems preceding it in the published book as part of the horizon of expectation of the original audience (43-59), but not as part of his own. He also never explains (just as Jauss did not) why he selected this particular poem in the first place; the answer presumably is that the Soracte Ode has given rise to a highly notorious, long-standing interpretative controversy in classical philology, and has been used before to stage a confrontation between 'philology' and 'hermeneutics'.[41] Edmunds sides emphatically with 'hermeneutics' against 'philolo-

---

[40] Cf. the commentary of Nisbet and Hubbard (1970) 116. But the owners of Roman villas set great store by views of the surrounding scenery, especially from the dining rooms; cf. e.g. Pliny the Younger, *Epistles* 2.17.5 and 5.6.19.

[41] See Kresic (ed.) (1981) 275-98. In Nauta (1991) I had selected the Soracte Ode independently of Edmunds.

gy', to the extent of trying to abandon his identity as a classical philologist
and to read the poem innocent of the *Geschichte der Forschung*. This leads
to the second deviation from Jauss.

Edmunds deals with the history of philological interpretation not in the
third reading, as Jauss did, but separately: "Scholarship" is a chapter not in
"Part One" of his book, called "The Jaussian Readings", but in "Part Two",
called "Other Approaches". So Edmunds radically separates scholarship from
reading. Even if we do not accept this, we can admit that modern philological scholarship has at least *changed* reading. Edmunds dates this change to
the nineteenth century (75), but further consideration will allow us to revise
this date and at the same time to demonstrate that scholarship is a form of
reading after all.

Even if philological 'interpretations' as we know them have not always
existed, commentaries on Horace were written already in Antiquity, and then
in great quantity in the Renaissance. These commentaries usually contain an
argumentum, which shows how the commentator understood the poem (as
apart from the local features picked out for comment). Thus Porphyrio, from
probably the third century, offers this summary: 'he exhorts Thaliarchus to
a more cheerful life, to enjoy the playful activities of youth, as long as his
age permits'. In the most influential Renaissance commentary, that of
Lambinus (1561), we find 'in winter one should indulge in pleasure', which
keeps recurring (with variants) in editions of the *Odes* until the beginning
of the nineteenth century.[42] It seems as if Lambinus' *sententia* is meant not
just as a summary of the speaker's advice to Thaliarchus, but also as an
application (in the Gadamerian sense) to the situation of the reader, because
the advice is now formulated generally, not limited to youth.[43] But
explication of the poem as poem, beyond the moral extracted from it, begins
only in the second half of the eighteenth century (at least in Germany), the
period which saw the rise both of aesthetics and of literary hermeneutics.[44]
The first such explication of the Soracte ode that I have found occurs in a
commentary by Jakob Friedrich Schmidt, published in 1776.[45] Interestingly
enough, this is a commentary in German, not in Latin, and it is addressed

---

[42] For the ancient commentaries see Nisbet and Hubbard (1970) xlvii-li and P.L. Schmidt
(1992) 498-500. A useful annotated list of editions from the Renaissance through the eighteenth
century is to be found in Mitscherlich (1800) xlii-cliv.

[43] A generalization with respect to gender seems not intended: as women generally were not
taught Latin, they were not reckoned with as readers of Horace. Only at the end of the
eighteenth century there appear vernacular adaptations of 'Horace for young ladies': cf. Pietsch
1988: 1 with n. 3.

[44] See the pioneering article of E.A. Schmidt (1981), which studies the changes in the
German commentaries on Horace's *Odes* from 1700 to 1850. The magisterial work of Weimar
(1989), although devoted to German philology, is also very important for the backgrounds to
classical philology.

[45] J.F. Schmidt (1776) 260-66.

to 'young people'; Schmidt moreover was by no means a leading classical philologist, but a preacher and a schoolmaster, as well as a poet and a critic of contemporary German literature.[46] This suggests that as long as the history of classical philology is written as a history of the great philologists (or as the story of the 'growth of knowledge'), an important dimension is omitted: that of the *history of reading*, which depends less on scholarly 'discoveries' than on larger cultural developments.

Schmidt is concerned with the order *(Ordnung)* of the ode: a degree of disorder is permitted, is even considered to be particularly 'lyrical' (according to the poetics of the time), but here 'one believes one observes a real disorder'. The problem is that the depiction of the outdoor entertainments in the final strophes does not seem to be consistent with the winter setting. Schmidt's solution is that the poem is not about the winter at all (the traditional *argumenta* are therefore incorrect), but about 'the favourite thought of the poet ... which is only occasioned by the winter'. In order to understand how this thought develops, one should be aware 'that *nunc* in verses 18 and 21 refers to *puer* in verse 16 and to *donec*, etc. in verse 17, but in no way to the winter time'. Schmidt does not explicitly ask in what situation the thought was expressed, but seems to provide an answer in his note on verse 8, where he maintains that Thaliarchus was 'a friend of Horace, who without doubt had a country house not far from Mt. Soracte, and whom the poet visited there'. Two years later (1778) Christian David Jani, another schoolmaster, explicitly states: 'It is probable that Horace composed this poem at the villa of Thaliarchus, not far from Mt. Soracte'; Jani also explains the connection of thought *(connexio)* and notes that *nunc* (18) refers to youth.[47] In Mitscherlich's commentary of 1800 this interpretation then enters the mainstream of academic philology.[48]

Nevertheless, many philologists have attacked the unity of the ode, most recently Eduard Fraenkel, who pronounced: 'This incongruity cannot be removed by any device of apologetic interpretation'.[49] Of course Fraenkel's *dictum* has stimulated rather than stifled 'apologetic interpretation', because interpretation in the modern sense is not deemed successful if no unity is found. One reaction to Fraenkel was to re-instate the old interpretation of J.F. Schmidt and Jani. This was done by (among others) David West, who insisted on two things: a correct reconstruction of the setting (a country house near Mt. Soracte, not Rome) and a correct reconstruction of the train

---

[46] See Johann Georg Meusel, *Lexikon der vom Jahr 1750 bis 1800 verstorbenen teutschen Schriftsteller*, vol. 12 (Leipzig 1812), 269-72.

[47] Jani (1778) 74-79. On Jani see Meusel (as in the preceding note), vol. 6 (Leipzig 1806), 228-29.

[48] Mitscherlich (1800) 104-11.

[49] Fraenkel (1957) 177.

of thought (*nunc* meaning 'now when you are young', not 'this instant').[50]
West called the poem a 'dramatic monologue' (with explicit reference to
Browning), and thereby separated the levels of communication which were
still conflated by Jani: whereas Jani asked where the poem was *written*,
West asks where it is *set*. The poet has constructed a situation (the 'setting')
in which a speaker (in this case 'the poet' himself, according to West) is
supposed to have uttered a certain speech act directed to an addressee; the
task of interpretation is to identify the situation and understand the speech
act. But the term "dramatic monologue" implies still more: it presumes that
we are primarily interested in the speaker, in the character and attitudes
revealed during the speech act, not in the intended effect on the addressee.
Thus another proponent of reading the ode as 'dramatic monologue',
Kenneth Quinn, believes that in the final strophes the speaker is reminiscing,
'pursuing vanished youth as much as giving advice to his companion'.[51]
Here the idea of 'monologue' is radicalized in opposition to the 'dialogical'
conception of the Horatian ode championed by Richard Heinze.[52] But both
the 'dialogic' and the 'monologic' emphases are articulated within one and
the same convention: that of reading lyric poetry as something spoken in the
context of a situation. This convention may be powerful; it is not
uncontested.[53]

A competing convention may again be introduced from an old German
interpretation, again written by someone who was not primarily a classical
philologist. In 1840 the German Goethe scholar Heinrich Düntzer argued
that the 'symbol', which played so important a role in his main object of
study, was also very important 'in the ancients generally and particularly in
Horace'.[54] When interpreting the 'Soracte Ode', he suggested that the
winter in the first strophe is an 'image' *(Bild)* of old age, to be connected
with the word *canities* in verse 17, which Düntzer paraphrases with 'winter
of life' *(Lebenswinter)*; 'the images of winter and of old age correspond, and
at the end there apparently is opposition *(Gegensatz)* between the joy of
youth and oppressive age'. The unity is sought in a system of correspon-
dences and oppositions, and this system can be built up with the help of
metaphorical (or 'symbolic') connections: winter can correspond with age
if the two are in some ways analogous or similar. If we look at the later

---

[50] West (1967) 1-12.

[51] Quinn (1980) 139-42. This view is very common: it is also found e.g. in Pöschl (1991)
30-51 and in Edmunds.

[52] See "Die Horazische Ode" (from 1923) in Heinze (1972) 172-89. Without reference to
Heinze, Gregson Davis has recently re-emphasized the rhetorical character of the communication represented in Horace's *Odes*: Davis (1991).

[53] For a theoretical criticism see Culler (1985).

[54] Düntzer (1840) 13; his general discussion on symbolism is at 13-19, on opposition at 19-
20, and his interpretation of the 'Soracte Ode' at 171-74. On his Goethe studies cf. e.g. Weimar
(1989), 404-406.

history of interpreting the 'Soracte Ode', we see that controversy arises about how far the system can be extended. L.P. Wilkinson submitted that the third strophe 'gains enormously in significance, and unites the whole poem, if we feel the storm to be the storm of life, and the calm the calm of death'; Steele Commager, among others, added that the ash-trees are 'old' and that cypresses have funerary connotations.[55] But it has been objected that the poem's argument demands that the calm be reassuring, so that this particular correspondence must be abandoned.[56] In this case, the rejection of symbolism is motivated by considerations of consistency, but we also find refusals to read the winter in the first strophe as symbolic of old age, although here consistency is not at stake; West, e.g., bluntly declares: 'Horace's snow is simply snow'.[57] His motive is a fear of reductionism: if many terms are metaphorically equated, they all become instances of the same overarching category, which is then often proposed as the 'theme' of the poem (as when Commager writes: 'mortality is the poem's real theme').[58] In somewhat technical terms one could state that Commager and others, by establishing connections of similarity and opposition between elements in the poem, convert the syntagmatic order of these elements into a paradigmatic order; this too is a powerful, but (as we see) contested convention.[59]

Now the two conventions I have identified are not logically incompatible. One can hold without contradiction that at the level of the communication between speaker and addressee the poem is uttered in a certain situation and reveals a certain frame of mind, whereas at the level of the communication between poet and reader it is constructed in such a way that symbolical connections obtain between elements of the text. Yet readers are often disinclined to be that catholic. I have already instanced West's refusal to read symbolically, but there are also many examples of refusals to reconstruct a situation in which the poem is a conceivable speech act.[60] This suggests that discussions about the interpretation of the 'Soracte Ode' cannot be resolved simply by looking harder at the poem, but have to take into account the framework within which the text is read, or (in Jaussian terms) the 'horizon'. But this also suggests that one cannot speak of 'the' horizon of a certain historical moment, as Jauss does, because the horizon is not in fact homogeneous. People negotiate about their various horizons, and in the modern age the main vehicle for this negotiation is interpretation.

But interpreters negotiate their horizons not only with the horizons of other interpreters, but also with what they know or think they know about

---

[55] See Wilkinson (1951) 131 and Commager (1962) 271.

[56] E.g. Pöschl (1991) 38-40.

[57] West (1967) 11; similarly e.g. Pöschl (1991) 45 and Nisbet and Hubbard (1970) 118.

[58] Commager (1962) 271.

[59] Roman Jakobson's famous description of the poetic function (Jakobson 1960) turns this convention of *reception* into a principle of *production*; cf. Posner (1982) 171-79.

[60] See e.g. Commager (1962) 271, Nisbet and Hubbard (1970) 117-18, Davis (1992) 152-53.

the horizon of the past. In practice critics usually support their refusal to read the 'Soracte Ode' in a certain way by reference to how they think poetry was read in Ancient Rome. This suggests that the 'history of reading' could and should be extended to Antiquity itself. Such a project, however, even if inspired by the aesthetics of reception, could not be considered an 'application' of anything Jauss has done.

Indeed, the possibilities for direct application of his work are, I believe, very limited. The *Provokation* essay has not provided a consistent and feasible model for literary history, even if some of its proposals can still (after 25 years) contribute to a reorientation of research. The "Spleen" essay has not offered an acceptable model for interpretation, either in its original form or in its adaptation by Edmunds. The value of the aesthetics of reception, therefore, seems to me to be not primarily historical or hermeneutical, but heuristic.

BIBLIOGRAPHY

Albrecht M. von (1992) *Geschichte der römischen Literatur von Andronicus bis Boethius mit Berücksichtigung ihrer Bedeutung für die Neuzeit* (2 vols., Bern-Munich: 1992).
Anz H. (1976) "Erwartungshorizont. Ein Diskussionsbeitrag zu H.R. Jauss's Begründung einer Rezeptionsästhetik der Literatur", *Euphorion* 70 (1976) 398-408.
Barner W. (1973) *Produktive Rezeption. Lessing und die Tragödien Senecas* (Munich: 1973).
—— (1977) "Neuphilologische Rezeptionsforschung und die Möglichkeiten der klassischen Philologie", *Poetica* 9 (1977) 499-521.
Commager S. (1962) *The Odes of Horace. A Critical Study* (New Haven-London: 1962).
Culler J. (1985) "Changes in the Study of the Lyric", in *Lyric Poetry: Beyond New Criticism*, ed. Ch. Hošek and P. Parker (Ithaca-London: 1985) 38-54.
Curtius E.R. (1948) *Europäische Literatur und lateinisches Mittelalter* (Bern-Munich: 1948).
Davis G. (1991) *Polyhymnia. The Rhetoric of Horatian Lyric Discourse* (Berkeley-Los Angeles-London: 1991).
Düntzer H. (1840) *Kritik und Erklärung der Oden des Horaz* (= *Kritik und Erklärung der horazischen Gedichte*, vol. 1) (Brunswick: 1840).
Edmunds L. (1992) *From a Sabine Jar. Reading Horace, Odes 1.9* (Chapel Hill-London: 1992).
Fraenkel E. (1957) *Horace* (Oxford: 1957).
Freund E. (1987) *The Return of the Reader. Reader-Response Criticism* (London-New York: 1987).
Fuhrmann M., H.R. Jauss and W. Pannenberg (eds.) (1981) *Text und Applikation. Theologie, Jurisprudenz und Literaturwissenschaft im hermeneutischen Gespräch* (= *Poetik und Hermeneutik*, vol. 9) (Munich: 1981).
Gadamer H.-G. (1986) *Wahrheit und Methode. Grundzüge einer philosophischen Hermeneutik* (Tübingen: [6]1986; first edition published 1960).
Galinsky K. (1992) "Introduction: the Current State of the Interpretation of Roman Poetry and the Contemporary Critical Scene", in Galinsky (ed.) (1992) 1-40.
Galinsky K. (ed.) (1992) *The Interpretation of Roman Poetry: Empiricism or Hermeneutics?* (Frankfurt am Main-Bern-New York-Paris: 1992).
Grimm G. (1977) *Rezeptionsgeschichte. Grundlegung einer Theorie. Mit Analysen und Bibliographie* (Munich: 1977).
Heinze R. (1972) *Vom Geist des Römertums. Ausgewählte Aufsätze*, ed. E. Burck (Darmstadt: [4]1972; identical with the edition Stuttgart: [3]1960).

Holub R.C. (1984) *Reception Theory. A Critical Introduction* (London-New York: 1984).

Ibsch E. and D.H. Schram (eds.) (1987) *Rezeptionsforschung zwischen Hermeneutik und Empirik* (Amsterdam: 1987).

Iser W. (1972) *Der implizite Leser. Kommunikationsformen des Romans von Bunyan bis Beckett* (Munich: 1972).

—— (1976) *Der Akt des Lesens. Theorie ästhetischer Wirkung* (Munich: 1976).

—— (1991) *Das Fiktive und das Imaginäre. Perspektiven literarischer Anthropologie* (Frankfurt am Main: 1991).

Jakobson R. (1960) "Closing Statement: Linguistics and Poetics", in *Style in Language*, ed. T.A. Sebeok (Cambridge, Mass.: 1960) (widely reprinted).

Jani C.D. (1778) *Q. Horatii Flacci Opera*, vol. 1 (Leipzig: 1778).

Jauss H.R. (1969) "Paradigmawechsel in der Literaturwissenschaft", *Linguistische Berichte* 3 (1969) 44-56.

—— (1970) *Literaturgeschichte als Provokation* (Frankfurt am Main: 1970).

—— (1972) *Kleine Apologie der ästhetischen Erfahrung* (Constance: 1972).

—— (1975) "Der Leser als Instanz einer neuen Geschichte der Literatur", *Poetica* 11 (1975) 325-44.

—— (1977a) *Ästhetische Erfahrung und literarische Hermeneutik*, vol. 1 (Munich: 1977).

—— (1977b) *Alterität und Modernität der mittelalterlichen Literatur. Gesammelte Aufsätze 1956-76* (Munich: 1977).

—— (1982) *Ästhetische Erfahrung und literarische Hermeneutik* (Frankfurt am Main: 1982).

—— (1983) "Historia calamitatum et fortunarum mearum. Oder: Ein Paradigmenwechsel in der Literaturwissenschaft", in *Forschung in der Bundesrepublik Deutschland. Beispiele, Kritik, Vorschläge*, ed. C. Schneider (Weinheim: 1983) 121-34.

—— (1987) *Die Theorie der Rezeption — Rückschau auf ihre unerkannte Vorgeschichte* (Constance: 1987).

—— (1989a) "Response to Paul de Man" (tr. A. Michel), in *Reading de Man Reading*, ed. L. Waters and W. Godzich (Minneapolis: 1989) 202-08.

—— (1989b) *Studien zum Epochenwandel der ästhetischen Moderne* (Frankfurt am Main: 1989).

Kresic S. (ed.) (1981) *Contemporary Literary Hermeneutics and Interpretation of Classical Texts/Herméneutique littéraire contemporaine et interprétation des textes classiques* (Ottawa: 1981).

Kuhn T.S. (1970) *The Structure of Scientific Revolutions* (Chicago-London: ²1970; first edition published 1960).

Link H. (1976) *Rezeptionsforschung. Eine Einführung in Methoden und Probleme* (Stuttgart-Berlin-Cologne-Mayence: 1976).

Mauch H. (1986) *O laborum dulce lenimen. Funktionsgeschichtliche Untersuchungen zur römischen Dichtung zwischen Republik und Prinzipat am Beispiel der ersten Odensammlung des Horaz* (Frankfurt am Main-Bern-New York: 1986).

Mitscherlich C.G. (1800) *Q. Horatii Flacci Opera*, vol. 1 (Leipzig: 1800).

Nauta R.R. (1987) "Seneca's *Apocolocyntosis* as Saturnalian literature", *Mnemosyne* 40 (1987) 69-96.

—— (1990) "Gattungsgeschichte als Rezeptionsgeschichte am Beispiel der Entstehung der Bukolik", *Antike und Abendland* 36 (1990) 116-37.

—— (1991) "Schrijven over lezen. Receptie-esthetica en Horatius-interpretatie", *Lampas* 24 (1991) 239-56.

—— (1994) *Poetry for Patrons. Literary Communication in the Age of Domitian* (to be published 1994).

Nisbet R.G.M. and M. Hubbard (1970) *A Commentary on Horace: Odes. Book I* (Oxford: 1970).

Pedrick V. and N.S. Rabinowitz (eds.) (1986) *Audience-Oriented Criticism and the Classics = Arethusa* 19:2 (1986).

Pietsch W.J. (1988) *Friedrich von Hagedorn und Horaz. Untersuchungen zur Horaz-Rezeption in der deutschen Literatur des 18. Jahrhunderts* (Hildesheim-Zurich-New York: 1988).

Pöschl V. (1991) *Horazische Lyrik. Interpretationen* (Heidelberg: ²1991; first edition published 1970).

Posner R. (1982) *Rational Discourse and Poetic Communication* (Berlin-New York: 1982).

Quinn K. (1980) *Horace: The Odes* (Basingstoke-London: 1980).

Rösler W. (1980) *Dichter und Gruppe. Eine Untersuchung zu den Bedingungen und zur historischen Funktion früher griechischer Lyrik am Beispiel Alkaios* (Munich: 1980).

—— (1984) "Die frühe griechische Lyrik und ihre Interpretation. Versuch einer Situationsbeschreibung", *Poetica* 16 (1984) 179-205.

Schmidt E.A. (1981) "Das Interesse am horazischen Einzelgedicht", in *Geschichte des Textverständnisses am Beispiel von Pindar und Horaz*, ed. W. Killy (Munich: 1981) 19-70.

Schmidt J.F. (1776) *Horaz lateinisch und deutsch mit Anmerkungen für junge Leute*, vol. 1 (Gotha: 1776).

Schmidt P.L. (1985) "Reception Theory and Classical Scholarship: a Plea for Convergence", in *Hypatia. Essays presented to Hazel E. Barnes*, ed. W.M. Calder III a.o. (Boulder: 1985) 67-77.

—— (1992) "Horaz", in *Reallexikon für Antike und Christentum* fasc. 124 (1992) 491-524.

Slater N.W. (1990) *Reading Petronius* (Baltimore-London: 1990).

Stückrath J. (1979) *Historische Rezeptionsforschung. Ein kritischer Versuch zu ihrer Geschichte* (Stuttgart: 1979).

Suleiman S.R. and I. Crosman (eds.) (1980) *The Reader in the Text. Essays on Audience and Interpretation* (Princeton-Guildford: 1980).

Tompkins J.P. (ed.) (1980) *Reader-Response Criticism. From Formalism to Post-Structuralism* (Baltimore-London: 1980).

Veeser H.A. (ed.) (1989) *The New Historicism* (New York-London: 1989).

Warning R. (ed.) (1975) *Rezeptionsästhetik. Theorie und Praxis* (Munich: 1975).

Weimar K. (1989) *Geschichte der deutschen Literaturwissenschaft bis zum Ende des 19. Jahrhunderts* (Munich: 1989).

West D. (1967) *Reading Horace* (Edinburgh: 1967).

Wilkinson L.P. (1951) *Horace and his Lyric Poetry* (Cambridge: ²1951; first edition published 1945).

POSTMODERNISM, ROMANTIC IRONY,
AND CLASSICAL CLOSURE

BY

DON FOWLER

> *'Irony is no joking matter'* F. Schlegel
> *'The opposite of irony is common sense'* R. Rorty

'Closure' in all its senses[1] has often been seen as a distinguishing characteristic of classicism. The classic work is a rounded organic whole, *simplex et
unum*: it ends in resolution, 'all passion spent'. Antiquity is a closed system,
providing a canon of texts whose perfection is beyond time: criticism of
those texts is an eternal return, the rediscovery of the timeless verities that
they contain. The Classical Tradition is a golden chain which enables us to
'take our journey back' as Edwin Muir puts it. And at the end of all our
journeying are those same everlasting Forms of Beauty that have always
been there and always will be.

No one, of course, has ever really believed this nonsense. There are much
messier stories to tell of the 'real' Classical Tradition, and classical studies
as a discipline have always been much more 'open', again in every sense.
We should not complain as professionals that others get it 'wrong': one of
the functions of the classical ideal has always been to enable rebellion from
it, to function as a dreary father-figure for the Oedipal revolt of Romantics
and Moderns. But many recent critics have rightly seen as one of their tasks
the demonstration that the texts of the classical canon can fail just as
successfully as other texts to attain classical perfection. Looking for a
contrast to the novel, the American critic R.M. Adams[2] was happy to write
in the 1950s of the *Oedipus Tyrannus* that:

> the play is a self-contained unit; there is nothing within it which calls attention to
> or criticises its aesthetic existence; there is no unresolved or discordant element to
> disturb its conclusion; in its psychological effects it is a unified and harmonious
> whole that passes the audience through a clear, easily defined and complete
> emotional cycle to a distinct logical and emotional conclusion.

---

[1] Cf. Fowler (1989). A revised version of that article will appear in a volume of essays on
closure that I am editing with D.H. Roberts and F. Dunn.

[2] Adams (1958) 26. See Fowler (1989) 80-1.

All that sentence requires to become consonant with the current orthodoxies of Sophoclean criticism is the insertion of a few negatives:[3] when Oliver Taplin ends his own discussion of the end of the *Oedipus Tyrannus* with the declaration that Sophocles, far from taking us through a clear, easily defined and complete emotional cycle, rather 'uses his theatre to stop *us* from finding a way out of his tragedy,[4]' the *différance* of meaning in his last words is seen as increasing, rather than diminishing, our respect for the play.

This sort of critical 'opening', however motivated — and I have quoted the last page of a piece by Taplin rather than of, say, Simon Goldhill's *Language, Sexuality, Narrative: the Oresteia* to make the point that we are not talking only of deconstruction — represents one pole of modern classical criticism, as of criticism in general. The other pole is of course historicism, old and new, with its stress on the closure of meaning by the realities of power: and the two form a pretty opposition onto which many other oppositions can be projected[5] — and which can itself be deconstructed. In this piece I want in one sense to write within the 'opening' tradition: I want to set some ancient endings against the theories of irony developed by the German Romantic critics in order to 'spoil' any sense of cool classical perfection, to show again that the images of classical closure held by people in other disciplines can be made to look misleadingly simple. But irony has also become central to postmodern attempts to cope with the abandonment of 'foundationalism'. I want to suggest that these attempts may help to alleviate some of the resistance to theory in a classical community which has similarly to face the loss of its foundations. Many classical scholars are attached to a rhetoric of presence because they feel that without it their activity has no point. If we are not trying to *discover* what Vergil meant or why the Peloponnesian War broke out: if we are only telling stories about the past: why bother? I cannot of course claim that there is *nothing* to fear, but I believe that one can be brought to feel that things are not quite as bad as they seem.

SELF — POLEMIC OVERCOME?

I would to heaven that I were so much Clay —
As I am blood — bone — marrow, passion — feeling —
Because at least the past were past away —
And for the future — (but I write this reeling
Having got drunk exceedingly to day
So that I seem to stand upon the ceiling)

---

[3] See especially Roberts (1988).
[4] Taplin (1983) 174.
[5] Cf. Fowler (1991) 33-5.

I say — the future is a serious matter —
And so — for Godsake — Hock and Soda water

Byron[6]

It is a cliché not without its ironies that the word 'irony' has become impossibly multiform.[7] The meaning, location, status, and value of the concept are all controversial. In particular, it is much disputed whether irony is a trope or a philosophy, a rhetorical device or a way of looking at the world (another opposition ripe for deconstruction by those who feel that tropes are all we have). Scholars play two familiar games: the creation of a range of distinctions, and the demonstration that those distinctions are inadequate. How many ironies dance on the end of a pin? The conceptual chaos repeats itself fractally as we descend to sub-types. My concern here is with Romantic Irony: it is true that this has been argued to be neither romantically ironic nor ironically romantic, but it remains one of the better defined sub-groups.[8] Its essence lies in a rupture of sublime illusion that nevertheless in some way retains sublimity. As the title suggests, the term was first brought to prominence by the German romantic critics, and its original context was that of German idealist philosophy as elaborated by Fichte. The *protos heuretes* is conventionally made Friedrich Schlegel, though he did not use the phrase in his published writings.[9] Here is one modern scholar's summary:

> Schlegel ... starts from the Fichtean philosophical position that the ego both posits the external world and is limited by it. But this limitation is overcome when, to simplify the terminology, the ego recognises what is going on and remembers that the non-ego is indeed its creature. Intelligence recognises that all its creations are relative. The poetic act analogous to the Fichtean process is that the artist, through

---

[6] Stanza rejected from *Don Juan* (McGann 5. 88): discussed in Garber (1988b) 153-6.

[7] The bibliography on irony is huge: the most comprehensive up-to-date bibliography I know is that in Seery (1990) (see especially notes 5 and 17 to ch. 3), but most of the works mentioned here and in note 7 have good bibliographies. As a general survey in English, Muecke (1969) remains invaluable: other classics include Knox (1972) (in part a review of Muecke) and Booth (1974), which is excessively reductive but for that reason usefully sceptical. In a similar vein is Dane (1991). For postmodern irony (to which I return at the end) see Rorty (1989), Seery (1990), and Hutcheon (1991).

[8] The most detailed treatment is that of Strohschneider-Kohrs (1977), but there is now a comprehensive volume of English essays in Garber (1988a): see especially the opening pieces by Behler and Immerwahr. See also Garber (1988b), Bourgeois (1974), Simpson (1979), Mellor (1980), Furst (1984), Finlay (1988), Prang (1989), Bishop (1989), Seery (1990) ch. 3, Dane (1991) chs 5-7. Immerwahr (1951) remains a classic clarification with regard to Schlegel himself. For the original texts, there is a useful collection in English translation, with good introduction, in Wheeler (1984): there is a handy two-volume edition of Friedrich Schlegel's works in the *Bibliothek Deutscher Klassiker* (Berlin and Weimar 1980).

[9] See especially Immerwahr (1951) and in Garber (1988a) 82-96, and Dane (1991).

his intelligence, frees himself from the limitations of what his enthusiasm has created.[10]

By rupturing the illusion — by in a sense destroying his own creation — the poet frees himself from being bound by the text he has created. As the text progresses, the possibilities narrow, as what has gone before determines what shall follow: the gesture of Romantic Irony reminds us that this is after all just the creation of a man like us, who can do what he likes with his material. The ultimate examples of this are novels like Diderot's *Jacques le Fataliste*, or Thomas Mann's *Doktor Faustus*, the example regularly taken as paradigmatic in modern discussions. As these examples suggest, while the original formulations of Romantic Irony were made in the specific context of German Romanticism, the problems the theory is attempting to address are general ones faced by all literature, and they are bound up with the notion of closure. To quote D. C. Muecke's formulation,[11] 'How can a work of art, which of its nature is something that can be finished and therefore something finite and static, express the infiniteness of life?' The answer of the Romantic Ironists was that 'the work of art should itself acknowledge its limitations and by doing so with irony it would take on the dynamic quality that life has and which art should therefore express'. This refusal of closure is not a negative act, but one which enables the reader to cope with seriousness and sublimity. Here are two more modern reformulations:

> The self-aware artist reveals his detached presence behind the work, calling attention to his creative role and thus to the fictional nature of the work; and thereby he undermines the credibility of the work as dramatic illusion (which at the same time undermines any illusion of godlike creativity). But by making the admission that his work is indeed fiction, by admitting art's representational limitations (and by admitting that he is indeed a 'buffoon' and not a god) the ironic artist creates the dramatic space for his art to unfold as a valid activity in its own terms. His 'mockery' of art reveals a combination of detachment *and* affirmation. A negative sets the stage for a 'positive'.[12]

More optimistically still:

> The authentic romantic ironist is as filled with enthusiasm as with skepticism. He is as much a romantic as an ironist. Having ironically acknowledged the fictiveness of his own patternings of human experience, he romantically engages in the creative process of life by eagerly constructing new forms, new myths. And these new fictions and self-concepts bear with them the seeds of their own destruction. They too die to give way to new patterns, in a never-ending process that becomes an analogy for life itself. The resultant artistic mode that alone can

---

[10] Hughes (1979) 142-3.
[11] Muecke (1969) 195.
[12] Seery (1990) 179-80.

properly be called romantic irony must therefore be a form or structure that simultaneously creates and de-creates itself.[13]

Now I am not concerned with the historical development of the concept of Romantic Irony, or with the adequacy of these formulations as a summary of the views of Schlegel or any of his followers. That historical development has its own stories, and they have their own structuring principles, in particular an opposition between 'optimistic' and 'pessimistic' views of the concept.[14] I want to concentrate on the most distinctive element in the concept: the view that the ironic unmasking of reality is not simply a negative act, but one in which the reader is enabled to accept a sublimity. This gesture has both a dynamic and a static aspect. Dynamically, it represents a *movement* from high seriousness or emotional pathos to what is in some sense seen as 'reality', a movement which is then 'transcended': hence the connection with closure. More statically, Romantic Irony may involve a constant, ever-present awareness of reality, and in particular of the reality of fictional creation. We are continually reminded that what is before us is made by man, not God: that even apparent 'showing' is really 'telling', that all narrative is discourse, that whether we ask 'who sees?' or 'who speaks?' the answer will always be: the author. In this form of Romantic Irony, the text is constantly self-conscious, with all the familiar devices of mise-en-abyme, and author and reader alike continually meet with doubles and surrogates in the work. Again, however, these are not simply devices of 'distancing': despite (or because of) it all, we take it seriously.

The relationship between these two aspects of Romantic Irony has its problems: if the essence of the dynamic form is a movement between sublimity and 'reality', is not that removed when reality is ever-present? In fact, the dynamic element is present in the pervasive form in terms of the *reader's* movement between a view *of the whole work* as sublime and a perception of it as just words on the page, *and back again* in a fruitful oscillation. The two forms have more in common than is first obvious. Nevertheless I want to look at them in turn. I also want to stress again at the outset, however, that whether to read a particular work in terms of Romantic Irony is a decision of the reader. The presence of various elements like a concluding deflationary turn or an authorial intervention may be more-or-less an objective feature of a text, but the interpretation of them has to be the reader's. It is a cliché to say that irony is above all a mode of reading, not a mode of writing. And of course the fragmentary nature of the Classical Tradition brings its own problems even with regard to apparently 'objective' elements (it is an enormously productive paradox that much of this literature of supposed formal perfection comes down to us already packaged as

---

[13] Mellor (1980) 5.
[14] Cf. e.g. Hélein-Koss (1988) 39.

Romantic Fragments like the *Satyricon*). I think that one of the clearest examples of Romantic Irony as closural gesture is Theognis' famous promise to Cyrnus in *Theognidea* 236-254:

σοὶ μὲν ἐγὼ πτέρ' ἔδωκα, σὺν οἷς' ἐπ' ἀπείρονα πόντον
πωτήσηι, κατὰ γῆν πᾶσαν ἀειρόμενος
ῥηϊδίως· θοίνηις δὲ καὶ εἰλαπίνηισι παρέσσηι
ἐν πάσαις πολλῶν κείμενος ἐν στόμασιν,   240
καί σε σὺν αὐλίσκοισι λιγυφθόγγοις νέοι ἄνδρες
εὐκόσμως ἐρατοὶ καλά τε καὶ λιγέα
ἄισονται. καὶ ὅταν δνοφερῆς ὑπὸ κεύθεσι γαίης
βῆις πολυκωκύτους εἰς Ἀίδαο δόμους,
οὐδέποτ' οὐδὲ θανὼν ἀπολεῖς κλέος, ἀλλὰ μελήσεις   245
ἄφθιτον ἀνθρώποις' αἰὲν ἔχων ὄνομα,
Κύρνε, καθ' Ἑλλάδα γῆν στρωφώμενος, ἠδ' ἀνὰ νήσους
ἰχθυόεντα περῶν πόντον ἐπ' ἀτρύγετον,
οὐχ ἵππων νώτοισιν ἐφήμενος, ἀλλά σε πέμψει
ἀγλαὰ Μουσάων δῶρα ἰοστεφάνων.   250
πᾶσι δ', ὅσοισι μέμηλε καὶ ἐσσομένοισιν ἀοιδή
ἔσσηι ὁμῶς, ὄφρ' ἂν γῆ τε καὶ ἠέλιος.
αὐτὰρ ἐγὼν ὀλίγης παρὰ σεῦ οὐ τυγχάνω αἰδοῦς,
ἀλλ' ὥσπερ μικρὸν παῖδα λόγοις μ' ἀπατᾶις.

I have given you wings on which you may rise and fly with ease over the endless sea and over the whole earth. You will be present at all feasts and banquets, on the tongues of many men; and young men will sing loud and clear of you during [their] lovely revels accompanied by their little clear-toned flutes. And, when you pass into the hiding places of the dark earth, into the house of Hades filled with lamentation, not even then, not even when dead, will you lose your glory, but, since your name will be undying among men, you will be famous, Cyrnus, as you circle around the land of Greece and the islands, crossing the unharvested fish-rich sea, not riding on mortal horses. The glorious gifts of the violet-crowned Muses will send you on your way, for you will be with all who care and who will care for songs, as long as there is earth and sun. Yet I do not have a little respect from you, but you deceive me with your talk, as if I were a little child (trans. Trypanis).

Reading this as a complete, self-contained poem, the structure is clear. The poem pivots at the reference to Cyrnus' name in 246-7: 245-6 has a strong closural force with its categorical assertion and reference to death and future fame (accompanied by some formal devices like the emphatic *Sperrung* ἄφθιτον ... ὄνομα). The poem then restarts in 247 with the actual name and recall of the opening (e.g. the recurrence of the γῆν ... πόντον opposition and of a pair of middle participles): 251-2 then recall both the opening and the false closure of 245-6 with yet more categorical assertion of future fame. The 'earth-sea' pairing is now hyperbolically replaced by 'earth-sun' (capping the reference in 243-4 to the darkness of Hades): the epic allusion in κλέος ... ἄφθιτον (245-6) is recalled with καὶ ἐσσομένοισιν ἀοιδὴ with its echo of Homeric passages like *Odyssey* 8.580 and 3.204.[15] After these grand promises of the power of poetry, the naked revelation in the last couplet[16] that this is all *werbende Dichtung* comes as a shock: one is surely not supposed to reveal so clearly that something was expected in return for the gift of immortality. Moreover, when we read of how Cyrnus deceives Theognis with words, it is difficult not to think of how Theognis has been deceiving Cyrnus, and more importantly us.[17] What else is poetry but deceptive words? It is not normally thought a good tactic for seducers in literature or life to bring up the subject of deception. Would you believe a man who declared his love like this? Can we allow ourselves to be taken in by a poem that so blatantly tells us it deceives? The answer of course is 'yes': that is the name of the game. The concluding shock of 253-4 does not affect the success of the lines either as a poem or as an expression of love. We have all learned in the postmodern age to say,[18] not 'I love you', but 'As Barbara Cartland would say ...'

This is a nice story — well, I like it. But of course it requires a lot of assumptions. The problems of the Theognid corpus need no rehearsal.[19] Is this a complete poem? What was its original context? How was it received? What is the status of this Englishman's dislike of explicit sexual bargaining? Is this ending a shock? Who says? These are questions worth discussing, but the provisional nature of any answer to them should not prevent us attempting readings. Naturally, in the end my reading is my reading, based on the stories I want to tell. I should like to convince others of it and them, and to argue: I should like to be forced to modify elements of my position, to be brought to see things I have missed. But it's no good pretending I didn't *make it all up*. Can we believe a critic who tells us this? Can we admit what we are doing, but take it seriously? I would argue that the answer is again 'yes'. And again, it seems to me particulary curious that classical scholars of all people should be determined to situate their stories so firmly 'out there' when even the most apparently objective features of their texts are up for grabs.

---

[15] The phrase will later be recalled in Theocritus 12.11, in an erotic context that merits attention: and a notable piece of Propertian Romantic Irony, 1.15.24 *tu quoque uti fieres nobilis historia*, is a further allusion — a line many have tried to make closural.

[16] The interpretation of the final couplet is disputed; 'Is the poet saying "I do not chance on even a slight respect from you" or "I chance on a good amount of respect from you," a meaning which effectively postpones the *aprosdoketon* to the final line' (Tarkow (1977) 114). I would favour the former view, but note the interpretation of Gentili (1977) favouring the latter: 'Non poco riguardo io attengo da te (Cirno), ma *in realta* (my emphasis) tu mi inganni coi tuoi discorsi come un fanciullo'.

[17] Cf. Tarkow (1977) 103, Adkins (1985) 152.

[18] The celebrated example of Eco (1984) 67-8, which finds its way into most discussions of postmodernism: quoted Fowler (1989) 113.

[19] On these lines, see especially Tarkow (1977) and Gentili (1977): more generally, Figueira and Nagy (1985). Note also the 'practical criticism' of the poem in Adkins (1985).

THE NEED TO BE STRAIGHT

The detection of Romantic Irony in Classical literature is not of course a novelty.[20] One of the most interesting and ambitious uses of the concept was by Douglass Parker in his 1969 *Arion* article on 'The Ovidian Coda'. He finds seven of Ovid's *Amores* — 1.7, 1.10, 1.13, 1.14, 2.13, 2.14, and 2.15 — 'distinguished by a common structural peculiarity':[21]

> each concludes with a brief coda which contradicts the main body of the poem more or less thoroughly. This coda is always marked by a shift of tone, which may be intensified by a change in the orientation of the elegiac *mise en scène* — in addressee, time, or place. In any case there is indicated a distinct change in viewpoint and sensibility. This change is impelled by, or constitutes, a return to *wie es eigentlich gewesen ist*: the *suasoria* addressed to the Dawn ends with her regular arrival; adumbrations of guilt, lost beauty, or abortion confront immediate distress; a fanciful transformation runs into physiological fact. The movement is always from more imaginative to less imaginative, from 'fictional' to 'real' — from, in a way, high to low. (Not that it is ever intentional bathos: Ovid may sink, but not too far). The illusion is broken, but it is the poetic illusion, which in some cases would be a perfectly free-standing poem without a coda. The coda by its very difference forces the comment, 'What I have said treat <as> not reality but an illusion'. The words neither cover nor solve the situation.

He expounds this closural device in terms of Romantic Irony, and uses it to support a serious reading of the *Amores* in the manner of Hermann Fränkel:[22]

> the poems of the *Amores*, by their wit rather than in spite of it, make quite serious points, points whose complexity are advanced rather than retarded by a specious simplicity and a surface slickness.

This is a first-rate account of how these endings *would* work if the codas represented true Romantic Irony. Parker's reading of 1.7, for instance, the poem in which Ovid agonizes over his violence to Corinna and then concludes by inviting her to wreak vengeance on his body — or at least tidy her hair, is of serious moral agony only at the conclusion subverted. Only the coda reveals the previous language and response to be overblown:[23]

> were the last distich lacking, the poem, even with the time-shift, would be quite different; its language would be, for the whole of the piece, admissible as somehow 'true'.

The trouble is, I cannot see it like that. For me, the poem is humorous from the beginning and the final throwaway only confirms our cynical

---

[20] Some references in Fowler (1989) 109 n. 126: add especially Schmitt (1989).
[21] Parker (1969) 93.
[22] Parker (1969) 81.
[23] Parker (1969) 87.

response.[24] Parker refers with apparent approval to Fränkel's interpretation of 1.7 as one of Ovid's 'deepest and most moving elegies'[25] but this, like the poem, seems to me ridiculous. Commenting on lines 61-2, for instance:

> ter tamen ante pedes volui succumbere supplex,
> ter formidatas reppulit illa manus

Parker remarks that 'the alienation of the lovers at this moment of spiritual juncture is put into relief by an epic tone, the triple frustration usually employed when a hero tries to clasp a goddess or a ghost',[26] but the gap between the situation of the text and the epic moments alluded to — and Parker omits the most obvious, Priam with Achilles' man-slaying hands — is too great for anything other than burlesque. Can any reader take Ovid seriously for a moment here or in most of the other poems mentioned? For me, the effect of the throwaway coda in them is not that of Romantic Irony.[27]

Why do I want to do this? My argument will of course appeal to 'objective' features of the poems, to plausible intertextual links, and generally to the context in the book of the *Amores*. But it will above all depend on the literary-historical narrative into which I want to insert the *Amores*. If we make the Ovid of the *Amores* an ironist, what do we do with Propertius? How do we make the *Amores* come after Propertius unless we are allowed to see Ovid pushing over into simpler burlesque the complex balance of humour and seriousness we ascribe to Propertius? My point is obviously again that what determines my reading is the larger stories I want to tell. One of the paradoxical effects of having stories like this is that one has to read some texts unironically: if one is seriously into irony, one has to be more than ironically into straightforwardness. This is one of the factors in the familiar phenomenon of literary history whereby texts pass in and out of complexity depending on whether they are serving as target or as model: the *Aeneid* of Vergilian scholars is very different from the *Aeneid* of Lucan specialists.

---

[24] Cf. McKeown (1989) 164.

[25] Fränkel (1945) 54.

[26] Parker (1969) 85.

[27] I confess, however, to feeling much less confident about *Amores* 1.13, which was Parker's starting-point: the address to dawn with a bid to delay which concludes with the couplet:

iurgia finieram. scires audisse: rubebat —
nec tamen adsueto tardius orta dies.

It is easier to 'take this seriously': a cynical, wholly humorous, reading of the opening is hard to sustain, there is hardly any Ovidian 'bad taste', and the poem, like 1.5, is a favourite amongst Ovidian critics like Fränkel, who expounds it at length. Even here, however, I feel rather inclined to take the path of heroic cynicism and thus to read the first part of 1.13 also as humorous. And naturally, I do not mean to imply that reading these poems humorously is an ideologically innocent act ...

Another celebrated example of Romantic Irony is Horace *Epode* 2, with
its praise of country life and shocking conclusion:

haec ubi locutus faenerator Alfius,
iam iam futurus rusticus,
omnem redegit Idibus pecuniam,
quaerit Kalendis ponere.

Having said these words, moneylender Alfius, always on the point of becoming
a farmer, calls in on the Ides all his money, and looks to place it again on the
kalends.

Like Ovid's aubade, *beatus ille qui procul negotiis* has a rich posterity, and
this one suspects is a further element in dissuading people from seeing the
first part of it as simply undermined by the concluding revelation that this
is all the hypocritical musing of *faenerator Alfius*. So Fraenkel suggests[28]
'that Horace seized upon the final surprise which he found in Archilochus
because this turn enabled him to mix the strong expression of what he really
cared for with a dose of that self-mockery without which he would not,
except in a moment of deepest emotion, feel that he was entirely true to his
own mind' — a classic exposition of at least one aspect of Romantic Irony,
in which, as he notes, Fraenkel is in substantial agreement with W. Y.
Sellar.[29] More recently, Stephen Heyworth[30] has joined Fraenkel in
endorsing the sincerity of the poem, particularly coming as it does
immediately after Horace's thanks to Maecenas for his rural retreat at the
end of *Epode* 1: 'are we to believe that he arranged his book of *Iambi* so
that a satire on love of the country should follow his expressions of thanks
for the very act which has enabled him to fulfil his own deeply felt love?'
His solution to the problems posed by the final couplet is to see Alfius
speaking the truth *malgré lui*, and criticised only for not acting on it: the
poem is thus an interesting combination of a description of the joys of
country life and a satirical attack on Alfius.

This will not do, because of the imbalance between the attention given to
the idyllic description and that devoted to the satire. Had they been more
equally balanced, we might talk of combination, but the four lines of satire
are insufficient in themselves, and can only function through their effect on
the first part. That is indeed how a coda employing Romantic Irony would
work, but I am afraid that again I am inclined to see *Epode* 2 rather
differently. Again it is possible to see the cynical criticism of the coda
anticipated in the body of the poem, albeit much less directly than in Ovid.
At first we may take the piece straight, but looking back we may see how
Alfius continually returns to images of wealth, from the *bubus ... suis* of line

---

[28] Fraenkel (1957) 60.
[29] Sellar (1892) 130.
[30] Heyworth (1988) 74.

2, through details like 10 *altas ... populos*, the numbers suggested by *prospectat errantis* in 12, the *distenta ubera* of 46, and the *pinguissimis ... ramis* of 55, to the final *ditis examen domus* of 65. One way of reading this in relation to *Epode* 1 is to stress how at the end of that poem Horace had rejected the economic aspect of farming:

> satis superque me benignitas tua
> ditavit: haud paravero
> quod aut avarus ut Chremes terra premam
> discinctus aut perdat[31] nepos

> Enough and more than enough the riches your kindness has given me: I shall not amass wealth to hide in the ground like miserly Chremes, or money for a dissolute grandson to lose.

With this, one can compare *Epistles* 1.16, where Quinctius is depicted as interested in the products of farming but Horace wants no more than a sunny valley, rich in only oak-leaves and shade:

> Ne perconteris fundus meus, optime Quincti,
> arvo pascat erum an bacis opulentet olivae,
> pomisne an pratis an amicta vitibus ulmo,
> scribetur tibi forma loquaciter et situs agri.
> continui montes si dissocientur opaca
> valle, sed ut veniens dextrum latus aspiciat sol
> laevum discedens curru fugiente vaporet,
> temperiem laudes: quid si rubicunda benigni
> corna vepres et pruina ferant? si quercus et ilex
> multa fruge pecus multa dominum iuvet umbra?

> To stop you asking, my dear Quinctus, whether my farm keeps its master fed through arable-land or enriches him through olives, through apples or meadows or elm-trees clad in vines, you shall have a detailed account of the disposition of my land. If continuous hills were broken by a valley, shady but such that the sun at his coming looked at the right side, breathed on the left when he departed in his chariot, you would praise the climate: what if the kindly thorns bore red cornel-berries, if the oaks pleased the cattle with abundant fodder and the master with abundant shade?

The effect of the coda in *Epode* 2 on this reading would not be to enable us to accept the initial moralising by relieving the tension inherent in serious-ness, but would be to expose the difference between what is said in *Epode* 2 and true love of the country: this would not be 'The countryside is a wonderful place — as a Barbara Cartland villain might say' but an instance of genuine subversion which forces us to go back and re-evaluate what we

---

[31] The manuscripts have *perdam*, but the efforts of the commentators to explain that are unconvincing, and Shackleton Bailey's *perdat* is an easy change.

have just read, to discover hints of Alfius' character already peeping through.

One way of reading *Epode* 2, without Romantic Irony: but there is another possibility. A given for both the interpretations mentioned is that Horace's affection for the countryside, reflected in Maecenas' gift of a country seat alluded to in the first *Epode*, cannot be other than wholly serious: and that there has to be a contrast between Horace and Alfius. But if we look again at the opening of *Beatus ille*, we see another way of reading the poem:

> Beatus ille, qui procul negotiis,
> ut prisca gens mortalium,
> paterna rura bubus exercet suis,
> solutus omni faenore,
> neque excitatur classico miles truci,
> neque horret iratum mare,
> forumque vitat et superba civium
> potentiorum limina.

> Happy the man who far from engagements, like the ancient race of mortals, works his father's fields with his own oxen, free of all debt, and is not stirred to become a soldier by the grim trumpet, nor stares with terror at the angry sea: avoids the forum, and the proud thresholds of powerful citizens.

This is like a parody both of Horace's life and of Maecenas', with whom, like Propertius in 3.9, Horace had in the previous epode insinuated a parallel (as Maecenas to Caesar, so Horace to Maecenas). When Horace imagines Maecenas' question (1.15-16):

> roges, tuum labore quid iuvem meo,
> imbellis ac firmus parum

> You may ask how I, unwarlike and infirm, could help your work with mine,

the reader is not going to miss the opportunity to ask the same thing about Maecenas and Imperator Caesar. Horace like his master lurks at the *superba civium potentiorum limina*, incurring debts to the great for their gifts of property, working fields not his father's with oxen scarcely his own: *procul negotiis*? *solutus omni faenore*? The irony in *Epode* 2 on this line of approach is much broader, and more disruptive: the reality of servile submission that is surfacing here is much less easily accommodated to a recuperation of the praise of country life. On this reading, the concluding gesture of *Epode* 2 does not help rehabilitate the poem's seriousness, nor does it draw a contrast between Alfius and Horace: rather it assimilates Horace and his money-grubbing surrogate (who seems to be an iambic poet, if we take 67 *locutus* seriously). What we do with that irony — and in particular, how we relate our reading to our reading of the rest of Horace's work — is of course up to us. We may wish to reintroduce Romantic Irony at a higher level, and see the exposure of Roman 'reality' as a way of legitimating the fictions that clothe that reality: by acknowledging his real position, Horace enables us accept the myths of Caesarism. Or we may feel in a more vandalistic mood, and choose to pick at the fissures and rents in Horace's discourse to stress how this doesn't work, how we cannot establish a stable view of the new imperial world from his poems.

What the problems of *Epode* 2 show is that the question of the poem's ending in relation to Romantic Irony is again ironically a very open one. They also show that as always in literary criticism, formalism inescapably leads us into the realm of the political and the ideological. To put it negatively, irony avoids commitment. What does Horace think about his relationship to the men of power? What story are we to tell of his engagement? It is not very clear, is it? More positively, irony can be viewed as a way of rendering commitment necessarily incomplete and unstable. When reality is exposed, we have to come to terms with it: and we may well feel that both acceptance and denial of our fictions are unacceptable. Somewhere in the middle is the ironist's stance.

Affirmations of Love

'Despite the difficulties of my story, despite discomforts, doubts, despairs, despite impulses to be done with it, I unceasingly affirm love, within myself, as a value. Though I will listen to all the arguments which the most divergent systems employ to demystify, to limit, to erase, in short to deprecate love, I persist. "I know, I know, but all the same ...' R. Barthes.[32]

Other poems of Horace are more easy to read as relatively straightforward Romantic Irony, notable the famous endings of *Odes* 2.1 and 3.3. The endings to some of the *Epistles* are similarly clear-cut in their effects: we meet the irony of the moralist, who breaks the tension of preaching with a joke, as in 1.1:

ad summam, sapiens uno minor est Iove, dives,
liber, honoratus, pulcher, rex denique regum;
praecipue sanus, nisi cum pituita molesta est.
In short, the wise man is inferior only to Jupiter, rich, free, honoured, beautiful, king of kings; healthy especially, except when a cold is troubling him.

and 1.4.:

inter spem curamque, timores inter et iras,
omnem crede diem tibi diluxisse supremum.
me pinguem et nitidum bene curata cute vises

---

[32] Barthes (1979) 22.

cum ridere voles Epicuri de grege porcum.

In the midst of hope and care, fear and anger, believe every day has shone the last for you: me you will see fat and shining with skin well-cared-for when you want to laugh at a pig from Epicurus' herd.

This will become a familiar trait also in Seneca, as with the famous ending to his diatribe on the resistance of the *sapiens* to noise in *Epistles* 56:

tunc ergo te scito esse compositum, cum ad te nullus clamor pertinebit, cum te nulla vox tibi excutiet, non si blandietur, non si minabitur, non si inani sono vana circumstrepet. 'quid ergo? non aliquando commodius est et carere convicio?' fateor. itaque ego ex hoc loco migrabo. experiri et exercere me volui. quid necesse est diutius torqueri, cum tam facile remedium Vlixes sociis etiam adversus Sirenas invenerit?

So you mustn't be sure of your equilibrium until no clamour affects you, no voice shakes your hold on yourself, whether it coax or threaten or boom emptily round you in meaningless uproar. 'Yes? and isn't it sometimes more convenient to be free from noise?' I admit it. That's why I shall shortly make a flit. I wanted to test and train myself. Why stay longer on the rack, when Ulysses discovered such a simple antidote for his ships company even against the sirens? (trans. Phillips Barker).

But the most obvious figure to employ Romantic Irony is not the moralist but the lover. Propertius has a number of celebrated examples, well discussed in recent years by Lefèvre and Papanghelis.[33] It is a lack of appreciation of the role of Romantic Irony in Propertius and Tibullus that is the most conspicuous deficiency in P. Veyne's otherwise excellent *Roman Erotic Elegy*. Too often he makes the humorous elements undermine or subvert the pathos of love:[34]

Here and there, in the middle of this picture of sharp, hardly harmonious colours, our attention is drawn to fragments full of a charming humanity ... But if we step back three paces, so as to grasp the whole picture, suddenly something ironic happens. When these quite human fragments are set along with everything else, which is so different, the contrast is so improbable that our eyes no longer know how to make sense of it, and the uncertainty retrospectively confers a humorous intention on the fragments. This art is not about human warmth; rather it is a fiction based upon a haughty sense of humour ... Instead of regretting that his best moments are ruined by bizarre digressions, bad taste, or an abuse of mythology, it would be better to acknowledge that he is doing what he meant to do ...

Romantic irony, however, offers a further alternative to 'regretting' the humorous or bizarre elements in Propertius or seeing them as undermining the seriousness, or indeed dismissing the whole game as merely piquant

---

[33] Lefèvre (1966) 152, 156, 172-3; Papanghelis (1987).
[34] Veyne (1988) 32-3.

titillation. In love this contrast of fiction and human feeling is untenable. Love cannot help but be a fiction, but it is a fiction by which we live: and it is this role as a supreme fiction which makes it a paradigm for human culture in general.[35] You do not have to read *ei mihi* in Propertius 2.28. 62 if you want to be moved by *sunt apud infernos tot milia formosarum*: you do not have to choose between humour and pathos. But rather than explore the well-worn path of the elegists' irony, I want to return to an example of lover's irony that I have touched on before,[36] Catullus 51, and to use it to enable me to move from the subject of closural Romantic Irony to more pervasive self-reflexivity.

In poem 51, Catullus translates Sappho Fr. 31 LP but then veers away at the end to address himself:

Ille mi par esse deo videtur,
ille, si fas est, superare divos,
qui sedens adversus identidem te
spectat et audit

dulce ridentem, misero quod omnes
eripit sensus mihi: nam simul te,
Lesbia, aspexi, nihil est super mi
<vocis in ore>

lingua sed torpet, tenuis sub artus
flamma demanat, sonitu suopte
tintinant aures geminae, teguntur
lumina nocte.

otium, Catulle, tibi molestum est:
otio exsultas nimiumque gestis:
otium et reges prius et beatas
perdidit urbes.

He seems to me the equal of a god,
he seems, if that may be, the gods' superior,
who sits face to face with you and again and again
watches and hears you

sweetly laughing, an experience which robs me
poor wretch, of all my senses; for the moment I set
eyes on you, Lesbia, there remains not a whisper
<of voice on my lips>,

---

[35] As brilliantly argued in connection with Ovid's *Ars Amatoria* by Myerowitz (1985).
[36] Fowler (1989) 112-13.

but my tongue is paralysed, a subtle flame
course through my limbs, with sound self-caused
my two ears ring, and my eyes are
covered in darkness.

Idleness, Catullus, is your trouble;
idleness is what delights you and moves you to passion;
idleness has proved ere now the ruin of kings and
prosperous cities. (Trans. G. Goold).

It was this self-address that persuaded Veyne[37] that we should read the 'I'
in Catullus like that of a pop-singer rather than an ego of anguished
sincerity: 'Catullus calls to himself under the name Catullus, but this is just
a fiction, for after all, we really do not address ourselves by name and say
to ourselves, "Listen, Veyne, stop this foolishness." Catullus took his own
name, Catullus, as his stage name.' Certainly this self-address marks a
strong break in the last stanza, a break so strong, indeed, that many have
thought of it as a separate fragment: and the translation of the previous
stanza has been manipulated to give it a strong closural force. Where
Sappho had talked merely of not seeing, Catullus talks more emphatically
of his eyes being covered in night,[38] a closural allusion which crams two
nouns into the final Adonean and which gains added force from the hints of
fainting and even death generated from the presence of Sappho's untrans-
lated fourth stanza,[39] and Lucretius' contemporary use of it in *DRN*
3.152-8:

ἀλλ' ἄκαν μὲν γλῶσσα †ἔαγε†, λέπτον
δ' αὔτικα χρῶι πῦρ ὑπαδεδρόμηκεν,
ὀππάτεσσι δ' οὐδ' ἓν ὄρημμ', ἐπιρρόμ-
βεισι δ' ἄκουαι,

†ἔκαδε μ' ἴδρως ψῦχρος κακχέεται†, τρόμος δὲ
παῖσαν ἄγρει, χλωροτέρα δὲ ποίας
ἔμμι, τεθνάκην δ' ὀλίγω 'πιδεύης
φαίνομ' ἔμ' αὔται· (ed. D. Page, *Lyra Graeca Selecta*)

my tongue has snapped, at once a subtle fire has stolen beneath my flesh, I see
nothing with my eyes, my ears hum, sweat pours from me, a trembling seizes me
all over, I am greener than grass, and it seems to me that I am little short of dying.

---

[37] Veyne (1988) 174.

[38] It is difficult to choose between the MSS *gemina ... nocte* and Schrader's *aures geminae*
printed by Goold. Certainly *aures geminae* is a familiar *iunctura*, but the collocation with
gemina might elegantly suggest the familiar phrase without saying it, and the bold hypallage
gemina ... nocte is more interesting. On the other hand, the simple *teguntur lumina nocte* has
a stronger closural force as unqualified 'categorical assertion'; two short and simple cola frame
two lengthier ones.

[39] Cf. Immisch (1933) 10, Lefèvre (1988) 327-8.

verum ubi vementi magis est commota metu mens
consentire animam totam per membra videmus
sudoresque ita palloremque exsistere toto
corpore et infringi linguam voemque aboriri,
caligare oculos, sonere auris, succidere artus,
denique concidere ex animi terrore videmus
saepe homines

> But when the intelligence is moved by more vehement fear, we see the whole
> spirit throughout the frame share in the feeling; sweatings and pallor hence arise
> over the whole body, the speech falters, the voice dies away, blackness comes
> before the eyes, a sounding is in the ears, the limbs give way beneath; in a word
> we often see men fall to the ground for mental terror.

But there is no way of knowing a priori whether the closure of the third
stanza in 51 is false closure[40] or reinforcement of the real end of the poem.
The problem is compounded by the loss of the last stanza(s) in Sappho, and
critics have naturally taken different views as to the relation of what Sappho
may or may not have said in them to the problem stanza of Catullus 51. The
tone of the last stanza has been interpreted very differently by different
critics, as humorous and as serious: but it has often been felt to 'spoil' the
poem, particularly by those who wish to see this as Catullus' expression of
love at first sight, his overture to Lesbia and the poem that explains her
name, a declaration of love later powerfully reversed in poem 11, the other
poem in the corpus in sapphics.

One answer to this question of the tone of the last stanza is that it is
indeterminate, because the tone of lovers discourse always is. There is in
principle no answer to the question of whether a lover is serious. Naturally
my own reading of Catullus 51 is in terms of Romantic Irony: the recall to
reality in the last stanza enables us to take the declaration of love 'seriously'. This is bound up, however, with the status of the poem as a translation.
The cause of Catullus' affliction is idleness, *otium*: having too much time
on one's hands, not attending to *negotium*, business. There has been much
discussion of what *otium* here means, and it is clearly a word to which both
context and intertext give great complexity. But I would suggest that this is
not only the *otium* produced by love and productive of it, the *otium* which
leaves Catullus with a mind too free of normal cares to avoid brooding on
his passion; it is also the *otium* in which he has produced this translation of
Sappho. As Charles Segal[41] and others have pointed out, this aspect of
otium is highlighted by the conjunction with poem 50 in the extant
collection. There Catullus and Calvus had been playing around writing
verses at leisure, *otiosi*: and a translation of Sappho is exactly the sort of

---

[40] Compare the false closure of poem 8, discussed in Fowler (1989) 98-101.
[41] Segal (1970).

trifle one might expect. The deviation at the end of 51 reminds us that this is just a translation: the trouble with Catullus is that he has too much time on his hands, the time to translate Sappho rather than getting on with life. But it is impossible to take the final stanza as simply deflating: this is the *otium* that has destroyed cities and kings, and the intertexts confirm the seriousness of Catullus' point. This is not only a translation: it is also a poem to Catullus' mistress, *lux mea, qua viva vivere dulce mihi est*. Yet, again, the exaggeration of Catullus' implicit comparison of his own fate to *reges ... et beatas ... urbes*, the contrast between *perdidit* and *molestum est* in both sense and register, underlines the irony. This is just a literary exercise: as all literature inevitably is.

The expanding circles of irony in Catullus 51 thus dramatise the inevitable dialectic between sublimity and reality which is built into literary discourse. Catullus, writing in an age of lost innocence, can only say: 'I love you madly — as Sappho might say'. That age of lost innocence began the second time Adam declared his love: but classicists like to situate it in 3rd century BC Alexandria. If a crucial element in Romantic Irony is an awareness of the anxiety of influence — that all saying is saying again — then the Hellenistic period is the 'natural' place in which to locate it. One of the models for Catullus' self-address in poem 51, the Cyclops' despair in Theocritus *Idyll* 11, is a celebrated example.[42] Theocritus begins with a framing address to his doctor-friend Nicias declaring that there ain't no cure for love except the Muses: the exemplum that proves this truth is that of ὁ Κύκλωψ ὁ παρ' ἁμῖν, ὡρχαῖος Πολύφαμος, and we are then given the song he used to sing to Galatea as he sat on the rock. His despairing song ends with a typical piece of lover's self-awareness (72-9):

ὦ Κύκλωψ Κύκλωψ, πᾷ τὰς φρένας ἐκπεπότασαι;
αἴ κ' ἐνθὼν ταλάρως τε πλέκοις καὶ θαλλὸν ἀμάσας
ταῖς ἄρνεσσι φέροις, τάχα κα πολὺ μᾶλλον ἔχοις νῶν.
τὰν παρεοῖσαν ἄμελγε· τί τὸν φεύγοντα διώκεις;
εὑρησεῖς Γαλάτειαν ἴσως καὶ καλλίον' ἄλλαν.
πολλαὶ συμπαίσδεν με κόραι τὰν νύκτα κέλονται,
κιχλίζοντι δὲ πᾶσαι, ἐπεί κ' αὐταῖς ὑπακούσω.
δῆλον ὅτ' ἐν τᾷ γᾷ κἠγών τις φαίνομαι ἦμεν.

O Cyclops, Cyclops, have you gone out of your mind?
You should be gathering browse to feed your lambs
Or plaiting baskets for cheese; that would show more sense.
Milk the beast you can catch; let the others range.
You will find another Galatea with lovelier looks.
The girls call after me, 'Shall I see you tonight?'

---

[42] See especially Schmitt (1989), an excellent discussion which argues that *Idyll* 11 is neither simply ludic nor exactly an example of Romantic Irony: although I take a different line, I find myself in agreement with much of what Schmitt says.

And laugh in a huddle as soon as I turn my head.
On land I clearly have something to show for myself. (trans. R. Wells).

Theocritus as narrator then returns and gets in a humorous dig at his addressee's profession (80-81):

Οὕτω τοι Πολύφαμος ἐποίμαινεν τὸν ἔρωτα
μουσίσδων, ῥᾷον δὲ διᾶγ' ἢ εἰ χρυσὸν ἔδωκεν

So Polyphemus shepherded his love by singing
And found more relief than if he had paid out gold.

Latin scholars like to contrast the humour of Theocritus' Cyclops with the darker tones of Corydon in *Eclogue* 2, who fails in his attempt at solace (5 *studio ... inani*), and ends on a more despairing note (69-73):

a, Corydon, Corydon, quae te dementia cepit!
semiputata tibi frondosa vitis in ulmo est:
quin tu aliquid saltem potius, quorum indiget usus,
viminibus mollique paras detexere iunco?
invenies alium, si te hic fastidit, Alexin.

A Corydon, Corydon, what madness has seized you! You have left the vine unpruned on the leafy elm. Why don't you get down to weaving something useful from withies and reed? You will find another Alexis if this one rejects you.

This opposition between light-hearted Hellenistic piquancy and Latin emotion is as suspect as any that we use to structure literary history, and I want for the moment to concentrate more on the similarities between Theocritus and Vergil. Both their lovers are singers, and as such surrogates for the poets: this is reinforced by the weaving metaphors both employ. In both poems, the status of poetry is thereby called into question: poetry is something sung by a comic monster or a lovesick shepherd. If Polyphemus is successful in shepherding his love, the imperfects ἄειδε (18) and ἐποίμαινεν (80) show that he nevertheless returned again and again to the shore: as with *veniebat* and *iactabat* in Vergil (5), they technically make our lover's discourse free direct speech,[43] a sample merely of what was said. In both Theocritus and Vergil, we are conscious that the singers are figures of 'unreality', and the reader possesses an obvious sense of superiority not merely at their naivety but also at the fact that they have no existence outside art. Art is unreal, and also useless, *studium inane* in contrast to things *quorum indiget usus*. The protestations of *Nützlichkeit* made by Theocritus emphasise this point even more than Vergil's denial.

All of this emphasis on the gap between poetry and reality is regularly summed up as 'distancing': it teaches us to look here not for love but for

---

[43] I owe the insight that the use of imperfects in speech introductions implies free direct speech to Andrew Laird.

art, not for feeling but for intellectual play. Again, Romantic Irony offers a different approach. Just as our lovers' absurdities are no obstacles to their love, so our awareness of the true nature of art need not invalidate an emotional response. As another of Theocritus' surrogates remarks, 'Even in empty[44] kisses there is sweet pleasure' (3. 20). Theocritus' famous 'deflationary' endings like those to *Idyll* 1:

πλῆρές τοι μέλιτος τὸ καλὸν στόμα, Θύρσι, γένοιτο,
πλῆρες δὲ σχαδόνων, καὶ ἀπ' Αἰγίλω ἰσχάδα τρώγοις
ἁδεῖαν, τέττιγος ἐπεὶ τύγα φέρτερον ᾄδεις.
ἠνίδε τοι τὸ δέπας· θᾶσαι, φίλος, ὡς καλὸν ὄσδεις·
Ὡρᾶν πεπλύσθαι νιν ἐπὶ κράναισι δοκησεῖς.
ὧδ' ἴθι, Κισσαίθα· τὺ δ' ἄμελγέ νιν. αἱ δὲ χίμαιραι,
οὐ μὴ σκιρτασῆτε, μὴ ὁ τράγος ὔμμιν ἀναστῇ.

Then, Thyrsis, you must stop your mouth with sweetness,
Eat only honeycomb and the best dried figs,
Since even as it is, you out-sing the cicada.
Here is the cup. Smell the scented wood, so fresh
You would think it had been dipped at the well of the Hours.
Cissaetha!
                    Yours for milking! Gently, my goats,
Down! or you'll have the billy force you down.

or *Idyll* 15:

Πραξινόα, τὸ χρῆμα σοφώτατον ἁ θήλεια·
ὀλβία ὅσσα ἴσατι, πανολβία ὡς γλυκὺ φωνεῖ.
ὥρα ὅμως κἠς οἶκον. ἀνάριστος Διοκλείδας·
χὡνὴρ ὄξος ἄπαν, πεινᾶντι δὲ μηδὲ ποτένθῃς.
χαῖρε, Ἄδων ἀγαπατέ, καὶ ἐς χαίροντας ἀφικνεῦ.

Praxinoa, what wouldn't I give to sing like that!
Time to go home. Diocleidas will be in a state.
it's more than my life's worth if his dinner's late.
Goodbye, Adonis. I pray that you find us here,
Healthy and happy, when you come back next year.

can be read as classic examples of Romantic Irony, enabling us to take them seriously rather than 'distancing' us from sublimity. But the best example of all is perhaps *Idyll* 10, with its contrast between the absurd lover-artist Boucaeus and the robust realist Milon, who comments at the end how much more real his art is (56-8):

---

[44] ἔστι καὶ ἐν κενεοῖσι φιλήμασιν ἁδεα τέρψις, parodied in [Theocritus] 27.5. Dover's note on 3. 20, 'Empty, i.e. not proceeding to sexual intercourse' is true enough of course as far as it goes: but the resonances in connection with art of words like κενός and *inanis* need not be restricted to the most obvious contexts (like *Aeneid* 1. 464).

ταῦτα χρὴ μοχθεῦντας ἐν ἁλίῳ ἄνδρας ἀείδειν,
τὸν δὲ τεόν, Βουκαῖε, πρέπει λιμηρὸν ἔρωτα
μυθίσδεν τᾷ ματρὶ κατ' εὐνὰν ὀρθρευοίσᾳ

That's how men should sing as they work in the sun.
But as for your hungry love, Bucaeus, keep it
For your mother's ears when she wakes you in bed at dawn.

But it is Boucaeus who is the surrogate for the Hellenistic poet. Art *is* absurd, unreal, derivative: but it still matters. Poet and reader alike accept 'the challenge of the past, of the already said' and both succeed, once again, 'in speaking of love'.[45]

THE POET IN THE TEXT

It would be easy to multiply instances of Romantic Irony in Hellenistic poetry: I have not, for instance, even touched on Callimachus.[46] But I want to deal more directly with the second, more pervasive aspect of Romantic Irony that I have already touched upon, and then to broaden the issue still further and to return to the political aspects of irony that I mentioned earlier. Theocritus' shepherd singers are surrogates for the poet himself: in some way they stand in for him. A poet within a poem is the most obvious form of *mise-en-abyme*. But there are many other possible authorial surrogates - and surrogates for readers, and the literary work. Any form of non-literary writing can obviously be read in this way, and is often linked with literary forms: so for instance Ovid's epistolary heroines in the *Heroides* and Byblis in *Metamorphoses* 9 are clearly figured like love elegists. Prophecy is so closely linked with poetry that it is almost not a trope to see 'Lucan in disguise'[47] when Appius consults the oracle in *Bellum Civile* 5. Works of art and handicrafts very frequently mirror in some way the texts that contain them — like the basket in *Idyll* 1, or any of the myriad figured objects of ekphrasis. And the reader's interpretative adventures may be similarly reflected in characters who face within the texts their own hermeneutic problems, even those like Aeneas who give up and *rerum ... ignarus imagine gaudet*. And ultimately there are the grandest tropes of all: the poet as God, creating order from chaos, the poet as ruler, lord of all she sways. These

---

[45] Eco (1984) 67-8: see above n. 18.

[46] See e.g. the end of the first episode in the *Aetia*, where the request to the Graces to 'come now and wipe your anointed hands upon my elegies that they may live for many a year' (fr. 7, trans. Trypanis) is both a piece of bizarrerie and a reference to the material reality of the book, anointed with cedar oil; or the end of the Acontius and Cydippe episode, with its reference to the source in Xenomedes (fr. 75), from where 'the maiden's story ran to my Calliope'.

[47] A sub-heading in Masters (1992) 133: his whole work is much concerned with surrogacy.

forms of surrogacy have been much explored in recent criticism, and their impact on the interpretation of some works — most obviously Ovid — has been considerable. Interpreters of Roman poetry in particular have become increasingly sensitized to the notion that the terms of the Callimachean aesthetic code continually violate the boundaries of the aesthetic and contaminate the whole field of discourse, from ethics to politics. Don't try to be innocently big or small in recent criticism: don't try crossing rivers, moving along paths, holding spears or drinking water. *Quidquid agunt homines* can be seen in terms of poetics: there is nothing but surrogacy.

Some people have welcomed these moves as ways of removing literature from the sphere of ideology, of getting us back to 'literary criticism'. Thank God for Callimachus. Others however have resisted these attempts to see poetry as everywhere about poetry. Poetry for them is not a game, not self-reflexive self-abuse: it's about real things, Life with a capital letter. No mise-en-abyme please, we're British. But the most productive criticism of ancient literature, especially Latin, has concerned itself precisely with the negotiation of the interactions between aesthetics and the 'real world': the word at war, in the phrase of John Henderson, who has done more than anyone else to make us take the politics of aesthetics seriously. Surrogacy cannot be restricted to a one-way process. Seeing the world in terms of poetics, of readers, works, and poets, inevitably involves seeing the components of fictional creation in terms of the world. In contaminating the field of discourse, poetics becomes itself contaminated by ideology. In the particular case of the criticism of Latin literature, the Callimachean code becomes politicised, and works like Ovid's amatory poems or *Fasti*[48] become 'political' poetry just as much as the *Aeneid*.

If Romantic Irony takes its beginning from the reader's recognition that the artist has 'made it all up', the ideological reading of aesthetics stresses the lack of innocence in that making. But irony has to reenter the picture when we scrutinise this ideological reading itself. What is its foundation? The fashionable political reading of poetics tends to be vague about how it is grounded. Is this the way authors and readers are supposed to have seen it in antiquity? The 'right' way to read the texts, *sub specie aeternitatis*? The 'right' way for us in our present historical situation? The view endorsed by an interpretative community which is in some way privileged? Or just another way to read? I began by offering hope to traditionally inclined humanist critics that maybe they could be brought to feel happy with the loss of foundations, but the urgency is the same for cultural materialists or new historicists. If there are no foundations, there are no foundations. The critic has to be aware not just that the work before her is a human construct, but that her readings of it, however sophisticated and however ideologically

---

[48] See especially Wallace-Hadrill (1987), Hinds (1992) and Feeney (1992), with Fowler (1992) on Feeney (1991).

alive, are also just ways of seeing. It is not simply a question of giving up believing that Propertius was 'really' in love with Cynthia: we have also to recognise that viewing her as an ideologically-loaded trope for the poetic book is just another story.

And it is here that Romantic Irony may again come to the rescue. The commonest criticism of that postmodernist anti-foundationalism whose most famous representative is Richard Rorty is that it makes political action impossible: just as the sceptic cannot live her scepticism, so the postmodernist cannot live her postmodernism. In *Contingency, Irony, and Solidarity*[49] Rorty attempted to answer that criticism by showing how a person who is a thoroughgoing nominalist and historicist can yet act in the world:

> The fundamental premise of this book is that a belief can still regulate action, can still be thought worth dying for, among people who are quite aware that this belief is caused by nothing deeper than contingent historical circumstance.

The political aspect of irony is taken further by J. E. Seery in his suggestively titled book *Political Returns, Irony in Politics and Theory from Plato to the Antinuclear Movement*,[50] in which he attempts to show how an anti-foundationalist can take part in the anti-nuclear movement through an ironic stance:

> Why is politics implicitly 'ironic'? Politics involves an affirmation of the idea of human community, but that affirmation grows out of, or is attendant upon, a profound awareness of human difference, as well <as> of human tragedy. Such an affirmation requires, I suggest, the kind of reversal of expectations typically associated with the concept of irony. To choose to affirm human community in the face of human mortality, to seek order against the background of chaos, to hold out for worldly justice even though death ultimately defeats or mocks all such efforts, to be dedicated when one is also deeply doubtful — all of this suggests a philosophical stance that involves a double perspective on things, though a stance in which one's affirmative side finally (if barely) triumphs over, that is, partially reverses, ones cynical expectations. Given a deep appreciation of tragedy, one would expect cynicism, scepticism, fatalism, even nihilism, to reign. That instead one affirms human association at all — human differences notwithstanding — entails what I think is best called an ironist attitude.[51]

Just as in reading a poem, one does not have to deny that it is a poem to be moved by it, so in writing about that poem one does not have to believe that one is finding the truth to be able to carry on as a critic. A typical trope of criticism is the unmasking of one's opponents assumptions, the revelation of how their views have been historically determined: but traditional humanist criticism has then liked to try to supplant these temporally

---

[49] Rorty (1989), esp. 189.
[50] Seery (1990).
[51] Seery (1990) 343.

bounded fantasies of its opponents with the solid truth. This rhetoric of presence is not unknown in more sophisticated and ideologically aware criticism. But such criticism may also more cautiously stop at the level of unmasking, at the revelation of the processes of the text and their political implications. One danger here is that we produce a negative rhetoric that can only be used up, that presupposes an *Endzeit*. Where do we go after we have seen ancient literature for the fraud and pretence it really is?

Another danger lies in the gulf that opens up between professional classicists and the subject in society. The popular image of antiquity is 'The Glory that was Greece, The Grandeur that was Rome', an image in which it is easy to acquiesce to pull in the money and the students. But our scholarly literature is all about revealing the backside of this sublimity, removing the props that hold up the shiny-white stage sets of Greece and Rome. This dissociation of sensiblity is unfortunate, but it is no good trying to recover lost innocence, to get back to a time before we knew what we were doing. Somehow we need to be able to acknowledge the absence of foundations but to carry on the tradition. We need Romantic Irony.

The ironist can acknowledge her own temporal grounding without feeling that this makes everything pointless. As with love, it is precisely because we are making it all up that we need to take our responsibilities so seriously: to argue, change our minds, take up new positions, teach and learn. The stories that we tell do not lose point: on the contrary, they have to become better ones if we are to get others to share the truths that we are inventing. In the end Romantic Irony is not a trope to be seen in a few classical poems, it is the only attitude towards antiquity that it is possible for us now to take. And that statement (like this) is as contingent as any other.[52]

BIBLIOGRAPHY

Adams R.M. (1958) *Strains of Discord: Studies in Literary Openness* (Ithaca: 1958).
Adkins A.W.H. (1985) *Poetic Craft in the Early Greek Elegists* (Chicago and London: 1985).
Barthes R. (1979) *A Lover's Discourse, Fragments*, trans. R. Howard (London: 1979) from *Fragments d'un discours amoureux* (Paris: 1977).
Bishop L. (1989) *Romantic Irony in French Literature: From Diderot to Beckett* (Nashville: 1989).
Booth W.C. (1974) *A Rhetoric of Irony* (Chicago-London: 1974).
Bourgeois F. (1974) *L'ironie romantique* (Paris: 1974).
Dane J.A. *The Critical Mythology of Irony* (Athens-London: 1991).
Eco U. (1984) *Postscript to the Name of the Rose* (New York-London: 1984).
Feeney D.C. (1991) *The Gods in Epic* (Oxford: 1991).

---

[52] I am grateful for comments to members of the London Institute of Classical Studies seminar on Greek Narrative, especially Nick Lowe and Michael Silk, and to Peta Fowler and Matthew Leigh: lovers of truth.

—— (1992) "*Si licet et fas est*: Ovid's *Fasti* and the problem of Free Speech under the Principate", in *Roman Poetry and propaganda in the Age of Augustus* ed. A. Powell (Bristol: 1992) 1-25.

Figueira T.J. and Nagy, G. (1985) *Theognis of Megara* (Baltimore-London: 1985).

Finlay M. (1988) *The Romantic Irony of Semiotics: Friedrich Schlegel and the crisis of representation* (Berlin-New York-Amsterdam: 1988).

Fowler D.P. (1991) "Narrate and Describe: the Problem of Ekphrasis", *Journal of Roman Studies* 81 (1991) 25-35.

—— (1989) "First Thoughts on Closure: Problems and Prospects", *Materiali e Discussioni per l'analisi dei testi classici* 22 (1989) 75-122.

—— (1992) "Subject Reviews: Roman Literature", *Greece and Rome* 39 (1992) 92-3.

Fraenkel E. (1957) *Horace* (Oxford: 1957).

Fränkel H. (1945) *Ovid. A Poet between Two Worlds* (Berkeley-Los Angeles: 1945).

Furst L.R. (1984) *Fictions of Romantic Irony* (Cambridge Mass.: 1984).

Garber F. (1988a) *Romantic Irony* (Budapest: 1988).

—— (1988b) *Self, text, and Romantic Irony, The Example of Byron* (Princeton: 1988).

Gentili B. (1977) "Addendum: A proposito dei vv. 253-254 di Teognide", *Quaderni Urbinati de Cultura Classica* 26 (1977) 115-6.

Hélein-Koss S. (1988) "Discours ironique et ironie dramatique dans *Salammbo* de Gustave Flaubert", *Symposium* 40 (1988) 16-40.

Heyworth S.J. (1988) "Horace's Second Epode", *American Journal of Philology* 109 (1988) 71-85.

Hinds S. (1992) "Arma in Ovid's *Fasti*", *Arethusa* 25 (1992) 81-154.

Hughes G.T. (1979) *Romantic German Literature* (London: 1979).

Hutcheon L. (1991) *Splitting Images, Contemporary Canadian Ironies* (Toronto: 1991).

Immerwahr R. (1951) "The Subjectivity or Objectivity of Friedrich Schlegel's Poetic Irony", *Germanic Review* 26 (1951) 173-91.

—— (1969) "Romantic Irony and Romantic Arabesque prior to Romanticism" *The German Quarterly* 42 (1969) 665-84.

Immisch O. (1933) "Catulls Sappho", *SB Akad Heidelberg* phil-hist. Kl. 1933/4, 2. Abh. (Heidelberg: 1933).

Itkowitz J.B. (1985) "On the Last Stanza of Catullus 51", *Latomus* 42 (1985) 129-34.

Knox N. (1972) "On the Classification of Ironies", *Modern Philology* 70 (1972) 53-62.

Lefèvre E. (1988) "Otium und Tolman: Catulls Sappho-Gedicht c. 51", *Rheinisches Museum* (1988) 324-37.

—— (1966) *Propertius ludibundus* (Heidelberg: 1966).

Masters J. (1992) *Poetry and Civil War in Lucan's Bellum Civile* (Cambridge: 1992).

McKeown J.C. (1989) ed. *Ovid Amores 1* (Leeds: 1989).

Mellor A.K. (1980) *English Romantic Irony* (Cambridge Mass.: 1980).

Muecke D.C. (1969) *The Compass of Irony* (London: 1969).

Myerowitz M. (1985) *Ovid's Games of Love* (Detroit: 1985).

O'Higgins D. (1990) "Sappho's Splintered Tongue: Silence in Sappho 31 and Catullus 51", *American Journal of Philology* 111 (1990) 156-67.

Papanghelis T.D. (1987) *Propertius, a Hellenistic Poet on Love and Death* (Cambridge: 1987).

Parker D. (1969) "The Ovidian Coda", *Arion* 8 (1969) 80-97.

Prang H. (1989) *Die romantische Ironie* (Darmstadt 1989).

Roberts D.H. (1988) "Sophoclean Endings: Another Story", *Arethusa* 21 (1988) 177-96.

Rorty R. (1989) *Contingency, Irony, and Solidarity* (Cambridge: 1989).

Schmitt A. (1989) "Ironie und Humor bei Theokrit", *Würzburger Jahrbücher für die Altertumswissenschaft* NF 15 (1989) 107-18.

Seery J.E. (1990) *Political Returns, Irony in Politics and Theory from Plato to the Antinuclear Movement* (Boulder, San Francisco, and Oxford: 1990).

Segal C. (1970) "Catullan Otiosi: The Lover and the Poet", *Greece and Rome* 17 (1970) 25-31.

Sellar W.Y. (1892) *Horace, Roman Poets of the Augustan Age* (Oxford: 1892).

Simpson D. (1979) *Irony and Authority in Romantic Poetry* (London: 1979).

Strohschneider-Kohrs I. (1977) *Die romantische Ironie in Theorie und Gestaltung* (Tübingen: ²1977).

Taplin O.P. (1983) "Sophocles in his Theatre", *Entretiens sur l'antiquité classique* XXIX (Geneva: 1983).

Tarkow T. (1977) "Theognis 237-254: A Reexamination" *Quaderni Urbinati di Cultura Classica* 26 (1977) 99-114.

Veyne, P. (1988) *Roman Erotic Elegy*, trans. D. Pellauer (Chicago-London: 1988) from *L'Élegie érotique romaine* (Paris: 1983).

Wallace-Hadrill A. (1987) "Time for Augustus" in *Homo Viator*, ed. M. Whitby, P. Hardie, and M. Whitby (Bristol 1987) 227-30.

Wheeler K. (1984) *German Aesthetic and Literary Criticism, The Romantic Ironists and Goethe* (Cambridge: 1984).

PHILOMELA'S WEB AND THE PLEASURES OF THE TEXT: READER AND VIOLENCE IN THE *METAMORPHOSES* OF OVID

BY

CHARLES SEGAL

INTRODUCTION: VIOLENCE AND PLEASURE

Generations of Romans were trained in the sadistic spectacles of the gladiatorial games.[1] This delight in watching pain being inflicted is one of those unpleasant features of Roman civilization that we would happily forget. Ovid is not immune to the influence of the amphitheater: witness the long catalogue of wounds in Perseus' battle against Phineus in *Metamorphoses* 5, the centauromachy in book 12, and the account of the mangling of Hippolytus by his horses in book 15.[2]

In fairness to the Romans, it must be said that there was occasional inquietude about these bloody spectacles. Lucretius, Cicero, Horace, and Virgil in the generations before Ovid express repugnance in various ways.[3] Even before the fulminations of the Christian fathers, the same Seneca who presented awful mutilations, blindings, and dismemberments in the *Tragedies* wrote about the corruption of the soul in the amphitheaters.[4] Social historians and literary scholars alike have often speculated on why the Imperial poets dwell at length on such scenes of physical suffering. But even if we can explain them as externalizing anxieties about individual identity, the arbitrariness of power, and personal helplessness in an ever-increasing

---

[1] See Seel (1961) 54ff. on some particularly ugly examples in Martial's book of *Spectacula*; also Williams (1978) 184ff.; Barton (1989); Richlin (1992a) 161 and 174-77; Brown (1992) 183ff.; Most (1992) passim, especially 400ff. I am grateful to Professor Most for allowing me to see his paper in advance of publication. The Roman interest in gory scenes of physical suffering is, however, well established even prior to the Empire: see Segal (1990c) passim, especially chaps. 5-7.

[2] On 6.552-60, for example, Bömer (1976) 151 remarks: "Hier beginnt ein Katalog von Scheusslichkeiten ..., den Ovid, ebenso wie anderswo, in genüsslicher Ausführlichkeit schildert ..." See also Galinsky (1975) 126-32; Diller (1968) 333f.

[3] Lucretius' disapproving account of wild beasts in warfare in *DRN* 5.1308-40 is sometimes attributed to the experience of the amphitheater. Cf. also Horace *C*. 3.13, on the mixture of the cold, pure water of the *fons Bandusiae* and the hot blood of the young goat sacrificed to it.

[4] Seneca, *Ep.* 7.2ff., 14.4ff. For other criticism of the contemporary taste for gladiatorial contests see Cic., *Tusc. Disp.* 2.17.41 and *Ad Fam.* 7.1.3; Pliny, *Ep.* 9.6. Seel (1961) 54-56 points out, however, that even these authors are not consistent in their disapproval of gladiatorial bloodshed.

bureaucracy,[5] there remains the problem of how *we* as readers respond to such violence.

In *Metamorphoses* 6.424-674 Ovid tells how Tereus rapes Philomela, cuts out her tongue, and then locks her up in a forest prison. Ovid makes the mutilation of Philomela part of Tereus' raping her; and, so far as we can tell, he has the dubious distinction of being the first to combine the mutilation with the repeated sexual violation. Is this episode, then, sadistic pornography adorned with epic dignity, pandering to the degenerate tastes of an audience that liked violence and liked it even more if it were spiced with some sex? Or, on the other hand, does Ovid know that the pleasures of this text are dangerous pleasures, appealing to base instincts for cruelty, sexual domination, and inflicting pain?[6] If so, does he show that he knows so that his reader can know it too? Where in his text is such an awareness located? Perhaps most important, who exactly is his reader and what kind of reader does he imply?

In trying to answer these questions I draw on an eclectic mix of reader-response, feminist, intertextual, deconstructionist, and even psychoanalytic approaches. I prefer eclecticism because no single method can adequately interpret the range of meanings of a complex literary work and therefore the critic should be free to choose any method or combination of methods that seem most helpful. It is better for the text to direct the critic to the most useful method(s) than to have the critic force the text into his or her Procrustean bed. This means, in practice, that the interpreter should be willing to adapt the method to the different levels and kinds of meaning in the work. In the text that I am considering here, the area of meaning with which I am most concerned centers on the problem of violence and the reader's response to a narrative of violence. As the violence in question is initially against women and as the reader envisaged by one account of the violence is female, reader-response and feminist criticism come together. My reading follows the order of Ovid's narrative in so far as this is possible; but a certain amount of back and forward movement is necessary in order to point parallels, symmetries, and contrasts.

RAPE AND THE GAZE OF TEREUS

As I have suggested elsewhere, Ovid does not always resolve the moral problems that his narratives raise, particularly when, as in this case, there is

---

[5] See Williams (1978) 153ff., 169ff.; Segal (1986) 315-36, especially 316f., 333ff.; also Most (1992) 402-8.

[6] Some of these problems are raised in an interesting way by Richlin (1992a) 158ff., with a useful bibliography of feminist scholarship, pp. 160f., 173-79. Unfortunately this work appeared only after my own essay was substantially complete, and I could not use it as fully as I should have liked.

so much innocent suffering and gratuitous violence.[7] The Tereus episode, however, does more than just exploit the *grand guignol* possibilities offered by a Thracian barbarian's goriness. Ovid provides a powerful and sympathetic depiction of the victim's suffering; and, as we shall see, he even implies a female reader.[8] The rape, he shows, has its origin in lust but soon becomes an attempt to control and degrade the victim. The very beginning, with the ill-omened wedding of Procne and Tereus, foreshadows the violated sanctity of family ties.[9] Later, Pandion's fateful handing of Philomela over to Tereus, who has been devouring her with his eyes (475-82), evokes the holy marriage rite of the *dextrarum iunctio*, the joining of right hands, a gesture of solemn trust that will be flagrantly violated (506-10; see Pavlock, 1991, 35).

Tereus' acts, moreover, are not just the crimes of a psychopath. Ovid presents them against a cultural background that reveals their implications for the nature of excessive desire, the social status of women, and the ambiguity of violence by women, even justified violence. Tereus himself is the "tyrant" par excellence, as we know him from the famous description of the tyrannical soul in the ninth book of Plato's *Republic*. He exemplifies the tyrant's monstrous, uncontrolled appetites, especially sexual appetites, which lead him to outrage the basic laws of humanity and transgress the boundaries between god, man, and beast (see Pavlock, 1991, 34ff.).

As tyrannical man, Tereus has the tyrant's desire for unlimited and therefore sadistic power over his victim. This is also a desire for the "tyrannical" power that males in this culture claim over women's bodies. The ultimate form of that power is to rape, degrade, and silence women. In Ovid's narrative it emerges as the dark side of the power of the Father/King (Father as King) to dispose of his daughters' bodies as objects of exchange with other males in marriage (see Joplin, 1991, 40-42, following Lévi-Strauss, 1969, 480ff.). The beginning of the story is King Pandion's exchange of Procne for Tereus' help in war (424-28). The turning point is Pandion's decision to permit her younger sister, Philomela, to visit Procne in Thrace (465-510). Both women, in fact, need male permission (cf. 440-44); but Ovid dramatizes the situation of Philomela because he can thereby show Tereus' lustful desperation to use all available means to secure her transfer from the *patria potestas* of Pandion to his own power.

---

[7] Segal (1971) passim, especially 377ff., 384ff.; Galinsky (1975) chap. 3, "Ovid's Humanity: Death and Suffering in the *Metamorphoses*," pp. 110-57, especially 138-40.

[8] See Curran (1978), especially 233-37. Richlin (1992a) 165 takes a less positive view of Ovid generally, arguing that Ovid makes up for the suppression of the physical details of rape by dwelling on meticulous descriptions of the female body undergoing ugly and painful deformations in metamorphosis (e.g. Io, Callisto, Cyane, Dryope, Byblis, Myrrha).

[9] Note the triple anaphora of *non* in 6.428f., followed by the double anaphora of *Eumenides* in 430f. and of *hac ave* in 433f.

Through the motifs of "joining" and uniting "right hands" this transfer of
Philomela from Pandion to Tereus is virtually a reenactment of Pandion's
marrying of Procne to Tereus at the beginning. The exchange is completed
by the sacred gesture of *dextrarum iunctio* between the father and the son-
in-law, so that Pandion seems to be marrying Philomela to Tereus and not
just entrusting her to his safekeeping.[10]

Tereus' "tyrannical" assertion of male domination over the female body
culminates, of course, in the rape and mutilation. But it is enacted symbolically through the aggressive penetration of the male gaze, which here
combines fetishistic scopophilia and sadism. I borrow these terms from the
celebrated essay of Laura Mulvey:

> Fetishistic scopophilia ... builds up the physical beauty of the object [hence Tereus'
> wild overvaluation of Philomela's beauty, which we view through *his* eyes],
> transforming it into something satisfying in itself... Sadism demands a story,
> depends on making something happen, forcing a change in another person, a battle
> of will and strength, victory/defeat, all occuring in a linear time with a beginning
> and an end.[11]

One could scarcely find a better account of the dynamics of the first stage
of Ovid's narrative. The sight of Philomela makes Tereus "blaze up" with
desire (*exarsit conspecta virgine*, 455). As he gazes on her, his very look is
an anticipatory rape. He violates her with his eyes and commits incest with
her, as it were, by lustfully watching her in her father's embrace (478-82,
especially *spectat eam Tereus praecontrectatque videndo*, 478, "Tereus
watches her and by seeing her handles her in advance").[12]

Tereus' external gaze of desire soon becomes the inner gaze of licentious
imagination as the look fuses with the appetitive "reaching for" or "seeking"
(repetens) the physical form (490-93):

> at rex Odrysius quamvis secessit, in illa
> aestuat et *repetens faciem motusque manusque*
> *qualia vult, fingit, quae nondum vidit*, et ignes
> ipse suos nutrit cura removente soporem.

---

[10] Cf. 6.506f.: *dextras utriusque poposcit / inter seque datas iunxit natamque nepotemque ...
rogat.* Note the previous uses of *iungere* of the marriage of Procne: *conubio Procnes iunxit*,
428; *coniuncti*, 433; *dexterae dextra / iungitur*, 447f.). The placement of the conjunctive phrase
natamque nepotemque directly after *iunxit* in 507 subtly reinforces the association with
marriage.

[11] Mulvey (1988) 64. I take Mulvey's terminology and descriptions as phenomenological
rather than psychological; their value as descriptive analyses is independent of the Lacanian and
Freudian frame in which they are embedded.

[12] The eroticization of the male gaze also inheres in Ovid's hint, conscious or not, of the
father's incestuous desire for his daughter, treated more explicitly, for instance, in the Myrrha
episode (10.437-41, 462-68).

The Thracian king, although he withdrew, seethes over her and *seeking her form
again and her movements and (the gestures of) her hands, imagines what he does
not see as what he wishes,* and he himself nourishes his own flames, while his
anxious passion takes away sleep.

Finally, scopophilia and sadism come together in the juxtaposition of
Tereus' gesture of conquest, *vicimus* (513), when he gets Philomela aboard
his ship. Now the desiring, scopophilic gaze becomes the sadistic gaze that
the predator relentlessly fixes on his prey (514-18):

exultatque et vix animo sua gaudia differt
barbarus et *nusquam lumen detorquet* ab illa,
non aliter, quam cum pedibus *praedator* obuncis
deposuit nido leporem Iovis ales in alto:
nulla fuga est capto, *spectat* sua praemia raptor.

He rejoices, and in his thoughts he can scarcely postpone his pleasures, the
barbarian, and *never does he turn his eyes from her,* not otherwise than when the
predatory bird of Zeus with his hooked talons places a hare in his nest on high:
the captive has no chance of flight; the ravisher *watches* his prize.

As this simile suggests, the gaze becomes increasingly aggressive (sadistic);
but the image becomes reality when the site of lust shifts from the male
viewer to the female body, for the image is now repeated to describe the
rape itself (529-30).

That first rape is then reenacted in a brutal upward displacement to the
mouth, violated by the insertion of the *forceps* and the sword (555-63). The
application of the verb *repetere,* now to the act of rape instead of the visual
anticipation of rape emphasizes the continuity of the progression from gaze
to act (*repetens faciem motusque manusque,* 491; *lacerum repetisse libidine
corpus,* 562).[13] The "tyrannical" assertion of sadistic power over the female
body now becomes total, as the double rape not only completes the victim's
degradation but also removes her voice. This second rape also completes the
transfer of authority over her body from father to tyrant/rapist as it nullifies
her "calling" for the name of the father (*et nomen patris usque vocantem,*
555). Neither the father nor his symbolical surrogates, the Olympian gods,
offer any help (547f.). Only at the very end of the story is there an answer;

---

[13] The rape scene has many parallels with the rape in Shakespeare's *Lucrece,* as is often
noted (e.g. *Lucrece* 414ff.). See also Richlin (1992a) 172. Kahn (1991) 145 notes "a connection
between his [the rapist's] gaze and his power over her" [Lucrece]. *Lucrece* 678f. also offers a
close, though less brutal, parallel to the upward displacement of the rape to the mouth: see
Kahn 149f. Fully applicable to the Philomela episode, *mutatis mutandis,* is Kahn's remark on
p. 150: "When Tarquin muffles Lucrece's cries with the folds of her nightgown, as he rapes her,
... he but repeats and reinforces the dominant tendency of the culture in concealing, sealing off,
muffling women's desire and women's speech."

and it comes in the form of a mutilated head that avenges the crime, as Tereus "calls again" for his son (*quaerenti iterumque vocanti*, 656; cf. 555).

Admittedly, these features of the narrative might be read as happening *despite* Ovid, as if we are reading against the grain of his intentions. Ovid, as we shall see, cannot be entirely exonerated of complicity in the exploitive lubricity of his narrative material. Yet there are ways in which Ovid indicates his distance and disapproval. He shows the victim's emotional as well as physical trauma: her shame and confusion of identity and her feelings of being cut off from her past life, including her ties to her sister (531-41, 601-609).[14] Her first impulse is rage and the demand for vengeance and the criminal's punishment, but her prayers to unheeding gods only exasperate her isolation and helplessness (542-48). She can break through her year-long silence, itself the direct result of the traumas of mutilation and imprisonment, only by the inspiration that comes from great suffering as she finally contrives a way of telling her story (574f.). This gradual escape from her isolation and enclosure in pain enacts in mythical terms the struggle that the victims of rape and incest experience in reporting the crimes against them; and her persistence and ingenuity in accusing her rapist correspond to the emotional effort and courage that such victims often acquire only slowly and gradually.

POINT OF VIEW AND MODES OF NARRATION

Context is an important clue to Ovid's mood and meaning. Here he tells the story of Philomela and Tereus, appropriately, amid other tales of cruelty, torture, and murder, especially within the family. Shortly before come the gods' killing of Niobe's children, the flaying of Marsyas, and Tantalus' alleged cannibalistic slaughter of his son (6.218ff., 385ff., 407ff.). Pelias' death at the hands of his daughters and Medea's killing of her children follow shortly after (7.297ff., 394ff.). Even among these stories, the tale of Philomela stands out for its sexual violence, including the scene that one critic has called "probably the most repellant passage in all of Ovid" (Curran, 1978, 219). At this point Ovid even intrudes his narrative presence, in the first person, to distance himself from the ugliest detail by a statement of disbelief (561, *vix ausim credere*).

What follows this incredulity is a refocusing of the story on belief and evidence. The excision of Philomela's tongue is paradoxically both the culmination of the savagery and a way of repressing the story into silence. This silencing of the protagonist raises the question of how the story will get itself told and what can be its proper mode of utterance: *quid faciat*

---

[14] For good observations on the emotional aspects of Philomela's suffering see Curran (1978) 223ff., 229; also Pavlock (1991) 38f.

Philomela: how to narrate this horror? To conceal his crime, Tereus utters fictitious groans, and with his tears wins "faith" or "credibility" for his version of Philomela's fate (565-67):

> dat gemitus fictos commentaque funera narrat;
> et lacrimae fecere fidem. velamina Progne
> deripit ...

> He gives forth feigned groans and tells of the death that he has falsely invented;
> his tears win him credence. Procne rends her veils.[15]

This narrator, like the poet himself, makes his tale convincing by adding an affective dimension. He enacts, in his own narrative role, as falsehood, that fulness of emotional life that the master-narrator, Ovid, needs in order to bring the tale to life for us his audience. This life-likeness *(vraisemblance)*, however, is purchased by a sacrifice, the graphic victimization of Philomela.

The craft, artistry, careful plotting, eloquence, pretence, masks, and multiple identities of Tereus coincide temporarily with those of his creator, the poet Ovid, with his plotting, his shifting perspectives, his ability to take on and imitate different roles and different voices. Lust makes the Thracian warrior eloquent *(facundum faciebat amor*, 469), so that he becomes craftily persuasive and seductive through both his words and his tears (470-74). Yet however much Ovid may identify with Tereus' skill in winning over and manipulating his hearers, he has little sympathy with the character as a whole. By stressing the contrast with his Athenian victims, Ovid establishes Tereus as the barbarian, the Other, the one whose desires and acts stand outside the limits of humanity. As the Other, Tereus also serves as the field upon which can be projected libidinal and aggressive wishes that the (male) Roman audience may be reluctant to accept consciously in themselves. The shift in focus from the male to the female characters, however, also marks a change from the buildup and release of uncontrolled (male) desire to female victimization and vengeance. This shift of sympathy to the female victims coincides with the narrative's turn from verbal communication to other forms of expression, now between women. This mixture of media also brings a heightened narrative self-consciousness, particularly as the text envisages, if only momentarily, a female recipient, a female "reader" of its story, namely Procne.

When Tereus "relates his invented (story of Philomela's) death" *(commentaque funera narrat)*, no verbal response from Procne is reported. Instead she turns at once to the gestures of mourning: she rips her rich garments from her shoulder, puts on black, and immediately begins funerary

---

[15] For the motif of *fides* and *pietas* in the episode and their corruption, see Ortega (1970) 217 and 220-22. The motifs run throughout the tale, signalled by the repetition of *pius* and *fides* and derivatives: cf. 474, 482, 496, 498, 503, 506, 535, 539, 566, 629, 635, etc.

rites (566-70). This is an appropriate response, of course, to the news of her sister's death; but her gestures also enact her sympathetic involvement and identification with her sister, whose suffering she now mimetically repeats in her sorrowful rituals. She thus prepares for the solidarity of the two women in the ensuing narrative.

There is also a shift to a perspective of self-conscious textuality here, aided by a major narrative break. Ovid introduces the artificial temporal marker, "The god had traversed twice six constellations as the year drove past" (571), all the more striking because of the absence of gods from the narrative proper. He thus calls attention to his narrative frame, but he also effects a sharp transition to the imprisoned Philomela.

What resumes the thread of the narrative after this break is Philomela's device of getting her story told and heard. Her mode of narration exactly corresponds to Procne's mode of reception, that is, silence. When the narrative shifts to a female teller and a female audience, in other words, the male skill in rhetoric and persuasion changes to a non-verbal, gestural and pictorial mode involving garments or cloth, typically the work of women. Procne, in silence, tears off her *velamina* (566); Philomela's "silent mouth lacks a witness to the deed" (*os mutum facti caret indice*, 574), but she "weaves purple marks upon the white threads in witness to the crime" (*purpureasque notas filis intexuit albis / indicium sceleris*, 577-78). This silent craft of weaving proves itself a match for the rhetorical craft of "tears" by which Tereus reinforced the verbal arguments of his lie and so won "credence" for his lie (566).

Weaving adds the element of gender to the implicit representation of poetic creation and reception (weaving is an ancient metaphor for poetic construction). Along with the related motifs of verbal and non-verbal media and modes of narrating, it calls our attention to the textuality of the work.[16]

---

[16] I draw here on the structuralist notion of "text" (e.g. in Barthes, 1974) that emphasizes the construction of codes and conventions from which the reader reconstructs meaning in an endless production of possible readings. Barthes (and other deconstructionists) emphasize the interactive process between text and reader that always refuses control or limit and so issues into an endless chain of further readings and writings: see "On Reading" (1976) in Barthes (1986) 33-43 and "From Work to Text" (1971), ibid. 56-64. Here meaning can never be fixed but is always created anew in an infinite series of displacements and a never-ending play between signifier and signified. Literature thus consists not of definitive "works," only of "text," which consists of "a multi-dimensional space in which are married and contested several writings, none of which is original: the text is a fabric of quotations, resulting from a thousand sources of culture" ("The Death of the Author," 1968, in Barthes, 1986, 53). My emphasis in "textuality," however, is on the way in which the work is continually creating and throwing off figures of its own processes of creation. At the same time, I would not say that these self-reflexive figures are the work's only or most important concern or that the work can refer only to itself. Rather, the production of such self-reflexive figures seems to be part of the creative activity of a self-conscious narrative poet like Ovid. Sometimes the self-reflexive impulse becomes central, as in the Arachne episode of book 6 or the Orpheus and Pymalion episodes

Behind Philomela's weaving is Ovid's own web of words *(textus)* that recreates events which are spectacular for their suppression of speech. The *notae* of Philomela's weaving are virtually the "letters" of a written message — in fact, a "song," or "poem," *carmen*, like the present one — which Procne "reads" (*legit*, 582), as if "unrolling" a scroll (581f.): *evolvit vestes saevi matrona tyranni / fortunaeque suae carmen miserabile legit* ("The consort of the cruel ruler unrolls the fabric and reads the woeful tale [song] of her misfortune").[17] But Procne immediately represses this communication into silence — a silence which another authorial intrusion marks as extraordinary (*mirum potuisse*, 583). Unlike Tereus, Procne does not weep, for she has neither words nor tears, but is totally absorbed in the "image" that those "purple marks" have made her see (583-86):

et (mirum potuisse!) silet: dolor ora repressit,
verbaque quaerenti satis indignantia linguae
defuerunt, nec flere vacat, sed fasque nefasque
confusura ruit poenaeque in imagine tota est.

And she keeps silent — a wonder that she could! Grief checks her countenance, and words of sufficient wrath were lacking to the tongue that sought them, nor was she free to weep, but she rushes about, going to mingle justice and crime, and is totally given over to the image of the punishment.

The self-reflexive nature of these gestures is interesting in itself, but particularly noteworthy is the contrast between Tereus' convincing oral performance of a plausible lie and Procne's silent response to a different version of the same story, a version whose form is itself a figure for a written text. This contrast creates the textual space in which doubts about the story can arise. By textual space I mean the awareness of the distance — analogous to Derrida's "space of writing" or "space of inscription" (Derrida, 1976, 289-91) — between the events and the representation of the events, between the effect of "reality" in the tale and the means of creating that effect, or between the signified (a coherent, believable story) and the narrative equivalent of the signifier (the conventions of reading and writing that join author and audience in the communicative act of story-telling and story-listening). This textual space is the area in which the reader can refuse the games of verbal eloquence and the smooth, convincing *vraisemblance* of narrative surface with which Tereus and Ovid himself are so facile.

In Ovid's tale the process of unravelling a false, constructed tale also rests with a gendered reader, the victim's sister. To what extent Ovid's female reader within the text reflects his awareness of and interest in actual female

---

of book 10; at other times, as in the Tereus episode, it is incidental or interwoven with moral concerns, like violence here.

[17] The identification of Philomela's web with a mode of writing seems to have been part of the tradition: see Bömer (1976) ad 582 (p. 158).

readers in his audience we can probably never know; but the silent, true version of Philomela's story, told only by the silent *notae*, dramatically refutes Tereus' specious oral narrative and creates the point of view of an emotionally involved and sympathetic onlooker. From this perspective, we can separate ourselves from the narrator of the false version and look critically at his point of view.

These *notae* are not just the "letters" of his text; they are also the "marks" of a brutal crime, to which their color bears "evidence," *indicium*.[18] They return at the end of the episode not just as the marks of textuality, but as the stains of blood that remain stamped upon the face of nature in perpetual witness of the savage deed (669-70):

> neque adhuc de pectore caedis
> excessere notae, signataque sanguine pluma est.

> Nor do the marks of the murder depart from the breast, and the plumage is stamped with blood.

The *notae* in this passage shift from being textual to being extra-textual marks. Earlier, in the middle the story, "purple signs woven into the white threads" (577) are virtually the "letters" of a woven "text": etymologically, that is what a "text" is (cf. Latin *textus*). At the end, in 669-70, the *notae*, still of the same bloody color, are the "marks" left in the world of nature as the "signs" of this crime. Ovid is thus able to look beyond the frame ("text") of his tale to the moral codes that surround it. Philomela's weaving is both the art-work of the tale and the agency of a vengeance that changes the face of nature.

The weaving exemplifies the mimetic skill that, in the depiction of sadistic sexual pleasure, may invite the male reader or hearer — or critic — to voyeuristic complicity in the crime,[19] as it perhaps may invite the female reader to complicity in the vengeance. But, as the web of words that calls attention to its textual origins, it objectifies the crime and in that way enables the reader to take the full measure of its horror. The statement of disbelief by the external narrator (i.e., Ovid) parallels the shocked reaction of the "audience" of the rape tale *(vix ausim credere)*, in directing us to the appropriate response.

This overdetermination of the horrified response stands in counterpoint to the fact that the crime is doubly repressed into silence. Tereus physically silences his victim by ripping out her tongue, and Philomela can re-present

---

[18] I should agree with Joplin (1991) 36 when she criticizes Hartman (1970) 337 for eliding the violence against the female body and making the focus language and the power of language. A reading centered on semiotics and a poetics of textuality is not an adequate interpretative tool for this episode. Ovid does not forget the message in the medium.

[19] See the comment on Shakespeare's version of the rape scene in *Lucrece* by Joplin (1991) 58, note 14: "The poet's eyes are hardly less lewd than the rapist Tarquin's ..."

the crime only through the silent, non-verbal medium, which itself defies a spoken response (583-85). We can gain access to the unspeakable crime only through a symbolical representation, an *imago*, which shocks and incites revenge (*poenaeque in imagine tota est*, 586). Procne, the tale's first "reader," unrolls *(evolvit)* the woven narrative as a contemporary of Ovid would unroll the poem; and she is the model for the later reader's immediate reaction. What she finds is a tale whose pain lies beyond the power of words: *silet: dolor ora repressit* (583).

Thus the double function of the weaving, as a tableau of unspeakable crimes and as a message that involves us in the demand and the necessity of its being read and understood, holds multiple contradictions. It holds in tension the possible pleasure of a male reader in the sexual violence of the rape, the moral satisfaction of the violent revenge, and the pleasure in the poetry which recreates all of this violence, both the moral and the immoral. These tensions and contradictions are played out in part in the alternation of speech and silence in the narrative, for this alternation reflects the problem of the poet's decision to retell this violent myth and to lend his grace and skill to its horrors.

The central role of language in the episode is closely related to Tereus' status as both a barbarian and a tyrant, that is, as a threat to the defining features of civilized humanity. In his "tyrannical" lust, he had destroyed language, along with the sanctities of kinship and marriage.[20] He attempted to destroy his victim's humanity by destroying her power to speak and then separating her from civilized society by imprisonment in the forest.[21] Philomela's role henceforth is to "struggle to speak" (*luctantemque loqui*, 555f.; cf. *tua facta loquar*, 545). Tereus had used all the means of persuasion at his command (cf. 460-66); but, having won Philomela by eloquent speech and by tears, he is moved by neither (535).[22] Philomela, made dumb, ultimately proves the more effective communicator. The women's revenge self-consciously echoes these inversions of speech and silence. Procne, as she prepares her response, "seethes with *silent* wrath" (*triste parat facinus tacitaque exaestuat ira*, 623). Her silence recalls Philomela's, but her "seething" links her with the violence of Tereus' lust (cf. *aestuat*, 491). Like Tereus too, she disregards the pleas of her victim, her child, Itys (640-42).

---

[20] Note Philomela's cry in 537, *omnia turbasti*, "You have overturned everything." Cf. also 537f. and 605f.

[21] There is also a cruel irony in the fact that Philomela's "last farewell" as she leaves Athens proves to be the last words that she will ever speak there or anywhere else: *supremumque vale pleno singultibus ore / vix dixit* (509f.).

[22] The inversion of cultural values in this failure of an Athenian princess to move a Thracian king by her plea would be appreciated by an audience for whom Athens was the home of rhetorical training. Ovid uses the victim's silence to depict the horror of rape also in the Lucretia episode of the *Fasti*, especially 2.823ff.: see Newlands (1988) 38-40.

The most intense longing for the speech comes at the climax of the vengeance. Philomela desperately wants the voice of which Tereus had robbed her (659f.): *nec tempore maluit ullo / posse loqui et meritis testari gaudia dictis* ("At no other time did she have a greater desire to be able to speak and to bear witness to her joy in the deserved words"). Her frustration, however, is compensated by Procne's inability to keep silent any longer as she announces her "cruel joy" (*gaudia*, 653 and 660) in the revenge (653-55):

> dissimulare nequit crudelia gaudia Progne
> iamque suae cupiens existere nuntia cladis
> "intus habes, quem poscis," ait.

> Procne cannot conceal her cruel enjoyment, and now, eager to stand forth as the messenger of the destruction, she says, "You have within the one you are asking for."

The failure to suppress her speech in these "joys" is not only the mirror-image of Philomela's situation; it also harks back to the eager joy of Tereus' victorious persuasion (514): *exsultatque et vix animo sua gaudia differt* ("He leaps in joy and in his thoughts scarcely defers his enjoyment"). The echoes suggest the moral structure of the tale: the crime begets its own vengeance. But they also link the three main figures together in a pattern of reciprocal violence, into which they are frozen forever by the metamorphosis (cf. 666-74).

These crimes within the house not only destroy the security of domestic space; they also fit the savagery of the deed to the savagery of the land. Ovid purposefully contrasts the center of the civilized world, Athens, with its dubiously civilized periphery, Thrace.[23] He introduces Tereus in a splendid verse-paragraph, listing the glorious cities of Greece, with Athens conspicuous by its absence (412-23). Athens is harassed by "barbarian troops," against whom "Thracian Tereus" offers his aid (424). Tereus enters the poem as *Threicius*, and as an ally against *barbara agmina* (423f.). The collocation proves ironical, for Tereus himself is the true *barbarus* and is so called as he carries out his crime (515, 533). *O diris barbare factis*, "O barbarian in your terrible deeds," Philomela calls him in the last speech that she will ever have (533).

Having entered the poem with the "victory of a glorious name" in a battle for Athens and against barbarians (*clarum vincendo nomen habebat*, 425), Tereus wins an evil "victory" (*vicimus*, 513) over his Athenian victim, proving himself truly a barbarian (*barbarus*, 515):

---

[23] On the Thracians as uncivilized, see Bömer (1976) ad 458 (pp. 131f.). As in the incestuous births of Byblis and Myrrha, Ovid chooses a setting at the edges of civilization for the violation of basic human laws (cf. 9.640ff., 10.476ff.).

"vicimus! exclamat "mecum mea vota feruntur!"
exsultatque et vix animo sua gaudia differt
barbarus ...

His cry of conquest marks a turning point. He now reveals the hidden savagery of his character and lifts the veil of assumed *pietas* (cf. 474 and 482). The first of the episode's four animal images follows at once, comparing him to an eagle carrying off a hare in its hooked talons (516-18). The animal imagery will recur for the horrors of his crime (527-29, 559) and for Procne's revenge (636f.), until it becomes reality in the metamorphosis at the end. In the tale's pattern of mimetic violence, the birds of prey initiate and close the cycle of crimes against kin (cf. 516f. and 673f.). Four interlocking motifs — suppression of speech, corrupted *pietas*, barbarian status, and animality — form the thematic armature of Ovid's tale. Together they shape the structure of reversals in which violence meets its condign punishment in an almost exact imitation of itself.

TIME, SPACE, AND MORAL ORDER

Ovid also uses a more formal articulation of the action, punctuating the human events by a larger divine framework of seasonal or sacral time:

(1) iam tempora Titan
quinque per autumnos repetiti duxerat anni
cum blandita viro Progne ... (438-40);
(2) iam labor exiguus Phoebo restabat equique
pulsabant pedibus spatium declivis Olympi (486f.);
(3) signa deus bis sex acto lustraverat anno:
quid faciat Philomela? (571f.);
(4) tempus erat quo sacra solent trieterica Bacchi
Sithoniae celebrare nurus: nox conscia sacris (587f.).

Of these temporal markers, the first sets the disaster into motion; the second introduces the success of Tereus' scheme; the third indicates the duration of Philomela's imprisonment; and the fourth leads her to freedom and vengeance. This temporal movement is measured by something grander than the impatience of human desire (cf. 514 and 653) or the necessary intervals of a long sea-voyage, although these too mark major stages of the narrative (cf. 422, 444-46, 511-20).[24]

---

[24] There is also a progression here from the more or less neutral statements of the first two voyages to the third, which takes place under the sign of Tereus' lust, as his predatory eyes never leave Philomela (515). The significance of this last voyage is also marked by the suddenness of the violence in a *cum-inversum* clause after his arrival: *iamque iter effectum iamque in sua litora fessis / puppibus exierant, cum rex Pandione natam / in stabula alta trahit* ... (519-21). For other aspects of narrative structure see Ortega (1970) 215f.; Otis (1970) 408-

This sacred time might suggest a larger world-order framing the events. Yet the very remoteness of these celestial phenomena (especially in items 1 through 3 above) also sets off the moral isolation of the human world and the absence of gods. This story takes us about as far from a clear divine justice as any tale in the poem.[25] We are immersed in the dark night of human passions, as Ovid carefully points out at the beginning and end:

> pro superi, quantum mortalia pectora caecae
> noctis habent ("O gods, how much dark night do mortal hearts contain," 472f.);

> tantaque nox animi est ("So great is the night of his mind," 652)

There is, to be sure, a kind of poetic justice in the fact that Procne's night of Bacchic rites on the mountain harks back to the nocturnal banquet of Tereus' deception (487-94 and 588-90, where *nox* is repeated three times). Yet the only god explicitly mentioned is Bacchus, in a brief apostrophe (596).[26] Even the metamorphosis at the end comes without benefit of divinity. It follows as the external manifestation, almost ratification, of the bestiality which the main actors have already been enacting among one another. Compared to an eagle seeking its prey with its talons (516f.), Tereus has already undergone an inner metamorphosis before he becomes, literally, the hoopoe with its "armed face" (*armata facies*, 673f.). The bestiality in his character has already been marked by adjectives like *ferus* and *saevus* (549, 557; 464, 581).

Procne undergoes an analogous change as she emerges from the Bacchic ritual with a new identity: not the "Procne sweetly coaxing her husband," but the "fearful Procne," goaded by the furies of her grief (*blandita viro Progne*, 440; *Progne terribilis*, 595). Tereus, for a moment, could imagine himself as a potential Paris, carrying off a Greek woman to a barbarian land for a second Trojan war: *aut rapere et saevo raptam defendere bello* (464). But Procne has a more sinister register of mythical echoes to play upon. She becomes an Agave who rends her child, a Medea who kills her offspring, and a Clytaemnestra who would inflict multitudinous wounds on her

---

10.

[25] Schmidt (1991) 123f. attributes the absence of the gods here to the organizational scheme of the poem, which here turns from gods punishing mortals to relationships between man and man. This view, however, fails to take account of Ovid's insistence on the divine indifference in Philomela's three appeals to divine help (526, 542f., 548).

[26] Cf. also the *insignia Bacchi* just afterwards (598) and the metonymic use of Bacchus for wine in 488f. *(Bacchus in auro / ponitur)*, to be discussed later. The absence of gods to help the innocent or bring justice is also in keeping with the implicit criticism of divine cruelty in the stories of Arachne, Niobe, and Marsyas earlier in the book.

faithless husband: *aut per vulnera mille / sontem animam expellam*, 617f.; cf. A. *Ag.* 866-68).[27]

To this demarcation of the story by temporal divisions corresponds an equally sharp set of spatial contrasts. The chief mechanism of Tereus' plot is to lure Philomela from the civilized city of Athens and from the safety of her father's house to the desolate forest in the wild land (520f.). This movement from a civilized house to the wild and from a great city to lonely Thracian forest also gains force from the comparison of Philomela, at her first appearance, to the naiads and dryads of the forest (451-54, *quales audire solemus / naidas et dryadas mediis incedere silvis* ...). We may be reminded of the lament of these forest-dwellers over their kinsman Marsyas at his bloody end shortly before (390-95). That lament created a contrast between painful physical violation and a tranquil sylvan or pastoral landscape: *nec quicquam nisi vulnus erat; cruor undique manat, / detectique patent nervi* (388ff.); *et nymphae flerunt, et quisquis montibus illis / lanigerosque greges armentaque bucera pavit* (394f.). For Philomela, likened to a naiad, the remoteness of nature is threatening. There are no compassionate Nymphs or Fauns in this deserted forest, and the mutilated woman is thrown entirely on her own resources.

The violence implicit in the shift from Athens to Thrace is also symmetrical with an abrupt spatial shift within Thrace. The two Athenian sisters move from enclosure to dangerous wildness, and then back to a domestic interior. But the return to the house via the forest leaves that domestic space changed forever. It is now a place of crimes, passions, and bloody acts as grim as those of Tereus' forest. With the female vengeance, this becomes a world of total violence, a world from which reason and restraint are gone. Procne's maenadic freedom on the mountainside puts an end to her previous identity as Tereus' complaisant wife (cf. 428ff., especially 440, *blandita viro Progne*). The "Bacchic" drink served in cups of gold when Philomela lived in the regal shelter of her own house (488) returns as Procne's vengeful Bacchic riot in the forests of Thrace (587, 596).[28]

Philomela's delicate weaving enabled her to find a way through her heavily walled prison: *fugam custodia claudit, / structa rigent solido stabulorum moenia saxo*, 572f.). She had initially threatened Tereus with just

---

[27] The episode also has a number of other intertextual allusions. Often noted is the echo of Apollo's pursuit of Daphne in Tereus' lust for Philomela: 6.455-57 and 1.492-95, on which see Jacobsen (1984/85) 45-52. The ill-omened wedding at the beginning (6.429ff.) is perhaps recalled in the story of Orpheus, 10.3-8. In both cases the resemblances set off the bestiality of Tereus and the violence of this tale. Cf. also the motif of the final farewell, 509, which also recurs in Orpheus' story (10.62), as well as elsewhere: see Bömer (1976) ad loc. (p. 141). Compare the seduction motif of 463f. with the story of Procris in the next book, 7.739f., and see Bömer (1976) p. 133.

[28] This passage is perhaps a possible reminiscence of the disastrous banquet of Dido at the end of *Aen.* 1, esp. 1.685f.; cf. Bömer (1976) ad *Met.* 6.488f.

such an exposure, filling the forest with her cries of accusation (544-47, especially 546f.: *si silvis clausa tenebor / implebo silvas et conscia saxa movebo*).[29] Now she breaches these walls not by sound but by a silent witness (cf. 574, *os mutum facti caret indice*), an act of communication that is the product of artfulness in more senses than one (cf. *ingenium, sollertia, callida tela*, 575f.).

Procne's first response to the message was stupefied silence (582-86, above); her second is a violent departure from the house at night (*nocte sua est egressa domo regina*, 590), to join the Thracian women on Mt. Rhodope. The toponyms *Sithoniae* and *Rhodope* underline the Thracian character of the ritual. Procne takes up *furialia arma* and makes her way *per silvas* (594). "Stirred up by the wild madness of grief" (594f.), she leads the women in bacchantic rage. Later, in the infectious spread of violence, she will dress Philomela in Bacchantic garb (598f.). Amid the Dionysiac howls (*exululat euhoeque sonat*, 597), she penetrates the remote forest, "breaks down the doors" of her sister's prison, and carries her off, amazed, "within her own walls" (*adtonitamque trahens intra sua moenia ducit*, 600). She thus exactly undoes the act of Tereus, who had "dragged" Philomela "into" the forest: *in stabula alta trahit silvis obscura vetustis* (521). Enclosure in the remote forest was previously in the service of lust. Now lust is punished by the criminal's metaphorical enclosure within his own body: if he could, he would "unlock" his breast and remove the accursed food within: *et modo, si posset, reserato pectore diras / egerere inde dapes immersaque viscera gestit* (663f.). A crime committed across vast distances is answered by a crime committed in his own intimate household and, finally, within his own interior flesh. Tereus' tears, feigned before, are now genuine (*flet modo*, 665).

The parallels and inversions between the beginning and end multiply as the tale goes on and clearly form part of the terrible mimetic violence of the revenge plot.[30] Tereus' helpful "conquest" of a barbarian army in Athens' behalf degenerates into a libidinous "conquest" of his sister-in-law (reversing the direction of his voyage) and then into his own being "conquered" by the collusion of two women (425, 483, 513, 525, 612).[31] The first appearance of Procne and her child Itys combines the motifs of the Eumenides, the marriage torch, and the figurative bird of prophecy (430-34); and all of these

---

[29] These lines may be a reminiscence of E. *Hipp.* 1253f., especially as accusation by non-spoken means are involved.

[30] This structure of infectious violence could be described in the terms of Girard (1977), especially 41ff., 158ff. But such an analysis would perhaps only show how little the moral issues of the myth are here resolved. For a criticism of such an approach see Joplin (1991) 42ff.

[31] This reversal may go back beyond Accius' *Tereus* to Sophocles' play on that subject: see Bömer (1976) 117f. and Otis (1970) 406f. If so, the plotting and vengeance of Hecuba against Polymestor in Euripides' *Hecuba* may give us an idea of how it might have been handled in Greek tragedy.

return as part of the crime and its punishment. The Eumenides at the beginning (430f.) become the Furies (literal or figurative) who avenge the violation of marriage later (591-95, 657, 662). The torches *(faces)* of marriage, coming straight from a funeral, overdetermine the ominous atmosphere *(Eumenides tenuere faces de funere raptas*, 430). They soon become the metaphorical "torches" of Tereus' desire (480) and then of Procne's lust for revenge (614). And the birds of course recur at the cardinal point of Tereus' victorious lust (the eagle-simile of 516-18) and its defeat and punishment in metamorphosis (666-74).

The *blanditiae* with which Procne appeals to Tereus for her sister's visit (440, *cum blandita viro Progne*) return in her horrible vengeance for the crime that she has thus innocently set into motion *(blanditiae*, 626, 632). The joyful "leaping about" of Tereus at the apparent success of his plot *(exsultat*, 514) becomes the "leaping" of his son's boiling flesh in the caldron *(pars inde cavis exsultat aenis*, 645). The displacement of speech into weaving becomes a female "unveiling" that transforms apparent feminine helplessness into decisive and bloody action (cf. 566f., 576ff., 604). The male weapon of the sword or iron *(ensis, ferrum)* undergoes a parallel shift from agent to victim (551ff., 611f., 617, 643), until it fixes Tereus forever in his role of aggressive pursuer (666). As we have already noted, the repeated motifs of *pietas*, tears, night, fire, conquest, joy, weaving, speech and silence mark the major stages of crime and punishment.[32]

FEMALE REVENGE AND ITS PROBLEMS: METAMORPHOSIS AS RESOLUTION OR IRRESOLUTION

These symmetries suggest the working out of an immanent moral law in the *Metamorphoses* as a crime produces its own punishment. Yet there is a harsh asymmetry since the parallelism between the male violence of lust and the female desire for revenge is not exact. Not only is the former individual and the latter collective, but the women's crime develops only as a response to Tereus'. He was the initiator and aggressor; the women are avengers. Horrible as their vengeance is, it has justice on its side. Yet the dehumanization of all three characters in the final metamorphosis does not discriminate between degrees of guilt, and in fact rather encourages us not

---

[32] For example, night: 472f., 486ff., 588-90, 652; fire: 455ff., 460, 466, 492, 609, 614f., 645f.; silence: 574, 583-85, 622f., 632, 660; joy: 514, 653, 660; tears: 471f., 504, 523, 535, 566, 585, 610f., 628, 665; pain or grief *(dolor)*: 574, 583, 595, 671. See Anderson (1972) ad 490 and ad 671-74. Note too how the motif of "not containing" one's passion moves from Tereus to Procne: *nec capiunt inclusas pectora flammas*, of Tereus' lust in 466; *ardet et iram / non capit ipsa suam Procne*, of Procne's vengeful wrath in 609f.: see Bömer (1976) and Anderson (1972), both ad 609f.

274   CHARLES SEGAL

to judge. The closest Ovid comes to recognizing the tragedy of Procne's transformation into a child-murderess is in her brief hesitation and monologue at 624-35. Once decided, she is almost as monstrous as Tereus. As Tereus was an eagle or a wolf, she is an Indian tigress killing a suckling fawn (636f.), and she does not even turn her face away as she strikes her child who stretches out his arms to his mother (639-42).[33]

The unsatisfactoriness of the metamorphosis as a moral resolution is compounded by the mechanism that underlies the women's revenge. In his account of Procne's *furor*, Ovid recollects the maenadic *furor* of Virgil's Amata and Dido.[34] In this way he assimilates Procne's terrible, if just, vengeance to the most familiar literary models for female violence: madness, rage, maenadism.

Behind the bacchantic imagery of the Dido and Amata episodes of Virgil lie the maenads of Greek tragedy, especially of Euripides' *Bacchae* and, to a lesser degree, his *Hecuba*. In both of these plays men do violence to women, with implications also of sexual violation. In the *Bacchae* Pentheus' voyeuristically spies on the Maenads; in *Hecuba* the Greeks at Troy sacrifice the virgin Polyxena to Achilles as a kind of posthumous bride. In both cases the women turn suddenly from total helplessness and subjection to murderous vengeance. In both cases that vengeance takes the form of collective violence: the band of maenads tears apart Pentheus, and the Trojan women band together to blind the treacherous Polymestor and murder his two (male) children. In the *Bacchae* the mother who leads her band of women on the mountains in the killing and mutilation of her son is literally a maenad. In *Hecuba* the Trojan queen's companions are compared to maenads when they lure the evil King Polymestor into their tent, kill his sons, and blind the father (1076; cf. 1150-75: see Segal, 1990a, 119-22 and 1990b, 314f.). Indeed the Tereus episode resembles the *Hecuba* even more closely because it combines the motif of a conspiracy of women (a motif also parodied in Aristophanes' *Thesmophoriazusae*, *Lysistrata*, and *Ecclesiazusae*) with the motif of bacchantic rage and collective violence. It is even possible that this bacchantic motif entered Ovid's tale via Sophocles' lost *Tereus*, though this is only conjecture.

Ovid explores the violence of the male criminal, Tereus, in terms of individual psychology (e.g. 458f., *sed et hunc innata libido / exstimulat*, "but his inborn lustfulness goads him on"). Female violence, however, in this highly androcentric world, has something uncanny or supernatural about it.

---

[33] Contrast 7.340-42, where Pelias' daughter, even with her good intentions, cannot look as she strikes. See Galinsky (1975) 131f. on the "untragic presentation of tragic material."

[34] See *Aen.* 7.385-405, 4.300-3. *Met.* 6.587, *quo sacra solent trieterica Bacchi*, seems to be a conscious echo of *Aen.* 4.302, *ubi audito stimulant trieterica Baccho* ... On Ovid's assimilation of Virgil's language of *furor* elsewhere, see Bömer (1968) 192f.; also Büchner (1968) 388f. On the Bacchantic imagery of Dido and Amata, see Suzuki (1989) 111ff., 130ff.

The women appear not just as agents of justice but are demonized as Furies (591, 595, 657, 662). As we view the narrative as a whole, we see them descending to increasingly subhuman forms, from maenad to Fury to wild creature. Ovid is still working in a tradition in which the violence of women is perceived as monstrous. We may recall the first stasimon of Aeschylus' *Libation Bearers* (585-651).[35]

The sudden shift, at the peripety, from forest to mountain to interior of the *domus* (cf. 601, *ut sensit tetigisse domum Philomela nefandam*) also destabilizes the image of woman as a helpless victim. Rape is answered by maenadic *furor*; violation of the ties between husband and wife and between sister and sister is answered by the violation of the bonds between mother and son and between father and son. Incest is answered by filicide and cannibalism.

As Bacchants, the women become embodiments of irrationality rather than representatives of a retributive moral order. Put another way, the shading of maenadism into subterranean *furor* reduces the sacrality of Procne's Dionysiac procession to pure violence. Instead of constituting a breakthrough to a new order from the disintegration of the old in an irruption of a fresh and different form of human energy, the maenadic is demonized as an eruption from the underworld. When Philomela completes the vengeance by throwing Itys' head at his father, she is not only bespattered with a Fury's gore (657) but is the target of Tereus' evocation of the "viper-covered sisters" from Hades (*vipereasque ciet Stygia de valle sorores*, 662).

Procne might have carried Philomela away to a Bacchantic community of "sisters" very different from those hellish "sisters" of Hades. This could be a paradisiacal world of women outside of male culture and free of male control, like the maenads in happy fusion with nature on Mt. Cithaeron in the *Bacchae* (680-713). Ovid precludes that possibility by anticipating the Fury-laden savagery in the midst of the maenadic rescue. Even as Procne leads her band of maenads, she is "fearful and driven on by the furies of her grief" (*terribilis Procne furiisque agitata doloris*, 595). Her Dionysiac implements are *furialia arma* (591), and she only "feigns" (*simulat*, 596) bacchantic ecstasy. As Joplin remarks, "The end of the tale represents an attempt to forestall or foreclose a moment of radical transition when dominance and hierarchy might have begun to change or to give way" (1991, p. 49).

Viewed in this way Ovid's combination of the Dionysiac pattern with the chthonic imagery, like the three-way bestial metamorphosis that follows it, evokes the deep ambiguities that this culture feels toward female emotion (especially violent and aggressive emotion). Procne put on the sacred garb of the god Dionysus to rescue Philomela from her forest prison (591-600).

---

[35] On the microcosmic level of diction, for example, Procne's anticipated revenge consists in *crudelia gaudia* (653), whereas Tereus' anticipated rape consists only in *sua gaudia* (514).

But when she takes off these bacchic insignia (603), she also takes off the sacral dimension of her task and instead blazes up in a vengeful fury that she can control no more than Tereus could the fire of his lust (*ardet et iram / non capit ipsa sua*, 609f.; cf. 466, *nec capiunt inclusas pectora flammas*). In place of a woman's tears she now demands a sword (611-18). For her, as for her sister, "hands" stand in the place of "voice" in more senses than one (*pro voce manus fuit*, 609). Amid Procne's threats to Tereus' tongue, eyes, and genitals, the infant Itys enters. Now the ties of "mother" and "wife" give way entirely to those of "sister" and "daughter" (630-35, 640, 666).

Tereus' wild overthrowing of the tables and his invocation of the Stygian Furies 662) confirm that we are indeed in the realm of the Furies (cf. 657, *furiali caede*). The association of the sisters with the Furies (made all the stronger by Tereus' "sisters" for the Furies in 662) reinforces the horror of Philomela's inner transformation. The presence of the Furies suggests that the crime of rape has robbed Philomela of her previous self, her identity as a young Athenian princess, and changed her into something terrible and scarcely human. The metamorphosis begins before her actual change of shape. Tereus' brutalization of her has made her into a demon of revenge as all the rage of his violation of her now turns against him. In a sense, then, Philomela is victimized even in the justice of her revenge as she is brought down to the level of her attacker's bestiality and so endlessly pursued by him in the non-human forms that all three actors now assume.

It is illuminating to compare this reading of the episode, which owes much to Joplin's feminist approach, with the traditional "humanist" reading of Brooks Otis. Otis gives a good description of the dehumanization of the two women, but regards the metamorphosis as the "solution of their catastrophe" rather than as the problematization of justice in this world of sub-human behavior (Otis, 1970, 215). Joplin reads the myth (she does not deal with Ovid in detail) as a narrative that needs to be deconstructed or subverted into a critique of patriarchy: "The Greek imagination uses the mythic end to expel its own violence and to avoid any knowledge of its process. Patriarchal culture feels, as Tereus does, that it is asked to incorporate something monstrous when the woman returns from exile to tell her own story" (Joplin 1991, 49).

The issue here can perhaps be reframed as the critic's decision about where to situate himself or herself in relation to the text. If one reads the episode from within the frame of the narrative, Ovid receives credit for his full depiction of Tereus' savagery and his sympathetic treatment of the victims. If one reads the episode from outside this frame, Ovid is open to the charge of perpetuating a cultural pattern of subjugating and exploiting women and of demonizing their rage at such subjugation. I cannot hope to resolve this issue here, for it is *the* issue for any interpretation that confronts the moral dimensions of literature. But facing these tensions fairly can lead us to rethink some basic interpretive categories like textuality, allusion, and aesthetic pleasure.

This tale's self-conscious allusiveness (particularly in its echoes of Greek tragedy and Virgil) marks its literariness and thereby takes us back to the problem of literary pleasure, the problematical pleasure of the text in this most unpleasant tale. These armed women on the mountainside, with the irresistible strength of maenads that we know from Euripides' *Bacchae*, show us an image of the female body very different from that desired (and violated) by Tereus. It is not the passive object of uncontrollable, lawless male pleasure, but is full of strange power and quite capable of murder. The Greek tragedies with similar endings — Euripides' *Medea*, *Hecuba*, *Bacchae*, and perhaps Sophocles' lost *Tereus* — do not opt for the facile solution of metamorphosis, but leave us in shocked contemplation of this enormity of female hatred and vengeful force. The *Hecuba* and *Bacchae* do contain metamorphoses at the end, but these serve to intensify rather than to mitigate the tragic suffering. In the case of Ovid our aesthetic pleasure might be less, but our moral pleasure might be deeper if that shock-effect were less tamed by the pseudo-resolution of metamorphosis to which the poem is committed.

There are, then, two elements in the tale that are difficult for Ovid to control within the aesthetic and moral framework of his poem: these are the shift to an implicit female reader and the problem of combining justice and metamorphosis. If these elements destabilize the narrative, Ovid restabilizes his poem and achieves closure in the book by reasserting the authority of the patriarchal order. The next episode, the last one in book 6, is the myth of Boreas and Oreithyia. It is virtually a comic mirror-image of the story of Tereus and Philomela.[36] The raped victim now ends up as bride and as the mother of Boreas' two sons, who, at the end, go off on an all-male quest, with brilliant prospects, thanks to the special attribute of wings that they inherit from their father.

The justice that is never mentioned in the case of the Procne and Philomela has a prominent place at the beginning of the Boreas story. Ovid introduces Pandion's successor in Athens, Erechtheus, as both strong and just (677f.):

sceptra loci rerumque capit moderamen Erectheus,
iustitia dubium validisne potentior armis.

Erechtheus — it is unclear whether he is more powerful in justice or in mighty arms — takes the kingdom's scepter and the control of affairs.

---

[36] For some of the parallels between the two tales, see Albrecht (1968) 432 and Anderson (1972) 237 and ad 6.717-18.

The weak king and father, Pandion, is now replaced by a powerful father-figure, Erechtheus, who will not surrender his daughter, Oreithyia, to a Thracian husband, even though the latter is a god (682ff.).[37] Like Tereus, Boreas resorts to violence. Indeed, his highly rhetorical soliloquy, in which he reminds himself that he is a big bad storm-god, full of potential *saevitia* and *vis* (687ff.), recalls Tereus' readiness to play the role of Paris and launch a massive war (cf. 461-66). Like Tereus too, he yields to the blazing fires of passion (708) and carries his Athenian beloved off to the snowy wilds of Thrace (707ff.).

Unlike Tereus, however, Boreas makes his Athenian captive his wife and the mother of twin sons. The bird-metamorphosis that follows is now gradual and happy rather than sudden and destructive (contrast 666-74 and 714-18). The two sons, Zetes and Calais, have their wings as part of the joint attributes of both parents (*gemellos / cetera qui matris, pennas genitoris haberent*, 712f.). For the young Itys, "likeness to father" meant death (*a! quam / es similis patri*, 621f.); here that likeness is the source of special powers that ensure heroic success. These bird-like qualities emerge only in the due course of the Boreads' maturation (714-18), just when they are useful for their spectacular and literally radiant breaking away on the Argonautic expedition (720f.):

> vellera cum Minyis nitido radiantia villo
> per mare non notum prima petiere carina.

> Along with the Minyans (the Argonauts), through an unknown sea and on the first ship, they seek the shining fleeece with its bright hair.

These are the closing lines of the book; and they offer an image of bright, happy, and expansive travel, in contrast to the movement toward enclosure and darkness in the tale of Tereus (cf. especially *iubet ille carinas / in freta deduci*, "He orders the ships to be brought down to the sea," 443f., of Tereus' ill-fated voyage from Thrace to Greece). They also show us the children of a Thraco-Athenian union reaching a glorious adolescence rather than being cut off horribly in childhood.

Ovid thus ends this grim book on a lighter and more pleasant note. If we read with the flow of Ovid's elegant and pleasant surface, the Boreas-Oreithyia episode allows us to see the murderousness of the preceding tale in comic relief. But if we read it in the light of the disjunctions and unsuccessful resolutions of the preceding tale, it appears as a strategy to smooth over the very difficult problems that the Tereus-Philomela episode has raised. The resolution that is impossible inside the Tereus story is made by a supplement from outside, as it were, in another story. But like all

---

[37] Note too the motif of *blanditiae* here, 685. Unlike those of the Tereus story (440, 626, 632), these do not succeed.

supplements, this one too reveals the lack and instability of what it completes.[38]

BIBLIOGRAPHY

Albrecht M. von (1968) "Ovids Humor und die Einheit der Metamorphosen" (1963), in Albrecht and Zinn (1968) 405-37.
—— and E. Zinn (eds.) (1968) *Ovid, Wege der Forschung*, vol. 92 (Darmstadt: 1968).
Anderson W.S. (1972) *Ovid's Metamorphoses: Books 6-10* (Norman: 1972).
Barthes R. (1974) *S/Z*, trans. R. Miller (New York: 1974).
—— (1986) *The Rustle of Language*, trans. R. Howard (New York: 1986).
Barton C.A. (1989) "The Scandal of the Arena", *Representations* 27 (1989) 1-36.
Bömer F. (1968) "Ovid und die Sprache Vergils", in Albrecht and Zinn (1968) 173-202.
—— (1976) *P. Ovidius Naso, Metamorphosen, Buch VI-VII* (Heidelberg: 1976).
Brown S. (1992) "Death as Decoration: Scenes from the Arena on Roman Domestic Mosaics" in Richlin (1992) 180-208.
Büchner K. (1968) "Ovids Metamorphosen" (1957), in Albrecht and Zinn (1968) 384-92.
Curran L.C. (1978) "Rape and Rape Victims in the Metamorphoses", *Arethusa* 11 (1978) 213-42.
Derrida J. (1976) *Of Grammatology*, trans. G.C. Spivak (Baltimore: 1976).
Diller H. (1968) "Die dichterische Eigenart von Ovids Metamorphosen" (1934), in Albrecht and Zinn (1968) 332-39.
Galinsky G.K. (1975) *Ovid's Metamorphoses: An Introduction to the Basic Aspects* (Berkeley-Los Angeles: 1975).
Girard R. (1977) *Violence and the Sacred*, trans. P. Gregory (Baltimore: 1977).
Hartman G. (1970) *Beyond Formalism* (New Haven: 1970).
Higgins L.A. and Silver B.R. (eds.) (1991) *Rape and Representation* (New York: 1991).
Jacobsen G.A. (1984-85) "Apollo and Tereus: Parallel Motifs in Ovid's Metamorphoses", *Classical Journal* 80 (1984-85) 45-52.
Joplin P.K. (1991) "The Voice of the Shuttle Is Ours" (1984), in Higgins and Silver (1991) 35-64.
Kahn C. (1991) "Lucrece: The Sexual Politics of Subjectivity", in Higgins and Silver (1991) 141-59.
Lévi-Strauss C. (1969) *The Elementary Structures of Kingship*, trans. J.H. Bell, R. von Sturmer, R. Needham (Boston: 1969).
Most G. (1992) "*Disiecti membra poetae*: The Rhetoric of Dismemberment in Neronian Poetry", in *Innovations of Antiquity*, ed. D.L. Selden and R.J. Hexter (New York: 1992) 391-419.
Mulvey L. (1988, 1975) "Visual Pleasure and Narrative Cinema", in *Feminism and Film Theory*, ed. C. Penley (New York: 1988) 57-68 (originally published in *Screen* 16, 1975).
Newlands C.W. (1988) "The Rape of Lucretius in Ovid's Fasti", *Augustan Age* 8 (1988) 36-48.
Otis B. (1970) *Ovid as an Epic Poet* (Cambridge: 1970).

---

[38] On the supplement, see Derrida (1976) 144f., 292ff. I have drawn some of the material in the present essay from a study that appeared in my *Ovidio e la poesia del mito: Saggi sulle "Metamorfosi"* (Venice-Marsilio: 1991) 185-200 and, somewhat abbreviated, in *The Two Worlds of the Poet: New Perspectives on Vergil*, Studies in Honour of A.G. McKay, ed. R.M. Wilhelm and H. Jones (Detroit: 1992); but I have greatly recast this material to focus more sharply on interpretive assumptions and problems of methodology.

Ortega A. (1970) "Die Tragödie der Pandionstöchter in Ovids Metamorphosen", in W. Wimmel (ed.) *Forschungen zur Römischen Literatur*, Festschrift Karl Büchner (Wiesbaden: 1970) 215-23.

Pavlock B. (1991) "The Tyrant and Boundary Violation in Ovid's Tereus Episode", *Helios* 18 (1991) 34-48.

Richlin A. (ed.) (1992) *Pornography and Representation in Greece and Rome* (Oxford-New York: 1992).

—— (1992a) "Reading Ovid's Rapes", in Richlin (1992) 158-79.

Seel O. (1961) "Ansatz zu einer Martialinterpretation", *Antike und Abendland* 10 (1961) 53-76.

Segal C. (1971) "Ovid's Metamorphoses: Greek Myth in Augustan Rome", *Studies in Philology* 68 (1971) 371-94.

—— (1982) *Dionysiac Poetics and Euripides' Bacchae* (Princeton: 1982).

—— (1983) "The Menace of Dionysus: Sex Roles and Reversals in Euripides' Bacchae" (1978), in *Women in the Ancient World: The Arethusa Papers*, ed. J. Peradotto and J.P. Sullivan (Albany: 1983) 195-212.

—— (1986) "Boundary Violation and the Landscape of the Self in Senecan Tragedy" (1983), in *Interpreting Greek Tragedy* (Ithaca: 1986) 315-36.

—— (1990a) "Violence and the Other: Greek, Female, and Barbarian in Euripides' Hecuba", *Transactions of the American Philological Association* 120 (1990) 109-131.

—— (1990b) "Golden Armor and Servile Robes: Heroism and Metamorphosis in the *Hecuba* of Euripides", *American Journal of Philology* 111 (1990) 304-17.

—— (1990c) *Lucretius on Death and Anxiety: Poetry and Philosophy in De Rerum Natura* (Princeton: 1990).

Suzuki M. (1989) *Metamorphoses of Helen* (Ithaca, N.Y.: 1989).

Williams G. (1978) *Change and Decline*, Sather Classical Lectures, vol. 45 (Berkeley-Los Angeles: 1978).

GENERAL BIBLIOGRAPHY

The bibliography consists of the following rubrics: 1. introductions and collections, 2. narratology, 3. intertextuality, 4. reader-response, 5. feminist criticism, 6. psycho-analytical criticism, 7. structuralist, poststructuralist and semiotic criticism, and 8. dialectical and dialogic criticism. Each rubric is divided into a. theory and b. classical application. The bibliographies under a. are selective, providing the classical scholar a first orientation in otherwise vast areas of discussion; those under b. are more inclusive, although inevitably studies will have escaped our notice. Further specific guidance will be found in the individual bibliographies to each essay in this volume.

I. Introductions and Collections

a. theory

Cohen R. (ed.) (1989) *The Future of Literary Theory* (New York-London: 1989).
Collier P. and Geyer-Ryan H. (eds.) (1990) *Literary Theory Today* (Cambridge: 1990).
Culler J. (1983) *On Deconstruction: Theory and Criticism after Structuralism* (London: 1983).
Davis R.C. and Finke L. (eds.) (1989) *Literary Criticism and Theory: The Greeks to the Present* (London-New York: 1989).
Eagleton T. (1983) *Literary Theory. An Introduction* (Oxford: 1983).
Lodge D. (ed.) (1988) *Modern Criticism and Theory. A Reader* (London-New York: 1988).
Lentricchia F. and McLaughlin T. (eds.) (1990) *Critical Terms for Literary Study* (Chicago: 1990).

b. classical application

Benjamin A. (ed.) (1988) *Post-Structuralist Classics* (London: 1988).
Galinsky K. (1992) (ed.) *The Interpretation of Roman Poetry: Empiricism or Hermeneutics?* (Frankfurt am Main: 1992).
Kennedy G. (1989) "Ancient Antecedents of Modern Literary Theory", *American Journal of Philology* 110 (1989) 492-498.
Kresic S. (ed.) (1981) *Contemporary Literary Hermeneutics and Interpretation of Classical Texts* (Ottawa: 1981).
Peradotto J. (1983) "Texts and Unrefracted Facts: Philology, Hermeneutics and Semiotics", *Arethusa* 16 (1983) 15-33.
Rosenmeyer T.G. (1988) *DEINA TA POLLA: A Classicist's Checklist of Twenty Literary-Critical Positions* (Buffalo: 1988).
Rubino C.A. (1977) "*Lectio difficilior praeferenda est*. Some Remarks on Contemporary French Thought and the Study of Classical Literature", *Arethusa* 10 (1977) 63-84.
Segal C. (1968) "Ancient Texts and Modern Criticism: Some Recent Trends in Classical Literary Studies", *Arethusa* 1 (1968) 1-25.
—— (1984) "Classics and Comparative Literature", *Materiali e discussioni per l'analisi dei testi classici* 13 (1984) 9-27.
Selden D.L. (1990) "Classics and Contemporary Criticism", *Arion, n.s.* 1 (1990) 155-178.

II. NARRATOLOGY

a. theory

Bal M. (1985) *Narratology. Introduction to the Theory of Narrative* (Toronto: 1985).
Chatman S. (1978) *Story and Discourse: Narrative Structure in Fiction and Film* (Ithaca: 1978).
Cohn D. (1978) *Transparent Minds: Narrative Modes for Presenting Consciousness in Fiction* (Princeton: 1978).
Genette G. (1972) "Discours du récit", in *Figures III* (Paris: 1972), 67-267=*Narrative Discourse. An Essay in Method*, transl. J.E. Lewin (Ithaca, N.Y.: 1980).
—— (1983) *Nouveau discours du récit* (Paris: 1983).
Martin W. (1986) *Recent Theories of Narrative* (Ithaca, N.Y.-London: 1986).
Prince G. (1983) *The Form and Functioning of Narrative* (The Hague: 1983).
Rimmon-Kenan S. (1983) *Narrative Fiction: Contemporary Poetics* (London-New York: 1983).
Stanzel F. (1979) *Theorie des Erzählens* (Göttingen: 1979).

b. classical application

Aelion R. (1984) "Les mythes de Bellérophon et de Persée. Essai d'analyse selon un schéma inspiré de V. Propp", *Lalies* 4 (1984) 195-214.
Andersen O. (1987) "Myth, Paradigm and 'Spatial Form' in the Iliad", in *Homer: Beyond Oral Poetry*, ed. J.M. Bremer, I.J.F. de Jong, and J. Kalff (Amsterdam: 1987) 1-13.
Barchiesi A. (1989) "Voci e istanze narrative nelle *Metamorfosi* di Ovidio", *Materiali e discussioni per l'analisi dei testi classici* 23 (1989) 55-97.
Bergren A.L.T. (1979) "Helen's Web: Time and Tableau in the *Iliad*", *Helios* 7 (1979) 19-34.
—— (1983) "Odyssean Temporality: Many (Re)turns", in *Approaches to Homer*, ed. C.A. Rubino and C.W. Shelmerdine (Austin: 1983) 38-73.
Bonfanti M. (1985) *Punto di vista e modi della narrazione nell' Eneide* (Pisa: 1985).
Beye C.S. (1991) "The Narrator's Addresses to the Narratee in Apollonius Rhodius' *Argonautica*", *Transactions and Proceedings of the American Philological Association* 121 (1991) 215-28.
Calame C. (1986) *Le récit en Grèce ancienne* (Paris: 1986).
Dewald C. (1987) "Narrative Surface and Authorial Voice in Herodotus' *Histories*", *Arethusa* 20 (1987) 147-70.
Effe B. (1975) "Entstehung und Funktion personaler Erzählweisen in der Erzählliteratur der Antike", *Poetica* 7 (1975) 135-157.
—— (1983) "Epische Objektivität und auktoriales Erzählen", *Gymnasium* 90 (1983) 171-186.
Fowler D. (1990) "Deviant Focalisation in Virgil's *Aeneid*", *Proceedings of the Cambridge Philological Association* 36 (1990) 42-63.
—— (1991) "Narrate and Describe: the Problem of Ekphrasis", *Journal of Roman Studies* 81 (1991) 25-35.
Fusillo M. (1985) *Il tempo delle Argonautiche: un analisi del racconto in Apollonio Rodio* (Roma: 1985).
—— (1988) "Le miroir de la lune. L'histoire vraie de Lucien de la satire à l'utopie", *Poétique* 73 (1988) 109-35.
Ginsburg G.N. (1977) "Rhetoric and Representation in the *Metamorphoses* of Apuleius", *Arethusa* 10 (1977) 49-61.
Görler W. (1974) "Undramatische Elemente in der Griechisch-Römischen Komödie. Überlegungen zum Erzählerstandpunkt im Drama", *Poetica* 6 (1974) 259-84.
—— (1976) "Die Veränderung des Erzählerstandpunktes in Caesars *Bellum Gallicum*", *Poetica* 8 (1976) 95-119.
Grillo A. (1988) *Tra filologia e narratologia* (Roma: 1988).
Hägg T. (1971) *Narrative Technique in Ancient Greek Romances* (Stockholm: 1971).

Hellwig B. (1964) *Raum und Zeit im homerischen Epos* (Hildesheim: 1964).

Hurst A. "Temps du récit chez Pindare (P.4) et Bacchylide (11)", *Museum Helveticum* 40 (1983) 154-168.

Jong I.J.F. de (1985) "Iliad 1.366-392: A Mirror Story", *Arethusa* 18 (1985) 1-22.

—— (1987) *Narrators and Focalizers. The Presentation of the Story in the Iliad* (Amsterdam: 1987).

—— (1987) "Silent Characters in the *Iliad*", in *Homer: Beyond Oral Poetry. Recent Trends in Homeric Interpretation*, ed. J.M. Bremer, I.J.F. de Jong, and J. Kalff (Amsterdam: 1987) 105-21.

—— (1987) "Paris/Alexandros in the *Iliad*", *Mnemosyne* 40 (1987) 124-128.

—— (1988) "Homeric Words and Speakers: an Addendum", *Journal of Hellenic Studies* 108 (1988) 188-189.

—— (1989) "The Biter Bit. A Narratological Analysis of *H.Aphr.* 45-291", *Wiener Studien* 23 (1989) 13-26.

—— (1991) "Narratology and Oral Poetry: The Case of Homer", *Poetics Today* 12 (1991) 405-423.

—— (1991) *Narrative in Drama. The Art of the Euripidean Messenger-Speech* (Leiden: 1991).

—— (1992) "The Subjective Style in Odysseus' Wanderings", *Classical Quarterly* 42 (1992) 1-11.

Latacz E. (1981) "Zeus' Reise zu den Aithiopen (zu *Il.*1,304-495)" in *Gnomosyne, Menschliches Denken und Handeln in der frühgriechischen Literatur*, ed. G. Kurz, D. Mueller, and W. Nicolai (München: 1981) 53-81.

Létoublon F. (1983) "Le Miroir et la Boucle", *Poétique* 53 (1983) 19-35.

Marincola J. (1987) "Herodotean Narrative and the Narrator's Presence", *Arethusa* 20 (1987) 121-37.

Newlands C. (1992) "Ovid's Narrator in the *Fasti*", *Arethusa* 25 (1992) 33-54.

Paardt R.Th. van der (1978) "Various Aspects of Narrative Technique in Apuleius' *Metamorphoses*", in *Aspects of Apuleius' Golden Ass*, ed. B.L. Hijmans and R.Th. van der Paardt (Groningen: 1978) 75-94.

Perutelli A. (1979) "Registri narrativi e stile indiretto libero in Virgilio (a proposito di *Aen.* 1, 279 sgg.)", *Materiali e discussioni per l'analisi dei testi classici* 3 (1979) 69-82.

Richardson S. (1990) *The Homeric Narrator* (Nashville: 1990).

Roberts D.H. (1988) "Sophoclean Endings: Another Story", *Arethusa* 21 (1988) 177-96.

—— (1989) "Different Stories: Sophoclean Narrative(s) in the *Philoctetes*", *Transactions and Proceedings of the American Philological Association* 119 (1989) 161-76.

Segal C. (1981) "Art and the Hero: Participation, Detachment, and Narrative Point of View in *Aeneid* 1", *Arethusa* 14 (1981) 67-83.

Stark I. (1984) "Zur Erzählperspektive im griechischen Liebesroman", *Philologus* 128 (1984) 256-70.

Suerbaum W. (1968) "Die Ich-Erzählungen des Odysseus. Überlegungen zur epischen Technik der *Odyssee*", *Poetica* 2 (1968) 150-77.

Winkler J.J. (1982) "The Mendacity of Kalasiris and the Narrative Strategy of Heliodoros' *Aithiopika*", *Yale Classical Studies* 27 (1982) 93-158.

—— (1985) *Auctor and Actor. A Narratological Reading of Apuleius's Golden Ass* (Berkeley-London: 1985).

—— (1990) *The Constraints of Desire: the Antropology of Sex and Gender in Ancient Greece* (New York: 1990).

III. INTERTEXTUALITY

a. theory

Genette G. (1982) *Palimpsestes: la littérature au second degré* (Paris: 1982).
Kristeva J. (1969) Σημειωτική: *recherches pour une sémanalyse* (Paris: 1969), a translation is found in *Desire in Language. A Semiotic Approach to Literature and Art*, transl. T. Gora, A. Jardine, and L.S. Roudiez (Oxford: 1980).
Plett H.F. (ed.) (1991) *Intertextuality* (Berlin: 1991).
Pfister M. and Broich U. (eds) (1985) *Intertextualität. Formen, Funktionen, anglistische Fallstudien* (Tübingen: 1985).

b. classical application

Barchiesi A. (1980) "Le molte voci di Omero. Intertestialita e trasformazione del modello epico nel decimo dell' Eneide", *Materiali e discussioni per l'analisi dei testi classici* 4 (1980) 9-58.
Blänsdorf J. (1986) "Senecas *Apocolocyntosis* und die Intertextualitätstheorie", *Poetica* 18 (1986) 1-26.
Conte G.B. (1986) *The Rhetoric of Imitation: Genre and Poetic Memory in Virgil and other Latin Poets* (Ithaca, N.Y.: 1986).
King K.C. (1985) "The Politics of Imitation: Euripides' *Hekabe* and the Homeric Achilles", *Arethusa* 18 (1985) 47-66.
Lyne R.O.A.M. (1987) *Further Voices in Vergil's Aeneid* (Oxford: 1987).
Pucci P. (1987) *Odysseus Polytropos. Intertextual Reading in the Odyssey and the Iliad* (Ithaca, N.Y.: 1987).
Segal C. (1984) "Underreading and Intertextuality: Sappho, Simaetha, and Odysseus in Theocritus' Second *Idyll*", *Arethusa* 17 (1984) 201-9.
—— (1985) "Scrittura, intertestualità e incesto nella *Fedra* di Seneca", in *Mondo Classico: Percorsi Possibili*, ed. F. Baratta and F. Mariani (Ravenna 1985) 233-41.

IV. READER-RESPONSE CRITICISM

a. theory

Eco U. (1979) *The Role of the Reader: Explorations in the Semiotics of Texts* (Bloomington: 1979).
Freund E. (1987) *The Return of the Reader. Reader-Response Criticism* (London-New York: 1987).
Grimm G. (1977) *Rezeptionsgeschichte. Grundlegung einer Theorie. Mit Analysen und Bibliographie* (München: 1977).
Holub R.C. (1984) *Reception Theory. A Critical Introduction* (London-New York: 1984).
Ibsch E. and Schramm D. (eds.) (1987) *Rezeptionsforschung zwischen Hermeneutik und Empirik* (Amsterdam: 1987).
Iser W. (1972) *Der implizite Leser. Kommunikationsformen des Romans von Bunyan bis Beckett* (München: 1972) = *The Implied Reader: Patterns of Communication in Prose Fiction from Bunyan to Beckett* (Baltimore-London: 1974).
—— (1976) *Der Akt des Lesens. Theorie aesthetischer Wirkung* (München: 1976)= *The Act of Reading: a Theory of Aesthetic Response* (Baltimore: 1978).
—— (1991) *Das Fiktive und das Imaginäre. Perspektiven literarischer Anthropologie* (Frankfurt am Main: 1991).
Jauss H.R. (1970) *Literaturgeschichte als Provokation* (Frankfurt am Main: 1970) = *Towards an Aesthetic of Reception*, trans. T. Bahti (Minneapolis: 1982).

—— (1977) *Ästhetische Erfahrung und literarische Hermeneutik*, vol. 1 (München: 1977)=
    Aesthetic Experience and Literary Hermeneutics, trans. T. Bahti (Minneapolis: 1982).
Link H. (1976) *Rezeptionsforschung. Eine Einführung in Methoden und Probleme* (Stuttgart-
    Berlin: 1976).
Rabinowitz P.J. (1986) "Shifting Stands, Shifting Standards: Reading, Interpretation, and
    Literary Judgment", *Arethusa* 19 (1986) 115-34.
Suleiman S. and Crosman I. (eds.) (1980) *The Reader in the Text; Essays on Audience and
    Interpretations* (Princeton-New York: 1980).
Tompkins J. (ed.) (1980) *Reader-Response Criticism: from Formalism to Post-Structuralism*
    (Baltimore: 1980).
Warning R. (ed.) (1975) *Rezeptionsästhetik. Theorie und Praxis* (Munich: 1975).

b. classical application

Arethusa 19.2 (1986), special issue on "Audience-Oriented Criticism and the Classics".
Barner W. (1973) *Produktive Rezeption. Lessing und die Tragödien Senecas* (München: 1973).
—— (1977) "Neuphilologische Rezeptionsforschung und die Möglichkeiten der klassischen
    Philologie", *Poetica* 9 (1977) 499-521.
Bartsch S. (1989) *Decoding the Ancient Novel. The Reader and the Role of Description in
    Heliodorus and Achilles Tatius* (Princeton: 1989).
Batstone W.W. (1988) "On the Surface of the *Georgics*", *Arethusa* 21 (1988) 227-45.
Block E. (1986) "Narrative Judgment and Audience Response in Homer and Vergil", *Arethusa*
    19 (1986) 155-69.
Doherty L.E. (1991) "The Internal and Implied Audiences of *Odyssey* 11", *Arethusa* 24 (1991)
    145-76.
Leach E.W. (1989) "The Implied Reader and the Political Argument in Seneca's *Apocolocun-
    tosis* and *De Clementia*", *Arethusa* 22 (1989) 197-230.
Martindale C. (1991) "Redeeming the Text: the Validity of Comparisons of Classical and
    Postclassical Literature (a British View)" *Arion n.s.* 1.3 (1991) 45-75.
Nauta R.R. (1980) "Gattungsgeschichte als Rezeptionsgeschichte am Beispiel der Entstehung
    der Bukolik", *Antike und Abendland* 36 (1990) 116-37.
Nicolai W. (1983) "Rezeptionssteuerung in der *Ilias*", *Philologus* 127 (1983) 1-12.
—— (1984) "Zu den politischen Wirkungsabsichten des Odyssee-Dichters", *Gräzer Beiträge*
    11 (1984) 1-20.
Pedrick V. (1986) "*Qui potis est, igitur?* Audience Roles in Catullus", *Arethusa* 19 (1986) 187-
    209.
Rabinowitz N. (1986) "Aphrodite and the Audience: Engendering the Reader", *Arethusa* 19
    (1986) 171-85.
Schmidt P.L. (1985) "Reception Theory and Classical Scholarship: a Plea for Convergence",
    in *Hypatia. Essays Presented to Hazel E. Barnes*, ed. W.M. Calder III a.o. (Boulder:
    1985) 67-77.
Scully S.P. (1986) "Studies of Narrative and Speech in the *Iliad*", *Arethusa* 19 (1986) 133-54.
Rösler W. (1980) *Dichter und Gruppe. Eine Untersuchung zu den Bedingungen und zur
    historischen Funktion früher griechischer Lyrik am Beispiel Alkaios* (München: 1980).
—— (1980) "Die Entdeckung der Fiktionalität in der Antike", *Poetica* 12 (1980) 283-319.
Slater N.W. (1990) *Reading Petronius* (Baltimore-London: 1990).
Sutton D.F. (1974) "The Reader's Role in *The Golden Ass*", *Arethusa* 7 (1974) 187-209.

V. FEMINIST AND GENDER CRITICISM

a. theory

Armstrong I. (1992) *New Feminist Discourse. Critical Essays on Theories and Texts* (London-
    New York: 1992).

Fetterley J. (1978) *The Resisting Reader. A Feminist Approach to American Fiction* (Blooming-ton-London: 1978).

Kolodny A. (1980) "Dancing Through the Minefield: Some Observations on the Theory, Practice and Politics of a Feminist Literary Criticism", *Feminist Studies* 6 (1980) 1-25.

Lauretis T. de (1988) *Feminist Studies/Critical Studies* (Houndmills-London: 1988).

Miller, P.A. (1989) *"Sive deae seu sint dirae obscenaeque volucres"*, *Arethusa* 22 (1989) 47-79.

Schor N. (1985) *Breaking the Chain. Feminism, Theory and French Realist Fiction* (New York: 1985).

Showalter E. (1981) "Feminist Criticism in the Wilderness", *Critical Inquiry* 8 (1981) 179-206.

—— (ed.) (1985) *The New Feminist Criticism: Essays on Women, Literature, and Theory* (New York: 1985).

b. classical application

Ancona R. (1989) "The Subterfuge of Reason: Horace, *Odes* 1.23 and the Construction of Male Desire", *Helios* 16 (1989) 49-57.

Arethusa 11.1-2 (1978), special issue on "Women in the Ancient World".

Arthur M.B. (1981) "The Divided World of Iliad VI", in *Reflections of Women in Antiquity*, ed. H.P. Foley (New York-London: 1981) 19-44.

—— (1983) "The Dream of a World without Women: Poetics and the Circles of Order in the *Theogony* Prooemium", *Arethusa* 16 (1983) 97-116.

Bergren A.L.T. (1983) "Language and the Female in Early Greek Thought", *Arethusa* 16 (1983) 69-95.

DuBois P. (1978) "Sappho and Helen", *Arethusa* 11 (1978) 89-99.

Hallett J.P. (1973) "The Role of Women in Roman Elegy: Counter-Cultural Feminism", *Arethusa* 6 (1973) 103-24.

Henry M. (1987) "Ethos, Mythos, Praxis: Women in Greek Comedy" in *Rescuing Creusa: New Methodological Approaches to Women in Antiquity*, ed. M. Skinner, special issue of *Helios* 13.2 (1987) 141-50.

Rabinowitz N.S. (1987) "Female Speech and Female Sexuality: Euripides' *Hippolytos* as Model" in *Rescuing Creusa: New Methodological Approaches to Women in Antiquity*, ed. M. Skinner, special issue of *Helios* 13.2 (1987) 127-40.

Richlin A. (1983) *The Garden of Priapus: Sexuality and Aggression in Roman Humor* (New Haven: 1983).

—— (1984) "Invective Against Women in Roman Satire", *Arethusa* 17 (1984) 67-80.

—— (1991) "Zeus and Metis: Foucault, Feminism, Classics", *Helios* 18 (1991) 160-180.

Winkler, J.J. (1981) "Gardens of Nymphs: Public and Private in Sappho's Lyrics", in *Reflections of Women in Antiquity*, ed. H.P. Foley (New York-London: 1981) 63-90.

—— (1990) "The Education of Chloe: Hidden Injuries of Sex", in *The Constraints of Desire* (London-New York: 1990).

Wyke M. (1989) "Mistress and Metaphor in Augustan Elegy", *Helios* 16 (1989) 25-47.

Zeitlin F.I. (1978) "The Dynamics of Misogyny: Myth and Mythmaking in the Oresteia", *Arethusa* 11 (1978) 149-184.

—— (1981) "Travesties of Gender and Genre in Aristophanes' *Thesmophoriazousae*", in *Reflections of Women in Antiquity*, ed. H.P. Foley (New York-London: 1981) 169-217.

—— (1990) "Playing the Other: Theater, Theatricality, and the Feminine in Greek Drama", in *Nothing to Do with Dionysos? Athenian Drama in Its Social Context*, ed. J.J. Winkler and F.I. Zeitlin (Princeton: 1990) 63-96.

—— (1992) "The Politics of Eros in the Danaid Trilogy of Aeschylus" in *Innovations of Antiquity*, ed. R. Hexter and D. Selden (New York-London: 1992).

VI. PSYCHO-ANALYTICAL CRITICISM

a. theory

Bloom H. (1973) *The Anxiety of Influence. A Theory of Poetry* (Oxford: 1973).
Felman S. (ed.) (1982) *Literature and Psychoanalysis. The Question of Reading: Otherwise* (Baltimore-London: 1982).
Wright E. (1984) *Psychoanalytic Criticism* (London: 1984).

b. classical application

Arethusa 7.1 (1974), special issue on "Psychoanalysis and the Classics".
Caldwell R.S. (1970) "The Pattern of Aeschylean Tragedy", *Transactions and Proceedings of the American Philological Association* 101 (1970) 77-94.
Devereux G. (1970) "The Psychotherapy Scene in Euripides' *Bacchae*", *Journal of Hellenic Studies* 90 (1970) 35-48.
Segal C. (1978-79), "Pentheus and Hippolytus on the Couch and on the Grid: Psychoanalytic and Structuralist Readings of Greek Tragedy", *Classical World* 72 (1978-79) 129-48.
Slater P. (1968) *The Glory of Hera: Greek Mythology and the Greek Family* (Boston: 1968).
Sullivan J.P. (1961) "The *Satiricon* of Petronius: Some Psycho-Analytical Considerations." *The American Imago* 18 (1961) 353-369.
—— (1961) "*Castas odisse puellas*: a Reconsideration of Propertius 1.1", *Wiener Studien* 74 (1961) 96-110.

VII. STRUCTURALIST, POSTSTRUCTURALIST AND SEMIOTIC CRITICISM

a. theory

Culler J. (1975) *Structuralist Poetics: Structuralism, Linguistics and the Study of Literature* (London: 1975).
—— (1981) *The Pursuit of Signs: Semiotics, Literature, Deconstruction* (London: 1981).
Eco U. (1976) *A Theory of Semiotics* (Bloomington-London: 1976).
—— (1990) *The Limits of Interpretation* (Bloomington-London: 1990).
Petitt P. (1975) *The Concept of Structuralism* (Berkeley-Los Angeles: 1975).
Scholes R. (1974) *Structuralism in Literature. An Introduction* (New Haven-London: 1974).

b. classical application

Arethusa 10.1 (1977), special issue on "Classical Literature and Contemporary Critical Perspectives".
Arethusa 16.1-2 (1989), special issue on "Semiotics and Classical Studies".
McCabe K. (1986) "Was Juvenal a Structuralist? A Look at Anachronism in Literary Criticism", *Greece and Rome* 33 (1986) 78-84.
Cupaiuolo F. (1979) "A proposito di alcuni recenti studi latini", *Bolletino di Studi Latini* 9 (1979) 93-125.
Decreus F. (1977-8) "Les possibilités d'application de l'analyse structurale dans l'enseignement secondaire. Application sur le c. 99 de Catulle", *Didactica Classica Gandensia* 17-18 (1977-8) 165-90.
Farenga V. (1977) "Violent Structure: The Writing of Pindar's *Olympian*", *Arethusa* 10 (1977) 197-218.
Galinsky K. (ed.) (1992) *The Interpretation of Roman Poetry: Empiricism or Hermeneutics?* (Frankfurt am Main-New York: 1992).
Goldhill S. (1984) *Language, Sexuality, Narrative: the Oresteia* (Cambridge: 1984).
—— (1986) *Reading Greek Tragedy* (Cambridge: 1986).

Nimis S. (1987) *Narrative Semiotics in the Epic Tradition. The Simile* (Bloomington: 1987).

Peradotto J.J. (1977) "Oedipus and Erichthonius: some Observations on Paradigmatic and Syntagmatic Order", *Arethusa* 10 (1977) 85-101.

—— (1990) *Man in the Middle Voice: Name and Narration in the Odyssey* (Ithaca, N.Y.: 1990).

Rose P.W. (1988) "Thersites and the Plural Voices of Homer", *Arethusa* 21 (1988) 5-25.

Rubin N. Felson (1978-79) "Eco's Semiotics: a Classicist's Perspective", *Helios* 6.2 (1978-79) 17-32.

Segal C. (1973-4) "The *Homeric Hymn to Aphrodite*: a Structuralist Approach", *Classical World* 67 (1973-4) 205-12.

—— (1978) "Le structuralisme et Homère: sauvagerie, bestialité, et le problème d'Achille dans les derniers livres de l'*Iliade*", *Didactica Classica Gandensia* 7 (1978) 175-87.

—— (1983) "Greek Myth as a Semiotic and Structural System and the Problem of Tragedy", *Arethusa* 16 (1983) 173-98.

—— (1986) *Interpreting Greek Tragedy: Myth, Poetry, Text* (Ithaca, N.Y.: 1986).

—— (1986) "Greek Tragedy: a Structuralist Perspective", in *Greek Tragedy and Political Theory*, ed. J.P. Euben (Berkeley-Los Angeles: 1986) 43-75.

Turner T.S. (1977) "Narrative Structure and Mythopoesis: A Critique and Reformulation of Structuralist Concepts of Myth, Narrative, and Poetics", *Arethusa* 10 (1977) 103-63.

Zeitlin F.I. (1982) *Under the Sign of the Shield. Semiotics and Aeschylus' Seven against Thebes* (Rome: 1982).

VIII. DIALECTICAL AND DIALOGIC CRITICISM

a. theory

Bakhtin M.M. (1988) "Epic and the Novel" in *The Dialogic Imagination*, trans. C. Emerson and M. Holquist (Austin: 1988).

Barthes R. (1966) *Critique et verité* (Paris: 1966).

Demetz P. (1967) *Marx, Engels, and the Poets*, trans. J.L. Sammons (Chicago: 1967).

Eagleton T. (1976) *Marxism and Literary Criticism* (Berkeley: 1976).

b. classical application

Arethusa 8 (1975), special issue on "Marxism and the Classics".

Arthur M.B. and Konstan D. (1984) "Marxism and the Study of Classical Antiquity" in *The Left Academy* vol. 2: *Marxist Scholarship on the American Campus*, ed. B. Ollman and E. Vernoff (New York: 1984).

Rose P.W. (1992) *Sons of the Gods, Children of the Earth: Ideology and Literary Form in Ancient Greece* (Oxford: 1992).

Thomson G. (1946) *Aeschylus and Athens* (London: 1946).

NOTES ON CONTRIBUTORS

Richard S. Caldwell has held teaching positions at the Universities of Minnesota and Texas. He is presently Professor of Classics at the University of Southern California. He has written extensively on the psychoanalytical interpretation of Greek myth and drama. He has produced a translation and commentary for Hesiod's *Theogony* (1987) and is the author of *The Origin of the Gods* (1989), a psychoanalytical study of Greek Theogonic myth.

Rip Cohen took his Ph.D. in Classics and Comparative Literature at the University of California, Santa Barbara. He is presently a Gulbelkian Fellow, doing research in Portugal. He is the author of *Thirty-two cantigas d'amigo de Dom Dinis* (London 1987) and has translated and co-edited (with Peter Bing) *Games of Venus. An Anthology of Greek and Roman Erotic Verse from Sappho to Ovid* (London 1991).

A. Maria van Erp Taalman Kip studied classics at the University of Amsterdam. She taught Greek and Latin at a secondary school and took her Ph.D. during this period. Since 1977 she is Associate Professor in Greek at the University of Amsterdam. She has published (both in Dutch and in English) on Homer, on archaic and Hellenistic poetry, and especially on Greek tragedy. Her latest book is *Reader and Spectator. Some Problems in the Interpretation of Greek Tragedy* (Amsterdam 1990).

Don Fowler is Fellow and Tutor in classics at Jesus College and Lecturer in Greek and Latin literature in the University of Oxford. He has published articles on Latin authors and literary theory. He is currently working on a book on the book in antiquity.

Simon Goldhill is Lecturer in Classics in the University of Cambridge and Fellow of King's College. He has published on Homer, archaic and Hellenistic poetry, and tragedy. He is the author of *Language, Sexuality, Narrative: the Oresteia* (1984), *Reading Greek Tragedy* (1986), and *The Poet's Voice. Essays on Poetics and Greek Literature* (1991).

Irene J.F. de Jong studied classics at the University of Amsterdam. Since 1988 she is a senior research fellow at that same university, appointed by the Royal Netherlands Academy of Arts and Sciences. She has published articles on Homer, the Homeric hymns, and Greek tragedy. She is the author of *Narrators and Focalizers. The Presentation of the Story in the Iliad* (Amsterdam 1987) and *Narrative in Drama. The Art of the Euripidean Messenger-Speech* (Leiden 1991). She is currently working on a narrative commentary on the *Odyssey*.

Marianne McDonald studied classics and music at Bryn Mawr before taking her M.A. in Classics at the University of Chicago and her Ph.D. in Classics at the University of California, Irvine. She has been a Research Fellow with *Thesaurus Linguae Graecae* at the University of California, Irvine (a project she helped found) and a Visiting Research Fellow at Trinity College, Dublin, where she helped initiate the *Thesaurus Linguarum Hiberniae* project. She is presently Adjunct Professor in the Department of Theatre at the University of California, San Diego. She is the editor of numerous Greek concordances and the author of *Euripides in Cinema: The Heart Made Visible* (1983) and *Ancient Sun, Modern Light: Greek Drama on the Modern Stage* (1991).

Glenn W. Most studied ancient and modern literature and philosophy at the Universities of Harvard, Oxford, Yale, and Tübingen. He is Professor of Greek at the University of Heidelberg. He has published articles on ancient Greek lyric, ancient philosophy (especially Plato, Aristotle, and the Stoics), modern literature (especially Romantic poetry), and literary theory. His books include *The Measures of Praise. Structure and Function in Pindar's Second Pythian and Seventh Nemean Odes* (Göttingen 1985) and a translation (with A.T. Grafton and J.E.G. Zetzel) of F.A. Wolf's *Prolegomena ad Homerum* (Princeton 1985). One of his current projects is co-editing the collected works of F. Nietzsche.

Ruurd R. Nauta studied classics and theory of literature at the Universities of Groningen and Leiden. After spending a year at the University of Constance, he now teaches Latin at the Free University of Berlin. He has published articles on various aspects of ancient literary history and has just completed a book: *Poetry for Patrons: Literary Communication in the Age of Domitian.*

Charles Segal is Professor of Greek and Latin at Harvard University, and has written widely on classics and comparative literature, notably in the areas of epic and tragedy. He is a Fellow of the American Academy of Arts and Sciences and was elected President of the American Philological Society in 1992. His books include *Tragedy and Civilization: An Interpretation of Sophocles* (1981); *Dionysiac Poetics and Euripides' Bacchae* (1982); *Interpreting Greek Tragedy* (1986); *Pindar's Mythmaking* (1986); *Language and Desire in Seneca's Phaedra* (1986); *Orpheus: the Myth of the Poet* (1989); and *Lucretius on Death and Anxiety* (1990). Forthcoming volumes are *Oedipus Tyrannus: Tragic Heroism and the Limits of Knowledge* and *Euripides and the Poetics of Sorrow.*

J.P. Sullivan taught at Oxford University and the Universities of Texas and New York at Buffalo. He was Professor of Classics at the University of California, Santa Barbara. He edited the journals *Arion* and *Arethusa* as well as several anthologies and volumes of critical essays, including *Women in Antiquity: The Arethusa Papers* (with John Peradotto). He is the author of literary and historical studies on Propertius, Petronius, Neronian literature, Martial and Ezra Pound.

INDEX LOCORUM

SUPPLEMENTS TO MNEMOSYNE

EDITED BY J. M. BREMER, L. F. JANSSEN, H. PINKSTER,
H. W. PLEKET, C. J. RUIJGH AND P. H. SCHRIJVERS

4. LEEMAN, A.D. *A Systematical Bibliography of Sallust (1879-1964)*. Revised and augmented edition. 1965. ISBN 90 04 01467 5

5. LENZ, F.W. (ed.). *The Aristeides 'Prolegomena'*. 1959. ISBN 90 04 01468 3

7. McKAY, K.J. *Erysichthon. A Callimachean Comedy*. 1962. ISBN 90 04 01470 5

11. RUTILIUS LUPUS. *De Figuris Sententiarum et Elocutionis*. Edited with Prolegomena and Commentary by E. BROOKS. 1970. ISBN 90 04 01474 8

12. SMYTH, W.R. (ed.). *Thesaurus criticus ad Sexti Propertii textum*. 1970. ISBN 90 04 01475 6

13. LEVIN, D.N. *Apollonius' 'Argonautica' re-examined*. 1. The Neglected First and Second Books. 1971. ISBN 90 04 02575 8

14. REINMUTH, O.W. *The Ephebic Inscriptions of the Fourth Century B.C.* 1971. ISBN 90 04 01476 4

16. ROSE, K.F.C. *The Date and Author of the 'Satyricon'*. With an Introduction by J.P.SULLIVAN. 1971. ISBN 90 04 02578 2

18. WILLIS, J. *De Martiano Capella emendando*. 1971. ISBN 90 04 02580 4

19. HERINGTON, C.J. (ed.). *The Older Scholia on the Prometheus Bound*. 1972. ISBN 90 04 03455 2

20. THIEL, H. VAN. *Petron. Überlieferung und Rekonstruktion*. 1971. ISBN 90 04 02581 2

21. LOSADA, L.A. *The Fifth Column in the Peloponnesian War*. 1972. ISBN 90 04 03421 8

23. BROWN, V. *The Textual Transmission of Caesar's 'Civil War'*. 1972. ISBN 90 04 03457 9

24. LOOMIS, J.W. *Studies in Catullan Verse*. An Analysis of Word Types and Patterns in the Polymetra. 1972. ISBN 90 04 03429 3

27. GEORGE, E.V. *Aeneid VIII and the Aitia of Callimachus*. 1974. ISBN 90 04 03859 0

29. BERS, V. *Enallage and Greek Style*. 1974. ISBN 90 04 03786 1

37. SMITH, O.L. *Studies in the Scholia on Aeschylus*. 1. The Recensions of Demetrius Triclinius. 1975. ISBN 90 04 04220 2

39. SCHMELING, G.L. & J.H. STUCKEY. *A Bibliography of Petronius*. 1977. ISBN 90 04 04753 0

44. THOMPSON, W.E. *De Hagniae Hereditate. An Athenian Inheritance Case*. 1976. ISBN 90 04 04757 3

45. McGUSHIN, P. *Sallustius Crispus, 'Bellum Catilinae'. A Commentary*. 1977. ISBN 90 04 04835 9

46. THORNTON, A. *The Living Universe. Gods and Men in Virgil's Aeneid*. 1976. ISBN 90 04 04579 1

48. BRENK, F.E. *In Mist apparelled. Religious Themes in Plutarch's 'Moralia' and 'Lives'*. 1977. ISBN 90 04 05241 0

51. SUSSMAN, L.A. *The Elder Seneca*. 1978. ISBN 90 04 05759 5

57. BOER, W. DEN. *Private Morality in Greece and Rome*. Some Historical Aspects. 1979. ISBN 90 04 05976 8

61. *Hieronymus' Liber de optimo genere interpretandi (Epistula 57)*. Ein Kommentar von G.J.M. BARTELINK. 1980. ISBN 90 04 06085 5

63. HOHENDAHL-ZOETELIEF, I.M. *Manners in the Homeric Epic*. 1980. ISBN 90 04 06223 8

64. HARVEY, R.A. *A Commentary on Persius*. 1981. ISBN 90 04 06313 7

65. MAXWELL-STUART, P.G. *Studies in Greek Colour Terminology*. 1. γλαυκός. 1981. ISBN 90 04 06406 0
68. ACHARD, G. *Pratique rhétorique et idéologie politique dans les discours 'Optimates' de Cicéron*. 1981. ISBN 90 04 06374 9
69. MANNING, C.E. *On Seneca's 'Ad Marciam'*. 1981. ISBN 90 04 06430 3
70. BERTHIAUME, G. *Les rôles du Mágeiros*. Etude sur la boucherie, la cuisine et le sacrifice dans la Grèce ancienne. 1982. ISBN 90 04 06554 7
71. CAMPBELL, M. *A commentary on Quintus Smyrnaeus Posthomerica XII*. 1981. ISBN 90 04 06502 4
72. CAMPBELL, M. *Echoes and Imitations of Early Epic in Apollonius Rhodius*. 1981. ISBN 90 04 06503 2
73. MOSKALEW, W. *Formular Language and Poetic Design in the Aeneid*. 1982. ISBN 90 04 06580 6
74. RACE, W.H. *The Classical Priamel from Homer to Boethius*. 1982. ISBN 90 04 06515 6
75. MOORHOUSE, A.C. *The Syntax of Sophocles*. 1982. ISBN 90 04 06599 7
77. WITKE, C. *Horace's Roman Odes*. A Critical Examination. 1983. ISBN 90 04 07006 0
78. ORANJE, J. *Euripides' 'Bacchae'*. The Play and its Audience. 1984. ISBN 90 04 07011 7
79. STATIUS. *Thebaidos Libri XII*. Recensuit et cum apparatu critico et exegetico instruxit D.E. HILL. 1983. ISBN 90 04 06917 8
82. DAM, H.-J. VAN. *P. Papinius Statius, Silvae Book II*. A Commentary. 1984. ISBN 90 04 07110 5
84. OBER, J. *Fortress Attica*. Defense of the Athenian Land Frontier, 404-322 B.C. 1985. ISBN 90 04 07243 8
85. HUBBARD, T.K. *The Pindaric Mind*. A Study of Logical Structure in Early Greek Poetry. 1985. ISBN 90 04 07303 5
86. VERDENIUS, W.J. *A Commentary on Hesiod: Works and Days*, vv. 1-382. 1985. ISBN 90 04 07465 1
87. HARDER, A. *Euripides' 'Kresphontes' and 'Archelaos'*. Introduction, Text and Commentary. 1985. ISBN 90 04 07511 9
88. WILLIAMS, H.J. *The 'Eclogues' and 'Cynegetica' of Nemesianus*. Edited with an Introduction and Commentary. 1986. ISBN 90 04 07486 4
89. McGING, B.C. *The Foreign Policy of Mithridates VI Eupator, King of Pontus*. 1986. ISBN 90 04 07591 7
91. SIDEBOTHAM, S.E. *Roman Economic Policy in the Erythra Thalassa 30 B.C.-A.D. 217*. 1986. ISBN 90 04 07644 1
92. VOGEL, C.J. DE. *Rethinking Plato and Platonism*. 2nd impr. of the first (1986) ed. 1988. ISBN 90 04 08755 9
93. MILLER, A.M. *From Delos to Delphi*. A Literary Study of the Homeric Hymn to Apollo. 1986. ISBN 90 04 07674 3
94. BOYLE, A.J. *The Chaonian Dove*. Studies in the Eclogues, Georgics and Aeneid of Virgil. 1986. ISBN 90 04 07672 7
95. KYLE, D.G. *Athletics in Ancient Athens*. 2nd impr. of the first (1987) ed. 1993. ISBN 90 04 09759 7
97. VERDENIUS, W.J. *Commentaries on Pindar. Vol. I. Olympian Odes 3, 7, 12, 14*. 1987. ISBN 90 04 08126 7
98. PROIETTI, G. *Xenophon's Sparta*. An introduction. 1987. ISBN 90 04 08338 3
99. BREMER, J.M., A.M. VAN ERP TAALMAN KIP & S.R. SLINGS. *Some Recently Found Greek Poems*. Text and Commentary. 1987. ISBN 90 04 08319 7
100. OPHUIJSEN, J.M. VAN. *Hephaistion on Metre*. Translation and Commentary. 1987. ISBN 90 04 08452 5
101. VERDENIUS, W.J. *Commentaries on Pindar. Vol. II*. Olympian Odes 1, 10, 11, Nemean 11, Isthmian 2. 1988. ISBN 90 04 08535 1
102. LUSCHNIG, C.A.E. *Time holds the Mirror. A Study of Knowledge in Euripides'*

'*Hippolytus*'. 1988. ISBN 90 04 08601 3
103. MARCOVICH, M. *Alcestis Barcinonensis*. Text and Commentary. 1988.
ISBN 90 04 08600 5
104. HOLT, F.L. *Alexander the Great and Bactria*. The Formation of a Greek Frontier in
Central Asia. Repr. 1993. ISBN 90 04 08612 9
105. BILLERBECK, M. *Seneca's Tragödien; sprachliche und stilistische Untersuchungen*. Mit
Anhängen zur Sprache des Hercules Oetaeus und der Octavia. 1988.
ISBN 90 04 08631 5
106. ARENDS, J.F.M. *Die Einheit der Polis. Eine Studie über Platons Staat*. 1988.
ISBN 90 04 08785 0
107. BOTER, G.J. *The Textual Tradition of Plato's Republic*. 1988. ISBN 90 04 08787 7
108. WHEELER, E.L. *Stratagem and the Vocabulary of Military Trickery*. 1988.
ISBN 90 04 08831 8
109. BUCKLER, J. *Philip II and the Sacred War*. 1989. ISBN 90 04 09095 9
110. FULLERTON, M.D. *The Archaistic Style in Roman Statuary*. 1990.
ISBN 90 04 09146 7
111. ROTHWELL, K.S. *Politics and Persuasion in Aristophanes' 'Ecclesiazusae'*. 1990.
ISBN 90 04 09185 8
112. CALDER, W.M. & A. DEMANDT. *Eduard Meyer*. Leben und Leistung eines
Universalhistorikers. 1990. ISBN 90 04 09131 9
113. CHAMBERS, M.H. *Georg Busolt. His Career in His Letters*. 1990.
ISBN 90 04 09225 0
114. CASWELL, C.P. *A Study of 'Thumos' in Early Greek Epic*. 1990. ISBN 90 04 09260 9
115. EINGARTNER, J. *Isis und ihre Dienerinnen in der Kunst der Römischen Kaiserzeit*. 1991.
ISBN 90 04 09312 5
116. JONG, I. DE. *Narrative in Drama*. The Art of the Euripidean Messenger-Speech.
1991. ISBN 90 04 09406 7
117. BOYCE, B.T. *The Language of the Freedmen in Petronius'* Cena Trimalchionis. 1991.
ISBN 90 04 09431 8
118. RÜTTEN, Th. *Demokrit ― lachender Philosoph und sanguinischer Melancholiker*. 1992.
ISBN 90 04 09523 3
119. KARAVITES, P. (with the collaboration of Th. Wren). *Promise-Giving and Treaty-
Making*. Homer and the Near East. 1992. ISBN 90 04 09567 5
120. SANTORO L'HOIR, F. *The Rhetoric of Gender Terms*. 'Man', 'Woman' and the
portrayal of character in Latin prose. 1992. ISBN 90 04 09512 8
121. WALLINGA, H.T. *Ships and Sea-Power before the Great Persian War*. The Ancestry of
the Ancient Trireme. 1993. ISBN 90 04 09650 7
122. FARRON, S. *Vergil's Æneid: A Poem of Grief and Love*. 1993. ISBN 90 04 09661 2
123. LÉTOUBLON, F. *Les lieux communs du roman*. Stéréotypes grecs d'aventure et
d'amour. 1993. ISBN 90 04 09724 4
124. KUNTZ, M. *Narrative Setting and Dramatic Poetry*. 1993. ISBN 90 04 09784 8
125. THEOPHRASTUS. *Metaphysics*. With an introduction, Translation and Commentary by Marlein van Raalte. 1993. ISBN 90 04 09786 4
126. THIERMANN, P. *Die* Orationes Homeri *des Leonardo Bruni Aretino*. Kritische
Edition der lateinischen und kastilianischen Übersetzung mit Prolegomena und
Kommentar. 1993. ISBN 90 04 09719 8
127. LEVENE, D.S. *Religion in Livy*. 1993. ISBN 90 04 09617 5
128. PORTER, J.R. *Studies in Euripides'* Orestes. 1993. ISBN 90 04 09662 0
129. SICKING, C.M.J. & J.M. VAN OPHUIJSEN. *Two Studies in Attic Particle Usage*.
Lysias and Plato. 1993. ISBN 90 04 09867 4
130. JONG, I.J.F. de, & J.P. SULLIVAN (eds.). *Modern Critical Theory and Classical Literature*. 1994. ISBN 90 04 09571 3
131. YAMAGATA, N. *Homeric Morality*. 1994. ISBN 90 04 09872 0